# CONNECTED COMMUNITIES

MATTHEW A. PEEPLES

# CONNECTED COMMUNITIES

*Networks, Identity, and Social Change in the Ancient Cibola World*

THE UNIVERSITY OF ARIZONA PRESS
TUCSON

The University of Arizona Press
www.uapress.arizona.edu

We respectfully acknowledge the University of Arizona is on the land and territories of Indigenous peoples. Today, Arizona is home to twenty-two federally recognized tribes, with Tucson being home to the O'odham and the Yaqui. Committed to diversity and inclusion, the University strives to build sustainable relationships with sovereign Native Nations and Indigenous communities through education offerings, partnerships, and community service.


First paperback edition 2021

ISBN-13: 978-0-8165-3568-2 (cloth)
ISBN-13: 978-0-8165-4472-1 (paper)

Cover design by Leigh McDonald

Support for this publication was provided by the Arizona Archaeological and Historical Society.

Library of Congress Cataloging-in-Publication Data
Names: Peeples, Matthew A., author.
Title: Connected communities : networks, identity, and social change in the ancient Cibola world / Matthew A. Peeples.
Description: Tucson : The University of Arizona Press, 2018. | Includes bibliographical references and index.
Identifiers: LCCN 2017042852 | ISBN 9780816535682 (cloth : alk. paper)
Subjects: LCSH: Pueblo Indians—Arizona—Social conditions. | Pueblo Indians—New Mexico—Social conditions. | Group identity. | Arizona—Antiquities. | New Mexico—Antiquities.
Classification: LCC E99.P9 P377 2018 | DDC 978.9004/974—dc23 LC record available at https://lccn.loc.gov/2017042852

Printed in the United States of America
∞ This paper meets the requirements of ANSI/NISO Z39.48–1992 (Permanence of Paper).

# CONTENTS

# ILLUSTRATIONS

## FIGURES

## TABLES



## ONLINE APPENDIX

Data and additional analytical details associated with this project are available as an online appendix through tDAR at the following permanent link: https://core.tdar.org/project/427899/.

# ACKNOWLEDGMENTS

I COULD NEVER have completed this book without the help of many generous people. This research started as a dissertation project, and I am forever in debt to my wonderful committee, Keith Kintigh, Michelle Hegmon, and Kate Spielmann. They have always been extremely supportive, and many of the best ideas in this book came out of conversations with them. I am also particularly grateful to Peggy Nelson, who hired me as a research assistant many years ago on the Long Term Vulnerability and Transformation Project. I learned so much through that project, and a substantial amount of data in this book was initially generated as part of that research. I would also like to thank Barbara Mills at the University of Arizona for serving as a wonderful postdoctoral advisor and collaborator. The focus on formal network analysis in this book and in much of my research in recent years began through my work with her. I also want to thank my colleagues at Archaeology Southwest. I was in awe of the amazing work that you did before I even met you, and I count my time working with Archaeology Southwest as one of the best experiences of my life. I want to say thanks in particular to Bill Doelle for his support and for the example he set for me and so many others.

A synthetic, collections-based project such as this could never have been completed without the assistance of numerous institutions and individuals. The list of people I have to thank is long, but this book would not be a fraction of what it is without each and every one of these people. Access to collections was facilitated by Arleyn Simon and Dolma Roder at the Archaeological Research

Institute (now the Center for Archaeology and Society repository at Arizona State University); Arthur Vokes and Mike Jacobs at the Arizona State Museum; Jamie Kelly and Jonathan Haas at the Chicago Field Museum of Natural History; Patricia Capone, Susan Haskall, and Viva Fisher at the Harvard Peabody Museum of Archaeology and Ethnology; Darrell Creel, Laura Nightengale, and Jim Neely at the Texas Archaeological Research Laboratory; Elaine Hughes at the Museum of Northern Arizona; Linda Matthews and Carol Farnsworth at the Casa Malpais Archaeological Park; Paul Stavast at the Brigham Young University Museum of Peoples and Cultures; Jim Shrieve at SWCA; and Jonathan Damp at the Zuni Cultural Resource Enterprise. I would like to thank Bob Roland for sharing his immense local knowledge and also for allowing me to camp on his beautiful property. Thanks also to Charles and Emily Dumler for providing access to and samples from the amazing archaeological sites on their land. The Bureau of Land Management Rio Puerco Office (Cynthia Herhahn, Gretchen Obenauf, and Dave Simons) and the National Park Service at El Malpais National Monument (Steve Bauman) facilitated access to sites and collections that sent this research in new and exciting directions. The wonderful staff at the Archaeological Records Management Section at the Museum of New Mexico provided assistance and expertise in compiling the archaeological site data used throughout this study.

Many people very generously shared data used in this study, including Jim Allison, Andrew Duff, Dennis Gilpin, Kelley Hays-Gilpin, Sarah Herr, Deb Huntley, Karl Laumbach, Toni Laumbach, Steve LeBlanc, Patrick Lyons, Barbara Mills, Greg Schachner, Jimmy Smith and all the folks in the Tarrant County Archaeological Society "Texas Crew," Jason Theuer, Scott Van Keuren, Dave Wilcox, Tom Windes, and everyone at the Pueblo of Zuni, the Zuni Cultural Resource Enterprise, and Archaeology Southwest. Jeff Ferguson and Michael Glascock provided essential support and guidance for the analysis and interpretation of the NAA data presented in this study. I would also like to thank the people who helped me with the ceramic technological coding over the years, including Kate Bishop, Ashley Bitowf, Sarah Oas, Will Russell, Greg Schachner, Reuven Sinensky, Kellam Throgmorton, Garrett Trask, Katie Whitmore, and Caitlin Wichlacz. I would not have been able to do it without your help.

The research in this book was funded through two National Science Foundation awards, including a Doctoral Dissertation Improvement Grant (BSC-9043134) and a Collaborative Archaeology Program Grant to Arizona State

University (#1642904), Archaeology Southwest, and UCLA (#1419678). Thanks in particular to my collaborators Greg Schachner and Paul Reed on the newest incarnation of this project. Additional work was funded by a Wenner-Gren Foundation Dissertation Fieldwork Grant (#09094295) and several internal grant programs through Arizona State University and the School of Human Evolution and Social Change. The NAA ceramic compositional study was supported through the Archaeometry Subsidy Program at the University of Missouri Research Reactor (SBR-9802366). The settlement database used in this study was originally compiled as part of the National Science Foundation Biocomplexity program funded Long Term Vulnerability and Transformation Project at Arizona State University (BCS-0508001; PI: Margaret Nelson). Funds from the Society for American Archaeology Fred Plog Memorial Fellowship allowed me to hire Garrett Trask as a research assistant; he helped with the organization and implementation of several of the analyses presented here. Catherine Gillman of Desert Archaeology, Inc., provided excellent base maps and formats for the maps appearing in this book and worked patiently with me as I produced the final products you see here.

Many people have provided insightful and useful comments on various drafts of this book, including (in alphabetical order) Wes Bernardini, Kate Gann, Michelle Hegmon, Keith Kintigh, Melissa Kruse-Peeples, Barbara Mills, Peggy Nelson, Paul Reed, Chris Roberts, John Roberts Jr., Greg Schachner, Katherine Spielmann, and four anonymous reviewers. Thanks also to everyone at the University of Arizona Press for helping to push this project forward. I could not hope to list the names of all the people who have been both friends and inspirations over the years. I hope you know who you are. I would like to thank my parents for always being there for me. Finally, I would like to especially thank Melissa and Owen. I could not have done this without your love and support.

# CONNECTED COMMUNITIES

# 1

# WHO ARE YOU?

"WHO WERE the people who lived here?" I often hear this question when I give site tours for the public or conduct fieldwork in places where locals might pay a visit. It is a question that probably sounds simple and straightforward to the person asking it. To an archaeologist like me who has spent a lot of time thinking about how social groups form and change, this question opens the door to all kinds of complexity.

If I suspect that my visitor is looking for a quick answer—or if we have a looming project deadline—I may give her the short and way-too-simple version. This usually means providing the typical archaeological cultural or regional designation ("they were Ancestral Pueblo people" or "they were Hohokam people" or "they were the ancestors of people living at Zuni today"). If I am feeling a bit more inspired—or looking for an opportunity to have a longer conversation in the shade—I may go into the particular social and demographic histories, describing archaeological evidence for migration streams or material evidence for how the nature and scale of families, communities, or larger social groups changed through time. In my experience, the long answer to this deceptively simple question resonates quite well with members of the public and archaeologists alike, provided that I can find a clear and compelling way to describe interesting patterns and processes in the data.

In an effort to come up with better ways of explaining the complexities inherent in social group identities, how they change, and how we study that process archaeologically, I have often found it useful to rely on analogy with contemporary events and institutions. Most people living in the world of nation-states and borders have a good sense of what it means to have multiple and nested identities. When I turn the tables and ask my inquisitive visitors "who are you?" I find that they seldom stop at one or two labels and often rattle off quite a few. These might include their nationality, state/territory/city/neighborhood of residence or birth, ethnic heritage, familial ties, religion, occupation, or many other designations. Importantly, some of these designations are based on their own direct relationships, while others link them to groups much larger than they could ever hope to know personally.

In the United States, where I do my research, most people are well acquainted with the metaphor of the "American melting pot"—the romanticized notion of how the diverse populations that make up the nation came to represent a coherent whole—and they probably also have some notion of the diversity of people living in the United States through its ethnic neighborhoods and the waves of immigration that shaped such places. Such contemporary examples make it much easier to explain how archaeologists document similar migration streams, identify socially diverse communities or enclaves, and track the ways people marked or masked differences in the past. We see archaeological evidence of the *same historical processes* that drive the formation, maintenance, or dissolution of social groups in the world today. Identity is a complicated tapestry for us, and there is no compelling reason to believe it was less so in the past.

Conversations with the public like these brought me to the research in this book. Since I first started studying archaeology, I have been interested in understanding how people form very large social groups, especially those that are so large that they include people who will probably never meet. Searching for analogues and new perspectives on such large-scale social groups, I turned to a body of literature focused on nationalism, ethnic identity, and the drivers of social change in the contemporary world. This work suggests that the formation of social groups and the process of social change are intrinsically linked, and, importantly, researchers working from this perspective have developed tools and theoretical frameworks for exploring such relationships (i.e., social network analysis). The more I read, the more the underlying processes and mechanisms at work felt familiar to me as an archaeologist studying social change at regional scales in the ancient Southwest.

At the same time, and somewhat to my dismay, I found that researchers working within this paradigm from a contemporary perspective often made assumptions about the supposed absence of certain kinds of identities and interactions in premodern societies that are, to my mind, unfounded (see Chapter 2). Still, I considered that the methods and models used to untangle the complicated web of identities in the contemporary world might have some utility for exploring social groups in the more distant past through archaeological evidence. Might such models push us toward new and interesting revelations about identity and social change in the past? Could archaeologists contribute to the broader debate in the social sciences by expanding the scope of such frameworks to kinds of societies that have not yet been considered or by using new kinds of evidence? I hope to take the first steps toward addressing these important questions in this book.

## SOCIAL IDENTITY AND SOCIAL CHANGE IN THE ANCIENT SOUTHWEST AND BEYOND

I have two primary goals with this book: one focuses on developing new method and theory for addressing the complex relationships among identity, material culture, and social change, and one focuses on addressing some enduring questions about the archaeology of the ancient Southwest. In order to address the first goal, I develop and evaluate a novel theoretical approach for tracking social identification at regional scales in the archaeological record. This model builds on a large body of empirical and theoretical work in the broader comparative social sciences focused on issues of collective identity and social change. I argue that this new framework offers greater analytical leverage for exploring the complex issues of how and why social identities form, persist, decline, or change than do many currently popular archaeological methods and models. I focus in particular on how we might best address the relationship between social identification and periods of major social transformation, though this approach to tracking social identity need not be limited to explorations of social change.

By way of example, I explore changes occurring across the late prehispanic period (ca. A.D. 1150–1325) in the Cibola region of New Mexico and Arizona. Using many lines of archaeological evidence generated through more than a century of research in the region, I explore how the nature and scale of social groups and identities changed across one of the most dramatic periods of demographic and social upheaval seen in the U.S. Southwest. The relatively short period (to an archaeologist) considered here was marked by a region-wide shift in the way people built communities: from dispersed hamlets, to clustered villages, and eventually to a small number of large towns (Huntley and Kintigh 2004; Kintigh 1985a, 1996, 2007; Kintigh et al. 2004; Lekson 1996). This truly revolutionary transformation entailed a fundamental reconfiguration of the relationships between individuals and social groups, both large and small, across the region as a whole. In the chapters that follow, I demonstrate that the changing nature and scale of shared group identities across this transition played a major role in determining how this social transformation played out across different parts of the region.

The methods and theoretical tools I develop in this book provide not only new insights into this important period of social change in the Cibola region and the greater Southwest but also a useful general framework and a set of concrete procedures for evaluating identity using material culture. This approach is relevant across a broad range of demographic, political, and organizational scales. In the next section, I briefly outline the theoretical framework that forms the basis of this study (which is elaborated in Chapter 2), beginning by defining a number of key terms and concepts that will guide this study. As I argue here and throughout this book, archaeologists have much to gain by exploring alternative perspectives on social identity and social change beyond traditional anthropological models. Importantly, archaeologists also have much to offer broader conversations on such topics in the comparative social sciences (see also Smith 2017; Smith et al. 2012).

## TRACKING IDENTITY THROUGH SOCIAL RELATIONS AND SOCIAL CATEGORIES

Despite considerable variation in specific definitions (see Brubaker and Cooper 2000), most contemporary researchers use the term "identity" or "identification" to broadly refer to the ways that individuals relate themselves and others to larger groups based on perceived similarities and differences that are socially recognized as important (e.g., Barth 1969:10; Calhoun 1995:193–197; Díaz-Andreu et al. 2005; Emberling 1997; Jenkins 2004:1–8; Jones 1997). Such similarities and differences may be discerned along a number of lines, including, for example, gender, class, age, or ethnicity. As was the case with my inquisitive visitor described above, individuals take on multiple identities simultaneously and at multiple social scales. From this perspective, identities never really exist as things but rather are in a constant state of flux mediated through the interactions of people. At the same time, some social identities may maintain strong *perceptions* of permanence that can influence the actions of individuals through time across many generations (see Bentley 1987:24–27; Jenkins 2000; Jones 1997:84–105). It is often because some kinds of group identities *seem* so timeless and permanent that they are so important. The tensions between fluidity and permanence are palpable.

My focus in this book is on the *processes* involved in social identification among groups of people at large geographic and demographic scales (i.e., scales larger than households, villages, or communities). Such large scales are typically defined as "regions" or "culture areas" in the archaeological literature; these areas typically are characterized by some degree of material homogeneity, usually assumed to represent a degree of shared cultural identity (Duff 2000; Kantner 2008). Historically, explorations of identity at regional scales have been fundamentally tied to anthropological perspectives on ethnicity (see Jones 1997:15–29; Shennan 1989; Veit 1989). Indeed, the terms "ethnicity" and "identity" have often been used interchangeably in regional-scale archaeological research (see Chapter 2). However, the equation of patterns of similarity in material culture with traditional anthropological models of ethnicity presupposes a set of assumptions regarding political organization, social boundaries, and the nature of relationships with similar groups that may not be appropriate for all times and places (see Comaroff and Comaroff 1992:49–69; Jones 1997; MacEachern 1998; Neitzel 2000; Smith 1986). I argue that parsing the concept of identity along different dimensions of variation may provide new insights into regional-scale social groups that have not traditionally been the subject of anthropological research.

Most recent archaeological studies of regional-scale identities in the U.S. Southwest and elsewhere have focused on three primary sources of information: evidence for the *spatial clustering* of settlements, houses, and population (e.g., Duff and Adams 2004; Smail 2000; Varien 1999); evidence for the *active expression* of similarity among groups through material culture (Asouti 2006; Braun and Plog 1982; Duff 2000, 2002; Wiessner 1985); and evidence for *shared practices* among individuals or larger units, most often characterized through technological aspects of style (Clark 2001; Gosselain 1998, 2000; Lyons 2003; bioarchaeological and linguistic data are also often employed where data are available, e.g., Ortman 2012). Each of these lines of evidence provides a window into different aspects of identity: geography, active signaling, and habitual practice. I argue that many debates regarding the nature of social identities and boundaries in specific archaeological contexts boil down to researchers privileging one of these kinds of evidence over others. Thus, the model I develop here explicitly considers all of these lines of evidence and, most importantly, their interplay.

My approach in this book builds on a large body of comparative social science research focused on the relationships between social identity, collective action, and social change (e.g., Calhoun 1995, 1997; Diani 2003; Emirbayer 1997; Emirbayer and Goodwin 1994; Nexon 2009; Pachucki and Breiger 2010; Polleta and Jasper 2001; Somers 1994; Stokke and Tjomsland 1996; Tilly 1978, 2001, 2002, 2004a, 2004b, 2005; White 1992, 2008a, 2008b). The theoretical framework I draw on generally falls within the realm of what Ann Mische (2011) has referred to as the "New York School" of relational sociology. This approach has many features in common with currently popular anthropological approaches to identity and ethnicity, but it also diverges in some key ways. In particular, researchers working from this perspective are not directly concerned with defining or describing discrete social groups at particular demographic or geographic scales but rather with exploring the general *modes* in which identification occurs. Specifically, in this framework, social identification is conceptualized as operating primarily in terms of two distinct but complementary processes: *relational identification* and *categorical identification*.

Relational identification refers to a process through which individuals identify with larger groups based on networks of interactions or persistently activated relationships such as kinship or exchange ties. Groups of people linked through relational connections can sometimes comprise named entities like lineages. However, a key feature of relational identities is that they are forged out of direct and indirect connections among people rather than out of their common membership in some social category that could be defined external to those relationships. In contrast, categorical identification refers to the process through which individuals identify with large formal units such as political groups, religious organizations, or states based on perceived similarities with others in these groups. Categorical identities, unlike their relational counterparts, are not defined directly from networks of interaction and thus can include far greater numbers of individuals (Calhoun 1994:26).

The relational and categorical modes of identification provide more than a convenient means for describing variation in the nature of collective identities. A number of researchers have linked these general modes of identification to the potential for and organization of widespread trajectories of collective action, social movements, and social transformation in many contemporary and recent historic contexts (e.g., Nexon 2009; Stokke and Tjomsland 1996;

Tilly 1978, 2004). Importantly, Charles Tilly (1978:62–69) describes relations and categories as separate dimensions of a whole, noting that they are not binary concepts. Thus, we can evaluate the strength of relational connections in terms of the number or character of consistently overlapping social ties or the degree of categorical commonality in terms of the degree of homogeneity of shared public expressions of identity. Empirical studies in a broad range of social contexts (Baldassarri 2009; Diani 2003, 2007; Diani and McAdam 2003; McAdam and Paulson 1993; Nexon 2009; Tarrow 1998; Tilly 1998, 2002, 2004a, 2004b, 2005) suggest that the particular configuration of relations and categories among large groups has an enormous impact on both the potential for sustained cooperation and the specific form it may take. Indeed, many proponents of this relational/categorical approach argue that these distinct modes of identification have too often been conflated (see Somers 1994; Tilly 2001) and that an explicit consideration of the interplay between relations and categories is *necessary* for understanding social change (Somers and Gibson 1995:64–69; Nexon 2009; Stokke and Tjomsland 1996:27–31; Tilly 1978; White 2008a).

I am particularly interested in the relationship between the relational and categorical modes of social identification and periods of widespread social transformation. Social transformation, as I define it for the purposes of this study, refers to a relatively rapid and lasting period of social change occurring through concerted and sustained collective effort (see Chapter 2 for more in-depth discussion). Comparative studies of contemporary and recent historical instances of social transformation suggest that collective action is most effective and transformative among groups that are highly connected in terms of both relational and categorical identities (Stokke and Tjomsland 1996:29; Tilly 1978:63). Tilly (1978), building on an earlier influential and widely cited unpublished manuscript by Harrison White from 1965 ("Notes on the Constituents of Social Structure" later published as White 2008a), calls such social settings *catnets* (a term combining *category* and *network*). Following these pioneering researchers, I argue that the more a given social setting conforms to a catnet, the greater the *potential* for truly transformative collective action is at that particular scale (Tilly 1978:62–69).

The catnet model and the dual focus on relational and categorical aspects of identity espoused by White, Tilly, and many other scholars were originally formulated as responses to the structural-functionalist sociological program of researchers like Talcott Parsons (1937) and his collaborators, who placed the locus of social action in the categorical attributes of individuals (in particular, attitudes and values). White (2008a) and later Tilly (1978) explicitly criticized this approach, suggesting that shared categorical attributes were not sufficient to generate coordinated social action. Instead, they suggested that mobilization and collective identification necessitated that individuals also be linked in dense networks of interaction and information flow. Although this approach toward integrating both social categories and social networks was first formulated more than 50 years ago, the intellectual impact of the concept has been mostly indirect until relatively recently (see Diani 2013). This is likely because once White and his students began to implement this new catnet research agenda, they quickly pivoted toward formal social network analytical methods, largely leaving the *cats* behind (see Santoro 2008). Indeed, one of the major criticisms of social network approaches in general has been the laser focus on network structure to the exclusion of categorical aspects of individuals and groups.

In recent years proponents of relational approaches to sociology and formal social network analysis in particular have made renewed efforts to bring *categories* back into the fold (e.g., Mische 2009; Tilly 2005; White 2008b; see also Emirbayer 1997; Emirbayer and Goodwin 1994 for similar arguments). Mark Pachucki and Ronald Breiger (2010) review this and related developments in relational sociology and suggest that there is a burgeoning interest in once again explicitly focusing on the cultural contingency of social network structural relationships in terms of social categories, norms, and practices. Thus, the time is ripe for anthropologists and archaeologists to engage with interdisciplinary debates at the intersection of social networks and culture. I argue that the exploration of categories and relations and their interplay may be an area where anthropologists are particularly well poised to contribute theory and methods to the broader social sciences by expanding the range of social settings and the kinds of societies included in comparative research (see also Peeples and Haas 2013:232–233).

## THE CASE STUDY

This study focuses on the greater Cibola region of New Mexico and Arizona during what is known as the Pueblo III (A.D. 1150–1275) and the early Pueblo IV (A.D. 1275–1325) periods. This large region has been the locus of a number of long-term intensive excavation and survey projects for over a century, including the first formal archaeological expedition in the U.S. Southwest (the Hemenway

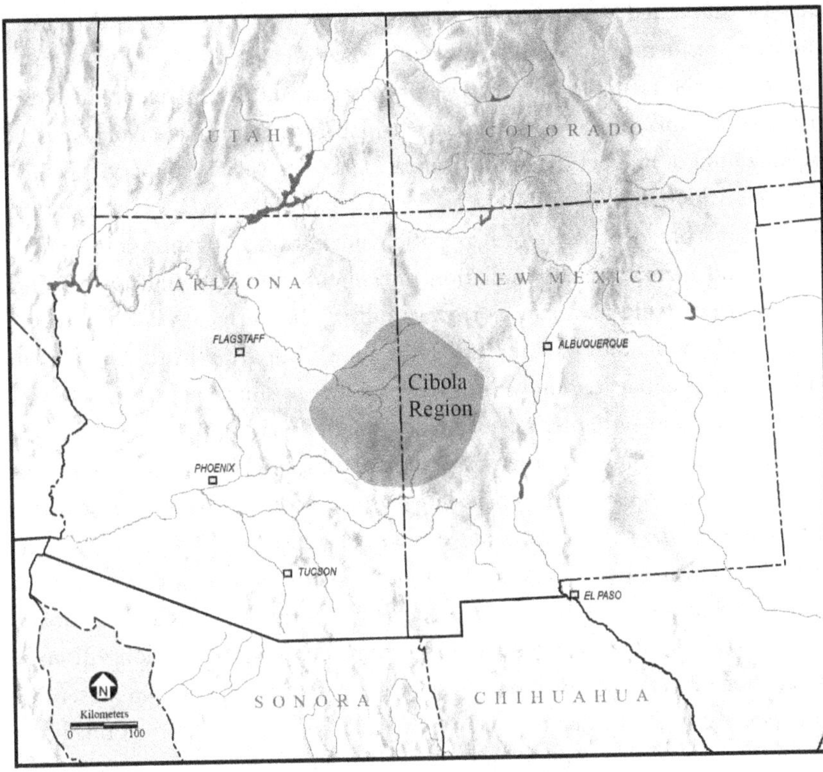


FIGURE 1. Map of the U.S. Southwest showing the greater Cibola region.

Southwestern Archaeological Expedition, beginning in the 1880s; see Cushing 1890). From the very beginning, research in the Cibola region has been regional in scope and directed toward issues of historical continuity and social identity (e.g., Cushing 1890, 1896; Spier 1917, 1918, 1919). Archaeologists working in the Cibola region are blessed with well-defined ceramic and dendrochronological sequences, which provide excellent chronological resolution for considerations of the pace of changes in settlement and material culture through time (see Peeples and Schachner 2012).

My period of interest for this study hinges around a well-documented interval of regional-scale social change occurring across the transition from the Pueblo III to the Pueblo IV periods (ca. A.D. 1275). During the last quarter of the thirteenth century, the inhabitants of the greater Cibola region rapidly abandoned thousands of small pueblos and constructed a small number of massive, nucleated structures, the largest of which may have housed nearly a thousand residents. This settlement reorganization was associated with major changes in the technology and styles of material culture, as well as the structure and organization of public spaces, which further suggest changes in the organization of interaction and identification among social groups at this time.

The Pueblo III to Pueblo IV transition in the Cibola region was also embedded within a broader pattern of aggregation, nucleation, reorganization of public spaces, and massive-scale population movement characterizing much of the U.S. Southwest and Mexican Northwest during the thirteenth and fourteenth centuries (Adams 1991; Adams and Duff 2004). Importantly, the inhabitants of the greater Cibola region were among the first to adopt new forms of social organization and settlement associated with the Pueblo IV period across the Southwest as a whole. Furthermore, within the central portion of the study area, this transition appears to have largely been a consolidation of the existing inhabitants of the region; it did not involve substantial immigration from outside of the greater Cibola region (Kintigh 1996; Kintigh et al. 2004). Thus, the Cibola region case study allows for a consideration of the trajectory of a major social transformation largely separate from the consequences of long-distance population movement, which has been a primary focus of research in most other portions of the Southwest for this time period. In the remainder of this book, I build the case that the rapid and widespread changes characterizing the late thirteenth century in the Cibola region can be profitably examined in relation to models focused on the drivers of social change typically applied to contemporary or recent historic settings.

## ARCHAEOLOGICAL PROXIES FOR SOCIAL TRANSFORMATION, RELATIONS, AND CATEGORIES

In order to explore the relationship between social identification and social transformation through archaeological data, I must face three primary challenges. First, I must demonstrate that a given transition in the archaeological record can be reasonably considered a social transformation in line with those explored in the contemporary comparative social science research that I draw on here. Next, I must document the primary patterns of relational connections and categorical commonality both before and after this transformation. Finally, I then must consider the divergent trajectories and pace of the social transformation through time in relation to different configurations of overlapping relational connections and patterns of shared categorical identities. In this final section, I outline the road ahead, including brief discussion of the specific methods and analyses that will be used to address these challenges.

In Chapter 2, I provide a more in-depth treatment of the theoretical framework that forms the basis of this study. In this overview, I further define and provide examples of how relational and categorical social identities intersect or diverge to form catnets and what impact this has on the potential for and nature of social transformation in general. Although, as I will show, this approach shares many features with currently popular archaeological methods and models, it also offers something new in that it reframes the investigation of identities in terms not of social boundaries or specific "kinds" of identity such as ethnicity or kinship but rather in terms of the processes through which identification can occur. I argue that this new framework helps to resolve a number of long-standing debates and dichotomies in the archaeological literature over the appropriate kinds of evidence for identifying social groups and social boundaries in the past (e.g., realist vs. constructivist perspectives on identity, primordialist vs. instrumentalist perspectives on ethnicity, passive vs. active notions of style, interaction vs. enculturation, structure vs. agency).

The first question that rises from the framework described above is, how might we identify a social transformation in the archaeological record? I argue that, in many cases, we already have. What archaeologists often so drably refer to as "phase transitions" (i.e., the Pueblo III to Pueblo IV transition; the Classic to Postclassic transition) very often represent truly revolutionary periods of social change. This is especially the case when we have evidence that a given transition occurred quickly (e.g., within one or two generations). Such transitions are often recognized as periods of rapid and widespread reorganization of settlement location, size, or structure and are sometimes associated with other abrupt changes in multiple domains of material culture (see Hegmon et al. 2008; Nelson et al. 2011; Torvinen et al. 2016). These changes often imply a fundamental reconfiguration of the relationships among individuals and larger social groups as well as how people chose to mark or mask social differences in a given social context (see Hegmon et al. 2016).

In Chapter 3, I document the massive shift in settlement along with numerous associated changes that marked the Pueblo III to Pueblo IV transition in the Cibola region. I argue that this period of jarring social change fits squarely within the realm of a social transformation as I have defined it here and likely involved the active participation (or opposition) of the entire population of the greater Cibola region and many areas even farther afield. In light of this, I suggest that it is appropriate to consider this archaeological case in terms of the model of relations and categories drawn from contemporary examples of social transformation.

Next, applying the relational/categorical framework described above using archaeological data necessitates defining material proxies for tracking relational connections and categorical commonality. As the brief outline below illustrates, this definition involves both developing new kinds of analyses and reframing more traditional archaeological analyses and data in new ways. Thus, the research in this book both adds to and extends the vast literature in archaeology on the appropriate methods and data for tracking social identity and social boundaries using traditional anthropological frameworks.

As described above, relational connections are forged out of networks of interpersonal interaction among individuals and larger groups. For the purposes of this study, I track the strength and direction of relational networks among the inhabitants of settlements across the study area using two complementary approaches. First, in Chapter 4, I track the movement of ceramic objects using geochemical compositional analyses focused on both painted and unpainted ceramics. These analyses take advantage of the massive amount of neutron activation analysis (NAA) data available from the Cibola region (Schachner et al. 2011; Peeples 2011), one of the largest regional samples in North America and anywhere in the world. These data allow me to track moderate to long-distance interactions (and, by extension, relational networks) across the study area and in nearby areas. I argue that settlements or groups of settlements involved in common spheres of ceramic circulation likely represent groups of individuals who were interacting on a regular basis, suggesting strong relational connections. I further argue that the circulation of different kinds of ceramics (unpainted vs. painted vessels) may provide insights into different kinds of social ties and identities among the inhabitants of the Cibola region.

The second approach consists of a series of detailed characterizations of technological style of both culinary ceramics and domestic architectural features. Numerous recent archaeological and ethnographic studies have focused on the potential of technological characterizations of material culture for assessing interactions, cultural origins, and social identities (e.g., Carr 1995; Clark 2001; Dietler and Herbich 1998; Gosselain 1998, 2000; Huntley 2008; Lyons 2003; Neuzil 2008; Sassman and Rudolphi 2001; Stark et al. 1998; see also Lechtman

1977; Lemonnier 1986). An ever-growing body of research suggests that attributes of material culture that are either invisible in the final product or located in contexts of low visibility more often vary in relation to the degree of interaction among producers in contrast to processes such as emulation (see Carr 1995; Clark 2001:6–22). Strong patterns of similarity in such low-visibility technological attributes provide important indicators of shared contexts of learning and shared "communities of practice" (e.g., Cordell and Habicht-Mauche 2012; Dietler and Herbich 1998; Gosselain 1998, 2000; Herbich 1987; Sassman and Rudolphi 2001; Stark et al. 1998; this approach also owes its origins to the chaîne opératoire approach to the anthropology of technology popularized by French researchers, in particular Leroi-Gourhan [1964] and Lemonnier [1986]). In this study, evidence for shared technological practices related to pottery production (Chapter 5) and the construction of domestic architectural spaces and features (Chapter 6) is interpreted as evidence of frequent interaction or common historical ties (strong *relational connections*) among the producers of those objects and spaces. The analyses presented in these chapters include both formal social network analyses and more traditional distributional analyses. As these analyses show, regional patterns of technological similarity and difference in both ceramic production and domestic architecture are quite similar, suggesting that both technologies were learned through similar vectors of frequent face-to-face interaction.

Categorical identities are built from perceived similarities with social roles or groups to which one can belong. Categorical identities do not depend on direct connections among individuals. Thus, categorical social groups typically require symbolization in order to facilitate the recognition of members vs. nonmembers of those groups (Calhoun 1995:193–230). The process of symbolization includes the kinds of active expressions of identity through material culture often referred to in archaeology as "emblemic" aspects of style (Wiessner 1983, 1984, 1985). In this study, I present two analyses directed at identifying patterns of shared categorical identities and such active expressions across the Cibola region through time: a stylistic analysis of certain decorated ceramic vessels and characterizations of the forms and locations of public architectural spaces across the region through time.

In the Cibola region, bold designs on the exteriors of large serving bowls have been suggested to be active signals of social identities (Mills 2007a, 2007b). A recent study by Barbara Mills (2007a) demonstrates that the size and boldness of the designs on these vessels in one portion of the study area tend to vary in relation to the sizes of the settlements and public spaces at these settlements through time. These large polychrome serving bowls are frequently found in settlements associated with evidence of communal feasting events (Mills 2007a, 2007b; Potter 2000; see also Spielmann 1998). Furthermore, specific communities also appear to have produced large numbers of vessels characterized by certain iconic designs and color combinations on bowl exteriors. The repeated use of design elements, the boldness of these designs, and their association with public ritual together suggest that visual information potential was an important consideration in their production and use. Thus, I argue that patterns of similarity and difference in designs associated with these polychrome bowls can be used as one indication of patterns of shared categorical identities among the inhabitants of settlements across the Cibola region. In Chapter 7, I address the expression of categorical identities through ceramics based on detailed stylistic analyses of a large sample of whole and partial bowls, along with a regional analysis of ceramic ware distributions.

Public architecture can be defined as highly visible built spaces with evidence for simultaneous use by large groups of individuals. Cross-culturally, the largest forms of public architecture are associated with public ritual or other specialized activities (Adler and Wilshusen 1990). Although public architecture is not inherently integrative, the scale of activities assumed to take place in these spaces brings large numbers of individuals into close proximity, fostering opportunities for other interactions (Hegmon 1989; Varien 1999:22–23). There are a variety of common types of public architecture in the Cibola region, often with multiple types appearing in individual settlements (e.g., Kintigh et al. 1996; Martin and Rinaldo 1950; McGimsey 1980). In Chapter 8, I explore the distributions of public architectural features across the greater Cibola region. Shared forms and attributes of public architectural spaces are interpreted as common contexts for public rituals. It is often the case that communities with similar public architectural spaces engage in similar kinds of public rituals (see Adams 1991; Adler and Wilshusen 1990). The public nature of these spaces further suggests that such features provide contexts for active expressions of social identities and social boundaries among individuals and larger groups at different scales. Thus, settlements or groups of settlements characterized by similar public structures are interpreted as areas occupied by people sharing a high degree of categorical commonality.

Finally, in Chapter 9, the results of the various analyses described above are combined in order to determine where they converge or diverge and to identify changes in the scales at which the relational and categorical modes of social identification operated and intersected across the Cibola region through time. Based on all of the analyses described briefly above, I argue that the Pueblo III to Pueblo IV transition in the Cibola region does constitute a major social transformation that was similar in both structure and trajectory to many well-studied contemporary examples. Furthermore, patterns of relational connections prior to this period of transformation appear to provide strong indications of the organization of collective action and the emergence of new categorical identities across the region as a whole. Interestingly, the strongest evidence for relational connections and the strongest evidence for categorical commonality are both highly consistent across multiple material proxies. At the same time, the trajectories of change in relations and categories are not entirely isomorphic (in other words, the strongest evidence for relational networks and the strongest evidence for shared expression of categorical identities do not always overlap). Such "mismatches" across different lines of evidence have often been treated simply as analytical noise or hindrances to exploring complex issues like identity through material culture alone (see Jones 1997:122–127; Eckert 2008:2–3). In this study, I argue instead that such mismatches also further suggest particular configurations of social relationships that would have defined the likely scales of organization and collective action across the region. Importantly, I document a trend toward increasing segmentation and consolidation across the Pueblo III to Pueblo IV transition along multiple lines of material evidence.

Overall, the patterns I document throughout this study suggest that collective identity, mobilization, and social transformation were increasingly tied to smaller geographic scales across the thirteenth-century social transformation in the Cibola region as populations aggregated into larger communities in fewer places. The changes that characterize this social transformation provide evidence that the same social processes and mechanisms were at work in this nonstate, nondemocratic, premodern context as have been documented in dramatically different contemporary and recent historic social settings. These similarities in trajectory and process suggest a need to reconsider the historical ubiquity of social movements and social transformation in general.

# 2

# LINKING SOCIAL IDENTITY AND SOCIAL CHANGE

HOW MIGHT we best evaluate the relationship between the process of social identification and social change at large geographic and social scales using material cultural data? In the discussion below, I attempt to move toward addressing this question by developing and evaluating a new framework drawing on both traditional anthropological perspectives on identity and models and methods from the broader comparative social sciences that have not previously been applied to archaeological research. This chapter sets the stage for the entire study by providing a historical perspective on how archaeologists have traditionally interpreted social identity and social groups at large scales and, further, by exploring what might be gained by considering alternative approaches. I argue that theoretical frameworks used to study the emergence and spread of social movements in the contemporary world may offer new insights into the processes involved in social change in the more distant past. Such approaches have the potential to help us get beyond the often static picture painted by the traditional culture area framework and, further, to allow us to more directly evaluate potential similarities and differences in how and why societies change in the past and in the present.

## ANTHROPOLOGICAL AND ARCHAEOLOGICAL PERSPECTIVES ON IDENTITY AND ETHNICITY

From the very beginnings of formal archaeological research archaeologists have been interested in exploring the nature and development of social groups in the prehistoric past, but the theoretical and methodological tools employed in such studies have changed dramatically over the last century and a quarter. Early archaeological studies of social identity, beginning in the late nineteenth and early twentieth centuries, used the distributions of material culture to define the discrete territories of *peoples*. The goal was typically to relate archaeological patterns to specific contemporary national or ethnic populations (see Fewkes 1891; Jones 1997:1–14; Meinander 1981; Veit 1989). Patterns in the distributions of pottery, lithics, house forms, or other objects provided the basis for delineating archaeological culture areas (or *Kulturkreis*), which were interpreted as the territories of bounded populations sharing a common culture, language, and identity (Childe 1929; Gladwin and Gladwin 1934; Kossina 1911:3; Kroeber 1939:2). Most archaeologists interpreted such archaeological cultures as past manifestations of contemporary ethnic populations. Thus, where patterns of material similarity were relatively consistent through time, it was assumed that there was a high degree of ethnic continuity (Jones 1997:16–17; Trigger 1989:163–167).

Ethnicity, as most contemporary researchers would define it, is one particularly important kind of collective social identity, based on a sense of shared culture, common history, and/or descent, that is most often activated in contexts of interaction among groups of socially defined difference (Barth 1969; Cohen 1978; Jenkins 2000, 2004; Jones 1996, 1997; Kaufman 2004). Ethnicity is not the only basis for collective social identification among large groups of people (see Calhoun 1997; Comaroff and Comaroff 1992; Ekeh 1990; Emberling 1997:304–306; Pohl 2004), but it has been by far the most pervasive in the archaeological literature for more than 100 years (see discussions of historical trends in Curta 2007; Jones 1997; Shennan 1989; Stark and Chance 2008). Indeed, the terms *ethnicity* and *identity* have often been used interchangeably, especially in regional-scale studies. My goal here is to provide a brief historical overview of changing perspectives on and uses of the concept of ethnicity and other closely related collective social identities in archaeology and anthropology as a means to introduce an alternate model for exploring collective social identity. Although ethnic identity is not the specific focus of the current study, many of the concepts, debates, and methods involving archaeological perspectives on ethnicity are relevant to the theoretical framework that forms the basis of this study.

The focus on bounded ethnic groups in early archaeological studies of identity draws from broader trends in anthropological research where individual ethnic populations (i.e., the Nuer, the Yanamami, the Zuni, etc.) were long considered the proper units of study, even in multiethnic settings (see Lewis

1991). Throughout most of the early twentieth century, ethnicity was seen by most anthropologists as a fundamental property of both individuals and social groups, understood to be based on a deep psychological and emotional sense of shared heritage that varied little through time (Geertz 1963; Shils 1957; see also Jones 1997:24, 65–72). This view is sometimes called the primordialist, realist, or essentialist perspective on identity. Relying on these relatively static concepts of collective identities, archaeologists most often interpreted abrupt and widespread changes in material culture as products of external forces such as migration, diffusion, or invasion rather than internal social processes (see Shennan 1989). Eric Wolf (1982:6) calls this the "billiard ball" model of social change, in which discrete and well-bounded groups of people, each characterized by a common culture, language, and identity, are seen as continually bumping up against each other and bouncing around on a global scale, all while somehow maintaining their internal coherence.

By the 1960s such static models of identity had increasingly come under attack on multiple fronts. First, through influential work by several anthropologists and sociologists, including Frederick Barth (1969), Michael Moerman (1965), and Raoul Narroll (1964), a consensus began to emerge that ethnicity and other similar collective social identities are not unchanging primordial properties of groups; instead, they are situational *constructs* used by individuals as a means to bind people together based on common interests and, often, to mobilize them toward common goals (see Cohen 1974). From this perspective, social identities are not attributes of individuals but are created and maintained through interactions. This view is known as the instrumentalist or constructivist perspective on ethnicity. Beginning about the same time as these instrumentalist critiques of ethnicity, many archaeologists also began to question the often assumed relationships between patterns in material culture and ethnic or cultural identity in general. Early critics of cultural historical approaches to archaeology such as Lewis Binford (1962, 1965; see also Clarke 1968) argued that variation in material culture could relate to a number of factors other than culture or ethnicity, including the intended function of objects, material availability, or the distribution of activities across space and time (see also Bordes 1973). Due in large part to the shift in focus in archaeology toward systematics and general processes during the 1960s, studies of identity waned, as many saw such efforts as the descriptive project of the old guard (Jones 1997:5–6).

As is often the case with theoretical debates, after swinging between two seemingly dichotomous extremes (primordialist vs. instrumentalist perspectives) the pendulum eventually began to settle somewhere in the middle. The recognition of the fluid and situational nature of social identities by instrumentalist scholars was an important step forward, but this perspective did not address the deep attachments of individuals to the historically persistent social identities recognized by the primordialist scholars. The question that remained then is, how can social identity both be a situational construct and have the durable qualities that allow individuals to recognize similarity and difference across generations?

By the 1980s, a number of researchers had made attempts to bridge the key insights of both the primordial and instrumental perspectives (e.g., Bentley 1987; Geary 1983; Jenkins 2000, 2004; Jones 1997; McKay 1982; Smith 1981, 1984). In one influential example, G. Carter Bentley (1987) attempted to address the problems associated with traditional concepts of ethnicity and other collective identities with reference to Pierre Bourdieu's (1977) theory of practice. Bentley argued that Bourdieu's concept of *habitus*, defined as habitual dispositions that both constitute and are constituted by the actions of individuals, provides the necessary linking argument between the situational and durable qualities of identity. Bentley (1987:27–29) interprets ethnic groups as social units that are mobilized around common experiences that tend to generate similar *habitus* among individuals. From this perspective, ethnic identification is situational in that it is driven by the specific practices of individuals. At the same time, however, similar habitual experiences tend to reproduce similar practices among individuals, giving ethnic identity a durable historical quality (see Yelvington [1991] and Bentley [1991] for further discussion and debate on the relationship between practice and ethnicity).

Drawing on these new theoretical advances, in particular practice-based approaches to identity, studies of social identification and group formation at regional scales once again began to regain popularity in archaeology in the late 1980s and later (see Jones 1997; Preucel 2005; Shennan 1989). Tammy Stone (2003; see also Hu 2013; Lyons and Clark 2008) argues that these more recent studies of ethnicity and social identity fall into two general approaches. The first approach, which she calls the interactionist approach, sees ethnic and other kinds of social boundaries as outgrowths of social interaction between groups socially defined as distinct (see also Cohen 1978; Duff 2002; Emberling 1997). From this perspective, ethnicity is a politically and socially negotiated identity that cannot be sustained outside of interethnic relations. The second approach, which Stone (2003) calls the enculturationist approach, focuses on cultural aspects of specific ethnic or cultural groups rather than the interactions between them (Clark 2001; Dietler and Herbich 1998; Jones 1997; Shennan 1989; Stark et al. 1998). Proponents of this approach argue that ethnic identity is built out of shared notions of habitual practice (i.e., *habitus*) learned through the process of enculturation. Although both positions are quite complex, in general, interactionist perspectives are focused on identifying the differences between groups, whereas enculturationist perspectives are focused on identifying the similarities within groups.

The divergent approaches toward ethnicity within archaeology described by Stone (2003) have fundamentally influenced the kinds of analyses directed toward studies of social identity in general (see Lyons and Clark 2008). Interactionist scholars have largely focused on evidence for interaction among bounded groups, particularly in the form of exchange, as the basis of ethnicity and other kinds of collective social identities (i.e., tribal, cultural, etc.). Working within this perspective, researchers most often use artifact distributions, stylistic analysis, or compositional data to infer the directionality of exchanges and the establishment, maintenance, or dissolution of social boundaries through time (e.g., Asouti 2006; Braun and Plog 1982; Duff 2002; Emberling 1997:319–325; Plog 1980, 1983; Upham 1982). This approach usually entails an active definition of stylistic variation in material culture (e.g., Plog 1980; Wiessner 1983, 1984; Wobst 1977; Wyckoff 1990; see also Hegmon 1992) in that stylistic differences are seen as active and conscious efforts at communicating social difference and marking social boundaries (e.g., Braun and Plog 1982:512–513; Duff 2002:187–192; Wells 1998).

Conversely, scholars working from the enculturationist perspective make a distinction between the kinds of boundary marking and purposeful ethnic signaling entailed in the interactionist perspective and enculturation, which is seen as a largely unconscious process of social learning. Enculturationist studies are most often focused on identifying groups of people characterized by common learning frameworks, particularly in terms of the production of technologies, which may reflect frequent interaction and shared *habitus* or enculturative backgrounds (e.g., Clark 2001, 2004; Dietler and Herbich 1998; Lyons 2003; Stark et al. 1995). This approach is often couched in terms of "communities of practice," which can be defined as groups of people who engage in a set of formal practices representing a common learning framework (Lave and Wenger 1991). The communities of practice model has proven useful and relevant to archaeological research in a number of contexts but perhaps most directly for research focused on technology and craft production (e.g., Cordell and Habicht-Mauche 2012) and more recently for research focused on consumption practices (Mills 2016; Mills, Clark, et al. 2013; Mills et al. 2015). Although the relationships between material culture, identity, social learning, and interaction are complex (e.g., Croes 1989; Dietler and Herbich 1989, 1998; Fennell 2000; Gosselain 1998, 2000; Hegmon 1998; Herbich 1987; Hodder 1982; Jones 1997; Lechtman 1977; Lemonnier 1986; MacEachern 1998; Wright 2005), a number of recent archaeological and ethnoarchaeological studies suggest that similarities in stylistic attributes of material culture that are of low physical or contextual visibility (e.g., subtle differences in ceramic forming techniques, interior domestic architecture, etc.) are infrequently imitated or used as active expressions of social identity (see Carr 1995; Clark 2001). From this, enculturationist scholars argue that commonalities in low-visibility attributes of material culture or spaces, often termed technological aspects of style, suggest shared communities of practice and common enculturative backgrounds among producers.

The enculturationist approach does not preclude the possibility of active expressions of identity through material culture but rather suggests that high-visibility objects, attributes, or spaces are more likely to be used for active and conscious efforts at signaling similarity and difference than less visible ones (Clark 2001:6–22). Groups of people characterized by common enculturative backgrounds do not necessarily constitute an ethnic group, but shared culture may provide the raw material from which ethnicities are built (see Dietler and Herbich 1998). The enculturationist approach has most frequently been used to identify groups characterized by divergent learning frameworks or communities of practice, suggesting distinct enculturative or historical backgrounds, especially in contexts characterized by immigration and the coresidence of multiple social groups (e.g., Clark 2001; Eckert 2008; Stark 2006).

Although the interactionist and enculturationist approaches to social identity have provided useful insights, both also have limitations for explorations of the process of social identification and social change at the broad geographic and demographic scales that are the focus of this study. For example, studies of interaction focus on the boundaries between ethnic and other social groups but do not necessarily address the nature of social identification outside of contexts of direct interaction where such identities may be less salient. Studies of enculturation focus on identifying groups with different enculturative backgrounds but are most frequently applied to contexts where multiple social groups characterized by sufficiently different material cultural traditions closely interact.

Although the degree to which social divisions defined through either approach are explicitly treated as ethnic or cultural distinctions varies among researchers, both approaches are fundamentally based on the premise that discrete and encompassing social groups, representing the scale at which interactions were concentrated and at which identities were expressed, *should* exist (see discussion in Hegmon 1998:271–273). In other words, the question is typically not whether large-scale bounded social groups were important in a particular context but rather at what spatial and social scales such groups or boundaries were defined. Although efforts at combining aspects of both the interactionist and enculturationist approaches have been made, to great effect (e.g., Burmeister 2000; Eckert 2008; Jones 1997; Lyons and Clark 2008; Parkinson 2006; Stone 2003, 2015), these models, heavily influenced by contemporary anthropological perspectives on ethnicity, may not be appropriate for considerations of large-scale collective social identities that are not necessarily ethnic in nature.

## ALTERNATIVE PERSPECTIVES ON SOCIAL IDENTITY AND SOCIAL CHANGE

The discussion above perhaps leaves the reader wondering if there might be a different approach to exploring the nature of social identity at large scales that gets beyond some of the analytical and theoretical issues of work focused on traditional ethnic models. Researchers studying the trajectories and development of contemporary and recent historical social movements or other instances of sustained collective action in the broader comparative social sciences have developed alternative perspectives for characterizing the creation and maintenance of social identities at large social scales. Although these perspectives have been informed in part by anthropological research on ethnicity and social identity in general, they have varied in emphasis in several important ways. In particular, such studies are not as directly concerned with defining social boundaries or identifying discrete groups but rather with exploring the general modes through which the process of identification occurs. As described briefly in the introductory chapter, within this framework, social identification is seen as operating in terms of two related processes referred to as relational identification and categorical identification. Importantly, the relationship between these two modes of social identification is a key factor in the organization of the kinds of widespread social transformations that are the focus of this study.

## RELATIONAL IDENTIFICATION

Relational identification refers to a process through which individuals identify themselves and others with larger social groups based on their positions within networks of interpersonal interaction. Relational networks are built out of social ties, which can be defined as routine and regular transactions between individuals or larger collectives that entail specific socially recognized rights and obligations (see discussions in Nexon 2009:25; Tilly 2002:80). Relational networks may include, for example, groups of people linked through regular face-to-face interaction in contexts of coresidence or people linked through somewhat more formal social ties such as kin relationships. Within any relational network, some people are more closely related than others (i.e., more directly connected); however, indirect connections are still considered structurally equivalent rather than a different type of relationship (at least across a limited number of removes; see White 2008a:1–2). Groups of people linked through relational connections can sometimes comprise named entities such as lineages, but a key feature of relational identities is that they are forged out of *direct* and *indirect connections* among people rather than out of their common membership in some social category that could be defined as external to individual relationships.

The character of social ties along which relational networks are built can influence the salience of relational identities in a given social context. In general, networks based on frequently activated social ties will tend to be more fundamental to the constitution of broader social structures and identities than networks built out of less frequent interactions. In this way, the importance of a given relational identity could be conceptualized as the frequency with which that identity is taken into account, by oneself or by others, in the sum of all social actions (e.g., Tilly 1978:64). Relations based on kinship or common historical origins, for example, are often closely tied to many other relationships and are major organizing factors for formal and informal social interactions. Relations forged through somewhat more limited contacts, such as the public exchange of goods, may have somewhat less influence on other social interactions. At the same time, such "weak ties" (sensu Granovetter 1973) are often important, as they connect distinct social settings that would otherwise be wholly separate and may provide the basis for the development of other kinds of social relationships.

Relational networks and the structural position of individuals within them are often described using formal tools developed by social network analysts (e.g., Emirbayer and Goodwin 1994; Scott 1991; Wasserman and Faust 1994). Social network analysis refers to a set of related approaches, derived from the mathematical field of graph theory, focused on characterizing and visualizing the structure of relationships among individuals or larger social entities. Social network analysis has been important in the social sciences in general for many decades, but only recently has the formal analysis of networks made a strong foothold in archaeology. Indeed, the number of articles per year focused on social networks and network science more broadly in archaeology has increased dramatically only in the last few years (Collar et al. 2015:Figure 2).

In its simplest form, a social network refers to a set of formally defined social relationships among a set of actors. Such formal networks are often depicted as graphs, with actors depicted as nodes (or vertices) and with lines connecting them representing social connections (often called ties or edges). Actors can represent individuals or larger collectives, and ties may entail a wide variety of relationships (e.g., friendship, exchange partnership, frequent interaction, etc.). One of the most important assumptions of network approaches is that the structure of relationships among actors, rather than simply attributes of those actors, is important for determining differences in outcome across that network (Borgatti and Halgin 2011).

The formal analysis of social networks provides a basis for cross-context comparisons on the basis of a factor such as network clustering (e.g., the tendency toward group formation in a given network) or the centrality of a particular actor (e.g., how well a node is connected to the rest of the network or how intermediate a given actor's position is). Archaeologists in recent years have developed a wide variety of methods for defining formal social networks through material cultural and geographic data (e.g., Bernardini and Peeples 2015; Blake 2014; Borck et al. 2013; Brughmans 2010, 2013; Golitko and Feinman 2015; Golitko et al. 2012; Hart and Engelbrecht 2012; Hill et al. 2015; Knappett 2011, 2013; Mills, Clark, et al. 2013; Mills et al. 2015; Mills, Roberts, et al. 2013; Pailes 2014; Peeples and Haas 2013; Sindbæk 2007). The creation of such formal networks has opened the door to a vast array of existing tools and network metrics useful for comparative research (e.g., Wasserman and Faust 1994). In contexts where only limited information is available it is not always possible to describe the structure of a relational network with such a high degree of resolution (see Peeples et al. 2016). It is, however, still often possible to identify and describe the strongest overlapping patterns of interaction in aggregate, even if the positions of individual units within relational networks cannot be articulated with a high degree of specificity. In this book, I use several lines of archaeological evidence to characterize relational social networks among individuals and larger social groups across the Cibola region at a variety of scales using both methods for formal social network analysis and more general concepts drawing on network theory (Borgatti and Halgin 2011).

## CATEGORICAL IDENTIFICATION

Categorical identification is the process through which individuals identify themselves and others with larger groups based on perceived similarities with socially defined categories or social roles to which an individual can belong. This includes membership in formal organizations such as states, religions, political parties, and even ethnic groups, as well as other broad social categories such as gender. An important distinction between relational and categorical identities is that categorical identities can be defined without reference to interactions among individuals or larger social units (although interactions among people sharing categorical identities may be common). For example, a person may be a "Catholic" or a "Protestant" irrespective of his or her kin ties or interactions with others. Membership in a categorical entity is not entirely arbitrary, however. Members of a categorical group must recognize their own common characteristics, and in most cases those characteristics must also be recognized by other members of a particular group. Because categories are not directly built out of relations, however, they need to be symbolized in order to facilitate such recognition (flags are a classic categorical symbol for modern nation-states; see Calhoun 1997:12). Thus, categorical identities are usually named social entities, often with specific material markers of membership or participation.

Although some categorical identities may overlap considerably with patterned relational connections among individuals, categories are not simply an extension of relations. For example, as discussed above, ethnic identities are collectives based on a sense of common origins or descent most frequently activated in contexts of interaction among similarly defined groups (see Barth 1969; Cohen 1978; Jenkins 2000; Kaufman 2004). Ethnic groups are often constituted among people linked in complex relational networks and characterized by other, smaller categorical divisions. At the same time, at the boundary between ethnic groups, each is seen as a unitary whole characterized by an "us" and a "them" (Calhoun 1997:40–41). In other words, although they are often made up of people sharing overlapping relational connections, ethnic groups are categorical identities because they are defined through a process of boundary making that occurs without direct reference to the internal structure of relations among members (see discussions in Stokke and Tjomsland 1996:27; Tilly 2004a).

As categorical identities are not directly built from relationships among people, they can be subject to manipulation and strategic use by individuals perhaps to a greater degree than relational connections. Thus, the boundaries of a given category or the salience of a categorical identity may change depending on the social context. For example, Ian Hodder (1979, 1982; see also Kimes et al. 1982) argues, based on his ethnoarchaeological research in the Baringo district of Kenya, that the active signaling of ethnic identities may be more pronounced in contexts characterized by severe economic stress and competition. Not all categorical identities are so easily manipulated, however. Richard Jenkins (2000:14–15, 2004) argues that certain categorical distinctions deeply embedded in the earliest process of socialization and learning (e.g., personhood, gender) may become "primary identities," which are both extremely robust to change and almost entirely taken for granted by individuals. Such robust categorical identities often maintain strong perceptions of persistence for both members and nonmembers of groups through time and across space.

Some scholars (Calhoun 1993, 1997:36–38; Foster 1974; Roosens 1989; Shennan 1989) argue that, in the relatively recent historical context of nation building, such robust "primary" categorical identities have taken on an increased importance that they probably never had in the past. From this perspective, the increasing importance of categorical identity in recent history is seen as a response to the creation of increased inequalities and the deconstruction of preexisting social relations (usually assumed to have been based almost exclusively on kinship) through the process of state expansion and political centralization. Such a perspective denies the existence of inequalities and factions in nonstate societies (see Stone [2003] for a similar argument regarding ethnic identity), a stance that has been thoroughly rejected by contemporary anthropologists and archaeologists (Brandt 1994; Brumfiel and Fox 1994; Flanagan 1989; McGuire and Saita 1996; Paynter 1989). I argue that there is no compelling reason to believe that robust large-scale categorical identities, ethnic or otherwise, did not exist in the premodern past, even within nonstate societies.

## COLLECTIVE ACTION AND SOCIAL TRANSFORMATION

The relational and categorical modes of identification described above provide more than a taxonomy for describing variation in the complex processes involved in the creation, maintenance, and dissolution of group identities. Importantly, a number of researchers have linked these general modes of social identification to the potential for and organization of widespread trajectories of collective action and social transformation in many contemporary and recent historical contexts. A large body of empirical research suggests that the particular configuration of relations and categories in a given social context influences the social scale at which collective action is most likely and potentially where it would be most transformative.

The term *collective action* refers to the wide variety of social processes through which large numbers of individuals cooperate toward a common outcome, often seen as some sort of public good (see Baldassarri 2009). Research on the development of and motivations for collective action in the social sciences has been extremely broad. Many have approached this topic from an evolutionary perspective, focusing on the processes through which groups of people overcome the rational economic obstacles to cooperation among individuals through repeated interactions (see Kollack 1998; Ostrom 2000, 2010). Such models of collective action have recently been applied to archaeology by a number of scholars primarily focused on ancient states (Blanton 2010, 2011; Blanton and Fargher 2008, 2009; Feinman 2011; see also Carballo 2012). Many other scholars have focused on explaining the emergence of seemingly spontaneous collective public behaviors such as crazes, mobs, riots, or panics (Rudé 1981). Among relational sociologists, collective action has more frequently been considered within the realm of research on political mobilization and social movements (Polleta and Jasper 2001). From this perspective, the primary question shifts from why collective action occurs to how dispersed populations are able to coordinate action across time and space to successfully negotiate fundamental changes within a particular social setting (e.g., Diani 1992; McAdam et al. 2001; Tarrow 1998; Tilly 1978). It is this last approach that provides the inspiration for the current study.

Successful campaigns of collective action can sometimes result in the emergence of social movements. I define social movements here as sustained collective actions that are embedded in local contexts and carried out by individuals linked together through both direct interaction and shared social identities (see Borck [2016] for a somewhat different perspective and further discussion). Importantly, social movements are built out of groups that share common identities that can extend beyond any specific event, action, or protest (see Diani 1992, 2003; see also Stokke and Tjomsland 1996:10–21; Tilly 1998). It is the extension through time and across space of a common identity among members that distinguishes groups involved in the kinds of social movements defined here from similar groups such as temporary coalitions. The ultimate goal of such a social movement is to fundamentally alter a particular social setting in line with the needs and desires of those involved. For the purposes of this study, I define a relatively rapid but lasting change brought about through such concerted collective action as a *social transformation*. Social movements and associated transformations may be prompted by either internal or external forces, but they invoke new or altered identities while at the same time reconfiguring the social, economic, and political relationships among people (see Hegmon et al. 2008; Kristiansen and Rowlands 1998; Schachner 2001; Spielmann et al. 2016; Torvinen et al. 2016; and Van Dyke 2008 for recent archaeological examinations of the process of social transformation based on archaeological evidence).

Not all social movements are organized in relation to the same forces. Researchers studying contemporary social movement processes often make a distinction between conflictual social movements and nonconflictual or consensus social movements (della Porta and Diani 2006:22–23; Diani 2003:301–302; McCarthy and Wolfson 1992; Schwartz and Shuva 1992). The primary difference is that conflictual movements are organized in direct opposition to a specific social group or organization, whereas nonconflictual movements are either broadly supported or not directed toward a distinct and identifiable opponent. Conflictual movements tend to be focused on specific political aims such as the abolishment of slavery, the extension of civil rights to a segment of society, or even armed rebellion. Well-known examples of conflictual movements include the American civil rights movement of the 1950s and 1960s (McAdam 1999), the Pueblo Revolt of 1680 (Liebman 2012), and the more recent Arab Spring. Nonconflictual movements, on the other hand, are most often focused on the transformation of social attitudes or practices toward somewhat broader issues such as environmental degradation, education, or religion. Examples include environmental movements developing across the world in the last 60 years (Michaelson 1994) and even religious movements such as the emergence and spread of Mormonism across the United States in the nineteenth century

(Michaelson 1977). Conflictual and nonconflictual varieties of social movement processes are not entirely distinct, nor are they mutually exclusive, however, and movements may oscillate between conflict and consensus depending on internal or external circumstances (e.g., Kuran 1989; McCarthy and Wolfson 1992:276–278). Importantly, empirical research on contemporary and more recent historical conflictual and nonconflictual movements suggests that they are driven by the same general mechanisms.

Some scholars of movement processes and social transformations limit their definitions of social movements to contentious political practices occurring in the relatively recent past, in particular in the wake of the expansion of democracy and market capitalism over the last few hundred years (e.g., Tarrow 1998; Tilly 2004a, 2004b).[1] I argue, however, that although the formal political or economic relevance of social movements may increase in relation to the consolidation of state authority, many of the same general movement processes are also important in nonstate and nondemocratic settings. For example, Polly Wiessner and Akii Tumu (1998; see also Wiessner 2002) provide a wonderfully detailed historical and ethnographic account of the establishment of the Tee ceremonial exchange system among the Enga of Papua New Guinea over the last 300 years after the arrival of the sweet potato. Before the sweet potato arrived in the Enga territory via exchange with their nearby neighbors, Enga tribes were relatively egalitarian and subsisted primarily through hunting and gathering or small-scale shifting horticulture. After the sweet potato, many Enga groups increasingly began to subsist as sedentary agriculturalists, and some were able to raise large surpluses of pigs fed on the production of potatoes. The establishment of sedentary communities and the expansion of potato and pig farming involved massive population relocations and intensified exchange among previously distinct social groups. Within a relatively short period, this intensified exchange formed the foundation for a series of complex ceremonial exchange systems, the largest of which was known as the Tee cycle. The establishment of these ceremonial exchange systems was associated with newly invigorated regional-scale categorical social identities (ancestor cults) defined in part through common participation in public ceremonial gatherings. These changes eventually led to the development of an entrenched regional social hierarchy that was based on wealth accumulated through exchange and pig production and that extended across generations through specific lineages.

All of the changes within the Enga region described here happened prior to contact with and without intervention from colonial state powers, but this change was marked by many of the same processes that characterize contemporary social movements and social transformations. Specifically, the establishment of the Tee cycle involved broad-scale and sustained collective action directed at creating social change (i.e., rapid settlement reorganization and relocation in relation to new economic opportunities), as well as the consolidation of newly important categorical social identities defined in relation to this trajectory of collective action (i.e., the establishment of ceremonial exchange systems and ancestor cults that cross-cut previous social boundaries). These processes brought about a fundamental and permanent reconfiguration of Enga society in a relatively short period of time. As this example suggests, although the degree of formal politicization and some of the specific dynamics may differ when compared with contemporary social movements, many of the same social movement processes documented in contemporary nation-states are arguably at work in nonstate settings as well. This suggests that models of social movement processes may also be generally relevant to examinations of periods of rapid social change in premodern archaeological contexts.

Although the concept of the social movement has a deep history in the social sciences, few archaeologists have attempted to directly explore the nature or trajectories of movements in the archaeological record. Notable exceptions include a few recent attempts at applying Anthony Wallace's (1956) influential model of the origin and spread of "social revitalization movements" to archaeological cases (see Bradley 1996; Glowacki 2011; Liebmann 2012; Turnbaugh 1979; see also McGuire 1989; Wallace 2014). For example, Matthew Liebmann (2012) used the concept of the social revitalization movement to explore the processes of culture change that occurred during the Pueblo Revolt of 1680 and its aftermath in the U.S. Southwest. By combining the concept of revitalization with a practice-based, semiotic approach to material culture, Liebmann argues that archaeological explorations of social movements provide a useful explanatory framework for understanding the rapid transformations in material culture and social organization that are frequently seen in the archaeological record. I argue that many other rapid transitions in the archaeological record can be considered in light of theoretical models derived from the broader body of social movement theory beyond Wallace's (1956) seminal ethnological work on revitalization.

There are certainly limitations to studying social movements and social transformations in the archaeological record. Features of movements that are key dimensions of study in the context of contemporary social transformations, such as the specific motivations of participants, the specific strategies employed, and broader perceptions of social change, are unlikely to be fully accessible through material remains alone. At the same time, I argue that it is still possible to track the dynamics of social transformation in the archaeological record in relation to models of contemporary movement processes, as there are commonalities in the trajectories of social transformations and identities that extend beyond any particular case.

## LINKING RELATIONS AND CATEGORIES TO SOCIAL CHANGE

The two general modes of social identification described above (relations and categories) are complementary rather than mutually exclusive. Social identities, from the perspective of the individual, are always cross-cutting and complex. However, these two idealized modes of social identification provide a means for exploring variation in the relationship between identity and social transformations, particularly at broad social and geographic scales. It is also important to note that relational and categorical dimensions of identity are not binary concepts. Thus, one may assess the strength of relational connections in terms of the number of consistently overlapping social ties or the degree of categorical commonality in terms of the degree of homogeneity of shared public expressions of similarity among groups of people.

Charles Tilly (1978:62–69), building on then unpublished work by Harrison White (later published as White 2008a), perhaps illustrates the relationship between relations and categories best by conceptualizing both as separate dimensions of a whole (see Figure 2 for a modified version of Tilly's original conceptualization). Tilly uses the four extremes of this two-dimensional diagram to characterize certain idealized configurations of social connections among individuals. Empirical studies of historical incidences of sustained collective action presented by Tilly (1978, 1998, 2002, 2004a, 2004b, 2005) and a number of other researchers (see Baldassarri 2009; Diani 2003, 2007; Diani and McAdam 2003; Gould 1993; McAdam and Paulson 1993; Nexon 2009; Stokke and Tjomsland 1996; Tarrow 1998) suggest that the particular configuration of relations and categories among large groups of people has an enormous impact on both the potential for the kinds of organized collective activities that can generate social transformation and the specific forms it may take. By way of an example, I describe here the general kinds of collective actions (and hindrances to collective actions) that these studies suggest are likely to characterize each of the four idealized extremes of Tilly's (1978) two-dimensional scheme.

This discussion draws heavily on Daniel Nexon's (2009; see also Stokke and Tjomsland 1996) thorough characterization of Tilly's key insights.

Among large groups of people who are weakly linked by relational connections and characterized by a low level of shared categorical homogeneity (the lower left quadrant of Figure 2), sustained collective action is rare. Under such circumstances, cooperation is subject to the kinds of constraints often placed under the rubric of collective action problems such as the classic "prisoner's dilemma" and the "tragedy of the commons" (see Kollock 1998). In such situations, where individual actors have few established connections to structure interaction and few cues of shared categorical identities to provide an indication of expected behaviors, there are substantial roadblocks to sustained collective action (Oliver and Marwell 1988; Ostrom 2010). Individuals will tend to respond to their own interests and carefully guard against exploitation by others. Nexon (2009:49–50) notes that this position is often incorrectly assumed to be the default situation from which all incidences of collective action emerge.

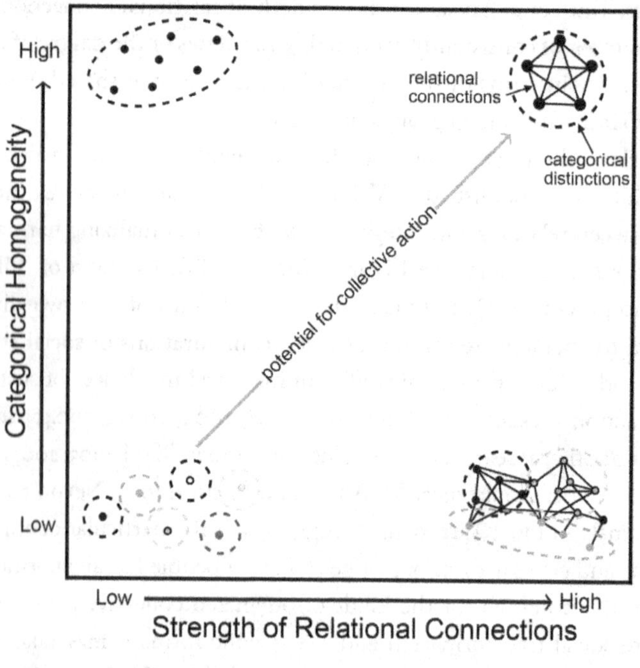


FIGURE 2. Schematic model of the relationships among relational connections, categorical homogeneity, and the organization of collective action (inspired by Tilly 1978: Figure 3-3).

In social contexts characterized by groups of people linked in dense relational networks but with little categorical commonality (the lower right quadrant of Figure 2), collective action is considerably more likely to arise than in the situation described above. Dense networks of interaction provide predefined pathways for cooperation among individuals, which can substantially lower the transaction costs associated with collective activity (Gould 1995; Kim and Bearman 1997; Siegel 2009). At the same time, the lack of significant shared categorical identities may create a situation where collective action is limited to dense subgroups of actors within more expansive relational social networks (divided along the lines of distinct categories) rather than spreading across a broader array of actors. If new and more inclusive categorical identities associated with a particular trajectory of collective action do not eventually emerge, collective action within such strong relational network / low categorical commonality situations may be relatively limited in scope and duration (see Nexon 2009:52).

Cases falling in the upper left extreme of Tilly's diagram represent situations where social groups share strong categorical identities but lack dense relational networks. Such groups can often be quite large, as is the case with national or religious organizations, and may include many more individuals than could reasonably interact on a regular basis (Calhoun 1997:42–44). In situations characterized by such weak relational connections but strong categorical identities, collective action usually emerges in response to a specific stimulus, whether internal or external, which in turn activates a specific shared categorical identity. Nexon (2009:51) provides the example of the broad array of collective activities and public categorical expressions occurring in the wake of the attacks on September 11, 2001 (e.g., flag flying, public demonstrations, etc.). However, lacking dense relational networks, such categorically based collective actions tend to be relatively ephemeral, often declining as the original stimulus to action declines in relevance.

The final idealized position in the upper right of Tilly's diagram is characterized by groups linked in dense relational networks of interaction that also share strong categorical identities. In such a situation, the costs of cooperation and collective action are low due to the strength of overlapping network ties. Networks provide well-established vectors for interaction that tend to promote continued collective action. At the same time, the high degree of categorical homogeneity discourages the subdivision of relational networks. Harrison White (1992, 2008a, 2008b) refers to social situations falling within this idealized quadrant as *catnets*, a term combining category and network. To White, such settings are important social forms specifically because catnets are conducive to collective action and social transformation. White (2008a) suggests that networks only truly become the drivers of social change when individuals in a relational network build up a formal categorical identity around their relations (there are certainly Marxist undertones in this formulation; see Crossley [2011:196]). Thus, when social settings approximate catnets, sustained, organized, and successful collective action of the kind that is often truly transformative becomes more likely at that scale (Nexon 2009:50–51; Tilly 1978:81–90).

Empirical research in a variety of contexts suggests that catnets can emerge through a number of distinct social processes. For example, categorical identities can provide the basis for new network connections through strong tendencies toward homophily (i.e., the development of networks among individuals with similar attributes; see McPherson et al. 2001). Conversely, dense relational connections can also facilitate the formation of new encompassing categorical distinctions. In other words, "nets" can beget "cats," or "cats" can beget "nets." In either case, the creation of new catnets at an expanded social or geographic scale is often a key part of the process of social transformation.

At this point, it is instructive to provide brief examples of how the general process of catnet formation described above plays out in particular social settings (in both the recent and more distant historic past). Perhaps the most frequently invoked example of the changing scope of relations and categories in social movement processes centers on the U.S. civil rights movement. As Doug McAdam (1999) characterizes the emergence of political action associated with the civil rights movement, during the 1940s through the early 1960s protests were initially largely organized in local communities around social groups connected by strong relational networks among black churches and ministers in particular. Through participation in specific actions and protests, these strong relational networks became increasingly subsumed under the categorical notion of "civil rights activists" in an attempt to include greater numbers of people. The creation of this new categorical identity built around the notion of social activism writ large provided opportunities for recruiting participants beyond the initial dense relational networks that had formed the nucleus of the early movement. As McAdam illustrates, this categorical distinction increasingly became the basis for increased participation of "ideologically available" new groups, including northerners and white students who were already tied to other networks of active political participation that had previously been operating separately. Large and increasingly inclusive campaigns like the "Freedom Summer" in turn fostered new relational connections among previously distinct sets of actors, expanding the social and demographic scale at which both relations and categories were shared. Thus, this new categorical notion of civil rights activism and the networks among new participants resulted in an expanded catnet setting focused on coordinated political action and protest at a large scale (McAdam 1999:146–180).

Nexon (2009) provides another excellent example in a very different context in his exploration of the changing face of politics and society in early modern Europe. He argues that early dynastic polities had been successful in maintaining rule for many centuries due in large part to the ability of dynastic rulers to divide their subjects both through geography and along class lines. Specifically, dynastic rulers worked to prevent successful campaigns of contention from ever emerging at large scales through a complex web of negotiations, contracts, accommodations, and suppression focused on *local* elites and factions that may otherwise have had reason to unite. This created a situation where most disputes were relatively localized and resistance to dynastic authority in one area did not often spread to other areas. Nexon argues that these dynastic polities were increasingly destabilized across the early modern period due in large part to the rise of Protestantism and the increasing relevance of religion as a source of identity and contention. During the Reformation, religion became a newly powerful categorical identity that cross-cut both political (geographic) and class boundaries where relational connections tended to be concentrated. This new categorical identity facilitated interaction and acts of political resistance among groups of people who previously had little contact. This process culminated in the emergence of new dense relational networks spanning the boundaries of polities and ultimately in the development of powerful "interregional" or "international" catnets that began to erode dynastic political rule.

As these two examples suggest, although the specific mechanisms involved in the emergence and spread of social change may vary from context to context, social transformations are often intrinsically linked with the creation of new and more pronounced categorical distinctions that further become the basis of identity and interaction (e.g., Aunio and Staggenborg 2011; McAdam et al. 2001, 2008; Nexon 2009; Tarrow and McAdam 2005). Many scholars focused on social transformation in the modern world assume, however, that the increasing importance of categorical distinctions in such settings is a product of contemporary (often read as post–A.D. 1500 Western) political realities and social boundaries and thus that such trajectories should be limited to modern polities and nation-states (e.g., Calhoun 1997:42–48; Stokke and Tjomsland 1996; Tilly 2004b). In this study, I contest this notion and instead argue that the social transformation processes described here are relevant across a broader range of social and political organizational settings than has typically been recognized.

The discussion of contemporary research on social identity and social change outlined above suggests that many major social transformations follow a particular trajectory of change through time marked by an increasing consolidation of relational social ties followed by the creation, elaboration, and spread of new and more distinct categorical identities. In the remainder of this book, I track changes in the configuration of and interplay between relational connections and categories through time in order to determine if such a trajectory characterized the late thirteenth-century social transformation in the Cibola region. If such a trajectory can be demonstrated in the Cibola region (a nonstate, nondemocratic, noncommercial, and noncentralized social context), it would suggest the need to expand the scope of cases typically considered relevant in comparative research focused on the dynamics of social transformation in general.

From the body of theory outlined in this chapter, I derive a few key principles that I argue will be useful in assessing the relationship between social identification and social transformation in the Cibola region and in archaeological contexts generally. First, the broad array of processes involved in collective identity formation and maintenance can be characterized in terms of the strength of relational connections and the shared categorical identities among groups of individuals. Importantly, groups characterized by strong relational connections or a high degree of categorical homogeneity are not necessarily coterminous. This observation stands in contrast to many traditional accounts of social identity at broad spatial and social scales in archaeology. Typically, archaeological investigations conflate relations and categories in favor of debates over the specific kind of collective identity a particular social setting entails (i.e., tribal vs. cultural vs. ethnic, etc.) or the demographic/geographic scale at which discrete and bounded groups can be identified. In this study, I argue that an explicit consideration of both relations and categories independently can provide new insights into the process of regional-scale social transformation in the Cibola region and other archaeological cases. Beyond this, I argue that many longstanding arguments over the nature of social identity in particular contexts are due in part to researchers privileging either relations or categories alone rather than their interplay.

The framework described above suggests that sustained collective actions that are truly transformative tend to be organized around catnets: groups of individuals who are highly connected relationally and who also share strong and homogeneous categorical identities. Importantly, strong relational connections among groups of people often precede the establishment of formal categorical identities. As Ann Mische (2011:86) puts it, new expansive categorical identities often develop from "an emerging awareness of structural equivalence in network position." From this, it follows that networks of frequent interaction or common historical ties prior to a period of transformation may predict the nature and scale of that social transformation.

Finally, related to the point above, many contemporary social transformations are characterized by a trajectory of change through time in which collective actions and social transformations either spread beyond their original contexts or become more deeply entrenched as new categorical identities emerge and become increasingly important and well defined at a given scale. This is not a simple diffusion of social change through an existing relational network; rather, this process involves a fundamental reconfiguration of the social identification through the creation of new, broader, and more distinct categorical identities. This process has often been seen as a product of modern political realities, but the examples I provide here suggest broader similarities in the trajectories of major social transformation across a wider variety of social contexts than have typically been considered. These general principles will provide avenues for assessing the applicability of the relational/categorical model of identity for the Cibola region case study and will also frame the concluding discussion in this book.

# 3

# SOCIAL TRANSFORMATION IN THE CIBOLA WORLD

FOR MORE than a century, the greater Cibola region, centered on the contemporary Pueblo of Zuni, has been the focus of research on issues of cultural identity (e.g., Cushing 1890, 1896; Ferguson and Hart 1985; Fewkes 1891; Green 1990; Mindeleff 1891; Spier 1917, 1918, 1919; Woodbury 1956). The core of the Cibola region has long been recognized as the ancestral homeland of the contemporary Zuni (A:shiwi) people (e.g., Kintigh 1985a, 2007; Woodbury 1956). The region also includes the traditional area of Zuni sovereignty and the vast majority of the named locations mentioned in Zuni migration histories (e.g., Cushing 1896; Ferguson 2007; Ferguson and Hart 1985; Frisbie 1984). Interestingly, the greater Cibola region also spans the traditionally defined boundaries between two archaeological culture areas: the Ancestral Pueblo culture area to the north and the Mogollon culture area to the south. The complexity of material distributions and social connections across the region makes this an ideal context within which to explore the relationships between social identification and social change at broad spatial scales.

My goals in this chapter are to (1) briefly describe the history of settlement and settlement organization across the greater Cibola region through time and (2) illustrate how the changes characterizing the late thirteenth century in particular can be profitably characterized as a social transformation. As I defined it in the previous chapter, a *social transformation* refers to a period of lasting and dramatic social change brought about through widespread collective action.

Thus, the task at hand is to demonstrate the dramatic impact, rapid pace, and coordinated nature of social change associated with the Pueblo III to Pueblo IV transition. As I illustrate here, within the span of *a single generation* the dominant patterns of local and regional interaction, social organization, and the nature of social boundaries were all fundamentally and permanently changed for the inhabitants of the greater Cibola region, though the specific changes differed in scope and scale across the region as a whole.

## THE GREATER CIBOLA REGION

I define the greater Cibola region here following Steven LeBlanc's (1989:338) delineation of the maximal extent of the region during the eleventh through the mid-thirteenth century. I view this regional designation as a useful archaeological construct but do not suggest this area necessarily relates to any meaningful cultural or social group in the past. As I have defined it here, the region comprises a physiographically diverse area marked by a common suite of painted ceramic types, as well as certain other similarities in architecture, settlement patterns, and economic strategies. As the following chapters illustrate, however, there are also key differences among specific portions of this large area.

In order to better highlight fine-grained similarities and differences across the region as a whole, I further divide the Cibola region into a number of smaller subregions. These subregions generally coincide with clusters of large settlements (>50 rooms) during the period considered here and also conform to archaeological districts that are commonly used in the regional literature (e.g., Adams and Duff 2004; Adler 1996; Duff 2002). The eight central subregions are treated as the core study area and are the focus of the vast majority of new data collection efforts and analyses discussed in the following chapters. The remaining subregions along the edges of the greater Cibola region are incorporated where possible largely through previously published information. All of these spatial designations are seen as just that and are not necessarily meant to represent the territories of discrete social or cultural groups unless explicitly stated otherwise.

The greater Cibola region includes large portions of the southern Colorado Plateau and the central mountain highlands of Arizona and New Mexico. Elevations across the region range from about 5,000 feet along the western boundary of the study area near Holbrook to over 9,000 feet in the Zuni, White, and

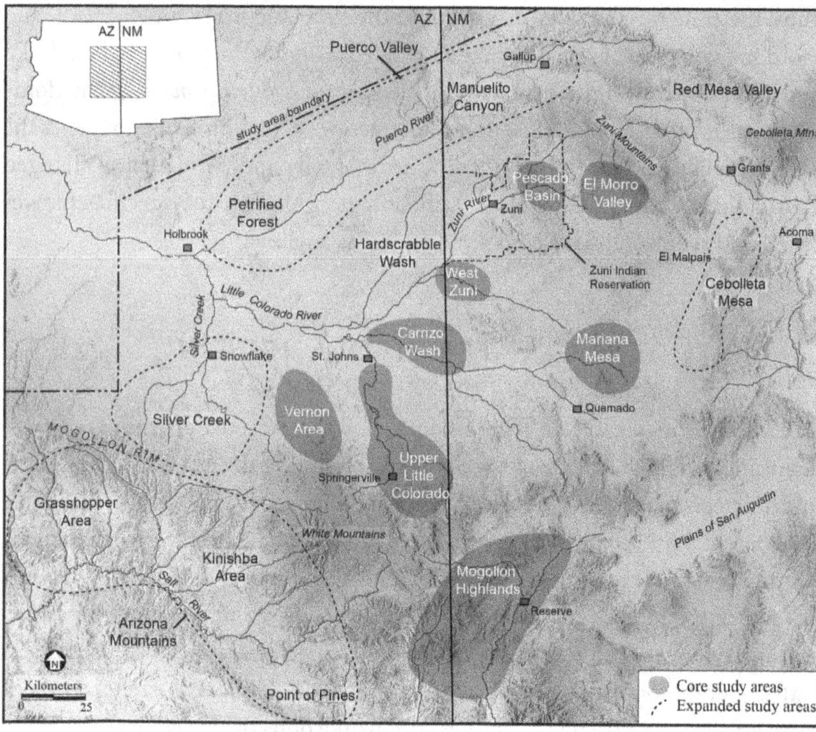


FIGURE 3. Map of the study area showing core and expanded subregions and other geographic features mentioned throughout the book.

Mogollon Mountains (with a few peaks as high as 11,000 feet). The vast majority of agricultural period habitation and land use was focused on areas below about 7,500 feet. As in most other portions of the semiarid U.S. Southwest, elevation and local land forms are both major determinants of other environmental factors that would have been important to agricultural populations in the region, including precipitation, temperature, and the availability of various resources.

Although there is substantial spatial variability, in an average year, most portions of the Cibola region do not receive enough direct precipitation during the growing season for adequate and predictable agricultural production. Thus, the inhabitants of the region relied on various forms of water management, including both runoff capture (Homburg et al. 2005; Muenchrath et al. 2002; Norton et al. 2003) and small-scale spring- or stream-fed irrigation in the locations where such strategies were feasible (see Damp et al. 2002; Kintigh

1985a:96–102).[1] Freezes are possible in most portions of the region during almost any month of the year (VanWest and Greenwald 2005:1.17–1.19). As would be expected, elevation strongly influences both mean annual temperatures and the length of the growing season. Many high-elevation portions of the Cibola region (>7,000 feet) may have experienced killing frosts on a periodic basis. In addition, both rainfall and temperature are locally sporadic and unpredictable, meaning that shortfalls in one area may not have coincided with shortfalls in another nearby area. Such spatial variability, high even by the standards of the U.S. Southwest (Hegmon et al. 2014), likely promoted regular interaction among the inhabitants of different portions of the greater Cibola region and beyond as a means to buffer the risks for local shortfalls (see also Borck et al. 2015; Cordell et al. 2007; Rautman 1993).

## SETTLEMENT HISTORY IN THE CIBOLA REGION: A.D. 1000–1325

The period considered in this study (ca. A.D. 1150–1325) was particularly dynamic in terms of settlement location and organization across the region. In just shy of two centuries, the inhabitants of the Cibola region went from residing in tens of thousands of small pueblos and dispersed hamlets, to increasingly clustered communities, and finally, to just a few dozen nucleated towns (see Duff 2002; Huntley and Kintigh 2004; Kintigh 1996; Lekson 1996). The establishment of the massive towns across the region was rapid and likely necessitated fundamental changes in social organizational strategies (see Kintigh 1985a, 1994). In order to set the stage for an evaluation of this social transformation, I provide here a brief overview of major trends in settlement through time ca. A.D. 1000–1325. This interval begins somewhat earlier than the period directly considered in the bulk of this study, but many of the patterns of settlement organization and regional interaction established at least by the eleventh century (and probably earlier; see Peeples et al. 2012; Schachner et al. 2012) continued to influence social developments in the Cibola region through the period of focus of this study and beyond.

### THE LATE PUEBLO II PERIOD: A.D. 1000–1150

The period from about A.D. 1000 to 1150 across the Cibola region was characterized in most areas by the occupation of relatively small hamlets that likely housed one or a few related nuclear families or households. The vast majority of settlements occupied at this time consisted of between one and ten masonry rooms and in areas above the Mogollon Rim perhaps one or two associated pit structures or kivas (e.g., Beeson 1966; Danson 1957; Dittert 1959; Howell 2000; Kintigh 2007; Longacre 1964; Varien 1990). This period also saw the maximum spatial extent of settlement across the greater Cibola region. Thousands of small sites dotted the landscape, primarily along major drainages and other well-watered areas. Although settlement density varied from place to place, most settlements were relatively dispersed (Peeples and Schachner 2008). There were, however, major gaps in this expansive regional distribution of settlements. Notably, the El Morro Valley in the northeastern portion of the Cibola region was virtually unoccupied at this time, despite becoming the major center of population in later decades (Watson et al. 1980).

In addition to the extensive distribution of small habitation sites across the region, there were several somewhat larger settlements constructed and occupied at this time, with different forms seen in different parts of the region. A number of large architectural complexes with strong similarities to the massive constructions in Chaco Canyon in the San Juan Basin were located in the portions of the Cibola region on the Colorado Plateau.[2] These complexes include Chacoan-style great houses (massively built room blocks usually of about 20–30 rooms; see Chapter 8), as well as other features such as circular great kivas, road segments, and earthen berms. Some of these Chacoan architectural complexes were associated with clusters of small habitation sites, while others were isolated (Duff 2005; Fowler et al. 1987; Mahoney et al. 1995; Roberts 1932, 1939). Several Chacoan architectural complexes are found along the Puerco and Zuni River Valleys, around Cebolleta Mesa, and between the Quemado area and the Arizona–New Mexico border (Duff and Lekson 2006; Duff and Schachner 2007). Although no Chacoan great houses have been identified in the western portion of the study area around Silver Creek, circular great kivas of a form similar to those associated with great houses were constructed at this time. Sarah Herr (2001) argues that these great kiva sites provide evidence for the extension of developments associated with Chaco and perhaps population movement into the Silver Creek area.

In the southern portions of the Cibola region, including the Mogollon Highlands, the Arizona Mountains, and the southern reaches of the Upper Little Colorado Valley, Chacoan architectural features are largely absent (but see discussions in Chapter 8; Duff 2002:67–69; Lekson 1991). In these areas there are, however, a few somewhat larger settlements consisting of masonry room blocks of about 15 to as many as 40 rooms (e.g., Danson 1957:36, 43, 54, 61–62; Rinaldo 1959). Some of these larger pueblos are associated with rectangular great kivas, a form of public architecture with a long history in the mountainous southern portions of the Cibola region (see Danson 1957:81–82; Haury 1950:29–39; Hough 1907:54; Oakes 1999; Olson 1960).

Despite the differences in the form of public architectural spaces in the northern and southern portions of the Cibola region, there is evidence for extensive interaction across these areas and likely some degree of population movement. Cibola White Ware was the dominant decorated ceramic ware across the Cibola region at this time, even though it was likely not produced in some portions of the study area (Mills 2007b:223–225; Wilson 1994, 2007; Wilson and Severts 1999). The widespread distribution of a common suite of decorated ceramics suggests a substantial amount of exchange and/or population circulation among the inhabitants of the entire region at this time.

## THE PUEBLO III PERIOD: A.D. 1150–1275

The Pueblo III period represents the beginning of the interval explicitly considered in this study. This was a period of increasing aggregation across the Cibola region and much of the greater Southwest (see chapters in Adler 1996). Unfortunately, the beginning of this period in the Cibola region is still fairly poorly understood. Absolute dates between about A.D. 1150 and 1200 are rare across the Cibola region as a whole, and with a few exceptions (e.g., Anyon et al. 1983; Eckert 1995; Martin et al. 1964; Westfall 1981), sites that likely fall within the early Pueblo III period are known primarily through surface information. This poorly understood interval coincides with a major hiatus in construction in Chaco Canyon and the San Juan Basin (Marshall et al. 1979; Powers et al. 1983; Windes and Ford 1996), as well as a prolonged dry and warm climatic interval (ca. A.D. 1131–1192; Van West and Grissino-Mayer 2005:33.18), both of which may have had far-reaching effects across the Southwest. More research is needed on issues of settlement and continuity in the early Pueblo III period.

By the beginning of the thirteenth century, patterns of regional settlement are much clearer. There are numerous well-dated sites with tree ring dates in the 1200s across most portions of the Cibola region (e.g., Duff 1999:Appendix A; Schachner 2012:Figure 4.5; Zier 1976). Major full coverage surveys (e.g., Anyon et al. 1983; Hogan 1985; Hunter-Anderson 1977; Kintigh 1980, 2007; Kintigh et al. 2004; Lightfoot 1984), as well as broader reconnaissance projects (Beeson 1966;

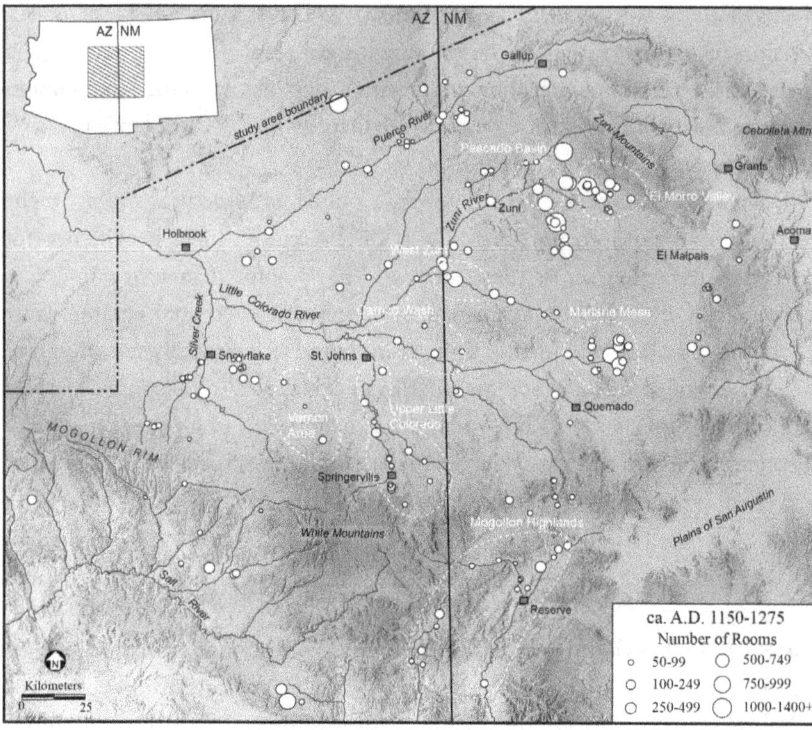


FIGURE 4. Distribution of major settlements during the Pueblo III period.

Danson 1957; Hough 1907; Spier 1917, 1918, 1919), suggest that this was a period of population growth across the region as a whole. Importantly, this era was marked by a large influx of population into the El Morro Valley, an area that was not intensively occupied prior to about A.D. 1225 or 1250 (Schachner 2012; Watson et al. 1980), as well as dramatic increases in population in many other high-elevation areas along the eastern edge of the Cibola region, including the Mariana Mesa and Cebolleta Mesa subregions (Danson 1957; Dittert 1959; Ruppé 1990). The shift of population into the El Morro Valley does not appear to have been associated with major depopulations in other portions of the Cibola region. The massive number of rooms constructed in such a short period in the El Morro Valley may instead reflect the extremely high degree of residential mobility practiced by the inhabitants of the Zuni area at this time (Schachner 2008).

Settlement organization during this period differed from place to place and was likely quite diverse, even at a local level. In general, however, there was a marked increase in site size from the Pueblo II period in terms of both individual structures and communities. In the northern Cibola region, including the Zuni area, Mariana Mesa, Cebolleta Mesa, and the Puerco Valley, a number of large communities were constructed at this time consisting of closely spaced clusters of small room blocks (e.g., Fowler et al. 1987; Kintigh et al. 2004; Kintigh et al. 1996; McGimsey 1980; Saitta 1994; Wozniak and Marshall 1991). These clusters typically ranged from about 100 to over 500 rooms within a small area. Some of these settlement clusters were centered on large structures with many architectural features harking back to the Chacoan era, including massive construction, blocked-in kivas, and circular great kivas (see Duff and Lekson 2006; Fowler et al. 1987; Kintigh et al. 1996; McGimsey 1980). These architectural complexes are often referred to as post-Chacoan great houses and are seen as extensions of Chacoan architectural symbolism into the thirteenth century. Interestingly, there appears to have been some innovation in the form of Chacoan-inspired architecture, as great kivas constructed during this period are larger than Chacoan era structures and unroofed. These large, open structures may have been designed to accommodate the increased size of residential communities (Kintigh 1994; Kintigh et al. 1996). The construction of Chacoan-inspired structures after the decline of Chaco Canyon as a regional center emphasizes the local importance of great house architecture in the Cibola region (Cameron and Duff 2008).

In the south, along the Upper Little Colorado, the Arizona Mountains, the Vernon area, Silver Creek, and the Mogollon Highlands, there are also a few closely spaced clusters of contemporaneous small sites, but the total number of rooms in clusters tends to be smaller, usually about 15 to 100 rooms. These groups of small sites are often also somewhat less spatially consolidated than northern clusters (e.g., Accola 1981; Danson 1957; Lekson 1996; Longacre 1964; Oakes 1999; Peckham 1969; Reid et al. 1996). After A.D. 1200, larger structures with about 50 to as many as 100 rooms were constructed in some areas in the southern Cibola region (Lekson 1996). These larger room blocks appear to have grown accretionally over time and typically consisted of irregular agglomerations of rooms with no evidence of large-scale planning. These large sites were often associated with a nearby or attached rectangular great kiva (DeGarmo 1975; Dungan 2015; Martin et al. 1957; Martin et al. 1956). By the end of the Pueblo III period, most of the population of the southern Cibola region was residing in one of these relatively large pueblos, and most other small sites had been abandoned (Lekson 1996:171).

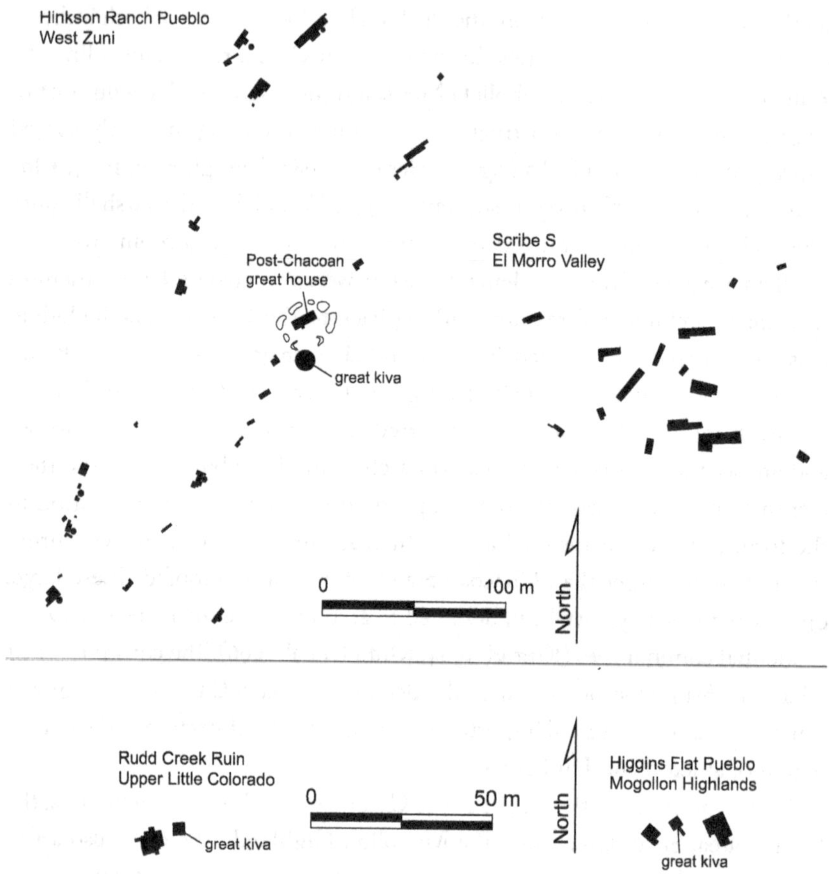


FIGURE 5. Examples of Pueblo III period settlements from the northern (*top*) and southern (*bottom*) Cibola region.

As the discussion above highlights, settlement organization and scale were quite varied across the study area at this time at both the local and regional levels. Overall, however, this period is marked by an increasing consolidation of the regional population into both larger structures and aggregated clusters of structures that likely formed residential communities. The increase in the size of individual structures and in the number of structures in close association with one another suggests that the scale of residential communities may have been greatly expanded compared to the previous century. As I describe below, this process ultimately culminated in the emergence of a new form of settlement consisting of nucleated villages or towns, where entire residential communities were encompassed within a single structure. Although a few nucleated villages appeared prior to A.D. 1275 in some portions of the region (see below), this new form of settlement was not common across the region until the last quarter of the thirteenth century.

## THE EARLY PUEBLO IV PERIOD: A.D. 1275–1325

The Pueblo III to Pueblo IV transition represents an interval of dramatic change across the Cibola region as a whole. By the end of the thirteenth century, virtually everyone in the Cibola region lived in one of about 40 large nucleated towns. The consolidation of population into these towns was associated with the depopulation of many other portions of the region, including the Vernon area, the lower Carrizo Wash area, and much of the Upper Puerco Valley, although those areas may have continued to be used in limited ways. In portions of the Cibola region with continued agricultural occupation, new settlements were established around the beginning of this period, but in some areas along the periphery of the Cibola region, such as the Mogollon Highlands, this period saw the continued occupation of a few of the largest villages (e.g., Lekson 1996; Rinaldo 1962; Robinson 1992).

As I previously suggested, the earliest large nucleated communities probably date to the final decades of the Pueblo III period (ca. A.D. 1240–1250; see Duff 2002:35–40; Duff and Schachner 2007; Lowell 1991), but this community form did not begin to characterize the bulk of the region until after A.D. 1275. Importantly, the specific forms of large, nucleated communities differed dramatically across the region as a whole. In the Zuni River Valley, in the El Morro Valley, and along the Puerco, early nucleated pueblos were rapidly constructed planned structures, indicating a high level of labor coordination (see Fowler et al. 1987; Huntley and Kintigh 2004; Kintigh 1985a; Kintigh et al. 2004). Additionally, a few of the earliest nucleated towns had over 1,000 rooms, suggesting they were formed through the consolidation of multiple smaller aggregated settlement clusters (e.g., Kintigh et al. 2004).

Many of the nucleated settlements in the northern Cibola area consist of distinctive oval and rectangular room blocks (some combining both forms), which some have suggested may represent different social groups or other underlying cosmological principles (Huntley and Kintigh 2004:70–71; Potter 1997). The majority of these villages were constructed around a large central plaza that was

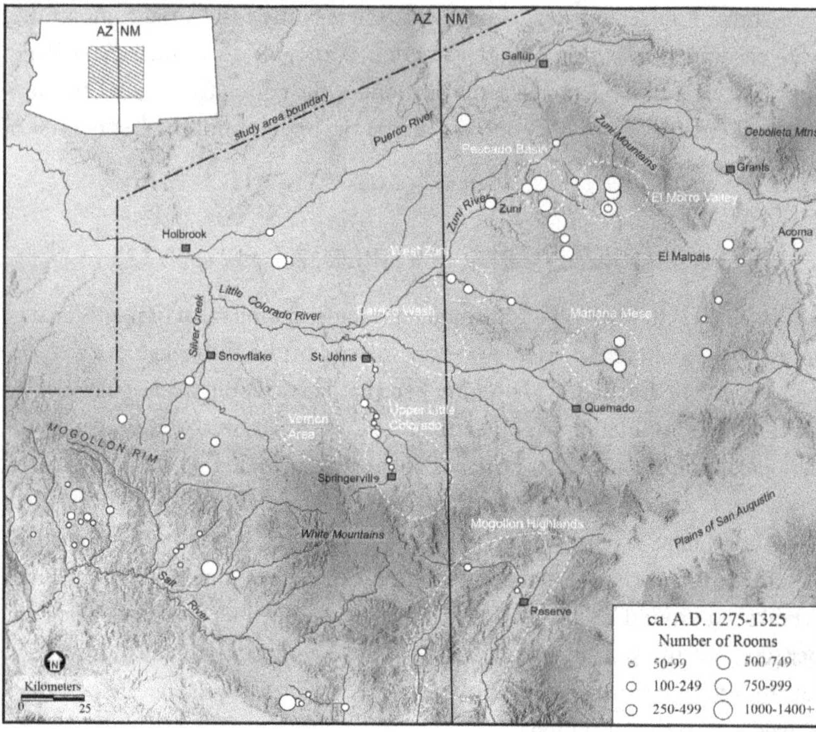


FIGURE 6. Distribution of major settlements during the early Pueblo IV period.

completely enclosed by the walls of the village. Despite their planned layouts and rapid construction, most of the first nucleated pueblos were depopulated within a single generation. Kintigh (1985:115–117) argues that the short-lived nature of the early nucleated towns may suggest that the inhabitants of the Zuni area had not yet developed the mechanisms for social organization and control necessary for life in these unprecedentedly large communities.

To the south, large nucleated pueblos established at this time were similar to the largest irregular agglomerations of rooms described above, but they were somewhat greater in size and began to incorporate open plazas and courtyards into their layouts. In some portions of the region, such as the southern Upper Little Colorado area, the size of these nucleated structures did not differ dramatically from the constructions of earlier decades (Duff 2002:39). Other settlements, such as the 250-room Bailey Ruin along the Silver Creek drainage (Mills et al. 1999), were considerably larger than any earlier communities in the area.

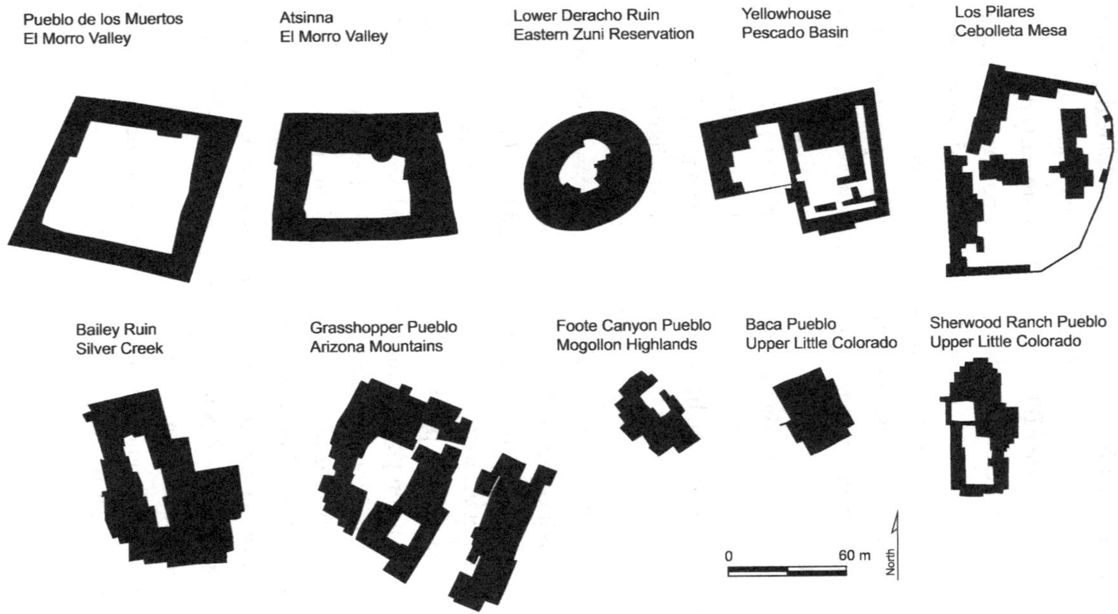


FIGURE 7. Examples of Pueblo IV period settlements from the northern (*top*) and southern (*bottom*) Cibola region.

This illustrates that transition to nucleated settlement may have been somewhat more gradual in the southern and western Cibola region than in areas near Zuni. Where good data are available, plaza-oriented nucleated communities in the Silver Creek, Arizona Mountains, Upper Little Colorado, and Mogollon Highlands areas appear to have grown accretionally rather than being planned and rapidly constructed (see Mills 1998). Furthermore, early nucleated pueblos in these southern and western portions of the Cibola region appear to have been somewhat longer lived than the massive nucleated communities of the Zuni area. These differences in the form of early nucleated communities and the pace of their construction in the northern and southern portions of the Cibola region may suggest differences in the nature or scale of social integration among populations prior to the construction of these communities.

In addition to changes in the nature and organization of settlements, the Pueblo III to Pueblo IV transition was also marked by several major changes in ceramic technology and design. In particular, this was a period of experimentation with glaze paint technologies. Early glaze-painted Cibola White Ware and White Mountain Red Ware ceramics, probably first produced in the mid–A.D. 1200s, may have been an unintentional product of increased firing temperatures and various minerals incorporated into paint recipes. After about A.D. 1275, relatively homogeneous and distinct recipes were established in different portions of the region (Fenn et al. 2006; Huntley 2006, 2008:44–59; Van Keuren et al. 2013). The transition to glaze-painted ceramics also coincided with a divergence in the painted designs on polychrome vessels found across the Cibola region. The widespread White Mountain Red Ware ceramics found across much of the Cibola region during the Pueblo III period diverged into two distinct series: the White Mountain and the Zuni series (often called Zuni Glaze Ware; Carlson 1970). These two distinct traditions have certain features in common but vary quite dramatically in terms of painted designs (see Chapter 7). The divergence between these ceramic traditions in terms of both design and technology may suggest the emergence of somewhat more distinct boundaries between the eastern and western portions of the Cibola region at this time.

## SOCIAL TRANSFORMATION IN THE CIBOLA REGION

As the brief overview above suggests, the Pueblo III to Pueblo IV transition was a dramatic and widespread period of change in the Cibola region. At an even broader spatial scale, the late thirteenth century was a turbulent period across the Southwest as a whole. This period was marked by the depopulation of the northern San Juan (Mesa Verde) region and most of northeastern Arizona, as well as major influxes of population into other areas to the south (Clark and Lyons 2013; Glowacki 2015; Hill et al. 2004). Although the core of the Cibola region around Zuni does not appear to have been a major destination for people leaving regions to the north at this time (Kintigh 1985a), there is substantial evidence for migration into many areas along the periphery of the study area, including but probably not limited to the Silver Creek area, the Arizona Mountains, Mariana Mesa, Cebolleta Mesa, and the Mogollon Highlands (see Kaldahl et al. 2004; Lyons 2003; Mills 1998; Wilcox et al. 2007). The scale of this population movement likely had dramatic consequences across the entire region even for the inhabitants of areas that did not see large numbers of new arrivals.

The pace of the Pueblo III to Pueblo IV settlement transformation across the Cibola region has been a topic of much debate, particularly in the Zuni area. Some argue that nucleation in the Zuni area was extremely rapid, occurring around ca. A.D. 1275–1280, perhaps even within a single year (LeBlanc 2001:30). Steven LeBlanc (1999, 2001; see also Watson et al. 1980) suggests that the transition to nucleated settlements was driven largely by increased conflict associated with regional climatic instability and large-scale population movements. While the available tree ring cutting dates from the El Morro Valley certainly do support the notion of a rapid transition (LeBlanc 2001:Table 2.2), other researchers have used seriations of dated ceramic types to argue that several nucleated pueblos may have been constructed somewhat earlier (ca. A.D. 1250; Huntley and Kintigh 2004; Kintigh 1985a:77–89; Schachner 2007:160–171). Unfortunately, there are no tree ring dates available for any of the nucleated pueblos in the Zuni area that are most likely to predate A.D. 1275. However, among the proposed early nucleated towns are all of the sites with more than 1,000 rooms and three sites associated with unroofed great kivas, a form of public architecture that likely fell out of use around A.D. 1275.[3] If a few nucleated towns in the Zuni area were constructed prior to A.D. 1275, as the limited available evidence suggests may be the case, this would mean that they were contemporaneous with the post-Chacoan great houses and clustered communities described above for a short period in the mid-thirteenth century. The earliest nucleated settlements in the Cibola region were likely constructed in the El Morro Valley and nearby areas to the west that were essentially unpopulated prior to the mid- to late

Pueblo III period (see Schachner 2012). From this, Gregson Schachner (2008; see also Duff and Schachner 2007) argues that the diversity of community forms in the El Morro Valley at this time was indicative of experimentation with different forms of social organization. Shortly after about A.D. 1275–1280, however, only nucleated towns remained across the entire Zuni area.

When considering the Cibola region as a whole, similar processes to those described for the Zuni area have been documented in many other areas, but the scale and timing are somewhat different from place to place. There are certainly some large communities in portions of the Cibola region first established prior to A.D. 1275, such as Turkey Creek Pueblo in the Point of Pines area, which was probably initially constructed in the 1240s (Lowell 1991). There are also a few pre–A.D. 1275 tree ring dates at other nucleated sites across the region (e.g., Casa Malpais, Horse Camp Mill, Los Pilares, Pinedale Ruin), but it is unclear if these dates represent earlier small sites that formed the core of nucleated villages, the initial establishment of nucleated villages, or the reuse of old wood. The available dates from the entire Cibola region suggest, however, that the scale of construction increased rapidly in almost every portion of the study area between A.D. 1275 and 1279 (see Bannister et al. 1970; Duff 1999:Table A.1; Kaldahl et al. 2004:Figure 9.4; LeBlanc 2001:Table 2.2; Riggs 2001:Figure 2.5). Furthermore, the transition to nucleated, plaza-oriented settlements was complete before A.D. 1300. Thus, although the transition may have been more abrupt in some places and more gradual in others, the available evidence suggests that this regional-scale transformation in settlement organization occurred *within a single generation* in the latter half of the thirteenth century.

LeBlanc (1999, 2001) has previously argued that the establishment of nucleated pueblos in the El Morro Valley and other areas across the northern Southwest along the Pueblo III to Pueblo IV transition may have been a response to increased warfare or, at least, the threat of conflict at this time. LeBlanc argues that conflict may have been driven by increasing climatic instability in the last half of the thirteenth century. Other researchers argue, based on reassessments of the nature and timing of the abandonment of Pueblo III period clustered communities, the establishment of Pueblo IV period towns, and the scale of burning at excavated sites, that direct evidence for conflict in the central Cibola region is lacking (Huntley 2008:76–77; Schachner 2007:240–242). The strong direct evidence for violence that does exist is from two nucleated sites along the edges of the Cibola region in the Mariana Mesa area (Techado Spring Pueblo [Smith et al. 2009] and Horse Camp Mill [McGimsey 1980]), but the episodes of violence at those sites date to the fourteenth century, ca. A.D. 1325. Evidence includes intense burning, de facto floor assemblages in numerous rooms (including whole vessels of ceramic types first produced around A.D. 1325), and unburied human remains with substantial evidence for skeletal trauma. The extent of conflict across the entire Cibola region in the late 1200s is currently unclear, but it is certainly likely that the inhabitants of this region were at least aware of conflict in areas to the north (e.g., Haas and Creamer 1996; Kukelman et al. 2000, 2002) that were emptying out during the mid- to late thirteenth century.

The transition in settlement size and layout likely also entailed fundamental changes in social organization. Unlike earlier centuries, when the building blocks of most communities were small room blocks that likely housed one or a few related households, nucleated settlements placed hundreds or in some cases more than a thousand people within a single structure, cheek to jowl. Although there were a few somewhat larger structures during the Pueblo III period, the bulk of the population still lived in small room blocks that may have housed one or a few households. Even where these small structures were part of larger clusters, the maintenance of distinct habitation space suggests some degree of household autonomy. After the transition, however, only large nucleated settlements remained, and most of these were substantially larger than the largest structures occupied prior to nucleation. In areas to the south, including the Mogollon Highlands, the Arizona Mountains, the Upper Little Colorado, and the Silver Creek areas, the transition to larger settlements may have been somewhat less dramatic, but Pueblo IV period sites are still often three to four times larger than Pueblo III period clustered communities and other large pueblos in these areas. Once the transition to nucleated settlement was complete, household autonomy was likely restricted as communal mechanisms for social monitoring and control were established and institutionalized (e.g., Bernardini 1998).

The Pueblo III to Pueblo IV transition also saw a major reorganization of public spaces. Prior to the Pueblo IV period, rectangular and circular great kivas and Chacoan great houses were the primary foci of ritual activity across the region. Over the course of the period considered here, public architectural spaces may have become somewhat more inclusive in portions of the region. In the areas along the Zuni River and along Mariana Mesa, roofed Chacoan great kivas were largely replaced by oversized unroofed great kivas in the late 1100s or early 1200s. These structures would have allowed more people to participate in events within their walls and also likely would have made the events visible to more members of a community (Kintigh et al. 1996). The trend may have gone in the other direction in other areas such as the Mogollon Highlands, where later great kivas were increasingly incorporated into other buildings and could have served an ever smaller fraction of growing communities (Dungan and Peeples n.d.). The beginning of the Pueblo IV period saw another shift in public architecture as enclosed plaza spaces become more common and great kivas declined in most portions of the study area. Plaza spaces were probably used for both daily activities and periodic ceremonies (e.g., Adams 1991). As nucleated structures housed entire communities, the ubiquity of plazas may suggest increasing integration and inclusiveness in community-scale ceremonies, though such spaces were likely also arenas of competition (Chamberlin 2012). At the same time, the creation of plazas completely enclosed by the walls of the community may have also limited the access of those outside of the residential community. This shift in the use of space may have been an active expression of newly developing notions of community.

Finally, the Pueblo III to Pueblo IV transition was also associated with major changes in the technology and styles of painted ceramics and other material culture described above. In particular, the rapid replacement of matte-painted ceramics with glaze-painted wares and the simultaneous divergence of designs and technological traditions may suggest the emergence or increasing importance of regional-scale social boundaries among the inhabitants of different portions of the greater Cibola region. This is a trend that characterizes much of the Southwest during the late thirteenth and early fourteenth centuries (Duff 2000).

Overall, the changes marking the late thirteenth century described above (Pueblo III to Pueblo IV transition) entailed the depopulation of many portions of the Cibola region, a rapid increase in community size, dramatic changes in public space, a fundamental reformulation of the relationship between households and communities, and an apparent increase in the importance of social boundaries at a regional scale. Although the timing and magnitude of this transformation may have differed somewhat from place to place, it appears that many of the most jarring changes probably occurred *within a single generation* and involved the active participation of people across the entire greater Cibola region. From this, I argue that this late thirteenth-century transition fits squarely within the definition of a social transformation as outlined in the previous chapter.

## ANASAZI, MOGOLLON, AND SOCIAL IDENTITY IN THE CIBOLA REGION

The patterns described above suggest not only many broad regional trends in settlement and interaction but also, notably, considerable local variation in how these trends play out from place to place. The nuanced picture provided above stands in contrast to the typical "short version" of the story, which is based purely on the culture area designations that have long structured thinking and research agendas in the Cibola region. As you can read in an introductory textbook on Southwest archaeology, the Anasazi were the people who lived on the Colorado Plateau, produced gray ware pottery, and made circular great kivas. The Mogollon people, on the other hand, lived in the mountainous highlands along the Mogollon Rim and in the Chihuahuan Desert, produced brown ware pottery, and built rectangular great kivas. This simple dichotomy belies the enormous amount of ink spilled in the debate over the nature of the archaeological constructs that have come to be known as Anasazi and Mogollon. In order to provide historical context to the discussion of large-scale social identities described in the remainder of this book, I provide a few brief comments on past and present thinking regarding the nature of archaeological "cultures" and their analytical and potential social meanings in the Cibola region. For those interested in a more detailed discussion of the specific issues covered here, J. Jefferson Reid and Stephanie Whittlesey (2010) have published a fascinating historical account of the Mogollon controversy and all of the personalities involved.

The term *Anasazi* has been abandoned by many Southwest archaeologists in recent years because it has negative connotations to many contemporary Puebloan peoples. This term has often been replaced by the more general term *Ancestral Pueblo*, which is often seen as a broader designation that includes the inhabitants of many areas that would be traditionally defined as both Anasazi and Mogollon in older schemes (e.g., Mills et al. 1999:3–4). In the context of this discussion, however, I use the terms *Anasazi* and *Mogollon* because I am referring to the historical archaeological concepts. I do not attribute any specific cultural or ethnic meaning to these concepts in general, although I do argue that these designations likely capture certain aspects of social interaction and identity at regional scales.

The debate over the nature and validity of distinct culture areas in the Cibola region began in earnest with the publication of Emil Haury's 1936 report, *The Mogollon Culture of Southwestern New Mexico*. In this influential publication,

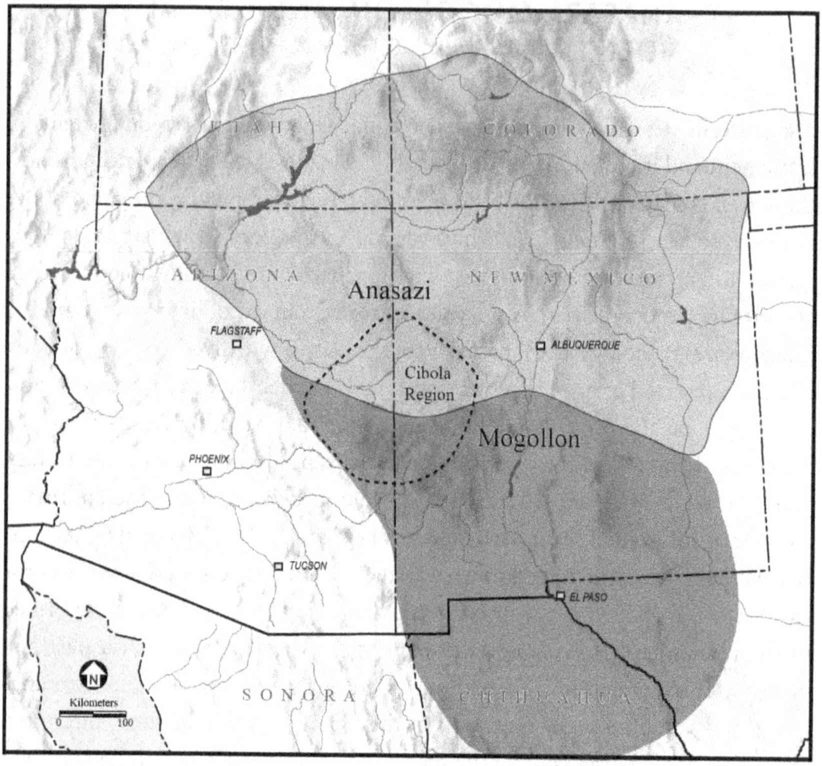


FIGURE 8. Map of the greater Cibola region in the U.S. Southwest showing the traditional boundaries of the Anasazi and Mogollon archaeological culture areas.

Haury argued that the pithouse dwellers of two villages in the highlands of southwestern New Mexico were culturally distinct from both Basketmaker-Pueblo (Anasazi) populations to the north and Hohokam populations to the west. He argued for the creation of a third major archaeological culture in the Southwest, which he named the Mogollon after the type site in the Mogollon Mountains along the Arizona–New Mexico border. Importantly, Haury also argued that Mogollon developments (i.e., pottery, pithouses, basketry, etc.) were at least as old as those documented in the Anasazi region to the north but that, due to cultural mixing with Anasazi groups, Mogollon populations were somewhat less distinct after A.D. 1000 (see also Haury 1985).

Haury's designation of the Mogollon as a distinct archaeological culture before A.D. 1000 set off a series of debates that fueled a great deal of primary archaeological research and theoretical arguments in the Cibola region and other nearby areas for decades to follow (e.g., Bullard 1962; Danson 1957; Haury 1985; Martin 1943, 1961; Martin and Rinaldo 1950, 1960; Martin et al. 1957; Martin et al. 1956; Martin et al. 1952; Martin et al. 1962; McGimsey 1980; Nesbit 1938; Rinaldo 1941, 1959; Wendorf 1953; Wheat 1955). Much of the disagreement centered on whether Mogollon populations were demonstrably distinct from Anasazi populations through time and across space. Some early critics argued that the suite of material traits that Haury and others had used to define the Mogollon culture were merely derivative of Anasazi traits, and thus the Mogollon region should be seen as the periphery of the Anasazi world rather than a separate cultural development (e.g., Nesbit 1938). Others argued that not only were Mogollon traits distinct, but they could be traced in time well past A.D. 1000 despite evidence for increasing Anasazi influence and "mixing" (e.g., Danson 1957; Martin and Rinaldo 1950; Wheat 1955). By the 1960s, once the dust had settled on the debate, the Mogollon concept was, in general, fairly uncontroversial. However, the Mogollon culture area of the mid-twentieth century was far larger in spatial extent and was applied to a broader temporal interval than Haury's original designation.

Despite the waning controversy over the existence of a distinct Mogollon archaeological culture, varying interpretations of the *cultural* nature and the analytical utility of this and similar archaeological constructs remain a source of disagreement even to this day. Some argue that designations like Anasazi and Mogollon should be abandoned because they tend to push researchers away from questions that span the traditional boundaries of archaeological cultures and because such constructs probably do not reflect cultural designations that would have had meaning in the past (e.g., Bernardini 2005; Dean 1988; Lekson 1996; Mills et al. 1999; Speth 1988; Tainter and Plog 1994; Wilcox 1988). Others argue that these archaeological cultures, which parse variability in material culture at regional scales, do have an underlying behavioral basis that may reflect patterns of social interaction and identity at some level (e.g., Reid 1989; Reid and Whittlesey 2010; Riggs 2005). In this book, I suggest that both of these arguments have merit.

Even within the brief regional overview provided in this chapter, it is immediately apparent that there are numerous differences between the northern and southern portions of the Cibola region representing areas traditionally seen as falling within the Anasazi and Mogollon regions, respectively. At a very basic level, the apparently persistent distinctions between these areas may suggest that the culture areas defined so long ago do capture real differences in material culture and settlement that almost certainly had some basis in patterns of social interaction and possibly identity in the period considered here. At the same time, I present data in the following chapters that suggest that differences across space were often gradational rather than being marked by discrete and well-defined cultural boundaries. Indeed, I agree with many other researchers who argue that the distinctions between these archaeological culture areas, which have structured archaeological research to a substantial degree (i.e., many researchers self-identify as Anasazi or Mogollon archaeologists, and there are separate annual conferences focused on Mogollon and Ancestral Puebloan archaeology, respectively), have sometimes hindered our ability to understand broader trends across the Southwest as a whole (see Lekson 1996:175). I argue that archaeological constructs like Anasazi and Mogollon can be useful, but only to the extent that they are understood as heuristics for describing broad patterns in the continuous regional variation of material culture rather than as models for cultural or ethnic groups that would have had any meaning in the past.

# 4

# TRACKING RELATIONS AND CATEGORIES THROUGH CERAMIC CIRCULATION

PERHAPS THE most direct way to track dynamic networks of interaction through material culture is to track the movement of the materials themselves. In the U.S. Southwest over the last several decades, studies of ceramic circulation in particular have provided many important insights into the nature and scale of networks of interaction at various spatial scales. I argue here that the inhabitants of settlements involved in common spheres of ceramic circulation (indicative of exchange, migration, and a host of other social/economic processes) represent groups of individuals who were likely interacting on a regular basis. From this, I suggest that the movement of ceramics can be used as a proxy for the nature, strength, and direction of *relational connections* across different portions of the greater Cibola region and beyond.

In this chapter I briefly outline a set of principles relating ceramic production and circulation to the creation and maintenance of relational connections at various social and spatial scales. In light of these general principles, I then present a series of analyses based on ceramic chemical compositional data generated through neutron activation analysis. The data used here represent one of the largest compilations of ceramic chemical characterizations ever published for such a regional study. The size of this sample and the high degree of geological diversity of the Cibola region mean that I am able to track the movement of both painted and unpainted ceramics across the region and beyond across relatively short distances (tens of kilometers). Importantly, these analyses demonstrate that the nature and scale of ceramic circulation differed for painted and unpainted ceramic wares through time, suggesting that these different wares circulated across different kinds of social relationships. As I argue below, so-called weak ties created through the exchange and circulation of painted ceramics in particular may provide evidence of participation of the inhabitants of various settlements in common spheres of public ceremonialism, contexts ripe for the creation and promotion of *categorical identities*. The analyses described below illustrate that ceramic circulation of both painted and unpainted wares changed dramatically across the late thirteenth-century social transformation in the Cibola region.

## TRACKING RELATIONAL CONNECTIONS THROUGH CERAMIC CIRCULATION

The overarching argument I make in this chapter is that communities and individuals involved in common spheres of exchange and ceramic circulation were likely involved in common *relational networks* of interaction at various scales. Ceramic circulation is not, however, a homogeneous social process and can involve a variety of different kinds of transactions both cooperative and competitive. Numerous studies in the Southwest and elsewhere suggest that the social transactions involved in the circulation of painted and unpainted ceramics in particular likely differed due in large part to the variable social values placed on these goods (e.g., Duff 2002:25–28; see also Abbott 2000:133–140; Graves 1991). Thus, I argue here that the spheres of interaction fostering the movement of different kinds of vessels should be treated separately and can be inferentially related to different kinds of social relationships.

In the U.S. Southwest, unpainted ceramics are typically interpreted as utilitarian goods assumed to have moved most frequently among relatively close relations, such as kin groups (Abbott 2000:139–140; Brunson 1985; Duff 2002:25–26; Reid and Montgomery 1998; Zedeño 1994). Indeed, previous studies of ceramic circulation in the Cibola region suggest that the movement of unpainted ceramics was relatively frequent within major river valleys but rare between valleys, suggesting that the kinds of transactions involving the movement of these vessels were primarily local in nature (Duff 2002:159–167). As the analyses below will show, however, unpainted ceramics do sometimes move across greater distances. Maria Nieves Zedeño (1994, 1995, 1998) has previously explored the various social and economic processes that have resulted in the movement of different kinds of ceramics in the U.S. Southwest. Her ethnographic and archaeological data suggest that the movement of unpainted vessels over vast distances may indicate particularly close relationships among the inhabitants of distant areas, including the kinds of relationships that may be forged through frequent and regular interaction and perhaps intermarriage (e.g., Zedeño 1994, 1995). Alternatively, the long-distance movement of unpainted vessels may also indicate migration (Zedeño 1998). Migrants into a new area may have maintained relationships with the inhabitants of the area that they left, leading to the continued reciprocal circulation of vessels across vast distances. Although it is difficult to separate exchange from migration through compositional data alone, when the movement of unpainted vessels is largely unidirectional, Zedeño (1998:15–21) suggests that population movement rather than exchange among groups residing in different areas may be more likely. Importantly, both of these potential processes (frequent long-distance interaction and migration) involve the kinds of sustained, informal relationships and shared historical connections that form the basis for strong and tight-knit relational connections among individuals and social groups. Thus, I interpret the movement of unpainted ceramics across the study area as a proxy for the degree and directionality of the *most frequently activated* relational social ties among populations across the study area.

Painted ceramic vessels are often circulated across far greater geographic distances than unpainted vessels. The most common painted ceramic type considered in this analysis, St. Johns Polychrome, is one of the most widely distributed ceramic types in the Southwest. It is found from southern Colorado to the north all the way to northern Mexico and from western Arizona to far eastern New Mexico (Carlson 1970:Figure 14). The spatial scale of this distribution alone suggests that such painted ceramic vessels likely did not circulate *only* through informal transactions among frequently interacting individuals or social groups.

Several researchers have suggested that painted ceramics in the Southwest were imbued with a higher relative social value than unpainted vessels due in part to their higher visibility in social settings and their use in public ceremonies (e.g., Duff 2002; Graves and Eckert 1998; Lyons and Clark 2012; Mills 1999, 2007a, 2007b; Potter 2000; Spielmann 1998; Van Keuren 2004). The color combinations and bold exterior designs of some painted ceramics in the Cibola region vary through time in relation to the sizes and configurations of public spaces (see Chapter 7; Mills 2007a, 2007b). This suggests that many vessels were produced with a fundamental concern for visual communication. Furthermore, several painted wares, in particular polychrome bowls, appear to have been used in contexts associated with feasting and/or public food consumption (see Mills 2007a; Potter 2000). Because of their high visibility and association with public contexts, painted vessels likely also served as common vehicles for the active and public expression of social identities (see Mills 2007a:220–228).

Andrew Duff (2002:26–27) argues that the long-distance circulation of painted vessels represents exchange among members of different communities taking place in public settings, perhaps as a means to formalize social connections and reciprocal obligations among the coparticipants in ceremonial gatherings. The formal and public nature of painted ceramic exchange and use suggests that the circulation of these vessels may provide an indication of patterns of long-distance, perhaps somewhat less frequently activated relational connections across the Cibola region. Such "weak ties" (sensu Granovetter 1973) among communities may have been important in fostering other kinds of relationships and commonalities among individuals and larger groups. Specifically, the association of painted vessels with the active expression of identities (see Chapter 7) suggests that the exchange and/or movement of painted vessels may also provide a venue for shared *categorical expressions* across the Cibola region. Stated another way, communities that were involved in common spheres of painted ceramic circulation were also likely involved in common spheres of public ceremonialism, providing contexts where categorical identities could have been expressed and contested.

## CHEMICAL CHARACTERIZATION USING NEUTRON ACTIVATION ANALYSIS

Recent archaeological studies of ceramic circulation have relied upon numerous methods, both chemical and mineralogical (i.e., optical petrography, LA-ICP-MS, XRF, NAA, PIXE), for identifying the likely production sources of ceramic materials at various spatial scales (for overviews, see Bishop et al. 1982; Glowacki and Neff 2002; Speakman 2005). Different methods (or combinations of methods; see Ownby et al. 2014) are more or less well suited for use in particular contexts depending on the diversity of clays and tempering materials used to produce vessels, the total number of samples to be analyzed, and the scale at which source determinations are required to address specific research questions. For regional studies focused on ceramic circulation, instrumental neutron activation analysis (NAA) has proven to be a particularly powerful method for defining groups of ceramic vessels that are compositionally similar. Further, through considerations of archaeological context and comparisons with raw materials, compositional groups defined through NAA can often be inferentially related to production sources at relatively small geographic scales.

NAA is a bulk radioisotopic method of chemical characterization, meaning that it provides element concentrations of the entire ceramic paste, including clay and temper particles (but excluding slips and paints; see Arnold et al. 1991; Neff and Glowacki 2002:7–9). This method of chemical characterization is particularly sensitive, allowing for the measurement of a large number of major, minor, and trace elements, many of which frequently occur below the detection limits of other methods. Perhaps most importantly, NAA has been extensively used for ceramic characterization across the greater Cibola region, providing a large existing database of chemical compositional data to which newly generated samples can be compared.

## THE SAMPLE

Several major studies focused on the Pueblo III and Pueblo IV periods in the primary portion of the study area conducted prior to this study (Duff 1999, 2002; Huntley 2004, 2008; Schachner 2012; Schachner et al. 2011) have resulted in a regional sample of over 1,400 ceramic sherds, as well as dozens of raw clay and temper samples. In addition to this, ceramics and clays have been analyzed for several complementary portions of the Cibola region study area (e.g., Ferguson 2008; Triadan 1997, Triadan et al. 2002; Zedeño 1994, 2002). This large existing regional database was expanded for this study by submitting an additional 600 ceramic samples for NAA characterization. Altogether, there are over 2,000 ceramic samples available for the primary portion of the study area and over 2,600 ceramic and clay samples, including those from the complementary portions of the study area, making this one of the largest regional NAA ceramic compositional databases anywhere in the world (the data are available in the online appendix to this book).[1]

The regional sample considered in this study includes several different wares and types. Sample selection criteria were somewhat different among the projects that produced the bulk of the existing data incorporated into this analysis. In general, however, all previous projects included both painted and unpainted wares, and specific types were typically selected at each site roughly *based on the proportions of individual types at the site as a whole* (Duff 1999:7.2–7.7; Huntley 2004:70–76; but see Schachner 2007:107–112). Site-wide samples from the primary portion of the study area range from 22 to 134 ceramic sherds and archaeological clays, roughly equally divided between painted and unpainted vessels. The vast majority of samples come from excavated contexts, but surface sherds were also included where other materials were not available. The 600 new samples analyzed for this study come primarily from the southern portion of the Cibola region, which had not been extensively sampled in the past, but also include additional ceramics from previously sampled areas for wares that were underrepresented in the existing data.[2]

The vast majority of sherds in the ceramic compositional sample are derived from contexts dating to the period directly considered in this study (ca. A.D. 1150–1325), but two projects from the primary portion of the study area also included ceramics from settlements dating somewhat later (ca. A.D. 1325–1400; see Duff 1999; Huntley 2004). Although these later samples were not produced during the period explicitly considered in this study, their inclusion in the initial analysis of the compositional database allows for a comparison of earlier ceramics with the compositional profiles of later assemblages. Since there are far fewer late Pueblo IV settlements, and they are found in fewer locations across the Cibola region, such a comparison helps to relate compositional groups to probable production zones at a somewhat finer geographic scale (see discussion in Schachner et al. 2011). The inclusion of late Pueblo IV ceramic materials also increases the total sample size, allowing more robust statistical methods to be used to evaluate compositional groups.

All ceramic samples included in this study were analyzed at the Archaeometry Laboratory at the Missouri University Research Reactor (MURR) with the exception of a small number of clay samples from existing datasets, which were analyzed at the Smithsonian Center for Materials Research and Education and the National Institute of Standards and Technology (SCMRE-NIST). Both the MURR and SCMRE-NIST facilities measure the same element abundances and use the same methods for sample preparation and standardization.

## GEOLOGY OF THE CIBOLA REGION AND CLAY AVAILABILITY

The geology of the Cibola region is particularly well suited to the identification of production zones through NAA. The region is geologically diverse, with discrete strata of varying geological ages exposed within limited geographic areas. Many major geological features of the region were created by faults, folds, and uplifts, which produced discrete zones of varying geomorphological properties that influence the arability of the landscape. Due in large part to the coassociation of geological features and arable land, areas of relatively dense prehistoric settlement are often strongly associated with discrete geological features. This makes attributions of ceramic compositional groups to specific areas somewhat stronger than would be the case in an area characterized by less geological diversity.

In addition to this, there is also a great deal of diversity in the clay resources that were selected for ceramic production. Previous clay resource surveys and technological studies of clay workability suggest that the clays used to produce different ceramic wares within the greater Cibola region were likely derived from somewhat different geological contexts (see Mills 1995:208–214; Wilson 1994, 2007; Wilson and Severts 1999). Specifically, most light paste ceramic wares produced during the period considered here, including Cibola White Ware, White Mountain Red Ware, Zuni Glaze Ware, and Cibola Gray Ware, were produced from sandstone- or shale-derived clays weathered from several major geological formations, likely including the widespread Triassic Chinle formation and various Cretaceous formations (see also Mills 1995). Dark paste Mogollon Brown Ware and Roosevelt Red Ware ceramics have substantially higher iron concentrations than the light paste wares and were likely produced from volcanic-derived alluvial and colluvial clays. Volcanic-derived clays would have been readily available to the inhabitants of settlements across most of the Cibola region, in particular south of the Colorado Plateau, but appear to have been used more extensively in some areas than others.

At a local level, there is a great deal of diversity in the specific materials that likely would have been available to potters. At the same time, there are also some broad regional trends that would have influenced the production and distribution of ceramics across the study area. Sandstone and shale outcrops that would have provided clay resources appropriate for producing light paste ceramic wares within the primary portion of the study area are available almost exclusively on the Colorado Plateau. This includes all of the areas along the Zuni River Valley, the El Morro Valley, the Mariana Mesa area, as well as the Silver Creek, Cebolleta Mesa, and Puerco Valley subregions within the complementary portion of the study area. Tertiary and Quaternary volcanic flows cover much of the southern portion of the study area, including the southern Upper

Little Colorado, the Mogollon Highlands, and the large Arizona Mountains subregion. Importantly, outcrops of Triassic and Cretaceous sandstone and shale that likely provided clays appropriate for producing light paste wares were also present within a short distance of most settlements in the Upper Little Colorado region as I have defined it here. Across the far southern reaches of the study area, however, the materials available for pottery production would have been limited to dark-firing clays primarily of volcanic origin (Triadan 1997; Wilson 1994; Wilson and Severts 1999; Zedeño 1994). One important implication of the distribution of clay resources across the Cibola region is that the inhabitants of the large Mogollon Highlands subregion and other nearby areas would not have had the appropriate resources within a reasonable catchment to produce the light paste painted wares (Cibola White Ware, White Mountain Red Ware, and Zuni Glaze Ware) recovered from sites dating to the period considered here.

## DEFINING COMPOSITIONAL GROUPS AND MAKING PRODUCTION INFERENCES

In order to define groups of ceramics with similar chemical compositions, I relied on a set of analytical heuristics commonly employed by MURR staff for analyzing large datasets (Neff 2002). The analyses presented here were conducted in close collaboration with Jeffrey Ferguson at MURR. The basic procedures involved five basic steps. I briefly explain these steps here (the details are left to the online appendix):

1. First, data were normalized by converting elemental concentrations to base-10 logarithms, and missing values were replaced. This procedure allows major and minor elements to be analyzed together by eliminating differences in magnitude.
2. Next, initial reference groups were constructed using a number of contextual and multivariate methods. For example, samples were grouped by ware/type, design style, and geographic location of recovery. Statistical methods of ordination and cluster analysis were used in order to determine whether such groups are compositionally distinct (Bishop and Neff 1989:68; Neff 2002:18). The most successful methods included hierarchical (average linkage and Wards method) and nonhierarchical (K-means and K-medoids) cluster analyses performed on a Euclidean distance matrix of the log-transformed

element concentrations or on standardized principal component scores. The goal of initial grouping was to develop groups of samples that are strongly associated across multiple methods of assessment.

3. Next, I assessed the probabilities of group membership through an iterative process of sample reassignment. This procedure involved calculating probabilities of group membership for each sample into each potential group using jackknifed Mahalanobis distances and Hotelling's $T^2$ statistic. Samples were iteratively removed or added to groups using probability cut-offs until stable core compositional groups were formed. The remaining unassigned samples were then projected against these core groups using log-transformed element data and principal components and were assigned as noncore members of those groups based on probability cut-offs.
4. After all of the group assignments were made, there were still some small groups of unassigned samples that consistently clustered together on element biplots, as well as on plots of PCA scores. Some of these small groups also appear to represent sherds primarily from one portion of the study area or one particular ware/type. Although groups with fewer than about 15–20 samples cannot usually be adequately evaluated in relation to all other groups using the most robust statistical methods, these small groupings may be the beginnings of other compositional core groups. For the purposes of this analysis, such small groups were considered provisional compositional groups.
5. After core groups were constructed, some groups still displayed a tendency toward division in terms of the concentrations of particular elements, suggesting that they could potentially be split into somewhat smaller units. The creation of subgroups can be important in the attribution of sherds to more specific geographic areas of production (e.g., Duff 2002:107–137). For this study, samples were divided into subgroups using procedures similar to those described above for the construction of core groups (i.e., cluster analysis, probability assessment and reassignment). The major exception is that, at this stage, individual groups were considered independently.

Based on the procedures described above, I defined a total of 13 core groups (several of which could be subdivided) and 5 additional provisional groups. Importantly, where the samples overlapped with previous compositional studies in the study area (Duff 2002; Huntley 2008; Schachner 2012; Schachner et al. 2011) there was a high level of parity between the groups defined here and those

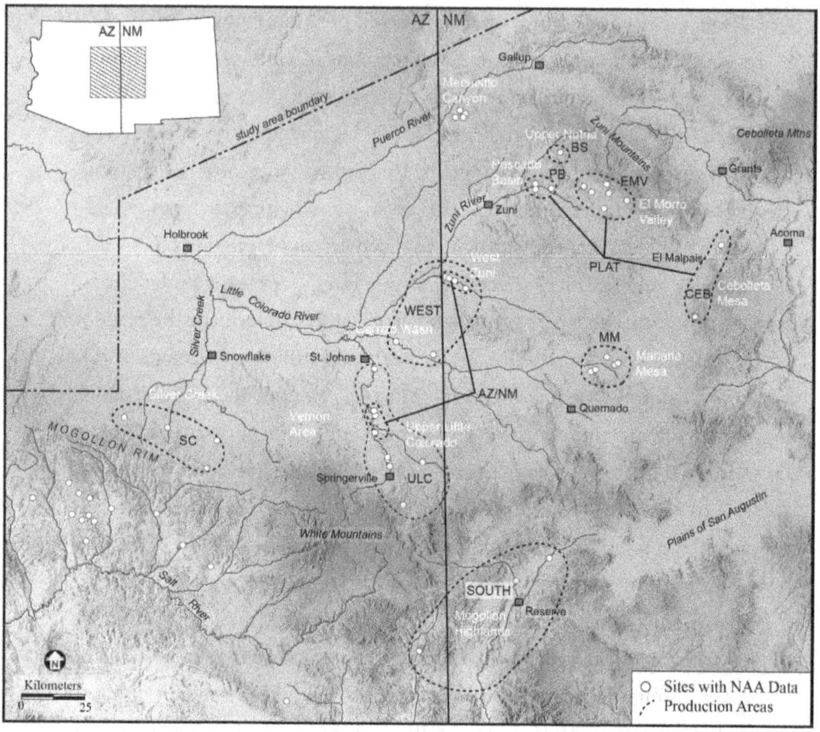


FIGURE 9. Map showing all sampled sites included in this study and major production zones defined based on compositional group assignments.

defined for previous analyses, though each researcher analyzed the data from scratch. This suggests that the patterns of ceramic compositional similarity are relatively robust.

Identifying chemical compositional groups based on element concentrations is not, however, the same as identifying discrete production sources. The chemical composition of a ceramic vessel is related to a number of complex factors, including the composition of the clay and tempering materials incorporated into the ceramic paste, how those materials were processed, and possible chemical alterations due to firing and diagenetic processes (see Arnold et al. 1991; Arnold et al. 2000; Neff et al. 2003; Neff and Glowacki 2002:5–9; Sterba et al. 2009). Discrete compositional groups defined based on element data may represent groups of ceramic vessels that were produced using distinct materials, different techniques for paste preparation, or some combination of both of these and other factors.

In order to attribute ceramic compositional groups to production in a specific geographic area, I relied on a number of different lines of archaeological and geological contextual evidence. These lines included comparison of ceramic chemical compositions to local geology and comparisons with chemically characterized unfired vessels (which are extremely fragile and unlikely to have been moved over any great distance). Another general principle that is commonly used to help link compositional groups to production in specific locations is known as the "criterion of abundance" (Bishop et al. 1982; Neff and Glowacki 2002:6). This principle assumes that ceramics will be most common in the areas in which they were produced. Thus, compositional groups can be inferentially related to production loci based on their distribution across the study area. There are, of course, a number of social processes that could potentially complicate this assumption (i.e., market exchange, long-distance movement of raw materials, major migrations, etc.), so it is also important to consider the broader regional context. Attribution of a compositional group to a geographic area based on abundance is strongest when multiple settlements within a particular geological zone have elevated proportions of that compositional group. For the purposes of this study, all of these general principles were used in concert to guide the attribution of compositional groups to specific loci of production.

## RESULTS

Using the procedures described briefly above (and in detail elsewhere; Peeples 2011; see online appendix), a total of 2,136 (>82 percent) of the 2,591 chemically characterized ceramic sherds from the primary and complementary study areas could be assigned to one of 26 core groups, subgroups, or provisional compositional groups defined from the regional sample. This rate of assignment is comparable to other studies relying on similar methods and criteria for large samples. Many of these compositional core and provisional groups were attributed to production in the same geographic areas. Thus, to simplify the discussion of patterns of ceramic circulation below, I combine multiple distinct compositional groups into larger regional production areas roughly coinciding with clusters of settlement across the study area. Figure 9 shows all of the sampled sites included in this study along with major production zones defined within the core and expanded study area. The specific assumptions and procedures used to define compositional groups and assign production areas are important, but those details are likely beyond the scope of interest for many readers. Thus, I have relegated detailed descriptions of individual compositional groups, production zones, and statistical procedures to the online appendix.

## REGIONAL PATTERNS OF CERAMIC CIRCULATION THROUGH TIME

### LOCAL VS. NONLOCAL POTTERY

Not surprisingly, most pottery included in this study was recovered from the general location where it was likely produced. Of all samples that could be confidently assigned to a particular production zone during both the Pueblo III and Pueblo IV periods in the core portion of the study area, approximately 74 percent were local. As Table 1 illustrates, however, there are substantial differences in the percentages of local and nonlocal ceramics for painted and unpainted vessels in the sample, as well as major changes through time. For the purposes of this study, ceramics were defined as local when they were recovered from a site within the likely zone of production, as illustrated in Figure 9.

In general, unpainted vessels are rarely recovered outside of the broad areas where they were produced during both the Pueblo III and Pueblo IV periods, and when they are, they are most frequently found in adjacent areas. This fits my general expectations outlined above, as unpainted vessels were presumably produced and consumed at the household level and exchanged primarily among close relations. The relatively low level of circulation of unpainted vessels suggests that such transactions occurred most frequently among groups of people

TABLE 1. Counts and percentages of local and nonlocal sherds

| WARE | PERIOD | LOCAL (%) | NONLOCAL (%) | TOTAL |
|---|---|---|---|---|
| Unpainted | PIII | 311 (85) | 52 (15) | 363 |
| | PIV | 164 (91) | 17 (9) | 181 |
| Painted | PIII | 217 (52) | 200 (48) | 417 |
| | PIV | 203 (79) | 55 (21) | 258 |
| Combined | PIII–PIV | 895 (74) | 324 (26) | 1,219 |

living in close proximity to one another. This inference is particularly important for analyses of unpainted ceramic technology presented in the next chapter.

Painted ceramics are frequently found outside of the areas where they were produced. Indeed, for the Pueblo III period sample, nearly half the painted vessels in the sample were recovered outside of their production zones. This number is perhaps somewhat inflated, as some areas included in the study (i.e., the Mogollon Highlands) imported nearly all of the painted wares included in the current NAA sample. Still, the much higher percentage of painted vessels that were transported over vast distances suggests that very different social processes were involved in the circulation of painted vessels. Consideration of the forms of painted vessels suggests that bowls were transported out of their production zones more frequently and over greater distances than painted jars (~39 percent of painted bowls were found outside of their production zone vs. ~19 percent of painted jars). The frequent long-distance transport of painted vessels, in particular polychrome bowls, may have been associated with public ceremonial gatherings involving food consumption and exchanges marking these public events (e.g., Duff 2002:26–27; Mills 2007a). Furthermore, as Deborah Huntley (2008) has argued, some communities may have specialized in the production of certain painted wares and vessel forms that were widely circulated across the region during both the Pueblo III and Pueblo IV periods.

The percentage of nonlocal vessels, both unpainted and painted, decreased across the Pueblo III to Pueblo IV transition. This decrease in ceramic circulation is also associated with a contraction in the total occupied area across the Cibola region. Across the Pueblo III to Pueblo IV transition, populations were increasingly concentrated into larger villages found in fewer places on the landscape. These large nucleated villages formed closely spaced clusters of settlements surrounded by largely uninhabited areas (see Chapter 3). The relative reduction in long-distance ceramic circulation suggests that interactions may have become increasingly internally focused across this transition (see Duff 2002; Huntley 2008; Schachner et al. 2011).

## THE CIRCULATION OF UNPAINTED CERAMICS

Table 2 lists the distribution of unpainted vessels from each major production zone for all sites by subregion. As this table illustrates, all well-sampled subregions within the core portion of the study area are strongly dominated by unpainted vessels that are presumably locally produced, but a small number of

TABLE 2. Production zone assignments by site and subregion for all unpainted ceramics

| REGION/ SETTLEMENT | EMV | PLAT | PB | CEB | BS | MM | WEST | AZ/NM | ULC | SOUTH | SC | UNK | TOTAL |
|---|---|---|---|---|---|---|---|---|---|---|---|---|---|
| *El Morro Valley PIII* | | | | | | | | | | | | | |
| Los Gigantes Cluster | 38 | 1 | 4 | 5 | | | 1 | 1 | | | | 10 | 60 |
| Togeye Canyon Cluster | 34 | 1 | 3 | 3 | | | 4 | | | | | 15 | 60 |
| Scribe S Cluster | 44 | | 4 | 1 | 1 | | | | | | | 10 | 60 |
| Tinaja Cluster | 57 | | 1 | 2 | | | | | | | | 0 | 60 |
| ***Known Sources %*** | *84* | *1* | *5.9* | *5.4* | *0.5* | | *2.4* | *0.5* | | | | | |
| *El Morro Valley PIV* | | | | | | | | | | | | | |
| Atsinna | 9 | | 1 | | | | | | | | | 1 | 11 |
| Cienega | 6 | | | | | | | | | | | 0 | 6 |
| Mirabal | 6 | | | | | | | | | | | 1 | 7 |
| Pueblo de los Muertos | 7 | | | | | | | | | | | 4 | 11 |
| ***Known Sources %*** | *97* | | *4.4* | | | | | | | | | | |
| *Pescado Basin PIII* | | | | | | | | | | | | | |
| Spier 81 Cluster | 5 | 2 | 14 | | | | | | | | | 4 | 25 |
| ***Known Sources %*** | *24* | *9.5* | *67* | | | | | | | | | | |
| *Pescado Basin PIV* | | | | | | | | | | | | | |
| Heshotauthla | | 2 | 4 | | | | | 1 | | | | 5 | 12 |
| Lower Pescado Village | 1 | | 4 | | | | | | | | | 5 | 10 |
| ***Known Sources %*** | *8.3* | *17* | *67* | | | | | *8.3* | | | | | |
| *Upper Nutria PIV* | | | | | | | | | | | | | |
| Box S Pueblo | 1 | 4 | 2 | | 3 | | | | | | | 2 | 12 |
| ***Known Sources %*** | *10* | *40* | *20* | | *30* | | | | | | | | |

| | | | | | | | | | | | |
|---|---|---|---|---|---|---|---|---|---|---|---|
| *Mariana Mesa PIII* | | | | | | | | | | | |
| UG481 | | | | | 8 | | | 1 | | 1 | 10 |
| Tri-R Pueblo | 1 | 1 | | | 17 | | | | | 7 | 26 |
| Hubble Corner | | | | 1 | 9 | | | 1 | | 4 | 15 |
| ***Known Sources %*** | ***2.6*** | ***2.6*** | | ***2.6*** | ***87*** | | | ***5.1*** | | | |
| *Mariana Mesa PIV* | | | | | | | | | | | |
| Horse Camp Mill | | | | | 13 | | | 1 | | 1 | 15 |
| Techado Spring Pueblo | 3 | 1 | | 2 | 24 | | | | | 6 | 36 |
| ***Known Sources %*** | ***6.8*** | ***2.3*** | | ***4.5*** | ***84*** | | | ***2.3*** | | | |
| *West Zuni PIII* | | | | | | | | | | | |
| Hinkson Ranch | | 1 | 2 | 1 | 1 | 11 | 1 | | | 3 | 20 |
| Jaralosa Pueblo | | | 2 | | | 8 | | | | 5 | 15 |
| ***Known Sources %*** | | ***3.7*** | ***15*** | ***3.7*** | ***3.7*** | ***70*** | ***3.7*** | | | | |
| *West Zuni PIV* | | | | | | | | | | | |
| Ojo Bonito | | | 1 | | | 9 | | | | 5 | 15 |
| Spier 170 | | | | | | 8 | | | | 2 | 10 |
| ***Known Sources %*** | | | ***5.6*** | | | ***94*** | | | | | |
| *Carrizo Wash PIII* | | | | | | | | | | | |
| Platt Ranch Settlement | | | 1 | | 1 | 4 | | | | 9 | 15 |
| Garcia Ranch Pueblo | | | 1 | | 2 | 10 | | 1 | | 6 | 20 |
| ***Known Sources %*** | | | ***10*** | | ***15*** | ***70*** | | ***5*** | | | |
| *Upper Little Colorado PIII* | | | | | | | | | | | |
| Coyote Creek Pueblo | | | | | | | | 12 | 1 | 2 | 15 |
| Rim Valley Pueblo | | | | | | | | 2 | | 0 | 2 |
| Rudd Creek Pueblo | | | | | | | | 18 | | 0 | 18 |
| ***Known Sources %*** | | | | | | | | ***97*** | ***3*** | | |

(*continued*)

TABLE 2. (*continued*)

| REGION/ SETTLEMENT | EMV | PLAT | PB | CEB | BS | MM | WEST | AZ/NM | ULC | SOUTH | SC | UNK | TOTAL |
|---|---|---|---|---|---|---|---|---|---|---|---|---|---|
| *Upper Little Colorado Early PIV* | | | | | | | | | | | | | |
| Baca Pueblo | | | | | | | | | 35 | | | 14 | 49 |
| Casa Malpais | | | | | | | | | 16 | 1 | | 4 | 21 |
| Hooper Ranch Pueblo | | | | | | | | | 14 | | | 1 | 15 |
| ***Known Sources %*** | | | | | | | | | ***99*** | ***1.5*** | | | |
| *Upper Little Colorado Late PIV* | | | | | | | | | | | | | |
| Sherwood Ranch Pueblo | | | | | | | | | 5 | 1 | | 4 | 10 |
| Rattlesnake Point Pueblo | | | | | | | | | 32 | | | 19 | 51 |
| Table Rock | | | | | | | | | 14 | | | 6 | 20 |
| ***Known Sources %*** | | | | | | | | | ***98*** | ***1.9*** | | | |
| *Mogollon Highlands PIII* | | | | | | | | | | | | | |
| Apache Creek Pueblo | | | | | | | | | | 15 | | 0 | 15 |
| Higgins Flat Pueblo | | | | | | | | | | 9 | | 1 | 10 |
| ***Known Sources %*** | | | | | | | | | | ***100*** | | | |
| *Mogollon Highlands PIV* | | | | | | | | | | | | | |
| Foote Canyon Pueblo | | | | | | 2 | | | | 6 | | 4 | 12 |
| ***Known Sources %*** | | | | | | ***25*** | | | | ***75*** | | | |
| *Complementary Areas PIII* | | | | | | | | | | | | | |
| Manuelito Canyon Sites | | 2 | 1 | 1 | | | | | | | | 11 | 15 |
| Cebolleta Mesa Sites | 1 | | | 8 | | | | | | | | 6 | 15 |

vessels were also recovered some distance from their production areas. In order to better visualize the strongest vectors of unpainted ceramic circulation across the study area, it is useful to display these data as a network graph. Figure 10 shows each major ceramic production zone, with arrows indicating the estimated volume of ceramics flowing among those areas in each direction. Thicker arrows represent a greater volume of ceramics moving from one source area to the other. Note that the production areas have been placed in their rough relative geographic locations.

There are numerous complex and overlapping patterns apparent in this network diagram and the associated table, but I limit my discussion here to a few trends that are most relevant to the current study. First, for the Pueblo III period there is a strong north/south component to the distribution of unpainted vessels produced in different zones across the core portion of the study area. Unpainted vessels produced in the Pescado Basin are found in moderate frequencies in all subregions along the Zuni River Valley and nearby drainages, including the El Morro Valley, the West Zuni area, and along Carrizo Wash, but in no areas farther to the south. Conversely, pottery produced in the Upper Little Colorado area is found at sites in both the Carrizo Wash and Mariana Mesa areas but in no sites farther north. Unpainted vessels likely produced in the Mariana Mesa area were recovered from sites in the West Zuni area and along Carrizo Wash in small amounts, potentially suggesting a few strong ties from east to west across the region.

A few vessels recovered from sites in the Mariana Mesa district were likely produced in the El Morro Valley, Cebolleta Mesa, and potentially other areas to the north along the Zuni River Valley. Although the number of vessels from northern sources is relatively small, this number is also probably too high. All of the vessels in question are Cibola Gray Ware sherds. Cibola Gray Ware vessels account for 0.5–3 percent of unpainted vessels recovered from the sampled sites in the Mariana Mesa area during the period considered here, but they account for approximately 19 percent of the NAA dataset from the Mariana Mesa area due to the large number of Cibola Gray Ware sherds submitted by Schachner (2012) in a previous study. Furthermore, there are limited data suggesting that some Cibola Gray Ware may have been locally produced in the Mariana Mesa area. Thus, the apparent strength of connections between the Mariana Mesa area and settlements to the north along the Zuni River and Cebolleta Mesa is likely somewhat exaggerated in the network graph.

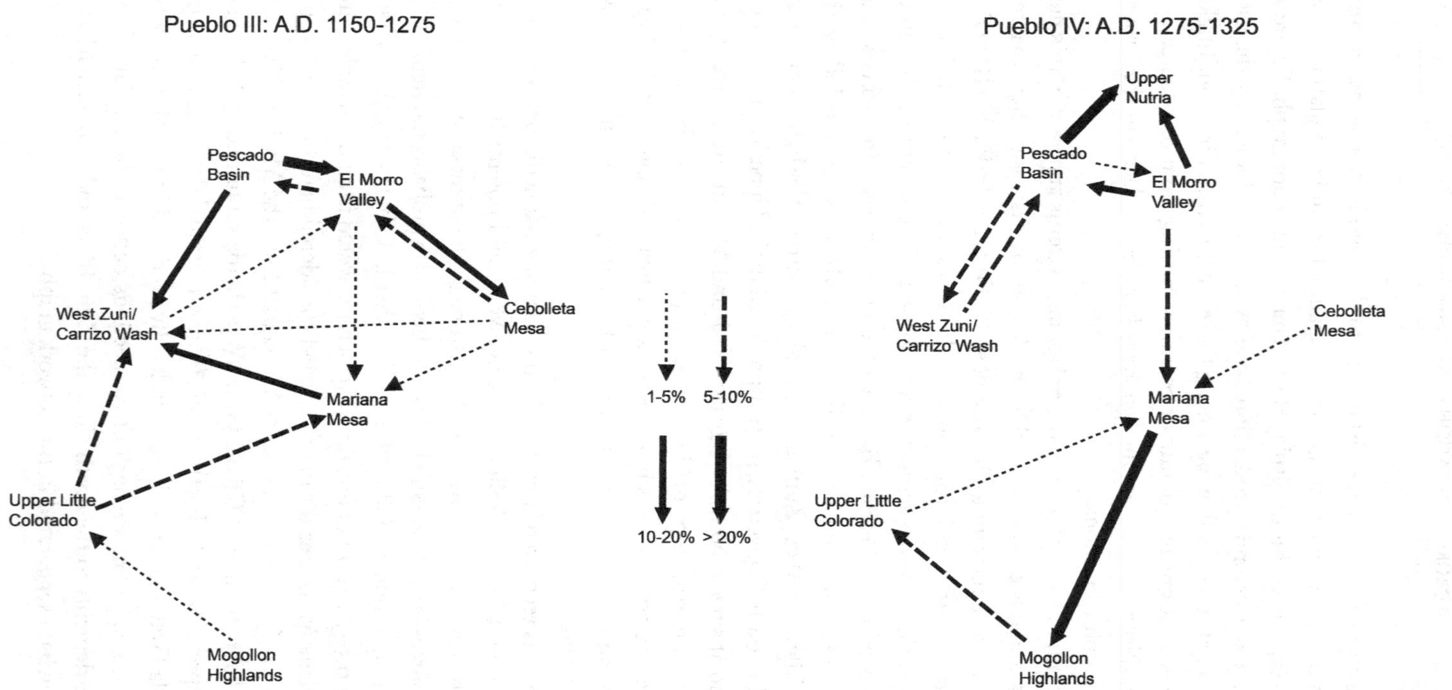


FIGURE 10. Network graph showing the primary vectors of unpainted ceramic circulation during the Pueblo III (*left*) and Pueblo IV (*right*) periods. Subregions are placed in their rough relative geographic positions.

During the early Pueblo IV period, there is substantially less evidence for the circulation of unpainted vessels among the inhabitants of different settlement clusters.[3] The few vessels that were transported out of their production zones suggest, however, that there was still a strong north/south division in the movement of vessels at this time. The circulation of vessels is most evident among sites in the core of the Zuni area (El Morro Valley, Pescado Basin, and Box S) and to a far lesser extent including the West Zuni area. There was also a small amount of movement of vessels among the Mariana Mesa, Upper Little Colorado, and Mogollon Highlands areas to the south. As was the case during the Pueblo III period, several vessels produced in the north were recovered from the Mariana Mesa area, but once again this relationship is likely somewhat exaggerated due to the overrepresentation of Cibola Gray Ware in the NAA dataset.

The patterns illustrated here suggest that unpainted vessels in the Cibola region circulated primarily in two relatively distinct spheres. The first includes settlements along the Zuni River Valley and the Carrizo Wash area in the north, and the second includes settlements along the edge of the Colorado Plateau and in the mountainous highlands farther south. Perhaps not surprisingly, these two spheres of ceramic circulation coincide with the distributions of Cibola Gray Ware to the north and Mogollon Brown Ware to the south, which have sometimes been interpreted as the markers of the Anasazi and Mogollon archaeological culture areas, respectively. However, the data presented here demonstrate that unpainted ceramic assemblages from sites along the edges of these two spheres of ceramic circulation were somewhat more variable in terms of the geographic sources of nonlocal unpainted vessels and included small numbers of nonlocal vessels produced both to the north and south. Overall, this suggests that there was a fairly consistent division between the northern and southern portions of the Cibola region through time, but the boundaries between the two overarching spheres of ceramic circulation were also somewhat permeable.

With the exception of the movement of vessels between the El Morro Valley and the nearby Pescado Basin, most unpainted ceramic circulation during both the Pueblo III and Pueblo IV periods was largely unidirectional, or at least heavily weighted in one direction, rather than reciprocal. This suggests that the long-distance movement of unpainted vessels may be partially attributable to regional-scale population movements rather than sustained patterns of interaction among distinct groups continually residing in different areas. Conversely, the consistent reciprocal circulation of unpainted vessels among the inhabitants of the El Morro Valley and the Pescado Basin suggests particularly strong relational connections and frequent interaction among the inhabitants of these nearby areas, or perhaps as Schachner (2012) has suggested, evidence that some households maintained residences in both areas.

## THE CIRCULATION OF PAINTED CERAMICS

Table 3 lists the distribution of painted vessels by production zone for all sites by subregion, and Figure 11 illustrates ceramic circulation as a network graph. This figure shows that there was a great deal of reciprocal circulation of ceramic vessels among the inhabitants of settlements along the Zuni River Valley, including the El Morro Valley, Pescado Basin, West Zuni, and Carrizo Wash areas, as well as the Cebolleta Mesa area beyond the core study area. Painted ceramics produced in the Pescado Basin are also quite common in most other portions of the region. In fact, painted vessels from the Pescado Basin production zone are found at almost every sampled site across the study area with the exception of sites in the Upper Little Colorado subregion. Upper Little Colorado area sites are dominated by locally produced painted vessels along with a small number of nonlocal painted corrugated ceramics (McDonald Painted Corrugated) likely produced to the south or west below the Mogollon Rim. Painted vessels produced in the Mariana Mesa area were primarily recovered locally but were also found in small amounts in the Carrizo Wash and Mogollon Highlands areas.

Although the patterns of circulation documented here for painted ceramics are quite different from the patterns documented for the circulation of unpainted vessels, there are also a few overarching similarities. First, there still appears to have been a strong division between the Upper Little Colorado area and areas farther north and east along the Zuni River during the Pueblo III period. As with the unpainted ceramics, settlements between the Upper Little Colorado and the central Zuni area have painted vessels from diverse sources to both the north and south. Unlike the patterns documented for unpainted vessels, however, ceramic assemblages for some Pueblo III settlements in the Mariana Mesa area are dominated by painted vessels produced in the Pescado Basin. This pattern is notable because, although the inhabitants of the Mariana Mesa area were apparently obtaining substantial amounts of painted pottery from the Pescado Basin, vessels exported from Mariana Mesa are primarily found in areas farther south. This may suggest that nonceramic items were being exchanged among the inhabitants of the Mariana Mesa and Pescado Basin areas or, possibly,

TABLE 3. Production zone assignments by site and subregion for all painted vessels

| REGION/SETTLEMENT | EMV | PLAT | PB | CEB | BS | MM | WEST | AZ/NM | ULC | SOUTH | SC | UNK | TOTAL |
|---|---|---|---|---|---|---|---|---|---|---|---|---|---|
| *El Morro Valley PIII* | | | | | | | | | | | | | |
| Los Gigantes Cluster | 16 | 3 | 32 | 1 | | | 3 | | | | | 20 | 75 |
| Togeye Canyon Cluster | 29 | | 22 | | | | 3 | 1 | | | | 7 | 62 |
| Scribe S Cluster | 26 | 6 | 24 | 1 | | | 4 | | | | | 13 | 74 |
| Tinaja Cluster | 43 | 1 | 12 | | | | 1 | 2 | | | | 6 | 65 |
| ***Known Sources %*** | ***50*** | ***4.3*** | ***39*** | ***0.9*** | | | ***4.8*** | ***1.3*** | | | | | |
| *El Morro Valley PIV* | | | | | | | | | | | | | |
| Atsinna | 11 | 4 | 6 | | | | | | | | | 6 | 27 |
| Cienega | 7 | | 5 | | | | | | | | | 4 | 16 |
| Mirabal | 7 | 1 | 5 | 1 | 4 | | | | | | | 2 | 20 |
| Pueblo de los Muertos | 11 | 1 | 15 | | | | | | | | | 2 | 29 |
| ***Known Sources %*** | ***46*** | ***7.7*** | ***40*** | ***1.3*** | ***5.1*** | | | | | | | | |
| *Pescado Basin PIII* | | | | | | | | | | | | | |
| Spier 81 Cluster | 3 | 3 | 17 | 3 | | | 2 | 1 | | | | 11 | 40 |
| ***Known Sources %*** | ***10*** | ***10*** | ***59*** | ***10*** | | | ***6.9*** | ***3.4*** | | | | | |
| *Pescado Basin PIV* | | | | | | | | | | | | | |
| Heshotauthla | | 2 | 29 | 1 | | | | | | | | 2 | 34 |
| Lower Pescado Village | 2 | 1 | 18 | | | | | 1 | | | | 3 | 25 |
| ***Known Sources %*** | ***3.7*** | ***5.6*** | ***87*** | ***1.9*** | | | | ***1.9*** | | | | | |
| *Upper Nutria PIV* | | | | | | | | | | | | | |
| Box S Pueblo | 2 | | 8 | | 8 | | | | | | | 0 | 18 |
| ***Known Sources %*** | ***11*** | | ***44*** | | ***44*** | | | | | | | | |

(*continued*)

TABLE 3. (*continued*)

| REGION/SETTLEMENT | EMV | PLAT | PB | CEB | BS | MM | WEST | AZ/NM | ULC | SOUTH | SC | UNK | TOTAL |
|---|---|---|---|---|---|---|---|---|---|---|---|---|---|
| *Mariana Mesa PIII* | | | | | | | | | | | | | |
| UG481 | | | 8 | | | | | | | | | 2 | 10 |
| Tri-R Pueblo | | 1 | 4 | | | 12 | | | | | | 4 | 21 |
| Hubble Corner | | | 10 | | | 5 | | | | | | 0 | 15 |
| ***Known Sources %*** | | *2.5* | *55* | | | *43* | | | | | | | |
| *Mariana Mesa PIV* | | | | | | | | | | | | | |
| Horse Camp Mill | | | 4 | | | 7 | | | | | | 4 | 15 |
| Techado Spring Pueblo | 4 | | 6 | | | 23 | | | 4 | | | 8 | 45 |
| ***Known Sources %*** | *8.3* | | *21* | | | *63* | | | *8.3* | | | | |
| *West Zuni PIII* | | | | | | | | | | | | | |
| Hinkson Ranch | | 1 | 11 | | | | 10 | | 1 | | | 7 | 30 |
| Jaralosa Pueblo | | 1 | 11 | 2 | | | 7 | | 2 | | | 2 | 25 |
| ***Known Sources %*** | | *4.3* | *48* | *4.3* | | | *37* | | *6.5* | | | | |
| *West Zuni PIV* | | | | | | | | | | | | | |
| Ojo Bonito | | 2 | 1 | | | | 5 | 18 | 1 | | | 14 | 41 |
| Spier 170 | | | | | | | 2 | 18 | | | | 5 | 25 |
| ***Known Sources %*** | | *4.3* | *2.1* | | | | *15* | *77* | *2.1* | | | | |
| *Carrizo Wash PIII* | | | | | | | | | | | | | |
| Platt Ranch Settlement | | 1 | 6 | 1 | | | 4 | | | | | 3 | 15 |
| Garcia Ranch Pueblo | | 2 | 1 | 2 | | 1 | | 5 | 5 | | | 4 | 20 |
| ***Known Sources %*** | | *11* | *25* | *11* | | *3.6* | *14* | *18* | *18* | | | | |

| | | | | | | | | | | | | |
|---|---|---|---|---|---|---|---|---|---|---|---|---|
| *Upper Little Colorado PIII* | | | | | | | | | | | | |
| Coyote Creek Pueblo | | | | | | | | 18 | | | 2 | 20 |
| Rim Valley Pueblo | | | | | | | | 7 | 4 | | 12 | 23 |
| Rudd Creek Pueblo | | | | | | | | 18 | | | 2 | 20 |
| ***Known Sources %*** | | | | | | | | ***92*** | ***8.5*** | | | |
| *Upper Little Colorado Early PIV* | | | | | | | | | | | | |
| Baca Pueblo | | | 1 | | | 1 | 28 | 28 | | 3 | 25 | 86 |
| Casa Malpais | | | 1 | | | | 2 | 20 | | | 13 | 36 |
| Hooper Ranch Pueblo | | | 1 | | | | 13 | 27 | | 3 | 10 | 54 |
| ***Known Sources %*** | | | ***2.3*** | | | ***0.8*** | ***34*** | ***59*** | | ***4.7*** | | |
| *Upper Little Colorado Late PIV* | | | | | | | | | | | | |
| Sherwood Ranch Pueblo | | | 1 | | | | 15 | 8 | | 7 | 4 | 35 |
| Rattlesnake Point Pueblo | | | | | | 2 | 40 | 25 | | 9 | 23 | 99 |
| Table Rock | | | | | | | 26 | 33 | | 6 | 15 | 80 |
| ***Known Sources %*** | | | ***0.6*** | | | ***1.2*** | ***47*** | ***38*** | | ***13*** | | |
| *Mogollon Highlands PIII* | | | | | | | | | | | | |
| Apache Creek Pueblo | | 1 | 3 | | 1 | | | 3 | | | 7 | 15 |
| Higgins Flat Pueblo | | | 3 | | | | | 5 | | | 7 | 15 |
| ***Known Sources %*** | | ***6.3*** | ***38*** | | ***6.3*** | | | ***50*** | | | | |
| *Mogollon Highlands PIV* | | | | | | | | | | | | |
| Foote Canyon Pueblo | | | 1 | | | | | 14 | | | 3 | 18 |
| ***Known Sources %*** | | | ***6.7*** | | | | | ***93.3*** | | | | |
| *Complementary Areas PIII* | | | | | | | | | | | | |
| Manuelito Canyon Sites | | 2 | 5 | | | 1 | 1 | | | | 6 | 15 |
| Cebolleta Mesa Sites | 5 | 1 | 8 | | | | | | | | 1 | 15 |
| Cañada Alamosa Sites | 4 | 3 | 14 | 11 | 11 | | | | | | 13 | 56 |

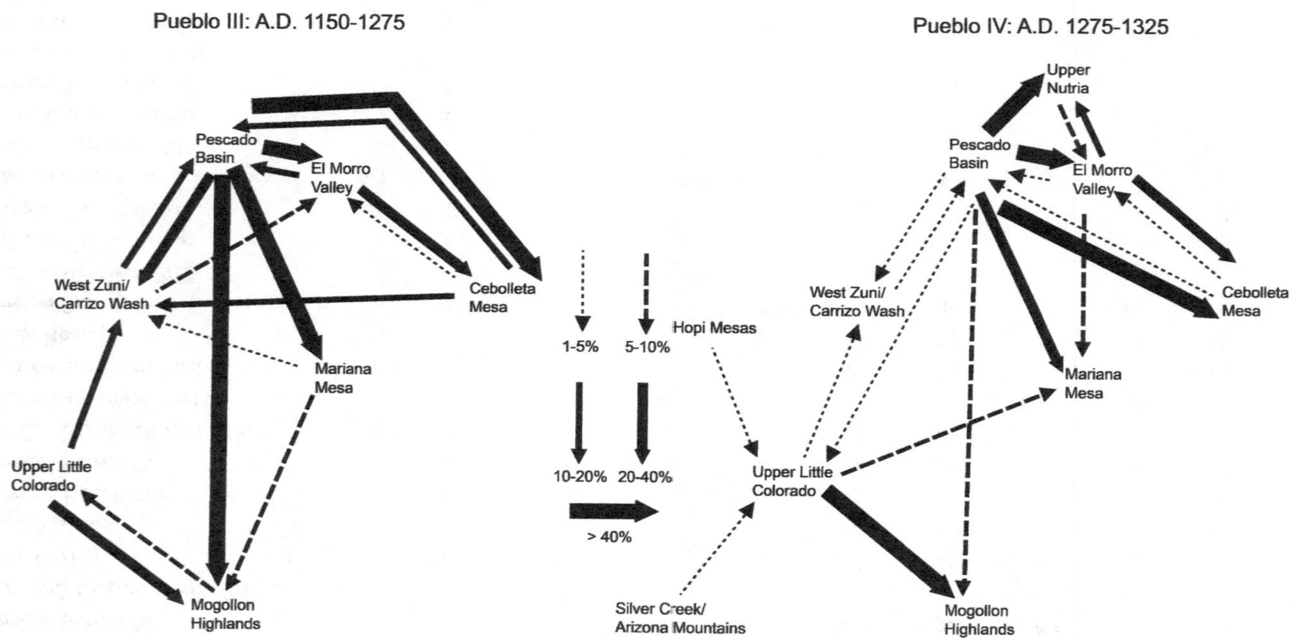


**FIGURE 11.** Network graph showing the primary vectors of painted ceramic circulation during the Pueblo III (*left*) and Pueblo IV (*right*) periods. Subregions are placed in their rough relative geographic positions.

that settlements in the Mariana Mesa area were somewhat peripheral to the sphere of exchange involving ceramics produced in the Pescado Basin. Considering the Mogollon Highlands area in the south, painted vessels in the sample are roughly equally split between those produced in the Pescado Basin and those produced in the Upper Little Colorado, although there are major differences in the wares represented by each production source. Painted vessels obtained from the Upper Little Colorado area are mostly Cibola White Ware jars (75 percent), whereas vessels obtained from the Pescado Basin area are mostly White Mountain Red Ware bowls (83 percent). Although the current sample is small, the differences suggest that the red ware bowls and white ware jars were obtained in different ways, possibly because jars would have been more difficult to transport than bowls. The number of vessels moving from the Pescado Basin into the Mogollon Highlands is likely somewhat overemphasized in the data presented here, however, as White Mountain Red Ware vessels are somewhat less frequent in site-wide ceramic assemblages than in the current small compositional dataset (White Mountain Red Ware typically makes up 5–30 percent of the painted ceramic assemblage at Pueblo III sites in the region and 43 percent of the current compositional dataset). Overall, the available data suggest that although White Mountain Red Ware was relatively rare at sites in the Mogollon Highlands, much of it may have been produced in the Pescado Basin area.

The patterns documented here for the Pueblo III period suggest that the inhabitants of a large portion of the Cibola region were involved in a broad sphere of painted ceramic exchange possibly centered on the Pescado Basin area. Reciprocal exchange relationships were strongest among the inhabitants of settlements in the Zuni area between Carrizo Wash and the El Morro Valley. Settlements to the south, in the Mariana Mesa and Mogollon Highlands areas, obtained pottery produced in the Pescado Basin, but if this movement of vessels represents exchange, it was likely not exchange in kind. At the same time, the Upper Little Colorado area appears to have been almost wholly isolated from this sphere of painted ceramic circulation. Although vessels produced in the Upper Little Colorado area did end up in nearby areas in small numbers, very few nonlocal painted vessels could be identified in the available compositional sample. This division suggests the maintenance of a relatively strong and persistent boundary between the inhabitants of the Upper Little Colorado and areas to the north and east.

For the early Pueblo IV period sample, most areas are dominated by locally produced painted vessels. It is important to note that although the Upper Little

Colorado and the West Zuni region share a common compositional group / production source (Arizona and New Mexico), most vessels within this group are likely local products where they were recovered, produced using different outcrops of the same geological formation (see the online appendix for additional analyses testing this possibility). In addition, all but one of the nonlocal samples recovered from the Mariana Mesa area were examples of types that potentially date to the very latest Pueblo III period (Tularosa Black-on-white and St. Johns Polychrome). Thus, the relative rarity of ceramic circulation among distant settlement clusters may have been even more pronounced after the transition to ceramic assemblages dominated by glaze-painted wares shortly after A.D. 1275.

By far, the largest numbers of vessels found outside of their production zone during the Pueblo IV period were Zuni Glaze Ware bowls moving from the Pescado Basin area into the El Morro Valley and the Box S area. After about A.D. 1275, the El Morro Valley was a major demographic center across the greater Cibola region and one of the most densely occupied areas in the northern Southwest. The largely unidirectional movement of vessels into the El Morro Valley may have been due to either population movement or intensified public ceremonialism associated with the establishment of the massive nucleated communities at this time (Huntley 2008:42–43; Schachner et al. 2011; see also Potter 1997, 2000). Either way, it appears that ceramic exchange in the Zuni area was increasingly focused on this newly developing demographic center.

The painted wares in the current sample recovered from the Mogollon Highlands area were also likely imports. All but one sample could be placed in a single compositional group attributed to production in the southern Upper Little Colorado area. This pattern, very different from that seen in the Pueblo III period, suggests that social relationships changed as interaction became increasingly localized. Alternatively, the changes between the two time periods also may relate to differences in the external relationships of the inhabitants of specific portions of the large Mogollon Highlands area. The Pueblo III sample was derived from sites in the Tularosa River / Apache Creek area, whereas the later Pueblo IV sample comes from Foote Canyon Pueblo (ca. A.D. 1250–1350) along the Blue River in Arizona. Most settlements in the Tularosa River / Apache Creek area were likely uninhabited by or shortly after the transition to the Pueblo IV period. There may have been a great deal of variability in the production sources represented among late sites in the Mogollon Highlands, as the latest ceramic wares and types present at individual sites differ quite a bit from place to place (cf. Rinaldo 1959:Table 2; Robinson 1992:Table 6.1; Zamora and Oakes 1999:Table 2.5). Although additional sampling could improve the picture, the currently available data do suggest an increasing focus on nearby production sources through time similar to the trend seen across the Cibola region as a whole.

Despite the relative isolation of settlement clusters during the Pueblo IV period, there is some evidence for the long-distance transport of painted ceramics. A small number of vessels from the Pescado Basin area were present in all of the other sampled subregions. Furthermore, a few Zuni Glaze Ware and White Mountain Red Ware vessels produced in the central and southern Upper Little Colorado were transported to relatively distant settlements in the West Zuni area and Mariana Mesa subregions. The rarity of the movement of vessels across great distances during the early Pueblo IV period suggests that the social contexts in which painted vessels were being exchanged were primarily organized among the inhabitants of proximate settlements. The demographic center of the Cibola region between the Pescado Basin and the El Morro Valley appears to have been particularly isolated in terms of long-distance ceramic exchange.

This picture of isolation may not have characterized all portions of the Cibola region equally, however, at least by the late Pueblo IV period (ca. A.D. 1325–1400). A small number of Fourmile Polychrome vessels, a Late White Mountain Red Ware type produced after A.D. 1325 almost exclusively in the Silver Creek area, were recovered from sites in the Upper Little Colorado area. A comparison of early and late Pueblo IV sites in the Upper Little Colorado area suggests that nonlocal Fourmile Polychrome from the Silver Creek area became somewhat more common through time. In addition, small numbers of Roosevelt Red Ware vessels likely produced in the Arizona Mountains and Hopi Yellow Ware vessels produced in the Hopi area were also recovered from a few late Pueblo IV sites in the Upper Little Colorado drainage. Daniela Triadan (1997; Triadan et al. 2002) has also documented substantial amounts of White Mountain Red Ware moving among different portions of the Silver Creek area and the Arizona Mountains. Available data suggest that, at least by A.D. 1325, the Upper Little Colorado area was part of an extensive western sphere of ceramic circulation involving sites in the Silver Creek drainage and the Arizona Mountains (see Duff 2002).

Andrew Duff (2002:166–167) argues that the inhabitants of this western zone, many of whom were relatively recent immigrants into the greater Cibola region, may have shared some level of common identity built upon the establishment of culturally diverse communities in a new land. Not all settlements were equally connected across this broad area. Different wares were present in varying proportions at individual settlements in the Upper Little Colorado, Arizona Mountains, and the Silver Creek area that likely reflect the varying historical ties among the inhabitants of distinct communities (Duff 2000). Despite this variability, the available data suggest that at least by the late Pueblo IV period, the Cibola region could roughly be divided into an eastern zone centered on the Zuni area and characterized by relative isolation and internally focused interaction, and a western zone marked by more extensive regional exchange relationships (Duff 2002:Chapter 7).

As painted vessels were likely used and perhaps exchanged in the context of public gatherings, these two largely distinct spheres of ceramic exchange may also represent separate spheres of broad-scale relational connections. Importantly, there is some evidence for an emerging boundary between the eastern and western portions of the study area as early as the Pueblo III period. The Upper Little Colorado area was largely isolated from the sphere of painted ceramic exchange focused on the Zuni area throughout the period considered in this study. Although additional sampling of earlier sites in the Silver Creek and Arizona Mountains areas could help to address this issue further (especially for St. Johns Polychrome bowls), the consistent separation between the Upper Little Colorado subregion and areas to the east may suggest that the distinct spheres of ceramic circulation characterizing the Pueblo IV period may have emerged several generations earlier. Intriguingly, a small number of samples of Cibola White Ware (Tularosa Black-on-white) submitted for NAA characterization by Zedeño (2002) from the Point of Pines area meet the criteria for membership in compositional groups attributed to the Upper Little Colorado, perhaps suggesting that ties to the mountainous western portions of the Cibola region may have also emerged somewhat earlier in time.

## CERAMIC CIRCULATION, RELATIONAL NETWORKS, AND SPHERES OF PUBLIC CEREMONIALISM

The analyses presented above demonstrate that a large number of ceramic vessels were transported across the greater Cibola region during the period considered in this study. I argue that these patterns of ceramic movement can be interpreted as proxies for the major vectors of social interaction and relational connections across the study area. Although the volume of ceramics moving over long distances changed through time, specific regional relationships were relatively consistent across the Pueblo III to Pueblo IV period transformation. In both periods, unpainted and painted wares were circulated in quite different spheres, perhaps suggesting that the different kinds of social relationships were involved in the movement of these vessels.

Unpainted vessels moved primarily in two relatively distinct spheres encompassing the northern (the Carrizo Wash, West Zuni, the Pescado Basin, and the El Morro Valley) and southern (the Mariana Mesa, the Upper Little Colorado, and the Mogollon Highlands) portions of the core study area. This strong north–south division was maintained across the Pueblo III to Pueblo IV period despite massive population movements and changes in settlement organization. Importantly, however, the inhabitants of settlements along the edges of these two overarching spheres obtained pottery from somewhat more diverse sources, including areas both to the north and to the south. Analyses presented in Chapter 5 further suggest that this pattern is not merely a product of geological diversity.

The most frequently activated relational connections were strongest among the inhabitants of spatially proximate areas both before and after the Pueblo III to Pueblo IV transition. Further, there was a persistent but also somewhat permeable boundary between the northern and southern Cibola region in terms of unpainted pottery circulation that may represent the separation between two distinct relational networks characterized by strong internal relationships and perhaps common historical ties. Interestingly, the two spheres of unpainted ceramic circulation generally coincide with the traditional Anasazi and Mogollon archaeological culture areas.

Painted vessels were frequently transported over much greater distances than unpainted vessels. I argue that, during the Pueblo III period, much of the Cibola region was involved in a common and extremely widespread sphere of ceramic circulation centered on the Pescado Basin. The inhabitants of widely dispersed communities were linked through ceramic exchanges, many of which likely took place in the context of public gatherings. Thus, members of distant communities may have established broad relational connections based on their common participation in periodic public events. Importantly, the association of painted ceramic exchange with public ceremonialism may also suggest that communities linked by weaker ties within similar spheres of painted ceramic circulation may have also shared a level of *categorical commonality*. The inhabitants of some areas, in particular the Pescado Basin, produced ceramic vessels that were apparently widely sought after across much of the region. Ceramic producers may have accrued a special position within this network of regional exchange and ceremonialism through the creation of objects that were ritually charged (e.g., Spielmann 2002). Notably, the Upper Little Colorado area was isolated from the regional sphere of painted ceramic exchange, perhaps suggesting an emerging social boundary between the eastern and western portions of the study area during the Pueblo III period.

Across the Pueblo III to Pueblo IV transition, the circulation of painted ceramics became increasingly locally focused within the central Zuni area (the Pescado Basin, the El Morro Valley, and the Box S area), whereas long-distance exchange was somewhat more common among settlements in the western portion of the region (the Upper Little Colorado, Silver Creek, and the Arizona Mountains). This transition also saw a major increase in the local production of red ware and polychrome vessels in many portions of the Cibola region, as well as a divergence in the ceramic production technology and decorative style associated with different portions of the study area (see Chapter 7). The brief discussion above necessarily downplays a great deal of regional variation, but there is a substantial east–west component to the dominant patterns of painted ceramic circulation at least by the early Pueblo IV period. This suggests that the eastern (Pescado Basin, El Morro Valley, Box S, West Zuni, and Mariana Mesa) and western (Upper Little Colorado, Mogollon Highlands, Arizona Mountains, and Silver Creek) portions of the study area were increasingly involved in different spheres of public ceremonialism. I argue that this indicates not only changes in long-distance patterns of relational "weak ties" but an increasing consolidation of distinct categorical social identities defined around periodic public ceremonies.

# 5

# THE TECHNOLOGY OF POTTERY PRODUCTION AND RELATIONAL NETWORKS

IN RECENT decades there has been an increasing interest among archaeologists in exploring the interplay between patterns of social interaction at various scales and the technological choices of individuals and larger groups (e.g., Cordell and Habicht-Mauche 2012; Killick 2004; Stark 1998). Recent work illustrates that investigations of shared technological practices can often provide a useful means for evaluating direct or historical relationships among individuals and larger social groups. In particular, an ever-growing body of ethnoarchaeological research suggests that attributes of material culture that are either invisible in the final product or located in contexts of low visibility tend to vary in relation to the degree of interaction among producers in contrast to other processes such as emulation (see Carr 1995; Clark 2001:6–22). Thus, strong patterns of similarity in such low-visibility technological attributes can provide important indicators of shared contexts of learning among producers and shared "communities of practice" (e.g., Cordell and Habicht-Mauche 2012; Dietler and Herbich 1998; Gosselain 1998, 2000; Herbich 1987; Sassman and Rudolphi 2001; Stark et al. 1998). This line of research further suggests that analyses designed to reveal shared technological practices also provide insights into patterns of frequent interaction and, by extension, shared *relational connections* among individuals and larger groups.

In this chapter, I describe and apply a new quantitative method for comparing the techniques used to produce unpainted ceramic vessels across the Cibola region. Unpainted ceramics in the Southwest are particularly well suited to investigations of technological practices because they are typically made at the household level and locally consumed (Chapter 4). The new method I use here draws on tools developed for social network analysis to produce a relative scale of ceramic technological similarity among a number of settlements across the Cibola region. I use this measure of technological similarity as a proxy for the direction and strength of *relational connections* among the inhabitants of settlements across the study area through time. In general, the analyses presented below suggest that the physical distance between settlements was a substantial factor influencing the frequency and/or intensity of interaction among potters. Furthermore, patterns of frequent interaction appear to have been consistent through time despite the massive changes of regional settlement marking the Pueblo III to Pueblo IV social transformation. The few deviations from this general regional trend may provide evidence of long-distance population movement into or within the greater Cibola region.

## PLAIN AND CORRUGATED POTTERY IN THE CIBOLA REGION

Culinary ceramic vessels produced across the Cibola region consist of unpainted and unslipped containers primarily used for food preparation and storage (e.g., Crown 1981; Hays-Gilpin and van Hartesveldt 1998; Rinaldo and Bluhm 1956). The vast majority of unpainted vessels produced during the period considered in this study have corrugated exterior surfaces (where coils used to produce the vessels remain visible), and thus they retain easily observable evidence for many of the specific forming and finishing steps used to produce them.

Corrugated and plain ware vessels are usually assumed to have been produced and consumed at the household level (Reid and Montgomery 1998; Zedeño 1994). Although these vessels did sometimes circulate, chemical characterizations presented in the previous chapter demonstrate that they were most frequently deposited in the general locations where they were produced. This suggests that the technological attributes of plain and corrugated vessels recovered from a settlement provide a reasonable proxy for the technological decisions and practices of local potters. Further, as these objects were likely made and consumed at the household level, I argue that such shared technological attributes provide evidence of relational connections among groups of

FIGURE 12. Examples of corrugated vessels from the greater Cibola region. The example on the left is Cibola indented corrugated gray, and the example on the right is Tularosa patterned corrugated brown. Photos by the author from collections at the Center for Archaeology and Society repository at Arizona State University.

local potters at various scales (e.g., settlement, subregion, etc.) and can serve as a proxy for relational connections among the inhabitants of those areas more generally.

Although there is some regional and temporal variation, sites within the Cibola region are generally dominated by vessels within two major ware categories. Cibola Gray Ware dominates assemblages at settlements along the Zuni River Valley and areas to the east and north, whereas Mogollon Brown Ware dominates assemblages along the southern edge of the Colorado Plateau and in the areas along the Mogollon Mountains. Sites in the zone between the mountains and the Zuni River sometimes contain varying frequencies of both major wares, but most sites are still strongly dominated by a single ware (see Clark et al. 2006; Crown 1981; Danson 1957; Duff 2005; Hagopian et al. 2004; Mills 2007a; Spier 1918:342).

Both Cibola Gray Ware and Mogollon Brown Ware vessels were constructed by coiling, but they differed in terms of the chemical characteristics of their pastes and the atmospheres in which they were fired (Crown 1981:267; Hays-Gilpin and van Hartesveldt 1998). Cibola Gray Ware vessels were typically produced from clays with low iron content, tempered with quartz sand and/or sherds, and fired in a neutral to reducing atmosphere, producing a grayish or whitish surface color. Mogollon Brown Ware vessels were constructed

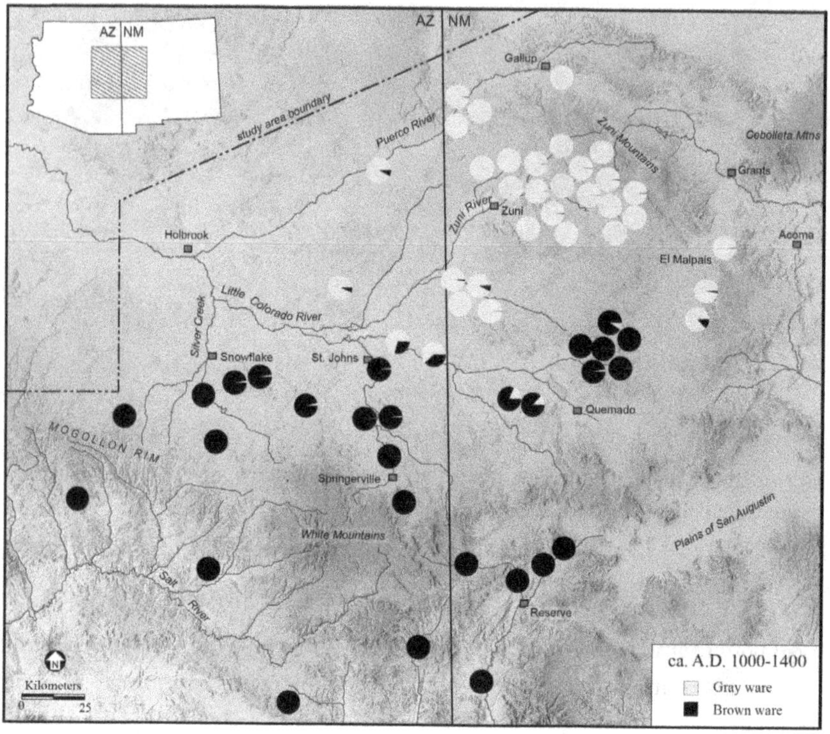


FIGURE 13. Map of the study area showing the relative proportions of brown and gray ware ceramics for sites dating ca. A.D. 1050–1400.

from iron-rich volcanic-derived clays, tempered with quartz sand, and fired in an oxidizing atmosphere, producing a reddish-brown or blackish-brown hue. Importantly, some vessels contain combinations of these common characteristics, and distinctions between these broad ware categories are not always clear cut (see discussions in Crown 1981:267–269; Hays-Gilpin and van Hartesveldt 1998:120–143).

The relatively discrete distributions of Cibola Gray Ware and Mogollon Brown Ware have, in the past, been interpreted as markers of a distinct boundary between the Anasazi and Mogollon culture areas (Colton 1939; Danson 1957; Gladwin and Gladwin 1934; Haury 1936; Wheat 1955). Opinions vary, however, as to the extent to which differences between brown and gray ceramics are products of cultural distinctions or material availability. For example, C. Dean Wilson (1994, 2007; Wilson and Severts 1999) argues that the distributions of brown and gray vessels may be defined largely by the availability of different kinds of clays across the Southwest (see also Chapter 4; Colton 1953; Lekson 1996; Martin 1951:233). Other researchers argue that consistent distinctions in the technology and surface treatments of brown and gray ware vessels suggest that the potters producing these wares were operating within distinct technological frameworks and represent distinct communities of practice (e.g., Crown 1981:269; Hays-Gilpin and van Hartesveldt 1998; Nauman 2007; Wichlacz 2009; Zedeño 1994:55–61). It is likely that both factors influenced the broad similarities and differences among vessels produced across the Cibola region, but no extensive regional-scale assessment of corrugated ceramic technology has previously been attempted.

In practice, archaeologists working in the Cibola region group sherds and vessels by ware based on surface color and paste characteristics and then place them into type categories based on specific surface treatments (see Rinaldo and Bluhm 1956). Importantly, the most commonly used type categories have analogues in both Mogollon Brown Ware and Cibola Gray Ware (see Hays-Gilpin and van Hartesveldt 1998; Rinaldo and Bluhm 1956:150–155). Indeed, plain and corrugated vessels do not fit well within the ware-type-variety system of classification that has long been used for painted ceramics across the greater Southwest (e.g., Colton 1953; Hays-Gilpin and van Hartesveldt 1998; but see Gifford and Smith 1978). Anna Neuzil (2008:28–29; see also Pierce 2005) argues that corrugated and plain ware pottery should instead be seen as falling along a stylistic and technological continuum with a great deal of overlap in many of the attributes that could potentially be used to define types. The analyses presented here are specifically designed to characterize the relative similarities and differences in ceramic production technology along this continuum that are usually masked by traditional typological analyses. I argue that the methods described here provide a better proxy for social interaction and relational connections at regional scales than either binary oppositions between brown/gray wares or considerations of ceramic attributes one at a time.

## CHARACTERIZING THE TECHNOLOGY OF POTTERY PRODUCTION

A number of recent studies from several regions across the Southwest have used technological assessments of plain and corrugated pottery to address questions relating to social interaction, population movement, and technological change (e.g., Brunson 1985; Clark 2001; Crown 1981; Dungan 2015; Hegmon et al. 2000; Kleinman 2010; Pierce 2005; McGarry 1975; McGimsey 1980; Nauman 2007; Neuzil 2001, 2005, 2008; Pierce 2005; Reid and Montgomery 1998; Schleher and Ruth 2005; Snow 1983; Stone 1986; Zedeño 1994). These studies have varied in their goals, but in general all suggest that characterizations of specific attributes of ceramic technology can reveal much that is missed through traditional typological analyses. Based on these past ceramic technological studies, a pilot study involving a detailed examination of whole vessels from the Cibola region, and my own and others' experimental reproductions of corrugated pottery technology, I define here a series of nominal, ordinal, presence/absence, and metric variables that can be consistently coded or measured on sherds and vessels of corrugated pottery from sites in the Cibola region. Table 4 lists all of the variables along with brief descriptions of their potential variable states (see the online appendix for additional details).

The coded variables were selected to include both the range of attributes typically considered in analyses of corrugated pottery and the variables that likely relate to specific steps in the ceramic production process.[1] However, not all of the measured and coded attributes are appropriate for exploring variation in the techniques employed by groups of potters. Several of the coded variables may relate more to the materials available or household composition than to production decisions among functional equivalents. For example, although temper selection is a fundamental technological choice involved in the preparation of a ceramic paste, different temper types have varying performance characteristics that depend on the properties of locally available clays (e.g., Arnold et al. 2000; Bronitsky and Hamer 1986; Sassman and Rudolphi 2001). Thus, a potter's decisions relating to tempering material are constrained to a degree by locally available clay resources (e.g., Meanwell 2015; Roper et al. 2010). Further, vessel size and shape can relate to the intended use of a vessel (Hally 1986; Skibo 1992) but are also influenced by other social factors such as household size and the context of food preparation or consumption (Blitz 1993; Mills 1999; Lesure 1998; Shapiro 1984). While both material selection and vessel size/form are likely strongly influenced by the technological frameworks of groups of potters, these factors cannot be easily separated from other potential constraints. For the purposes of the quantitative analyses described below, the variables included were limited to those 13 that likely primarily relate to choices among functional equivalents.

TABLE 4. Technological variables and variable states measured for this study

| VARIABLE | VARIABLE STATES |
|---|---|
| **All sherds** | |
| Ware/type | Traditional ware and type name |
| Portion of vessel | Body, rim, base, rim and body, rim and base, partial/ whole vessel |
| Vessel form | Jar, bowl, ladle, other |
| Sooting | Presence/absence of sooting on the vessel surface |
| Type of surface indentations | Finger, tool, multiple, none |
| Direction of indentations | Parallel, perpendicular, or oblique to direction of coils |
| Indentation alignment | Vertically aligned, diagonally aligned, unaligned |
| Elaborations | Scoring, punctations, appliqué, multiple, other, none |
| Indentation patterning | Presence of zoned or patterned indentations |
| Smudging | Presence or absence of interior smudging |
| Interior surface treatment | Ordinal scale from 1 (no polishing / limited smoothing) to 4 (highly polished) |
| Vessel wall thickness | Average thickness of sherd (not measured on rim or basal sherds) |
| Coil width | Average width from coil juncture to coil juncture (three measurements per sherd) |
| Indentation depth | Average depth of indentations from surface (three measurements per sherd) |
| Indentation width | Average width of indentations at coil juncture (three measurements per sherd) |
| Indentations per square cm | Measured using a 3 × 3 cm cardboard template |
| Obliteration | Ratio of fully obliterated coils to total coils visible in 3 × 3 cm cardboard template |
| **Rims** | |
| Rim diameter | Measured using standard rim diameter template |
| Distance to first coil | Distance from the top of the rim to the first exposed corrugated coil |
| Rim form | Flaring, straight, collar, inverted, recurved, etc. |
| **Bases** | |
| Coil direction | Direction of coiling (clockwise, counterclockwise, undetermined) |

*Note*: Only highlighted variables are included in the quantitative analyses described in the text.

## DEFINING THE SAMPLE AND CONTROLLING FOR BIAS

Because several of the variables considered in this study require relatively large sherds for consistent characterization, I rely primarily on excavated assemblages. Furthermore, the quantitative methods described below are specifically designed to deal with missing measurements. For each vessel or sherd, as many as possible of the selected variables were measured.

Many of the settlements included in this study are relatively large, but in most cases, the excavated samples come from a small number of contexts, limiting the potential for exploring intrasite patterns of ceramic technological similarity. Thus, settlements are the basic units in the analysis. Samples from each settlement were selected from as many different contexts as possible in an attempt to characterize the site-wide diversity of ceramics present. Additionally, vessels within each context were sorted by paste characteristics, surface treatment, vessel size, and other identifiable features. Any sherds that likely came from the same vessel were grouped, and only a single example was coded and measured. Whenever possible, all whole or partial vessels from floor or roof contexts were also included.

All of the measurement and coding was conducted by a small number of individuals working closely together using a standardized set of instruments and coding criteria. Before beginning the general data recording, all analysts were trained and then required to code and measure a calibration sample of 100 sherds in order to assess interobserver measurement reliability. After training, metric measurements among analysts on this calibration data set were highly correlated, and nominal, presence/absence, and ordinal variables showed agreement in the great majority of cases (see Peeples 2011:Table 6.4). Agreement among analysts was periodically retested over the course of the project, with similar results. This suggests that the potential effects of interobserver bias are likely minimal.

Finally, it is important to characterize the relationships among all of the variables included in the quantitative portion of the analyses described below to ensure that none of the coded or measured attributes are determined strictly by the mechanics of pottery production or consistently correlated with other attributes. The inclusion of highly correlated variables would have the effect of essentially double counting the specific production decision that led to both associated attributes. In general, although there are a few moderate associations among specific pairs of variables, these associations are not strictly determined

TABLE 5. Numbers of sherds and whole vessels from each excavated or extensively collected site included in the ceramic technological study

| SITE NAME | SUBREGION | EXCAVATED (E) OR SURFACE (S) | SHERDS | PARTIAL OR WHOLE VESSELS | TOTAL |
|---|---|---|---|---|---|
| Apache Creek Pueblo | MH | E | 27 | 15 | 42 |
| Atsinna | EMV | E | 56 | 1 | 57 |
| Baca Pueblo | ULC | E | 40 | | 40 |
| Casa Malpais | ULC | E | 92 | 1 | 93 |
| Cienega | EMV | E | 87 | 7 | 94 |
| Coyote Creek | ULC | E | 77 | 23 | 100 |
| Foote Canyon Pueblo | MH | E | 74 | 8 | 82 |
| Garcia Ranch | CW | S | 31 | | 31 |
| Heshotauthla | PB | E | 90 | | 90 |
| Hinkson Ranch | WZ | E | 90 | 2 | 92 |
| Hooper Ranch | ULC | E | 95 | 1 | 96 |
| Horse Camp Mill | MM | E | 82 | 24 | 106 |
| Hubble Corner | MM | E | 75 | | 75 |
| Jaralosa | WZ | E | 39 | 2 | 41 |
| Los Gigantes | EMV | E | 77 | | 77 |
| Mirabal | EMV | E | 98 | 5 | 103 |
| Ojo Bonito | WZ | E | 25 | 1 | 26 |
| Platt Ranch Pueblo | CW | E | 106 | | 106 |
| Pueblo de los Muertos | EMV | E | 103 | 2 | 105 |
| Rudd Creek Ruin | ULC | E | 37 | 2 | 39 |
| Scribe S | EMV | E | 89 | 2 | 91 |
| Spier 81 Cluster | PB | E | 129 | | 129 |
| Spier 170 | WZ | S | 32 | | 32 |
| Techado Spring Pueblo | MM | E | 66 | | 66 |
| Tinaja | EMV | E | 33 | 2 | 35 |
| Tri-R Pueblo | MM | E | 63 | | 63 |
| UG481 | MM | E | 89 | 4 | 93 |
| UG494 | MM | E | 18 | 7 | 25 |
| Vernon area sites | VA | E | 64 | 5 | 69 |
| WS Ranch Pueblo | MH | E | 77 | 24 | 101 |
| Yellowhouse | PB | S | 7 | | 7 |
| **TOTAL** | | | **2,068** | **138** | **2,206** |

*Note*: CW = Carrizo Wash, EMV = El Morro Valley, MH = Mogollon Highlands, MM = Mariana Mesa, PB = Pescado Basin, ULC = Upper Little Colorado, VA = Vernon Area, and WZ = West Zuni.

by the physical mechanics of ceramic production. For example, across all samples, the number of indentations per unit area is moderately negatively correlated with the average width of indentations (Pearson's $r = -0.63$). This relationship makes intuitive sense, as the larger the indentations get, the fewer will fit in a given space. At the same time, when considering individual settlements, the relationship between these variables is much more pronounced at some settlements than others. This suggests that potters were choosing to space indentations somewhat differently. In other words, these two variables still preserve the signatures of two distinct technological choices, and both merit inclusion in the analyses presented below.

## MEASURING RELATIVE TECHNOLOGICAL SIMILARITY

Each of the ceramic technological variables coded for this study provides information relating to specific steps in the production of vessels across the Cibola region. In order to characterize variation in the techniques of pottery production related to the degree of social interaction among potters in different portions of the study area, it is necessary to develop a procedure for measuring technological similarity across all variables simultaneously. The methods developed for this study are based on techniques used by quantitative morphologists and geneticists for defining groups among hybridized or closely related biological species (Dibble et al. 1998; Hawkins et al. 1999; Moeller and Schaal 1999; see also Edgar 2004).

The analyses presented below can be summarized in four basic steps. First, the coded variables for all samples are converted into a matrix of distances between samples. Second, the matrix is subjected to principal coordinates analysis to highlight strong relationships among cases. Third, clusters of pottery produced using similar methods are then defined based on the principal coordinate scores for each case. Finally, a relative scale of assemblage similarity is defined based on the shared proportions of each of the clusters created in step 3. Each of these steps is described in greater detail below.

1. The first step in this analytical procedure is to construct a matrix of relative similarities of every sherd or vessel against every other sherd or vessel in the sample based on the measured and coded attributes. J. C. Gower's general coefficient of similarity was selected for this analysis because it can be calculated using multiple classes of data (presence/absence, nominal, ordinal, and continuous) and because it can incorporate cases with missing data (see Gower

1971; Howell and Kintigh 1996:547). For each continuous and ordinal variable, Gower's coefficient $G_{ij}$ between two cases (*i* and *j*) is defined as:

$$G_{ijk} = 1 - \frac{|x_{ik} - x_{jk}|}{r_k}$$

where $r_k$ is the absolute range of values for the *k*th variable. For the presence/absence and nominal variables, the initial value of Gower's similarity coefficient is defined as the total number of included variables for which two cases have the same value (not including missing observations). All of the variables are then combined by summing the similarity contributions for each continuous and ordinal variable with the total number of co-occurrences in presence/absence and nominal variables. The value of Gower's coefficient between two cases is obtained by dividing this sum by the total number of variables for which both cases have data. Calculating Gower coefficients across all included cases (sherds/vessels) creates a symmetrical $n \times n$ matrix of similarities between cases ranging from 0 (no similarity) to 1 (perfect similarity) where $n$ is the total number of samples included in the analysis. For subsequent steps, this similarity matrix was converted into a distance matrix by simply inverting the scale (i.e., 1-similarity).

2. Next, the distance matrix produced in the previous step is subjected to principal coordinates analysis (PCoA). PCoA is a mathematical method of ordination similar to principal components analysis or correspondence analysis, except that it is calculated based on a matrix of distances rather than raw count/measurement data. PCoA can be used to reduce the dimensionality of a distance matrix by combining the correlated effects of all of the pair-wise interrelationships into a smaller number of axes that explain a large proportion of the variation present in the data as a whole. This allows for a low-dimensional representation of patterning that highlights the strongest associations among cases.

3. Groups of vessels that are similar in terms of the coded and measured variables are defined by conducting a cluster analysis on the PCoA scores for each case produced in step 2. For the purposes of this analysis, groups are defined using K-medoids cluster analysis on the first three PCoA axes defined above. K-medoids cluster analysis is a divisive, nonhierarchical method of cluster analysis that defines clusters based on Euclidean distances so as to reduce the distance between individual cases and their cluster medoid (or center) while maximizing the distance between clusters. The K-medoids clustering algorithm is closely related to the K-means algorithm but is more robust for data sets with outliers or noise (Kaufman and Rousseeuw 1990; Zhang and Couloigner 2005;

see also Everitt et al. 2001:100–105; Kintigh 1990; Kintigh and Ammerman 1982:39). Following methods described by Keith Kintigh and Albert Ammerman (1982; Kintigh 1990), I tested the strength of all clustering solutions from 1 to 15 through assessments of the sum of squared error and comparisons to random permutations of the original data. Based on these assessments, I selected the 10 cluster solution for this analysis, as higher numbers of clusters produced little reduction in error, and this solution also represented the greatest departure from randomized data (see Peeples 2011:188–193 for more details).[2]

Figure 14 displays plots of the first three axes of the PCoA for all variables selected for the quantitative analyses with cluster designations indicated. Each point on the plot represents a single sherd or vessel. The distance between any two points on these plots is a graphical representation of the relative technological similarity between those sherds or vessels. Figure 15 displays the proportions of these same clusters by subregion. This figure illustrates that there is some degree of spatial structure to the distribution of technological clusters. For example, clusters 2 and 3 appear to decline gradually from north to south, and, in general, southern subregions are more diverse than northern subregions.

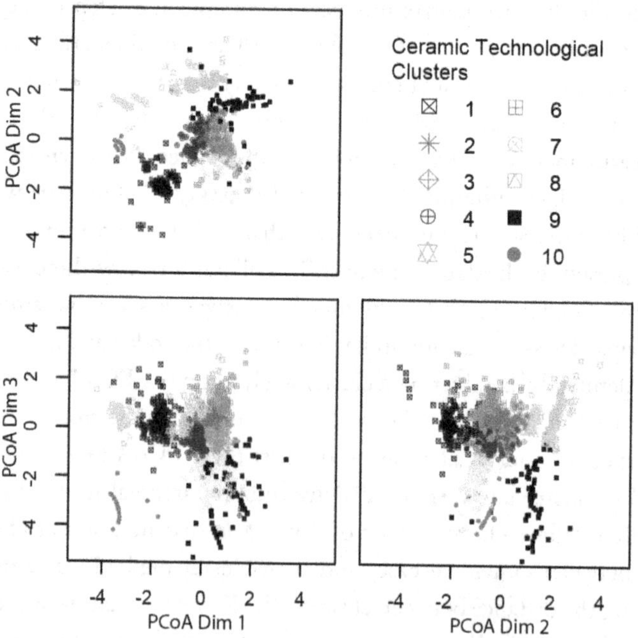


FIGURE 14. Principal coordinates plot showing technological cluster assignments.

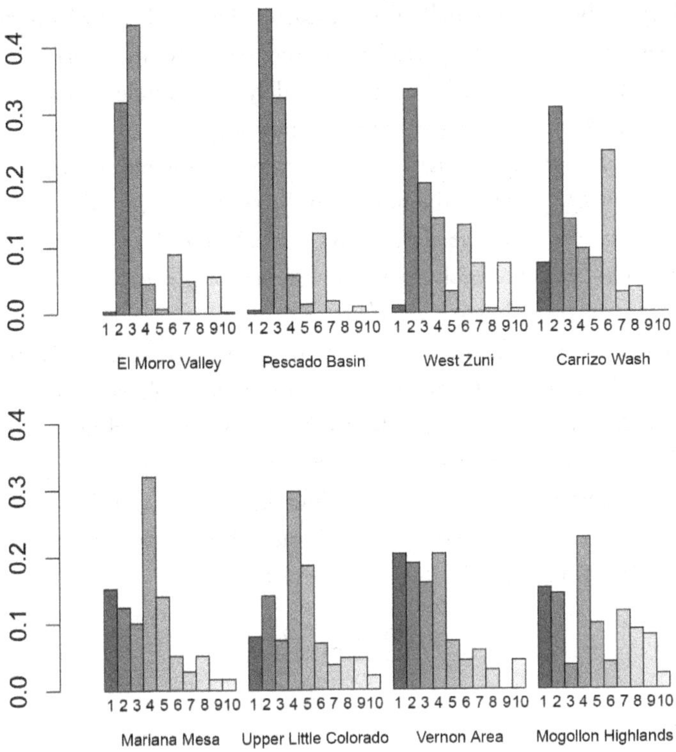


FIGURE 15. Barplots showing relative proportions of the 10 ceramic technological clusters by subregion. The top row represents subregions in the northern half of the study area, and the bottom row represents the southern half.

Although there is considerable variation within each region and even at the level of individual sites, the differing distributions of technological clusters yield information about some broad regional trends in the specific techniques and practices used to produce ceramics across the greater Cibola region. To summarize just some of the complex patterns represented here, potters in the southern portions of the region (including the Mariana Mesa, Mogollon Highlands, Vernon, and Upper Little Colorado subregions) more often tended to produce vessels characterized by smaller coils (<4 mm in width) with a high frequency of indentations per unit area (and often with marks left by fingernails in the process of producing indentations). In these same regions, elaborations of corrugated surfaces were also more common, as were interior polishing and smudging. In the northern half of the region, including the El Morro and Pescado Basin subregions, corrugated vessels were typically characterized by wider coils (5–6+ mm in width) with deep and widely spaced indentations. Also, the indentations were most often produced by pushing down from the top of each coil rather than wiping across the coil juncture, as was more common to the south. Interestingly, areas in the middle of the study area (in West Zuni and to an even greater extent in the Carrizo Wash area) were characterized by vessels with attributes typical of both the north and the south and even evidence for a mixture of traits on individual vessels.

4. The final step in this analysis is to create a relative scale of similarity among assemblages based on the technological clusters defined above. A modified version of the Brainerd-Robinson (BR) coefficient was selected for defining this scale (Brainerd 1951; Robinson 1951; see also Mills, Clark, et al. 2013; Mills et al. 2015; Mills, Roberts, et al. 2013; Peeples and Roberts 2013). BR is a city-block metric of similarity based on the sum of absolute differences in the proportional representation of individual categories calculated as:

$$S_{ab} = \frac{200 - \Sigma_k \mid P_{ak} - P_{bk}}{200}$$

$k$ = all clusters

$P_{ak}$ = percent of cluster $k$ at site $a$

$P_{bk}$ = percent of cluster $k$ at site $b$

This measure has been scaled to range from 0 to 1, where 1 is perfect similarity and 0 is no similarity. The basic assumption of this final step in the analysis is that *settlements with similar proportions of the ceramic technological clusters defined above represent settlements occupied by potters who shared similar suites of technological practices related to pottery production.*

## RESULTS

The procedures described above allow for the creation of a matrix of similarities between pairs of settlements and subregions that can be used as a proxy for the relative degree of social interaction among potters and other groups at different spatial and social scales. For a given unit of comparison (settlement, subregion, etc.), I argue that similarity coefficients closer to 1 suggest a greater likelihood of frequent interaction and stronger relational connections among the inhabitants of those areas.

It is first useful to directly examine the scale of ceramic technological similarity defined above. Table 6 shows the similarity scores for comparisons among all subregions divided by time period, with relatively high values of similarity highlighted (≥70 percent of possible similarity). An examination of the highlighted BR coefficients suggests that there are two groups of subregions characterized by consistently high similarity scores across both the Pueblo III and Pueblo IV periods: Group 1 (El Morro Valley, Pescado Basin, West Zuni, and Carrizo Wash) and Group 2 (Mariana Mesa, Vernon Area, Mogollon Highlands, and Upper Little Colorado). These two groups essentially conform to the northern (Group 1) and southern (Group 2) portions of the core study area. Interestingly, the locations of these two groups also roughly correspond with areas that have traditionally been associated with Anasazi populations to the north and Mogollon populations to the south. I return to this issue briefly at the end of this chapter. The consistent similarities among the same spatially contiguous groups of subregions through time suggest that there was likely a spatial component to the strength of relational connections among potters across the study area.

In order to evaluate this spatial pattern further, it is instructive to consider the relationship between technological similarity and the physical distance between settlements. Figure 16a displays a scatter plot of the distances between all settlements included in this analysis (in kilometers) against the similarity coefficients among pairs of settlements. Each point represents a comparison between a pair of sites. In general, this plot shows a weak negative relationship between physical distance and technological similarity ($r = -0.54$). There are, however, several outliers that have a substantial influence on the results. A detailed examination of the relationships among specific pairs of settlements suggests that the vast majority of the most extreme outliers involve settlements in the Mariana Mesa subregion. Indeed, as Figure 16b demonstrates, the negative linear relationship between spatial distance and technological similarity is substantially more pronounced when comparisons involving the Mariana Mesa area are removed ($r = -0.80$).

Importantly, the spatial patterns documented among all settlements included in this study are equally strong when comparing only sites dating to the Pueblo III or Pueblo IV periods independently, as well as when comparing

TABLE 6. Similarity coefficients for comparisons among subregions divided by time period

| | EMV PIII | EMV PIV | PB PIII | PB PIV | WZ PIII | WZ PIV | CW PIII | MM PIII | MM PIV | ULC PIII | ULC PIV | VA PIII | MH PIII |
|---|---|---|---|---|---|---|---|---|---|---|---|---|---|
| EMV PIII | | | | | | | | | | | | | |
| EMV PIV | 0.92 | | | | | | | | | | | | |
| PB PIII | 0.88 | 0.81 | | | | | | | | | | | |
| PB PIV | 0.80 | 0.73 | 0.85 | | | | | | | | | | |
| WZ PIII | 0.74 | 0.71 | 0.68 | 0.81 | | | | | | | | | |
| WZ PIV | 0.78 | 0.79 | 0.71 | 0.77 | 0.76 | | | | | | | | |
| CW PIII | 0.64 | 0.60 | 0.60 | 0.72 | 0.78 | 0.63 | | | | | | | |
| MM PIII | 0.41 | 0.39 | 0.37 | 0.44 | 0.59 | 0.41 | 0.62 | | | | | | |
| MM PIV | 0.36 | 0.34 | 0.30 | 0.38 | 0.54 | 0.36 | 0.55 | 0.81 | | | | | |
| ULC PIII | 0.35 | 0.33 | 0.32 | 0.39 | 0.53 | 0.35 | 0.56 | 0.83 | 0.86 | | | | |
| ULC PIV | 0.42 | 0.47 | 0.36 | 0.46 | 0.63 | 0.49 | 0.61 | 0.82 | 0.83 | 0.85 | | | |
| VA PIII | 0.49 | 0.50 | 0.45 | 0.54 | 0.69 | 0.52 | 0.69 | 0.82 | 0.68 | 0.72 | 0.69 | | |
| MH PIII | 0.26 | 0.32 | 0.20 | 0.29 | 0.47 | 0.44 | 0.45 | 0.74 | 0.71 | 0.68 | 0.74 | 0.68 | |
| MH PIV | 0.48 | 0.45 | 0.43 | 0.52 | 0.63 | 0.47 | 0.68 | 0.71 | 0.59 | 0.64 | 0.64 | 0.69 | 0.58 |

*Note*: Pairwise comparisons ≥0.70 are highlighted. CW = Carrizo Wash, EMV = El Morro Valley, MH = Mogollon Highlands, MM = Mariana Mesa, PB = Pescado Basin, ULC = Upper Little Colorado, VA = Vernon Area, and WZ = West Zuni.

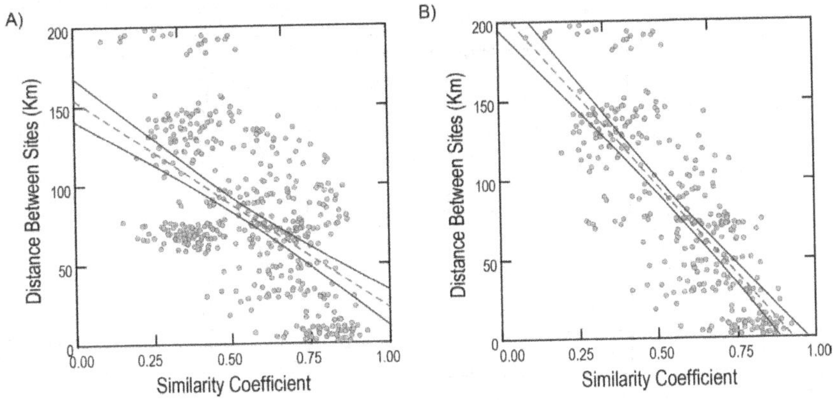


FIGURE 16. Plot of ceramic similarity against the linear distance (A) between all sites and (B) with sites in the Mariana Mesa subregion removed.

sites occupied in different time periods. This suggests that the physical distance between groups of potters may account for much of the variation in technological similarity seen across the region through time and that other processes may also have been at work, in particular in the Mariana Mesa area.[3] The consistency of this pattern despite widespread population movement and major upheavals in the organization of communities is intriguing. The lack of major changes could be interpreted as evidence that the nucleated towns constructed across the Pueblo III to Pueblo IV transition in the Cibola region were occupied in large part by individuals and groups that were already interacting on a regular basis prior to the settlement reorganization (see Huntley and Kintigh 2004; Kintigh 2007; Kintigh et al. 2004). This finding has important implications for considerations of the scale of population movement associated with the late thirteenth century in the region.

The ceramic technological similarities between the Mariana Mesa subregion and areas along the Zuni River Valley are lower than might be expected based on their spatial proximity alone. Further, the Mariana Mesa subregion shows strong similarities with relatively distant areas in the Mogollon Highlands to the south and along the Little Colorado River to the west. These patterns of technological similarity are particularly interesting because there is substantial evidence for the circulation of decorated ceramics (Chapter 4) as well as strong similarities in public architectural features (Chapter 8) between Mariana Mesa and the nearby areas to the north along the Zuni River. The

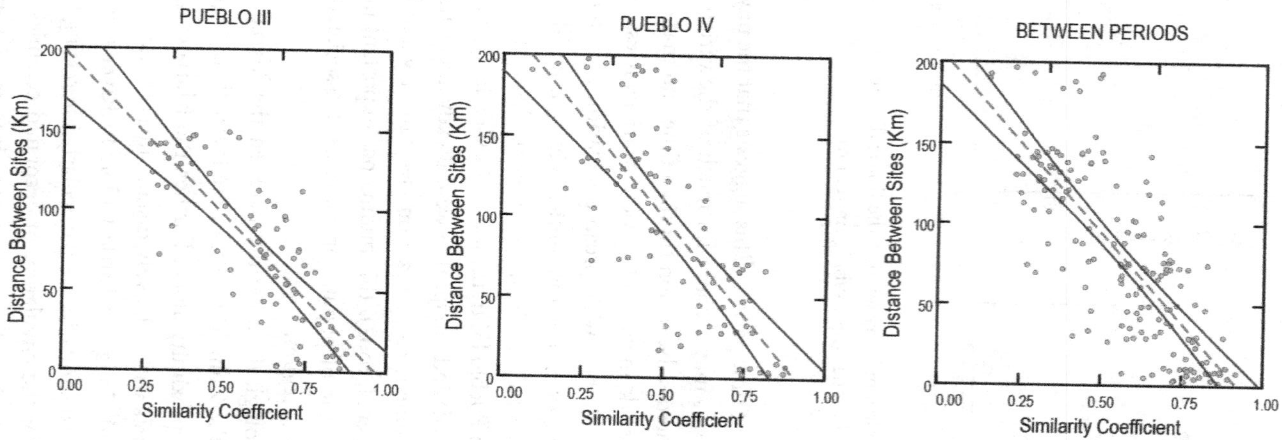


**FIGURE 17.** Plot of ceramic similarity against the linear distance between sites for the Pueblo III and Pueblo IV periods, as well as for comparisons between periods (excluding the Mariana Mesa subregion).

contrasting patterns of ceramic technological similarity and the frequency of painted ceramic exchange documented here suggest that the inhabitants of the Mariana Mesa region maintained strong relational connections with relatively distant areas, likely indicating historical ties with those areas. As subsequent chapters illustrate, several other lines of evidence, including unique wall construction styles and design layouts on painted vessels, also suggest that the Mariana Mesa region was likely occupied by a diverse group of individuals, including migrants from a number of areas in the western or southern portions of the Cibola region or even farther afield (see also Smith et al. 2009). The data presented here provide additional support for such a scenario and demonstrate the potential utility of the method of ceramic technological characterization used here for identifying patterns of population movement in the archaeological record.

## RELATIONAL CONNECTIONS AND SOCIAL NETWORKS

The discussion of general trends in ceramic technological similarity so far suggests that (1) there is a substantial spatial component to the strength of relational connections among the inhabitants of the region, and (2) patterns of technological similarity are relatively consistent across the major transformation in settlement across the Pueblo III to Pueblo IV transition. At this point, it is necessary to consider how such relationships play out for particular settlements. This is important because previous studies in the Cibola region have demonstrated that even tightly clustered groups of sites sometimes exhibit diverse external connections (e.g., Duff 2000, 2002; Huntley 2008; Schachner 2007). For the purposes of this analysis, I apply methods from social network analysis to visually explore patterns of interaction and relational connections among settlements across the study area. I use the relative measure of ceramic technological similarity defined above as the basis for a series of network graphs that efficiently summarize the strongest patterns of relational connections among settlements across the Cibola region through time.

For the purposes of this study, individual settlements were designated as nodes, and ties between these nodes were then assigned by defining a threshold similarity value for the scale of relative technological similarity created above. The specific threshold value was selected using a Monte Carlo simulation of the expected range of similarity values. Ten thousand column randomized matrices of the actual proportions of each of the technological clusters at each settlement were created, and similarity scores were calculated for each randomized matrix. Because the ceramic technological clusters were randomized by column, every cluster has the same mean and standard deviation in each of the randomized matrices. The distribution of similarity scores for the randomized data sets provides an estimate of the range and frequency of values that we might expect by chance given the number of clusters and the overall frequency of each cluster. It is then possible to compare this random distribution to the values obtained from the actual data.

As Figure 18 illustrates, similarity scores for the randomized data are normally distributed, whereas the scores for the original data are bimodal. Not surprisingly, this suggests that the underlying structure of relationships among

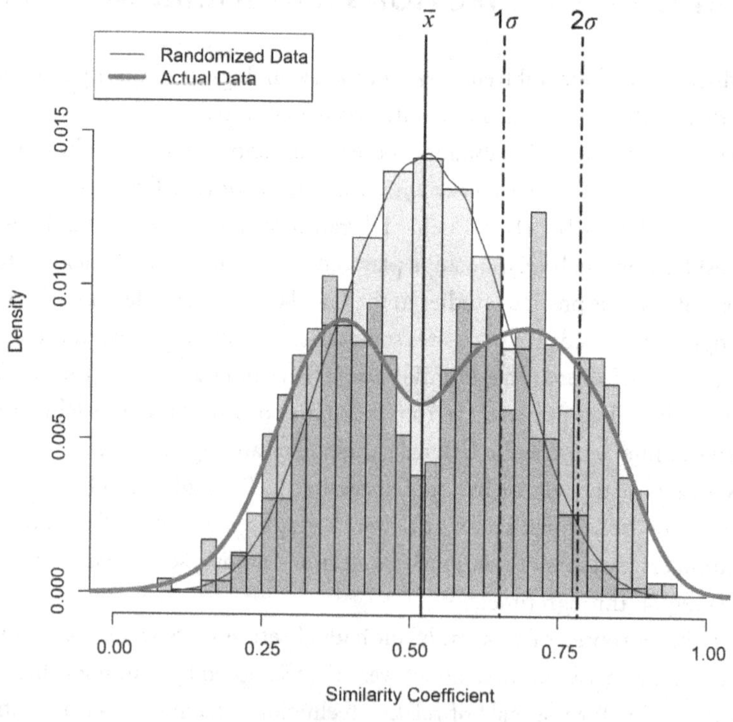


FIGURE 18. Distribution of similarity values for actual and randomized data sets.

settlements is substantially different from what might be expected by chance. For the purposes of this analysis, a tie between two settlements (nodes) was defined as a similarity score greater than one standard deviation above the mean score for the randomized data sets (0.66 in this case). This means that when visualizing these networks, a tie was defined between all pairs of sites that shared 66 percent or more of their totals of the 10 technological clusters defined above. The selection of this threshold is somewhat arbitrary, but the value used here falls in the upper mode in the observed similarity scores for the original data, and this selection was informed by the expectations generated through the Monte Carlo procedure. Additional analyses not described here suggest that the general relationships among settlements are similar across a range of potential thresholds, although the density of the network (total proportion of all possible ties that are active) does vary.

It should be noted that the network graphs displayed here are simply an efficient means of visually displaying the complex interrelationships among the settlements included in this study. I do not argue that a particular threshold similarity score represents a particular kind of social relationship that was absent between two settlements that do not share a tie (see also Mills, Clark, et al. 2013; Mills et al. 2015; Mills, Roberts, et al. 2013; Peeples and Roberts 2013). By using a common criterion for defining ties among settlements for various combinations of variables, however, the most robust relationships among settlements and groups of settlements across the region can be efficiently visually evaluated using network graphs.

Figure 19 shows the network graph for all sites included in this analysis. The relative size of each node is determined by the total weight of ties involving that settlement (i.e., weighted degree centrality defined as the sum of all similarity scores for that site). Point locations are determined using an algorithm that attempts to make as many of the ties as possible approximately the same length while limiting the number of crossing ties.[4] The overall effect of this algorithm is that highly connected groups of nodes will cluster together in the network graph. As this network graph shows, there are two well-defined groups of settlements characterized as numerous within group ties and fewer between group ties. These groups, which I designate simply Group 1 and Group 2, can further be confirmed via a K-means cluster analysis of the underlying matrix of raw similarity scores. Interestingly, the subregions within which settlements in these two clusters are located coincide with the sets of subregions defined above. In

TABLE 7. Similarity coefficients for comparisons among all sites

| | | GROUP 2 | | | | | | | | | | | | | | |
|---|---|---|---|---|---|---|---|---|---|---|---|---|---|---|---|---|
| | | APC | BACA | CMAL | COY | FOOT | HOOP | HCM | HUBB | RCR | TECS | TRIR | U481 | U494 | VA | WSR |
| GROUP 2 | APC | | | | | | | | | | | | | | | |
| | BACA | 0.45 | | | | | | | | | | | | | | |
| | CMAL | 0.71 | 0.56 | | | | | | | | | | | | | |
| | COY | 0.78 | 0.53 | 0.82 | | | | | | | | | | | | |
| | FOOT | 0.57 | 0.46 | 0.62 | 0.64 | | | | | | | | | | | |
| | HOOP | 0.83 | 0.49 | 0.75 | 0.84 | 0.60 | | | | | | | | | | |
| | HCM | 0.87 | 0.55 | 0.80 | 0.84 | 0.59 | 0.82 | | | | | | | | | |
| | HUBB | 0.80 | 0.53 | 0.75 | 0.84 | 0.72 | 0.78 | 0.78 | | | | | | | | |
| | RCR | 0.75 | 0.57 | 0.77 | 0.82 | 0.61 | 0.73 | 0.86 | 0.70 | | | | | | | |
| | TECS | 0.84 | 0.48 | 0.70 | 0.80 | 0.55 | 0.77 | 0.83 | 0.70 | 0.81 | | | | | | |
| | TRIR | 0.79 | 0.53 | 0.78 | 0.79 | 0.70 | 0.79 | 0.78 | 0.88 | 0.71 | 0.73 | | | | | |
| | U481 | 0.81 | 0.60 | 0.81 | 0.87 | 0.68 | 0.83 | 0.88 | 0.86 | 0.84 | 0.80 | 0.82 | | | | |
| | U494 | 0.72 | 0.44 | 0.53 | 0.63 | 0.62 | 0.68 | 0.64 | 0.73 | 0.50 | 0.57 | 0.73 | 0.66 | | | |
| | VA | 0.73 | 0.59 | 0.63 | 0.71 | 0.69 | 0.71 | 0.71 | 0.80 | 0.69 | 0.64 | 0.76 | 0.81 | 0.80 | | |
| | WSR | 0.59 | 0.63 | 0.48 | 0.58 | 0.55 | 0.63 | 0.58 | 0.59 | 0.59 | 0.60 | 0.61 | 0.64 | 0.59 | 0.64 | |
| GROUP 1 | ATS | 0.34 | 0.58 | 0.37 | 0.33 | 0.38 | 0.32 | 0.42 | 0.36 | 0.40 | 0.27 | 0.33 | 0.43 | 0.43 | 0.51 | 0.40 |
| | CIEN | 0.30 | 0.47 | 0.42 | 0.32 | 0.47 | 0.29 | 0.39 | 0.37 | 0.36 | 0.25 | 0.36 | 0.42 | 0.40 | 0.50 | 0.31 |
| | GARR | 0.60 | 0.47 | 0.72 | 0.66 | 0.69 | 0.62 | 0.68 | 0.62 | 0.66 | 0.53 | 0.61 | 0.70 | 0.59 | 0.69 | 0.39 |
| | HESH | 0.37 | 0.45 | 0.51 | 0.38 | 0.52 | 0.35 | 0.44 | 0.43 | 0.40 | 0.30 | 0.42 | 0.47 | 0.44 | 0.55 | 0.26 |
| | HINK | 0.60 | 0.63 | 0.71 | 0.62 | 0.65 | 0.57 | 0.68 | 0.67 | 0.66 | 0.54 | 0.65 | 0.71 | 0.56 | 0.72 | 0.48 |
| | JAR | 0.29 | 0.46 | 0.47 | 0.29 | 0.44 | 0.27 | 0.37 | 0.34 | 0.33 | 0.22 | 0.34 | 0.39 | 0.38 | 0.47 | 0.26 |
| | LG | 0.26 | 0.35 | 0.37 | 0.27 | 0.41 | 0.24 | 0.35 | 0.32 | 0.31 | 0.20 | 0.32 | 0.37 | 0.32 | 0.43 | 0.15 |
| | MIR | 0.29 | 0.36 | 0.41 | 0.31 | 0.43 | 0.25 | 0.36 | 0.36 | 0.33 | 0.22 | 0.35 | 0.38 | 0.33 | 0.44 | 0.17 |
| | OB | 0.38 | 0.66 | 0.46 | 0.39 | 0.51 | 0.37 | 0.46 | 0.44 | 0.42 | 0.31 | 0.41 | 0.48 | 0.48 | 0.56 | 0.47 |
| | PESC | 0.29 | 0.34 | 0.40 | 0.31 | 0.43 | 0.25 | 0.35 | 0.37 | 0.32 | 0.21 | 0.35 | 0.37 | 0.33 | 0.45 | 0.15 |
| | PR | 0.50 | 0.42 | 0.63 | 0.52 | 0.65 | 0.48 | 0.56 | 0.57 | 0.52 | 0.43 | 0.56 | 0.58 | 0.53 | 0.62 | 0.35 |
| | PDM | 0.30 | 0.46 | 0.37 | 0.31 | 0.41 | 0.26 | 0.38 | 0.36 | 0.35 | 0.23 | 0.33 | 0.40 | 0.35 | 0.46 | 0.26 |
| | SCS | 0.38 | 0.43 | 0.47 | 0.39 | 0.50 | 0.34 | 0.43 | 0.44 | 0.40 | 0.29 | 0.42 | 0.45 | 0.42 | 0.53 | 0.23 |
| | S170 | 0.29 | 0.56 | 0.39 | 0.30 | 0.44 | 0.28 | 0.38 | 0.35 | 0.34 | 0.23 | 0.35 | 0.40 | 0.39 | 0.48 | 0.40 |
| | TIN | 0.35 | 0.45 | 0.47 | 0.36 | 0.49 | 0.31 | 0.43 | 0.41 | 0.39 | 0.28 | 0.40 | 0.45 | 0.39 | 0.51 | 0.29 |
| | YH | 0.24 | 0.29 | 0.41 | 0.26 | 0.37 | 0.20 | 0.28 | 0.32 | 0.26 | 0.15 | 0.29 | 0.31 | 0.28 | 0.39 | 0.09 |

*Note*: Pairwise comparisons ≥0.66 are highlighted. Group 2: ApC = Apache Creek, Baca = Baca Pueblo, CMal = Casa Malpais, Coy = Coyote Creek, Foot = Foote Canyon Pueblo, HCM = Horse Camp Mill, Hoop = Hooper Ranch, Hubb = Hubble Ranch, RCr = Rudd Creek, TecS = Techado Spring, TriR = Tri-R Pueblo, U481 = UG481, U494 = UG494, VA = Vernon Area, WSR = WS Ranch; Group 1: Ats = Atsinna, Cien = Cienega, GarR = Garcia Ranch, Hesh = Heshotauthla, Hink = Hinkson Ranch, Jar = Jaralosa Pueblo, LG = Los Gigantes, Mir = Mirabal, OB = Ojo Bonito, Pesc = Spier 81 Cluster, PdM = Pueblo de los Muertos, PR = Platt Ranch, ScS = Scribe S, S170 = Spier 170, Tin = Tinaja, YH = Yellowhouse.

| GROUP 1 | | | | | | | | | | | | | | |
|---|---|---|---|---|---|---|---|---|---|---|---|---|---|---|
| ATS | CIEN | GARR | HESH | HINK | JAR | LG | MIR | OB | PESC | PR | PDM | SCS | S170 | TIN |
| 0.77 | | | | | | | | | | | | | | |
| 0.54 | 0.63 | | | | | | | | | | | | | |
| 0.62 | 0.73 | 0.72 | | | | | | | | | | | | |
| 0.57 | 0.70 | 0.79 | 0.74 | | | | | | | | | | | |
| 0.57 | 0.75 | 0.61 | 0.80 | 0.66 | | | | | | | | | | |
| 0.72 | 0.84 | 0.59 | 0.80 | 0.64 | 0.74 | | | | | | | | | |
| 0.74 | 0.83 | 0.62 | 0.78 | 0.66 | 0.71 | 0.93 | | | | | | | | |
| 0.74 | 0.76 | 0.67 | 0.77 | 0.74 | 0.76 | 0.68 | 0.68 | | | | | | | |
| 0.65 | 0.80 | 0.61 | 0.85 | 0.64 | 0.72 | 0.89 | 0.89 | 0.65 | | | | | | |
| 0.46 | 0.60 | 0.73 | 0.70 | 0.72 | 0.74 | 0.58 | 0.61 | 0.63 | 0.60 | | | | | |
| 0.86 | 0.83 | 0.58 | 0.68 | 0.64 | 0.63 | 0.85 | 0.88 | 0.73 | 0.78 | 0.55 | | | | |
| 0.79 | 0.80 | 0.68 | 0.78 | 0.71 | 0.62 | 0.86 | 0.90 | 0.72 | 0.83 | 0.65 | 0.87 | | | |
| 0.71 | 0.82 | 0.61 | 0.75 | 0.67 | 0.75 | 0.75 | 0.74 | 0.88 | 0.71 | 0.60 | 0.75 | 0.69 | | |
| 0.77 | 0.86 | 0.68 | 0.72 | 0.72 | 0.67 | 0.84 | 0.88 | 0.70 | 0.82 | 0.63 | 0.90 | 0.84 | 0.78 | |
| 0.51 | 0.69 | 0.58 | 0.81 | 0.59 | 0.83 | 0.79 | 0.76 | 0.62 | 0.82 | 0.72 | 0.65 | 0.69 | 0.69 | 0.69 |

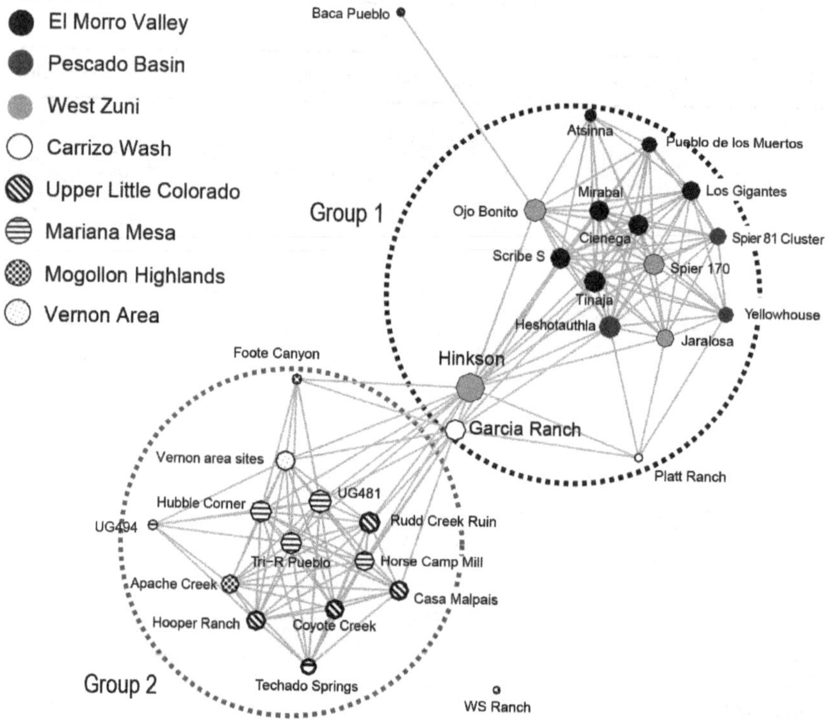


FIGURE 19. Network graph for all settlements. Node size represents weighted degree centrality.

other words, there are far more strong connections among sites in the northern half of the Cibola region and among sites in the southern half of the Cibola region than there are connections spanning the northern and southern Cibola region. At the same time, there are some strong cross-cutting ties between these groups, in particular among sites in the Upper Little Colorado, Carrizo Wash, West Zuni, and Vernon subregions. This suggests that the relational connections among the inhabitants of settlements in areas along the edges of these two overarching groups of subregions may have been somewhat more diverse than in areas within the core of these groups.

To further illustrate the relationships among these sites and to explore change through time, Figure 20 displays network graphs divided by time period. As this figure illustrates, in both the Pueblo III and Pueblo IV periods, there are two fairly discrete groups of settlements (network components) characterized by many interconnections that conform to Group 1 and Group 2 defined above. Interestingly, the division between the northern and southern portions of the study area appears to widen across the Pueblo III to Pueblo IV transition.[5] This is not necessarily surprising, as many of the areas along the edges of these two areas were depopulated across the Pueblo III to Pueblo IV transition. Overall, the patterns described here suggest that as clusters of settlements became increasingly spatially isolated across the Pueblo III to Pueblo IV transition, there was less interaction and weaker relational connections among the inhabitants of the northern and southern portions of the study area. This finding is in line with the increasingly restricted patterns of ceramic circulation documented in the previous chapter.

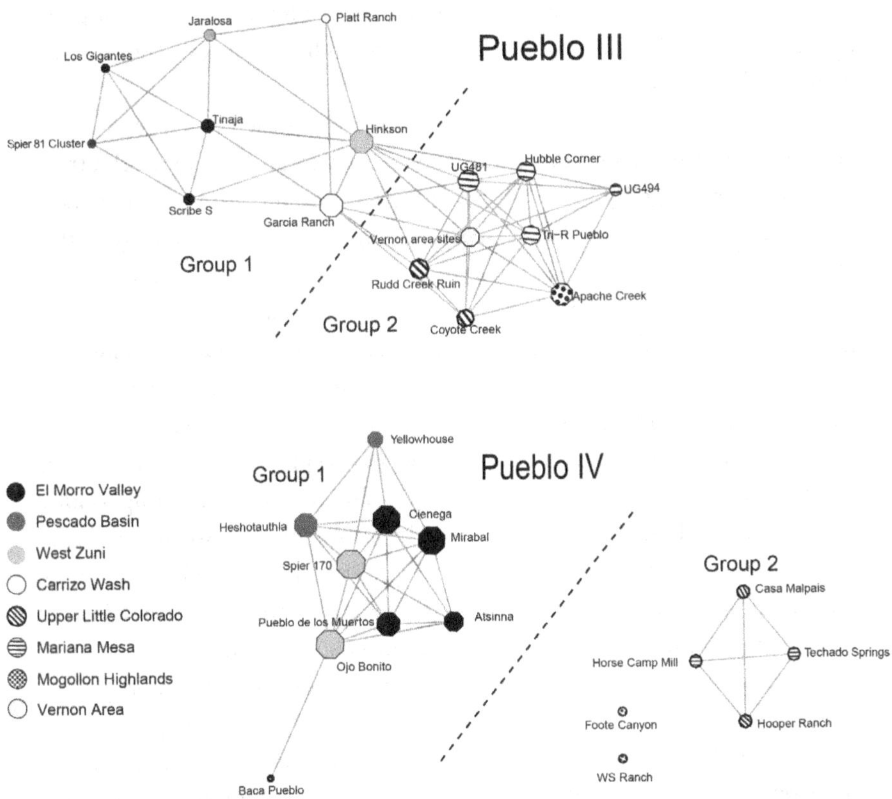


FIGURE 20. Network graphs for all settlements divided by time period. Node size represents weighted degree centrality.

As noted above, several sites spatially located along the edges of the two overarching groups of settlements defined here have somewhat more diverse network connections (including connections that span both groups) than sites farther away from the edges of these zones. These sites, which mediate connections among settlements within the network that would otherwise be entirely unconnected, play an important role in defining overall network structure and topology. Beyond this, settlements in such intermediate positions within regional networks of interaction may have controlled or facilitated interaction among somewhat more socially distant settlements (see Peeples and Haas 2013). One formal way to assess and rank the intermediate positions of settlements in the networks described above involves the use of a SNA metric known as betweenness centrality. Betweenness centrality is a metric that formally characterizes the degree to which a node sits along the shortest path between other unconnected nodes and is defined as the sum of the number of shortest paths between all possible pairs of nodes that pass through a given node (see Wasserman and Faust 1994:188–192).

Table 8 shows the betweenness centrality scores for the network containing all sites, as well as for sites divided by time period. In all three networks, there are a few sites (highlighted) with betweenness centrality scores two or more times greater than those of other sites within each network. This suggests that these sites were potentially key nodes for mediating connections among settlements across the region. The highest-scoring sites are all located in the West Zuni and Carrizo Wash subregions near the center of the study area and along the edges of the two overarching groups of settlements and subregions defined above. Although there are potential problems with interpreting absolute values of betweenness centrality in a sampled network (Peeples and Roberts 2013), the difference between the high and low centrality sites here is striking. Importantly, not all sites in these intermediate subregions have high betweenness scores. Of particular note, the two sites with the highest overall centrality scores both for the full network and for the Pueblo III period network are post-Chacoan great house communities with oversized unroofed great kivas. This suggests that these settlements may have been the locations of somewhat more diverse interactions than other sites within the regional networks, perhaps driven in part by periodic public gatherings focused on the public architectural spaces at these settlements. Importantly, this suggests that it is not the physical location of these settlements alone that is responsible for their intermediate positions in ceramic technological networks.

TABLE 8. Betweenness centrality scores for all sites and for sites divided by time period

| SITES | SUBREGION | ALL SITES | PIII | PIV |
|---|---|---|---|---|
| Atsinna | EMV | 0 | | 0 |
| Cienega | EMV | 16.07 | | 2.57 |
| Los Gigantes | EMV | 2.52 | 0.50 | |
| Mirabal | EMV | 16.07 | | 2.57 |
| Pueblo de los Muertos | EMV | 0.57 | | 0.40 |
| Scribe S | EMV | 30.71 | 15.87 | |
| Tinaja | EMV | 32.13 | 17.28 | |
| Heshotauthla | PB | 31.21 | | 1.50 |
| Spier 81 Cluster | PB | 1.14 | 0.50 | |
| Yellowhouse | PB | 4.35 | | 0 |
| Hinkson | WZ | 284.66 | 68.28 | |
| Jaralosa | WZ | 12.52 | 12.94 | |
| Ojo Bonito | WZ | 82.01 | | 14.40 |
| Spier 170 | WZ | 16.07 | | 2.57 |
| Garcia Ranch | CW | 117.41 | 33.61 | |
| Platt Ranch | CW | 5.59 | 0.92 | |
| Horse Camp Mill | MM | 18.10 | | 0 |
| Hubble Corner | MM | 23.90 | 6.12 | |
| Techado Springs | MM | 0.00 | | 0 |
| Tri-R Pueblo | MM | 23.90 | 6.12 | |
| UG481 | MM | 34.05 | 10.94 | |
| UG494 | MM | 0 | 0 | |
| Baca Pueblo | ULC | 0 | | 0 |
| Casa Malpais | ULC | 17.65 | | 0 |
| Coyote Creek | ULC | 6.57 | 2.31 | |
| Hooper Ranch | ULC | 2.25 | | 0 |
| Rudd Creek Ruin | ULC | 18.10 | 4.89 | |
| Vernon Area | VA | 25.71 | 10.94 | |
| Apache Creek | MH | 2.25 | 0.80 | |
| Foote Canyon | MH | 0.50 | | 0 |
| WS Ranch | MH | 0 | | 0 |

*Note*: Values greater than one standard deviation above the mean are highlighted for each column. CW = Carrizo Wash, EMV = El Morro Valley, MH = Mogollon Highlands, MM = Mariana Mesa, PB = Pescado Basin, WZ = West Zuni.

## CONNECTING CERAMIC TECHNOLOGY AND RELATIONAL IDENTITY

Overall, the analyses above suggest that one of the major factors influencing the degree of ceramic technological similarity among settlements across the study area is the spatial distance between them. The inhabitants of the Cibola region interacted most frequently with their closest neighbors, and these interactions likely included the kinds of close relationships that resulted in the sharing of knowledge related to the technology of pottery production. The Mariana Mesa area, however, appears to represent a departure from this general region-wide pattern. Settlements in the Mariana Mesa area exhibit strong similarities with relatively distant settlements to the west and south despite evidence for other forms of interaction with the spatially closer subregions along the Zuni River Valley. This deviation from the general regional spatial pattern, along with other lines of evidence discussed in subsequent chapters, suggests that the inhabitants of the Mariana Mesa region included people with historical relationships to a diversity of origins, likely including many migrants from the western or southern portions of the Cibola region and farther afield.

The patterns of ceramic technological similarity documented here remained relatively consistent across the thirteenth-century social transformation. The same two groups of northern and southern subregions and settlements are quite apparent in patterns of ceramic similarity both before and after this transformation, and the negative relationship between spatial distance and ceramic similarity is equally strong in both the Pueblo III and Pueblo IV periods, even for comparisons among sites dating to different periods. This suggests that relational connections among the inhabitants of different portions of the Cibola region were remarkably consistent through time despite the massive scale reorganization of settlement occurring across the Pueblo III to Pueblo IV transition. The consistency in patterns of technological similarity across the transition considered here suggests that this social transformation was organized largely along the lines of individuals and social groups that were already frequently interacting before the transformation.

Examinations of ceramic technological similarity in relation to specific settlements reveal that a few settlements along the edges of the overarching northern and southern groups of subregions defined above may have had ceramic technological practices that were somewhat transitional between the dominant patterns within the core of each group. Such fine-grained patterns of technological differentiation would not be accessible using traditional typological methods alone. Furthermore, the transitional nature of assemblages found in the area along the central portion of the study area provides a very different picture of interaction at a regional scale than considerations based on the distributions of Mogollon Brown Ware and Cibola Gray Ware alone. Although I do not argue that a network tie between two settlements represents a particular kind of social relationship, the consistency in the connections among sites across a range of technological variables suggests that the relationships documented across the study area as a whole are extremely robust.

Finally, it is important to note that the two overarching groups of settlements and subregions defined above roughly conform to areas that are traditionally placed within the northern Anasazi and the southern Mogollon archaeological culture areas. The fact that the groupings defined here, which are based on a detailed ceramic technological characterization, do coincide reasonably well with the traditional boundaries between these archaeological constructs suggests that the culture areas defined so long ago likely do have some basis in more nuanced patterns of social interaction at regional scales. However, the analyses presented here suggest that the boundaries of these archaeologically defined regions were somewhat more diffuse than has previously been suggested based on the distribution of distinct ceramic wares alone. Rather than being characterized by interactions between two "cultures," this study suggests that social relations across the Cibola region were more likely negotiated on a relatively local scale.

# 6

# DOMESTIC ARCHITECTURAL SPACES AND RELATIONAL NETWORKS

STRONG SIMILARITIES in domestic architectural spaces and features are frequently cited as particularly good indicators of interaction or common historical origins among the individuals or larger groups that produced those structures (e.g., Burmeister 2000:541–542; Clark 2001; Hegmon et al. 1998; Hillier and Hanson 1984; Riggs 2005). Such built spaces provide the physical contexts in which many daily social activities are conducted. The form and use of domestic architecture tend to be highly conservative, even in contexts where multiple distinct social groups are present (Clark 2001; Jordan and Kaups 1987; Rapoport 1990). Drawing on recent studies linking domestic architectural features to social distance, I argue that the degree of similarity in domestic structures and features can be used as a proxy for the frequency of interaction and historical connections among the inhabitants of the study area at various scales.

In this chapter, I characterize several aspects of the organization of domestic space and architectural features at excavated settlements across the study area. These analyses are designed to serve as a complement to the more detailed ceramic technological study presented in the previous chapter. I argue that robust patterns of similarity in terms of the form, size, and placement of domestic architectural features, which relate to the technological learning frameworks of those who produced them, reveal insights into the nature and direction of *relational connections* among individuals and communities across the Cibola region.

## THE ARCHITECTURAL DATASET

The architectural data used in this study were gathered from published sources and original field notes from 35 excavated sites dating between ca. A.D. 1150 and 1325 within the core portion of the study area. These data include details such as room dimensions, wall and floor construction styles, hearth form/placement, and mealing feature form and size for over 700 aboveground pueblo rooms. For the purposes of this chapter, subterranean structures were not included in this sample, nor were large, potentially public architectural spaces (see Chapter 8). For each site, data were recorded for as many variables as was possible for all excavated or thoroughly documented rooms dating to the period considered here. Features were coded independently for each floor surface within a room when multiple floors were present. These detailed architectural data were supplemented with additional information from a smaller number of sites in the expanded study area. Only a limited range of variables that could be easily obtained from site plan maps or descriptions was recorded for sites in the expanded study area.

The remainder of this chapter is divided into four sections. First, I characterize the distribution of room sizes for sites across the study area in order to explore potential variation in household size, as well as the scale of organization and planning involved in the construction of settlements across the study area. Following this, I consider the construction and placement of intramural domestic features, specifically, hearths and mealing bins. Similarities in the styles and placement of these features are interpreted as one measure of the degree of social interaction and relational connections among the inhabitants of the region. Next, I consider the distribution of relatively rare wall construction styles that may suggest patterns of population movement across the region. Finally, I summarize the results of these brief architectural analyses and compare them with the patterns of interaction and relational connections suggested by the ceramic technological analyses described in the previous chapter.

## ROOM SIZE AND SITE CONSTRUCTION

Although there are key differences in some of the specific details and materials used, pueblo rooms are reasonably consistent in terms of basic form and construction across much of the Colorado Plateau and the mountainous areas along

TABLE 9. Sites included in the architectural analyses

| SUBREGION | SITE NAME | SITE NUMBER | NUMBER OF RECORDED ROOMS | REFERENCES |
|---|---|---|---|---|
| | | **Core Area** | | |
| El Morro Valley | Atsinna | LA 99 | 15 | Watson et al. 1980; Woodbury/CARP |
| El Morro Valley | Pueblo de los Muertos | LA 1585 | 17 | Watson et al. 1980; CARP |
| El Morro Valley | Tinaja | LA 427 | 4 | Watson et al. 1980; CARP |
| El Morro Valley | Cienega | LA 425 | 3 | Watson et al. 1980; CARP |
| El Morro Valley | Mirabal | LA 426 | 7 | Watson et al. 1980; CARP |
| El Morro Valley | Scribe S | LA 59321–59331 | 24 | Watson et al. 1980; CARP |
| El Morro Valley | Los Gigantes | LA 56159 | 9 | Schachner 2007; EMVPP |
| El Morro Valley | LA 132353 | LA 132353 | 9 | Howell 2004 |
| El Morro Valley | Pettit | LA 1571 | 57 | Linthicum 1980 |
| Pescado Basin / Zuni | Heshotauthla | LA 2114 | 4 | Kintigh et al. 2004; HARP |
| Pescado Basin / Zuni | NM 12:K3:108 | NM 12:K3:108 | 6 | Varien 2000 |
| Pescado Basin / Zuni | NA 11527 | NA 11527 | 10 | Zier 1976 |
| Pescado Basin / Zuni | NA 11530 | NA 11530 | 25 | Zier 1976 |
| West Zuni | Hinkson Ranh | LA 11439 | 3 | Eckert 1995; OBAP |
| Carrizo Wash | Platt Ranch | AZ Q:7:26 (ASM) | 12 | Westfall 1981 |
| Carrizo Wash | Platt Ranch | AZ Q:7:27 (ASM) | 6 | Westfall 1981 |
| Upper Little Colorado | Rim Valley | AZ Q:15:73 (ASM) | 9 | Martin et al. 1962; CFM |
| Upper Little Colorado | Hooper Ranch | AZ Q:15:6 (ASM) | 21 | Martin et al. 1961; CFM |
| Upper Little Colorado | Coyote Creek Pueblo | AZ Q:16:3 (ASM) | 35 | DeGarmo 1975 |
| Upper Little Colorado | Rudd Creek Ruin | AZ Q:16:63 (ASM) | 12 | Clark 2006; RCAP |
| Mariana Mesa | Sandstone Hill | NA 11233 | 19 | Barnett 1974 |

|  |  |  |  |  |
|---|---|---|---|---|
| Mariana Mesa | Horse Camp Mill | LA 10983 | 22 | McGimsey 1980 |
| Mariana Mesa | UG481 | UG481 | 32 | McGimsey 1980 |
| Mariana Mesa | UG494 | UG494 | 12 | McGimsey 1980 |
| Mariana Mesa | Fisher Site | LA 12133 | 18 | Bice 2004; AAS |
| Mariana Mesa | Techado Spring | LA 2148, LA 6010 | 245 | Smith et al. 2009 |
| Mariana Mesa | Tri-R Pueblo | n/a | 8 | Jimmy Smith field notes, 2010; TCAS |
| Vernon Area | Chilcott Ranch I | n/a | 6 | Martin et al. 1962; CFM |
| Vernon Area | Mineral Creek | n/a | 5 | Martin et al. 1961; CFM |
| Mogollon Highlands | Apache Creek | LA 2949 | 9 | Martin et al. 1957; Peckham et al. 1956; CFM |
| Mogollon Highlands | Higgins Flat | LA 8682 | 13 | Martin et al. 1956; CFM |
| Mogollon Highlands | Foote Canyon Pueblo | LA 4425 | 11 | Rinaldo 1959; CFM |
| Mogollon Highlands | WS Ranch | LA 3099 | 13 | Tomka 1988; Robinson 1992; UT |
| Mogollon Highlands | Hough 70 | LA 3279 | 11 | Zamora and Oakes 1999 |
| Mogollon Highlands | DZ Site | LA 70185 | 2 | Zamora 1999 |
| *Subtotal* |  |  | *714* |  |
|  |  | **Expanded Study Area** |  |  |
| Silver Creek | Pottery Hill | AZ P:12:12 (ASM) | 4 | Mills et al. 1999 |
| Silver Creek | Bryant Ranch | AZ P:11:133 (ASU) | 4 | Mills et al. 1999 |
| Silver Creek | Bailey Ruin | AZ P:11:1 (ASM) | 7 | Mills et al. 1999 |
| Hay Hollow Valley | Joint Site | Longacre 151 | 33 | Hansen and Schiffer 1975 |
| Hay Hollow Valley | Broken K | Longacre 156 | 90 | Hill 1968, 1970; Martin et al. 1967 |
| Hay Hollow Valley | Carter Ranch | Longacre 155 | 23 | Longacre 1970; Martin et al. 1964 |
| Arizona Mountains | Grasshopper Pueblo | AZ P:14:1 (ASM) | 103 | Riggs 2001 |
| Arizona Mountains | Turkey Creek Pueblo | AZ W:9:123 (ASM) | 280 | Lowell 1986 |
| Hardscrabble Wash | Hardscrabble Ruin | NA 14650 | 17 | Stebbins et al. 1986 |

(*continued*)

TABLE 9. (*continued*)

| SUBREGION | SITE NAME | SITE NUMBER | NUMBER OF RECORDED ROOMS | REFERENCES |
|---|---|---|---|---|
| Cebolleta Mesa | Los Pilares, Calabash | LA 1331 | 12 | Forester 1964, 1966; Dittert 1959; Ruppé 1990 |
| Cebolleta Mesa | LP 2:25-V | LP 2:25-V | 8 | Dittert 1959; Ruppé 1990 |
| Cebolleta Mesa | LP 2:13-B | LP 2:13-B | 7 | Dittert 1959; Ruppé 1990 |
| Mount Taylor area | LA 2639 | LA 2639 | 9 | Wendorf 1956 |
| Mount Taylor area | LA 2640 | LA 2640 | 15 | Wendorf 1956 |
| Manuelito Canyon | NM 12:U2:108A | NM 12:U2:108A | 8 | Anyon et al. 1983 |
| Petrified Forest | Puerco Ruin | AZ Q:1:22 (ASM) | 29 | Burton 1990; Jennings 1967 |
| *Subtotal* | | | *649* | |
| ***TOTAL*** | | | ***1,363*** | |

*Note*: AAS = Albuquerque Archaeological Society, CARP = Cibola Archaeological Research Project, CFM = Chicago Field Museum, EMVPP = El Morro Valley Prehistory Project, HARP = Heshotauthia Archaeological Research Project, OBAP = Ojo Bonito Archaeology Project, RCAP = Rudd Creek Archaeological Project, TCAS = Tarrant County Archaeological Society, UT = University of Texas.

the Mogollon Rim after A.D. 1100. Rooms are almost exclusively rectangular, with masonry or adobe walls that bear at least some of the weight of their roofs. Pueblo roofs are usually constructed of large wooden beams (vigas) spanning the shorter dimension of the room, with smaller wooden elements, thatching, and earth used to fill in the remaining gaps. Rooms are usually part of larger units consisting of multiple adjacent rooms that share walls (for extended discussions, see Riggs 2001:35–111; Mindeleff 1891:137–219). Some settlements in the Cibola region have multiple stories, with upper rooms generally conforming to the plan of ground-floor rooms.

The size of rooms may be constrained to a certain degree by the specific materials or methods used in construction, including the availability of different varieties of large trees suitable for use as primary roof beams or posts (Ciolek-Torrello 1985:46–47), the specific methods used for constructing interior roof supports (James 1997:435–438), or the load-bearing capacity of materials available for wall construction (Cameron 1999:203–208). In general, however, the range of materials and construction methods commonly employed across the Cibola region study area does not differ dramatically from place to place.

Due to the basic similarities in construction materials and methods across much of the Puebloan Southwest, differences in the sizes of rooms have more frequently been attributed to social factors than technical ones. For example, Steven James (1997) noted that room sizes are typically somewhat smaller at Puebloan settlements north of the Mogollon Rim than at settlements to the south. This broad pattern appears to be consistent throughout the prehispanic period. Based on comparisons with ethnographic data on room size from a number of historic populations across the Southwest, James (1997) argues that these differences may relate to differences in postmarital residence patterns and descent rules. Specifically, he argues that larger rooms typical of areas south of the Mogollon Rim may have been constructed and owned by males, representing a patrilineal descent pattern, whereas smaller rooms above the rim may have been constructed and owned by women in matrilineal societies. James attributes differences in room size to the differing agricultural processing and storage practices that he associates with each descent pattern.

In another study, Catherine Cameron (1999) points out that the organization and size of construction task groups may have also played a major role in the distribution of room sizes. Specifically, some pueblo settlements were constructed or expanded by simply adding rooms either singly or in small groups along existing rooms. Such additions would likely have been built by a relatively small social unit, such as a nuclear or extended family. This method of construction tends to lead to what are known as "agglomerative" settlement layouts, where rooms of various sizes are massed together with no apparent overall settlement plan. In other settlements, large numbers of rooms were constructed simultaneously using what is known as the "ladder-type" construction method (see Cordell 1998:27). Ladder construction entails laying out two or more long linear walls, which are then subdivided into individual rooms by creating walls along the short axis of the rooms. As Cameron (1999:207–208) notes, this method of construction tends to produce settlements with long, linear blocks of rooms that are usually reasonably consistent in size because one dimension is the same for all rooms. The size of the units that are often simultaneously built using ladder construction suggests some degree of coordinated construction labor perhaps beyond one or a few households (see also Mills 1998:66–71).

In order to explore variation in room size across the greater Cibola region, I compiled available information on room dimensions for a large number of excavated sites across the core study area. I obtained these room dimensions only for fully excavated or exposed rooms from published sources, original notes, and scaled plan maps where available. Figure 21 displays mean room sizes by the subregions defined in Chapter 3, as well as for a few additional areas in the expanded study area where data were available. As this map illustrates, there is a general trend toward increasing room size from north to south. Not surprisingly, this is the same general trend documented by James (1997) using data gathered from across the Southwest as a whole. This regional-scale pattern may suggest broad differences in household size or the specific construction methods used across the study area.

Since rooms can sometimes vary considerably in size within a single site, it is also important to examine the distribution of room sizes. Figure 22 shows histograms of room size for each of the core subregions included in this study, as well as for several portions of the expanded study area where data were available. The West Zuni region is excluded, because very few rooms have been excavated in this area. As these histograms illustrate, room sizes in the northern Cibola region, including the El Morro Valley, Pescado Basin, Carrizo Wash, and Mariana Mesa subregions within the core study area, as well as the Cebolleta Mesa, Mount Taylor, Hardscrabble Wash, and Petrified Forest areas, are strongly unimodal, with the vast majority of rooms less than 10 $m^2$ in area. Room sizes at settlements to the south, including sites in the Upper Little Colorado, Vernon Area, and Mogollon Highlands subregions in the core study area, as well as the

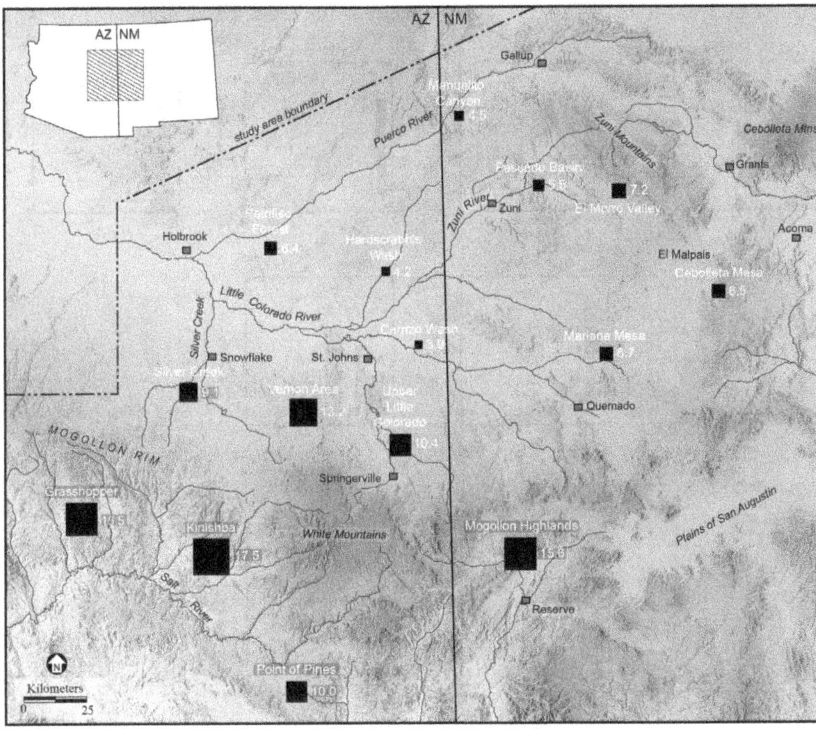


FIGURE 21. Mean room sizes by subregion across the study area.

Silver Creek, Hay Hollow Valley, and Arizona Mountains areas, are somewhat more diverse, with two or perhaps three modal sizes. Modes in the distribution of pueblo room sizes have frequently been interpreted as categories of rooms with different intended functions (e.g., Hill 1970:37–47). Typically, the smallest rooms are assumed to have been used for storage, larger rooms for habitation, and the largest rooms for ceremonial purposes (see the discussion in Cameron 1999:209–210). There are some data supporting this interpretation in the Cibola region, as featureless rooms with other evidence for use as storage areas do tend to be smaller than rooms with intramural features. At the same time, however, the frequency of remodeling and repurposing of rooms muddles the relationship between room size and function (Lowell 1991:36–38; Riggs 2001:176–178). At the very least, the differences between the subregions characterized by a single modal room size and the subregions with more diverse room sizes suggest that the inhabitants of various portions of the Cibola region were constructing

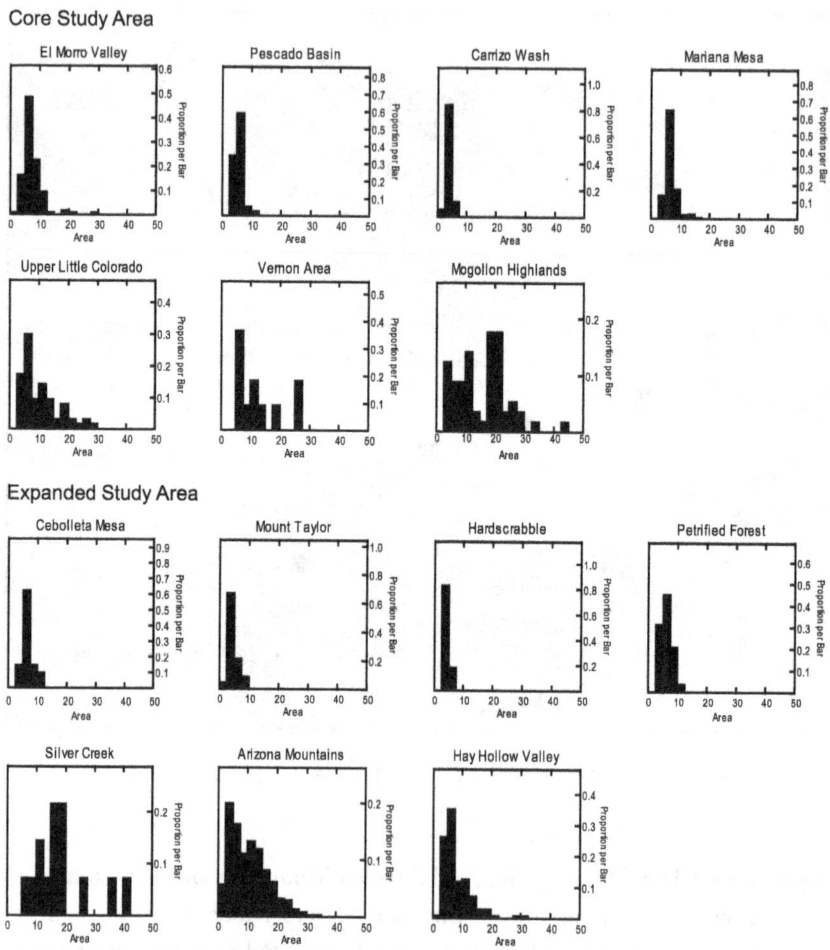


FIGURE 22. Histograms of room size for core subregions and nearby areas.

dwellings using somewhat different methods or criteria for organizing domestic space. Interestingly, excluding the Mariana Mesa area, these two groups of subregions within the core portion of the study area defined based on room size distributions conform to the overarching groups defined in the previous chapter based on similarities in the methods used to produce plain and corrugated ceramic vessels.

As Cameron (1999:230) points out, however, it is also necessary to consider the prevalence of ladder-type construction when interpreting room size distributions because ladder construction tends to produce rooms of similar sizes. Although the ladder construction has been studied in detail at few sites, a general examination of the plans of sites included in this study, as well as other published site plans (e.g., Fowler et al. 1987; Kintigh 1985a), suggests that ladder construction was much more prevalent in the subregions characterized by unimodal distribution of room sizes (El Morro Valley, Pescado Basin, Carrizo Wash, Mariana Mesa, Cebolleta Mesa) than in the other areas considered here.[1] For example, the site plans of large structures from across the region illustrated in Chapter 3 (see Figure 7) clearly demonstrate that sites from the northern and eastern portions of the Cibola region tend to be characterized by long, linear blocks of rooms, whereas sites in the south tend to be much less regular in plan.

Cameron (1999:226–230; see also Mills 1998) goes on to argue that ladder-type construction is an efficient means of building a large number of rooms simultaneously. The prevalence of ladder construction may provide evidence for the scale of coordinated effort that characterized the construction of dwellings across the Cibola region. Thus, although differences in room size distributions may have some basis in specific construction practices among different social groups, the patterns noted here are also likely partly functions of the size of the groups inhabiting these areas. In line with Cameron's (1999) expectations, the subregions characterized by a prevalence of ladder construction, indicating a high degree of labor coordination, were also the portions of the Cibola region with the greatest population densities during the interval considered here (see Peeples and Schachner 2008; Wilcox et al. 2007:Figures 12.6–12.8). Modular ladder constructions may have provided an efficient means for the large populations in these areas to accommodate increasing aggregation.

## INTRAMURAL DOMESTIC ARCHITECTURAL FEATURES

Across the greater Cibola region, a wide variety of intramural architectural features has been recorded, including formal hearths, mealing bins, ovens, storage bins/pits, post supports, stepped entryways, and pottery-drying features. Although many such features are common across much of the Southwest, similarities and differences in the specific form and placement of these features within rooms provide an indication of patterns of shared technological learning frameworks across the study area. I argue that similarities in the style and configuration of intramural domestic architectural features can be used as one proxy for strong relational connections among individuals and larger social groups across the Cibola region. For the purposes of this chapter, I focus primarily on hearths and mealing bins, as these are the only features that have been consistently recorded with enough detail and enough frequency to allow for comparison at a regional scale. Because the total sample of excavated rooms at most settlements is relatively small, comparisons are limited to the subregional scale.

Excavated hearths and mealing bins from settlements across the Cibola region take a wide variety of forms, sometimes even within a single settlement. These different forms relate to differences in the intended function of features (Lowell 1999), the size or composition of the social group using them (Ciolek-Torrello and Reid 1974; James 1994:250–252; Ortman 1998), or differences in cuisine (Crown 2000:241–249). In the context of this study, I interpret similarities in the form or placement of heating, cooking, and mealing features, which may be influenced by any or all of the factors listed above, as broadly indicative of similarities in daily activities revolving around food preparation. Practices relating to foodways are particularly useful avenues through which to explore relationships among social groups because cuisine tends to be conservative, learned through direct face-to-face interaction, and closely related to group membership (Clark 2001:12–22). Thus, I interpret similarities in attributes of hearths and mealing bins as evidence for the nature of relational connections among individuals and social groups across the study area.

## HEARTH FORM AND PLACEMENT

Interior domestic hearths found in the Cibola region heated interior spaces, provided light, and were used for food preparation. Several different forms of hearths have been recorded at settlements across the study area, and available paleoethnobotanical and ethnohistoric data suggest that different forms of these features may have been used for somewhat different purposes, including various styles of wet or dry cooking (e.g., Cushing 1920; Lowell 1999). In addition, there is considerable variation in the placement of hearth features within rooms at settlements across the study area. The location of interior hearths would have structured the interactions among members of the households occupying those spaces to some degree. Similarities in the design and placement of hearths may provide an indication of underlying similarities in the organization of domestic activities.

In order to characterize variation in hearth form, a series of categories of common feature types were defined based on a general assessment of available descriptions, feature plan illustrations, and photographs (see also Hegmon et al. 1998). In some cases, these categories could be parsed more finely at specific settlements, but the groups used here were designed to allow for consistent application across all sites included in this study. The analyses presented below include only formal hearths and exclude informal burned floor areas, as such features have not been consistently recorded during excavations across the Cibola region. In addition to placing excavated hearths into these broad form categories, the locations of hearths within rooms were recorded in three broad categories: along a wall, in a room corner, or in the room interior.[2] Due to the relatively small sample sizes available for most regions, sites were not divided by time period. Additional analyses not described in detail here suggest, however, that patterns of hearth design and placement were highly consistent in each subregion with data from multiple time periods.

Figure 23 displays the proportions of each major hearth type for all subregions included in this study area. The Carrizo Wash and West Zuni subregions were combined for this comparison, and the Vernon Area was excluded due to the low counts of excavated features in these regions. As this map illustrates, the most common form for every region is a rectangular slab-lined hearth. This type of feature accounts for the majority of excavated features in all subregions with enough examples to be included in this analysis. Rectangular slab-lined hearths have been interpreted as cooking features that are particularly well suited to pot boiling (Lowell 1999:460–462). Thus, the widespread distribution of this particular kind of feature during the period in question may suggest broad similarities in methods of food preparation and the degree of agricultural reliance across much of the region.

The proportions of other hearth types across the study area are generally similar, with the Mogollon Highlands and West Zuni / Carrizo Wash areas representing possible exceptions. In the available sample from both of these subregions, clay-lined hearths and hearths with adobe copings are more common than in other subregions. The size and contents of these clay and adobe features suggest that they were also used primarily for food preparation (see descriptions in Martin et al. 1956; Martin et al. 1952; Rinaldo 1959; Westfall 1981). The differences in form may indicate different cultural notions of proper hearth construction methods or differences in the intended use. Overall, however, the overwhelming dominance of rectangular, slab-lined hearths across the

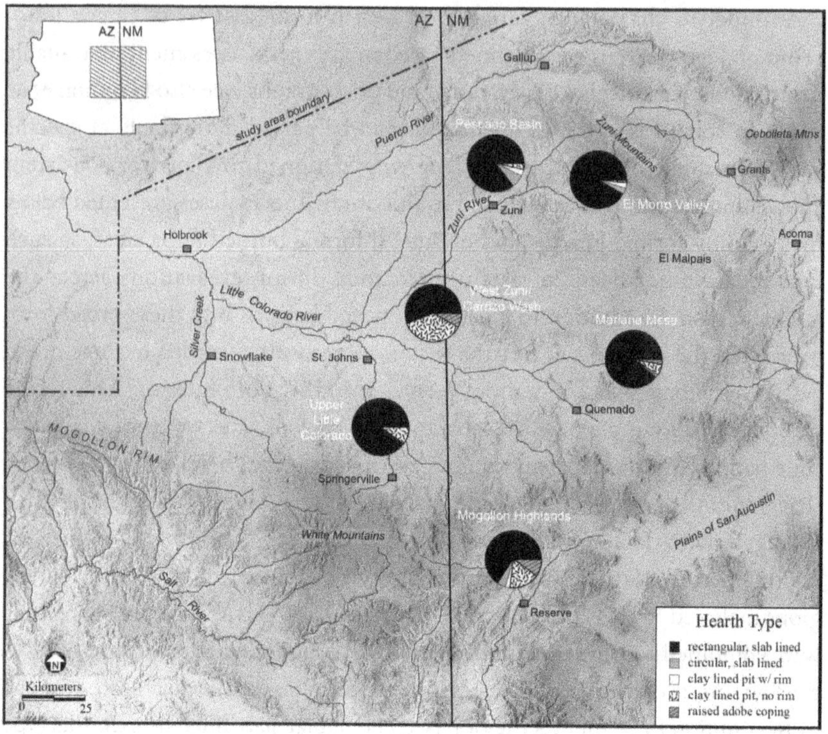


FIGURE 23. Map showing the percentages of hearth type categories across the region.

entire Cibola region suggests that the primary feature most commonly used for daily cooking was generally similar across the study area. This pattern is also consistent with published information from the expanded study area (see plan maps in Burton 1990; Dittert 1959; Hill 1970; Lowell 1991; Mills 1999; Riggs 2001; Ruppé 1990).

Patterns of hearth placement show substantially more variation than hearth form. Figure 24 shows the frequency of hearths found in each of the three general location categories for the core study area, as well as for several portions of the expanded study area. As this map illustrates, in most portions of the study area north and east of Carrizo Wash, hearths are typically placed along room walls or in room corners. In many cases, one or more walls of a hearth are actually formed by the walls of the room itself. Conversely, in the southern and western portions of the study area, hearths are typically located away from walls and in the interiors of rooms, usually near the room center. The Mariana

Mesa subregion in the eastern Cibola region is also dominated by hearths constructed in room interiors, in contrast to other nearby areas. Importantly, there is somewhat more diversity in hearth placement in areas along the edges of the two general groups, including the Carrizo Wash, Hardscrabble Wash, and Cebolleta Mesa areas, perhaps suggesting that individuals in these areas variously ascribed to methods of feature construction dominant to the north and to the south, respectively.[3]

Differences in the placement of hearths within rooms likely would have structured interactions among the members of households occupying these rooms to some degree. Cooking over wood fires using clay pots can be a time-consuming endeavor (e.g., Cushing 1920:289–316). In the northern portions of the study area, where hearths are typically found against walls or in corners, the members of the household responsible for preparing food may have spent long periods of time focused on maintaining fires, potentially isolated from

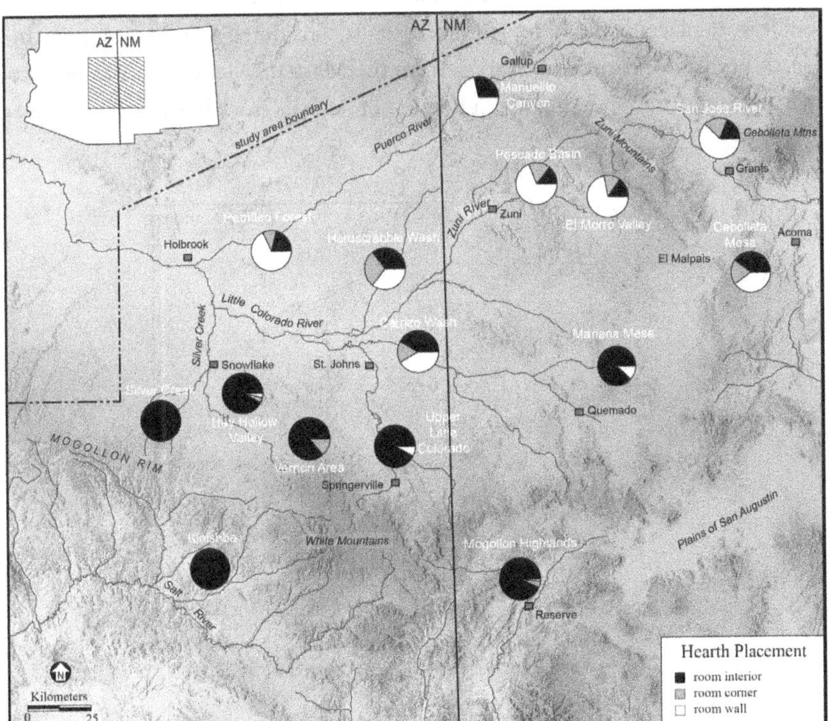


FIGURE 24. Map showing proportions of hearth placement categories across the region.

other activities occurring within the same room or adjacent habitation rooms. In the southern and western portions of the study area, where hearths are usually centrally located in large rooms, individuals may have more easily engaged with others while performing daily cooking activities. Although it is virtually impossible to determine how space was allocated as tasks were being performed, such differences in the locations of features may indicate underlying differences in the potential for socialization revolving around the common daily activity of cooking.

An additional consideration with regard to the pattern of hearth placement is the relationship between feature placement and room size. It could be argued that hearths are more likely to be found along walls or in corners in smaller rooms with less interior space. As Figure 25 shows, when considering the study area as a whole, it is indeed the case that rooms with hearths along walls or in corners do tend to be somewhat smaller than rooms with interior hearths. A general assessment of the data included here divided by subregion suggests, however, that there is no consistent patterned relationship between room size and feature placement when each subregion is considered separately. For example, 93 percent of excavated hearths from the Mariana Mesa region are located in room interiors, whereas only 14 percent of hearths from the El Morro Valley

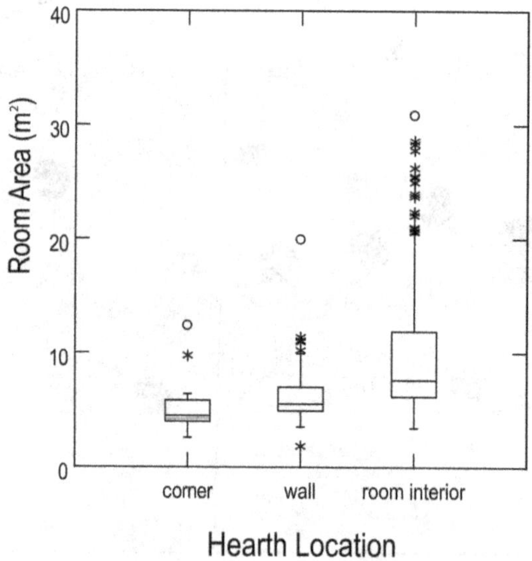


FIGURE 25. Boxplots of room area for each hearth location category.

and Pescado Basin are in room interiors. This represents a strong and statistically significant difference in hearth placement between Mariana Mesa and Pescado / El Morro ($X^2 = 126.14$, df = 2, $p < 0.00001$). At the same time, however, these subregions all have unimodal distributions of room sizes, and the average room sizes are not statistically significantly different ($t = -0.70$, df = 243.05, $p = 0.484$). Figure 26 illustrates this point further. The three site plans shown in this figure are all characterized by rooms of similar sizes but quite different patterns of hearth placement. Overall, this suggests that the regional patterns of hearth placement documented above are more likely related to specific technological decisions or cultural notions of the use of space than any physical constraints on feature placement due to room size or construction.

## GRINDING FACILITY FORM AND SIZE

Across the Southwest, the primary method for processing corn for consumption was grinding kernels into flour using a mano and metate. During the interval considered in this study, grinding facilities most often consisted of slab metates set into some form of permanent mealing facility, often with an associated flour receptacle. Such permanent grinding facilities are particularly well suited to efficiently grinding corn for long periods of time (Adams 1993:334; see also Crown 2000:243–249). Historically, Pueblo women spent as much as three to five hours per day grinding corn in similar permanent facilities (Cushing 1920:289–316). Osteological and other evidence suggests that women were engaged in a similar level and intensity of corn grinding in the prehispanic past (see discussion in Spielmann 1995:96). The time commitment involved preparing cornmeal emphasizes the importance of such features in the food system and the daily activities of women in general.

Following the analysis of hearth form described above, several categories of grinding facilities were defined based on available illustrations, photographs, and notes. These categories include only formal facilities, such as stone- or adobe-lined bins and flour receptacles embedded in floor surfaces. Rooms with loose metates that are not part of any formal grinding facility and rooms with no identified metates were grouped into a single category.

As Table 10 shows, across the core portion of the study area, although most rooms have no formal grinding facilities, rooms that do are dominated by upright slab-lined bins in all subregions. The Mogollon Highlands subregion is unique, however, in that it is the only area within the larger study area where

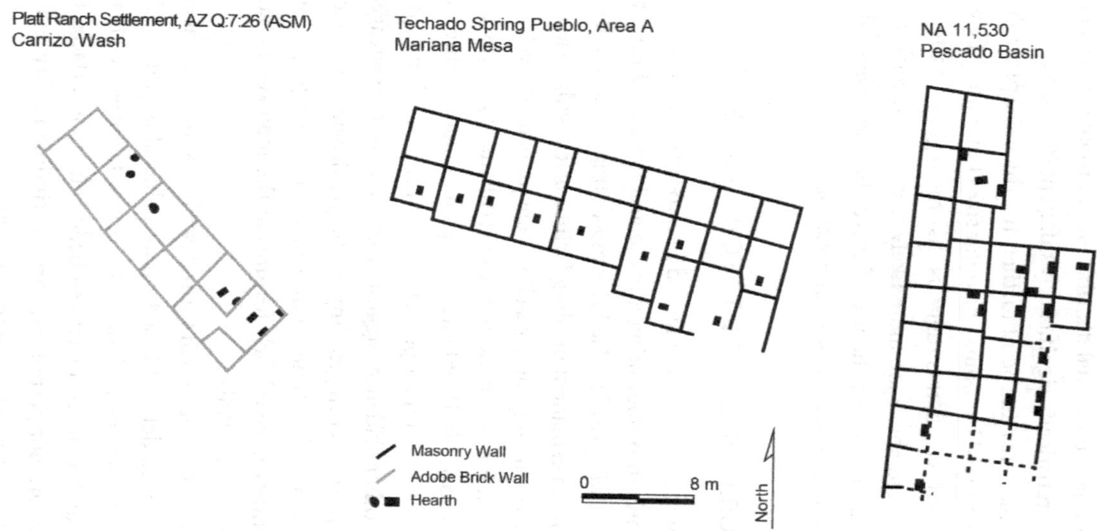


FIGURE 26. Examples of structures with similar room sizes but different patterns of hearth placement.

Table 10. Counts of grinding facilities by type

| REGION | SLAB-LINED BIN | BIN WITH ADOBE COPING | BOWL EMBEDDED IN FLOOR | EXCAVATED ROOM WITH NO FORMAL FACILITY |
|---|---|---|---|---|
| El Morro Valley | 5 | 0 | 0 | 87 |
| Pescado Basin | 4 | 0 | 0 | 39 |
| West Zuni | 4 | 0 | 0 | 19 |
| Carrizo Wash | 2 | 2 | 0 | 15 |
| Upper Little Colorado | 12 | 1 | 0 | 55 |
| Mariana Mesa | 15 | 0 | 0 | 81 |
| Vernon Area | 1 | 0 | 0 | 4 |
| Mogollon Highlands | 7 | 3 | 7 | 46 |

ceramic bowls set into the floor as flour receptacles have been documented. This particular type of mealing feature is also found in earlier and contemporaneous sites in other areas to the south, including in the Mimbres Valley, along the Upper Gila River near Cliff, New Mexico, and along the eastern slopes of the Black Range (e.g., Hegmon et al. 1998).

In addition, formal mealing bins are found in a somewhat smaller proportion of rooms in settlements in the El Morro Valley and Pescado Basin subregions than in areas to the south (see also James 1994:255–260). It could be argued that the lower frequency of mealing bins in the excavated sample from the El Morro Valley and Pescado Basin areas may be due in part to the greater frequency of upper-story rooms in these areas. Among the historic Western Pueblos, grinding did sometimes take place in upper-story habitation rooms, where bins would have been less likely to have been preserved (Adams 1993:Figure 1; see also Mindeleff 1891:Plate LXXIX). At this point, however, there is little direct evidence for the presence of formal grinding facilities either on roofs or in upper-story rooms (see also James 1994:253–254), so differences in the frequency of recorded features likely instead indicate a distinction in the use of space for grinding activities across the study area.[4]

Another attribute of grinding facilities that may indicate similarities and differences in the organization of daily food preparation activities across the study area is their size in terms of the number of bins within a single context. Mealing features often occur in groups of two to as many as eight within a single interior architectural space. Early historic accounts of such bin sets have often attributed each separate metate to a different stage of the grinding process, with surfaces graded from coarse to fine, indicating early- to late-stage grinding (Baxter 1882:83–84; Kidder 1932:67–68; Mindeleff 1891:208–214). Although this functional interpretation may have merit in certain contexts, other researchers have argued that the size of grinding facilities may instead relate to the size of the domestic unit involved in corn grinding (Adams 1993:41–42; James 1994:250–253; Ortman 1998).

Table 11 shows the counts of grinding facilities of various sizes (number of facilities per context) across the study area. As this table demonstrates, in the El Morro Valley and Pescado Basin subregions all recorded grinding facilities consist of three or fewer mealing bins per room. To the south in the Carrizo Wash, Mogollon Highlands, Mariana Mesa, and Upper Little Colorado areas, grinding facilities containing four or more mealing bins are also found. This suggests that daily grinding activities performed by the inhabitants of settlements in the southern portions of the study area may have more frequently involved somewhat larger groups of women working together simultaneously. The higher number of bins per architectural unit to the south may also suggest differences in household size across the study area (a possibility also suggested by patterns of room size) or differences in the organization of women's labor. Some of the largest grinding facilities in the Mariana Mesa area contain as many as eight bins, perhaps suggesting specialization in food preparation by some women within these communities (see a similar suggestion by Crown 2000:247–248 regarding Chaco Canyon).

TABLE 11. Counts of grinding facility by size (number of features per context)

| | NUMBER OF BINS PER CONTEXT | | | | |
|---|---|---|---|---|---|
| REGION | 1 | 2–3 | 4–5 | 6+ | TOTAL |
| El Morro Valley | 4 | 1 | 0 | 0 | 5 |
| Pescado Basin | 1 | 2 | 0 | 0 | 3 |
| West Zuni | 3 | 1 | 0 | 0 | 4 |
| Carrizo Wash | 2 | 1 | 1 | 0 | 4 |
| Upper Little Colorado | 6 | 4 | 3 | 0 | 13 |
| Mariana Mesa | 29 | 10 | 5 | 3 | 47 |
| Vernon Area | 0 | 1 | 0 | 0 | 1 |
| Mogollon Highlands | 4 | 10 | 3 | 0 | 17 |

Across the greater Southwest as a whole, Scott Ortman (1998) documented a trend in the size of grinding facilities through time. Specifically, he argues that the average number of bins per context decreased in most areas across the Pueblo III to Pueblo IV transition. Ortman suggests that this change may reflect the decreasing importance of extended family residential units in the context of large Pueblo IV villages. However, Ortman notes (1998:173) that this macroregional pattern does not play out particularly well in the central portion of the Cibola region around Zuni and Mariana Mesa, a finding that the additional data collected for this study support. In the southern and western portions of the study area, including the Upper Little Colorado, Mogollon Highlands, Silver Creek, and Arizona Mountains area, however, a pronounced decrease in grinding facility size through time does occur (Ortman 1998:Table 9.2). This may suggest differences in the organization of residential units across the Pueblo III to Pueblo IV transition between different portions of the Cibola region.

## WALL CONSTRUCTION METHODS

The vast majority of pueblo rooms in the Cibola region were constructed using some form of masonry. The style of masonry varied, from roughly shaped cobbles set in substantial amounts of mortar to well-shaped banded wall rocks with prepared interior wall faces. Some of the variation in wall construction from place to place is likely due to the availability of materials appropriate for cobble, slab, or shaped masonry construction, while some differences may also represent culturally specific technological building practices. However, the use of adobe, which is possible virtually anywhere mud and water are available, cannot easily be explained as simply a function of material availability. The distribution of this relatively rare construction method may provide insights into patterns of interaction and population movement across the study area.

Two basic methods of adobe construction have been documented in the Cibola region: coursed adobe construction and adobe brick construction. Coursed adobe walls are constructed by building up a thick mud in layers, allowing each layer to dry before applying the next (Cameron 1999:204; Stubbs and Stallings 1953:25–26). Coursed adobe construction is known from many portions of the greater Southwest but is particularly prevalent in the Hohokam region of Arizona, in the northern Rio Grande, and in the Mimbres region after the mid-twelfth century (Cameron 1998). Prehispanic adobe bricks in the Southwest were produced from a clay matrix similar in consistency to that used for pottery. These bricks were either hand formed or formed in a mold and then air dried rather than fired. Adobe brick construction has a somewhat more limited distribution than coursed adobe walls and has been documented only in areas above the Mogollon Rim, primarily in northeastern Arizona and along the Little Colorado River Valley, including portions of the Cibola region (see Gann 1996). Both adobe bricks and coursed adobe walls appear to be most common in contexts dating after about A.D. 1150–1200 in and around the Cibola region, although there are earlier examples in some areas (see Cameron 1998).

Within the core portion of the study area, there are only two settlements with direct evidence for adobe brick construction. These are the Platt Ranch settlement in the Carrizo Wash area (Westfall 1981:Figure 46) and the Horse Camp Mill site in the Mariana Mesa area (McGimsey 1980:45–46). Adobe brick construction is also known from a few sites to the west in the expanded study area, including Fourmile Ruin in the Silver Creek area (Van Keuren 2006:5), at least two of the late Pueblo IV period villages of the Petrified Forest area (Stone Axe Pueblo and Wallace Tank Pueblo; see Schachner et al. 2016), as well as just outside the study area in the Homol'ovi pueblos near Winslow, Arizona (Gann 1996). Walls constructed of coursed adobe have been documented at the Techado Spring site in the Mariana Mesa area (Smith et al. 2009:17–18), at several sites in the southern Cebolleta Mesa area (Dittert 1959:234–235; Ruppé 1990), as well as in the Homol'ovi area west of the study area.[5] At almost all of the sites where coursed adobe or adobe brick architecture is present, other portions of the same structures are constructed from stone masonry. This coassociation of adobe and masonry suggests that material availability was not the primary motive for adobe construction; instead, these various forms of adobe construction were likely culturally specific building practices.

Across the Cibola region and slightly beyond, sites with evidence for coursed adobe or adobe brick construction primarily fall along an west–east line running roughly from Winslow, Arizona, along the Little Colorado and Carrizo Wash to Mariana Mesa and into the southern Cebolleta Mesa area. The appearance of adobe brick and coursed adobe architecture in the thirteenth century in the Carrizo Wash and Mariana Mesa subregions may suggest interaction or historical ties between settlements in these areas and the more western portions of the Cibola region. In Chapter 5 I argued, based on ceramic technological

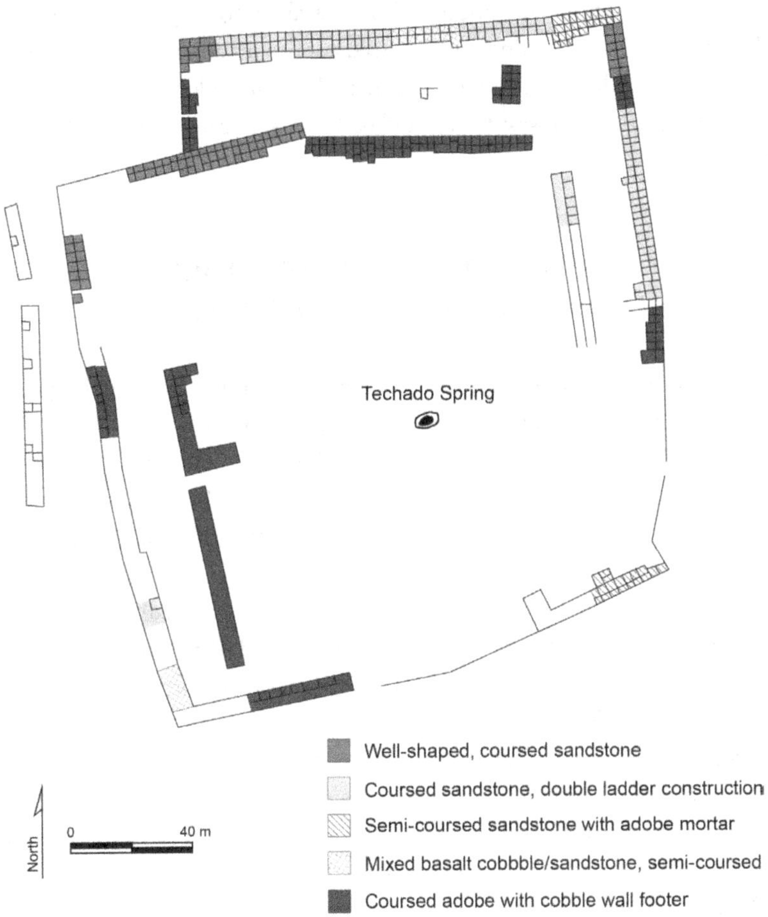


FIGURE 27. Map of Techado Spring Pueblo in the Mariana Mesa subregion showing the distributions of different styles of construction.

similarities, that the Mariana Mesa subregion in particular may have been inhabited by a diverse group of migrants, including many people from the southern and western portions of the study area. The diversity of methods used for wall construction in the Mariana Mesa area provides additional evidence for this scenario (see McGimsey 1980; Smith et al. 2009). Importantly, distinct wall construction styles are spatially contiguous at several well-documented large settlements in the Mariana Mesa area, suggesting that segments of settlements with multiple construction styles may represent the residences of small groups of households with diverse origins (Smith et al. 2009:35–73). The diversity of architectural styles, including both coursed adobe and adobe brick architecture, in the Mariana Mesa area provides some additional evidence for the hypothesized connections from west to east and patterns of migration across the Cibola region.

## DOMESTIC ARCHITECTURE AND RELATIONAL IDENTITY

The analyses described above provide a general overview of several aspects of domestic architectural construction that suggest patterns of frequent interaction and historical connections and, by extension, relational connections among the inhabitants of different portions of the study area. Some of the patterned variation noted here is difficult to interpret due to problems of equifinality. For example, the mean and distribution of room sizes across the study area may variously be due to differences in household size, particular technological practices related to domestic construction, or other factors such as the size or organization of construction task groups. Other variables, such as the form, size, and placement of domestic architectural features, are more easily interpreted as products of specific technological decisions among functional equivalents. In this final section, I briefly summarize some of the results discussed above and then place these results within the context of the analysis of ceramic technological similarity presented in the previous chapter.

Although hearth forms are generally similar across most of the study area, patterns of hearth placement differ dramatically from place to place. In the northern portions of the study area, hearths along walls and in corners are most common, whereas in the southern portions of the study area, including the Mariana Mesa subregion, hearths are usually in room interiors (usually centrally located). This pattern is not simply a product of room size and may represent a fundamental difference in notions of domestic spatial organization among the inhabitants of different portions of the study area. The consistent differences between these two large areas suggest that the inhabitants of these zones maintained the strongest relational connections with others within the same zone. Importantly, sites in areas along the edges of the two broad zones are somewhat more diverse in terms of the design and placement of intramural domestic features, perhaps suggesting that the boundaries between the two networks of relational connections were relatively permeable.

Similarly, although the forms of grinding facilities across the study area are fairly similar among all subregions except for the Mogollon Highlands, there are slight differences in the frequency and size of these features, which may provide some evidence for the directionality of interaction across the region. Specifically, bins are somewhat less frequent in the El Morro Valley and Pescado Basin subregions than in the areas to the south for which data are available (Upper Little Colorado, Carrizo Wash, Mariana Mesa, and Mogollon Highlands). Furthermore, in the El Morro Valley and Pescado Basin, documented grinding facilities are limited to groups of three or fewer bins, whereas in areas to the south, grinding facilities that include four or more bins are also common. These differences in the frequency and size of grinding facilities suggest that the northern and southern portions of the study area may have also been characterized by broad differences in the organization of women's labor. This is suggestive of differences in social organization among the inhabitants of these different portions of the Cibola region.

Wall construction methods vary considerably across the Cibola region as a whole, but for the most part, it is difficult to separate variation due to material availability from variation due to specific technological practices. The distribution of adobe construction, however, may provide one indication of a specific technological practice that suggests interaction or historical connections among populations across the study area. Coursed adobe and adobe brick construction are rare but have primarily been documented along a west–east line running from the Homol'ovi area to the Mariana Mesa and the southern Cebolleta Mesa areas. The patterned distribution of adobe architecture across the study area provides evidence for strong connections among the inhabitants of settlements in these areas possibly established through migration from west to east across the Cibola region.

Overall, the patterns of domestic architectural feature forms, frequency, and placement across the Cibola region for areas with available data suggest that the core study area can be divided into two groups of subregions: (1) the El Morro Valley and Pescado Basin to the north and (2) the Upper Little Colorado, Mariana Mesa, Vernon Area, and Mogollon Highlands to the south. The Carrizo Wash / West Zuni area appears to be somewhat transitional in that individual sites contain attributes that typically dominate areas to the north and to the south in roughly equal proportions. The groups of subregions defined here based on architectural data coincide well with the groups of subregions defined in the previous chapter based on ceramic technological similarities. Indeed, in terms of both the ceramic technological data and domestic architectural data, the Carrizo Wash and West Zuni subregions are somewhat transitional between dominant patterns to the north and to the south. The similarities in the patterns of ceramic production and domestic architectural construction suggest that both of these domestic crafts were likely taught and learned through similar vectors of strong relational connections.

# 7

# CERAMIC DESIGN AND THE EXPRESSION OF CATEGORICAL IDENTITY

THERE IS a voluminous literature in archaeology focused on stylistic variation in material culture, as well as the relationships between different kinds of style and social identities (e.g., Bowser 2000; Conkey and Hastorf 1990; Hegmon 1992, 1998, 2000; Sackett 1977; Wiessner 1983; Wobst 1977). This body of research suggests that although the specific factors that drive stylistic similarities and differences in a particular social setting are quite diverse, there are also certain regularities that cross-cut a wide variety of contexts (Hegmon 1998:277). For example, highly visible objects or designs found in public settings are often used to actively express social identities (e.g., Bowser 2000; Carr 1995; Hodder 1982; Mills 2007a, 2007b; Wobst 1977). Furthermore, design styles that span multiple media (e.g., ceramics, rock art, murals, clothing, etc.) are also often symbolically charged (see DeBoer 1991 on pervasive styles). Such broad regularities suggest that, through a careful contextualization of production and use, it may be possible to identify certain kinds of objects or designs that were actively manipulated as a means to express social distinctions in a given context.

As described in detail in Chapter 2, categorical identification refers to the process through which people identify with larger groups based on perceived similarities with social roles or categories to which an individual can belong. As categorical distinctions are not necessarily built out of direct and frequent interactions among people, identities must be symbolized in order to facilitate recognition among members and nonmembers of such groups. The process of symbolization often involves the kinds of active expressions of identities through material culture described above. From this, I argue that patterns of similarity and difference in highly visible objects and designs, when appropriately contextualized, can be used as one indication of patterns of shared categorical identities at various social and spatial scales.

This chapter presents a series of related ceramic stylistic analyses directed at documenting the strongest patterns of identity expression across the Cibola region during the Pueblo III to Pueblo IV transition. Through the discussion below, I argue that patterns of similarity in ceramic design, in particular for large polychrome serving bowls used and exchanged in the context of public gatherings (see Chapter 4), provide evidence for the shared public expressions of categorical identities among the inhabitants of various portions of the study area. The geographic and demographic scales at which categorical identities were expressed changed dramatically across the Pueblo III to Pueblo IV transition. This transition increased the social scale and distinctiveness of categorical distinctions overall, but as I describe here, different portions of the Cibola region were marked by different trajectories of change through time.

## PAINTED CERAMICS IN THE CIBOLA REGION

A wide variety of painted ceramics were produced and used across the greater Cibola region during the period considered in this study. Table 12 provides dates and references for the most common ceramic wares from the region (see Figure 28 for images), and I highlight a few additional temporal trends in design, technology, and vessel form that merit additional discussion in this section. As the discussion below illustrates, painted ceramics produced and used in the Cibola region became both more visually distinctive and regionally diverse across the Pueblo III to Pueblo IV transition.

In the primary portion of the study area, most painted ceramics fall into one of two overarching wares/ceramic traditions: Cibola White Ware and White Mountain Red Ware. Cibola White Ware vessels were slipped in white clay and painted with elaborate geometric designs in black. Cibola White Ware was produced across most of the greater Cibola region until about A.D. 1325 (see Goetze and Mills 1993; Hays-Gilpin and van Hartesveldt 1998), probably excluding a few areas south of the Mogollon Rim (Wilson 1994, 2007; Wilson

TABLE 12. Date ranges and references for Pueblo III and Pueblo IV period wares/types in the greater Cibola region

| WARE/SERIES | TYPE | DATE RANGE (A.D.) | REFERENCES |
|---|---|---|---|
| Cibola White Ware | Reserve Black-on-white | 1100–1200 | Hays-Gilpin and van Hartesveldt 1998 |
| | Snowflake Black-on-white | 1100–1275 | Hays-Gilpin and van Hartesveldt 1998 |
| | Tularosa Black-on-white | 1175–1300 | Hays-Gilpin and van Hartesveldt 1998 |
| | Pinedale Black-on-white | 1275–1325 | Hays-Gilpin and van Hartesveldt 1998 |
| Early White Mountain Red Ware | Wingate Black-on-red | 1050–1200 | Hays-Gilpin and van Hartesveldt 1998; Carlson 1970 |
| | Wingate Polychrome | 1100–1200 | Hays-Gilpin and van Hartesveldt 1998; Carlson 1970 |
| | St. Johns Black-on-red | 1200–1300 | Hays-Gilpin and van Hartesveldt 1998; Carlson 1970 |
| | St. Johns Polychrome | 1200–1300 | Hays-Gilpin and van Hartesveldt 1998; Carlson 1970 |
| | Springerville Polychrome | 1250–1300 | Hays-Gilpin and van Hartesveldt 1998; Carlson 1970 |
| | Techado Polychrome | 1250–1300 | Smith et al. 2009 |
| Late White Mountain Red Ware | Pinedale Black-on-red | 1280–1330 | Mills et al. 1999; Carlson 1970 |
| | Pinedale Polychrome | 1290–1330 | Mills et al. 1999; Carlson 1970 |
| | Cedar Creek Polychrome | 1300–1350 | Mills et al. 1999; Carlson 1970 |
| | Fourmile Polychrome | 1330–1390 | Mills et al. 1999; Carlson 1970 |
| | Show Low Polychrome | 1330–1390 | Mills et al. 1999; Carlson 1970 |
| Zuni Glaze Ware | Heshotauthla Black-on-red | 1275–1450+ | Eckert 2006; Smith et al. 1966 |
| | Heshotauthla Polychrome | 1275–1450+ | Eckert 2006; Smith et al. 1966 |
| | Kwakina Polychrome | 1280–1450+ | Eckert 2006; Smith et al. 1966 |
| | Pinnawa Glaze-on-white | 1350–1450+ | Eckert 2006; Smith et al. 1966 |
| | Pinnawa Red-on-white | 1350–1450+ | Eckert 2006; Smith et al. 1966 |
| | Kechipawan Polychrome | 1370–1450+ | Eckert 2006; Smith et al. 1966 |
| Puerco Valley Red Ware | Showlow Black-on-red | 1030–1280 | Mills and Herr 1999 |
| Mogollon Brown Ware | Tularosa White-on-red | 1200–1350 | Rinaldo and Bluhm 1956 |
| | McDonald Painted Corrugated | 1150–1280 | Mills et al. 1999 |
| **Additional Rare Wares/Series** | | | |
| Winslow Orange Ware | Multiple | 1260–1350 | Hays-Gilpin et al. 1996; Lyons 2001 |
| Kintiel-Klagetoh types | Multiple | 1250/1275–1300+ | Hays-Gilpin and van Hartesveldt 1998; Fowler et al. 1987 |
| Maverick Mountain Series | Multiple | 1275–1450 | Neuzil and Lyons 2005 |

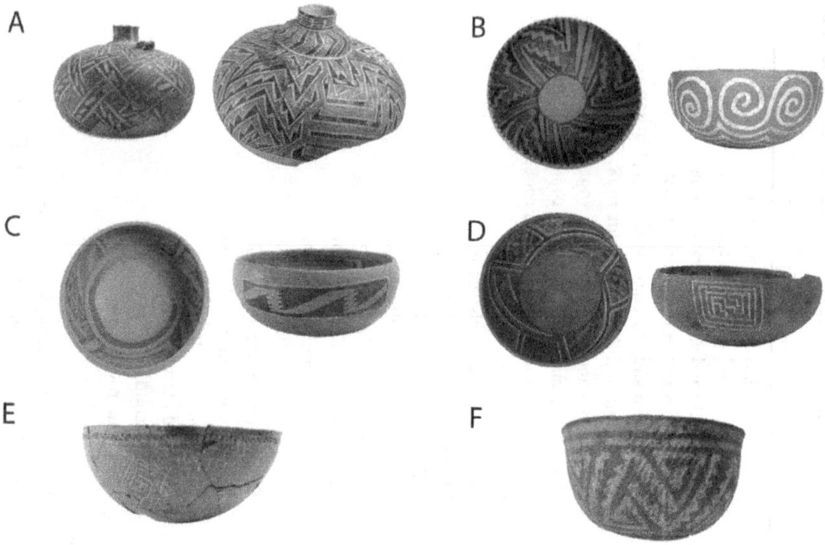


FIGURE 28. Examples of painted ceramics from the Cibola region: (A) Cibola White Ware, (B) Early White Mountain Red Ware, (C) Late White Mountain Red Ware, (D) Zuni Glaze Ware, (E) Tularosa White-on-red, and (F) McDonald Painted Corrugated. All photos by the author from collections at the Center for Archaeology and Society repository at Arizona State University except for D, which was provided by Paul Stavast at the Brigham Young University Museum of Peoples and Cultures.

and Sevrets 1999). Although many different vessel forms were produced (jars, bowls, pitchers, ladles, scoops, effigies, etc.), the most frequent form was large jars used for storage. Cibola White Ware declined in frequency throughout the Pueblo III and Pueblo IV periods as it was gradually replaced by the closely related red ware and polychrome types described below.

White Mountain Red Ware ceramics consist of a set of related red-slipped ceramic types produced ca. A.D. 1000–1450. The surfaces of these vessels were slipped with a thick and well-polished layer of red to orange clay and painted with black or black and white paint (Carlson 1970). The production of White Mountain Red Ware was considerably more restricted than that of Cibola White Ware and probably limited to areas along the Zuni River, the El Morro Valley, the Mariana Mesa, and the Upper Little Colorado and perhaps additional areas along the Puerco of the West and Cebolleta Mesa during the Pueblo III period (see Chapter 4). Specific varieties were also produced in the Silver Creek area during the Pueblo IV period (see Mills et al. 1999). White Mountain Red Ware vessels occur in many different forms but are overwhelmingly dominated by hemispherical bowls with complex geometric designs painted on their interiors and, in polychrome varieties, visually distinctive designs in white or black and white on their exteriors.

White Mountain Red Ware ceramics are often divided into three distinct series based on differences in technology and design through time and across space: Early White Mountain Red Ware (ca. A.D. 1000–1275), Late White Mountain Red Ware (ca. A.D. 1275–1390), and Zuni Glaze Ware (A.D. 1275–1450; see Mills 2007; Mills, Clark, et al. 2013; Mills et al. 2015). Early White Mountain Red Ware vessels are painted with a matte black mineral paint on the interiors of bowls, with bold repeating geometric designs painted in thick white lines on polychrome bowl exteriors. Late White Mountain Red Ware vessels were produced primarily in the western half of the study area in the Silver Creek and Upper Little Colorado areas in particular (and perhaps only in the Silver Creek area after A.D. 1325; see Duff 2002; Triadan 1997; Triadan et al. 2002; Zedeño 1994). These vessels were characterized by dense black designs painted in glaze paint and complex unit designs or life forms painted in black or black and white on the exteriors of bowls prior to about A.D. 1325 (with later varieties showing simple banded exterior designs; Carlson 1970). Zuni Glaze Ware vessels were produced primarily in the eastern half of the region along the Zuni River Valley, in the El Morro Valley, and in the Upper Little Colorado area (and likely also in the Petrified Forest area). These vessels were painted with distinctive dense designs in glaze paints that differed in recipe from those of Late White Mountain Red Ware (Fenn et al. 2006; Huntley 2006, 2008:44–59). The exteriors of polychrome bowls were painted with simple geometric designs, most often with thin white lines. Exterior designs were similar to those on Early White Mountain Red Ware bowls but typically somewhat more open.

In the southern portions of the study area along either side of the Mogollon Rim, a few distinct varieties of painted Mogollon Brown Ware vessels with similar design treatments were produced during the period considered here. These vessels incorporated bold designs in white on the exteriors of bowls in a format similar to those characteristic of the White Mountain Red Ware vessels described above. Many of these bowls had unpainted and often smudged interiors. Vessel forms and surface treatment often differed with bowls with exterior designs in the Mogollon Highlands (Tularosa White-on-red; Nesbit 1938:139; Rinaldo and Bluhm 1956:173, 177, 179), consisting of recurved bowls with a fillet of corrugated coils below the rim and other forms in the western portions of the study area (McDonald Painted Corrugated; Martin et al. 1967) consisting of white designs painted over a brown or red-slipped corrugated surface.

Across the greater Cibola region as a whole, the period considered here was marked by an increase in the prevalence of both polychrome vessels and bowls specifically through time. By the late Pueblo III period, bowls often made up 80 percent or more of painted ceramic assemblages. Most of these bowls had bold designs on their exteriors, suggesting that potters were increasingly concerned with the visual communication potential of the vessels they produced (see discussion below). This increasing focus on the exterior of bowls was a trend seen across multiple wares and ceramic series produced in the Cibola region, as well as on vessels imported from other areas. Finally, as I demonstrate in more detail below, there was a marked diversification in the ceramics produced across the Cibola region as a whole associated with the Pueblo III to Pueblo IV transition as the western and eastern halves of the region diverged (see also Hegmon et al. 2016).

## CERAMICS AND VISUAL COMMUNICATION

Aspects of the decorative styles associated with painted ceramic vessels in the Cibola region may provide an indication of the scales at which potters and those who obtained pots chose to signal similarity and difference in the contexts of public gatherings where these vessels were used and exchanged. In order to link the production and use of painted vessels to the expression of categorical identities more directly, it is important to first demonstrate that these vessels were made with a concern for their visual communication potential. In this section, building on analyses previously presented by Mills (2007a), I demonstrate that the size and boldness of painted designs on the exteriors of polychrome bowls in the Cibola region changed through time in relation to changes in the size and configuration of public spaces. From this, I argue that patterns of similarity in these polychrome bowls can be used as a proxy for shared categorical expressions among the inhabitants of different portions of the Cibola region.

For a number of reasons, painted serving bowls produced and circulated across the Cibola region during the Pueblo III and Pueblo IV periods are particularly good candidates for objects that were used to actively express social distinctions among large groups of people. First, painted bowls in the greater

Cibola region, at least by the twelfth century, were most often produced with a red slip on both the interior and exterior surfaces, in contrast to the unslipped or white-slipped surfaces that were most common on other vessel forms. Red-slipped vessels in the northern Southwest are often larger, more widely circulated than other painted vessels, and also frequently associated with evidence for feasting and public food consumption at least as early as the ninth century A.D. (see Blinman 1989; Hegmon 1995; Mills 2007a, 2007b; Potter 2000). In addition, red-slipped bowls in the greater Cibola region during the twelfth and thirteenth centuries were among the first bowls produced in the northern Southwest with designs painted on both their exteriors and interiors (see also Carlson 1970; Mills 1999; Robinson 2005). Mills (2007a) notes that the increased focus on exterior designs would have meant that, even when full of food, the designs on these bowls would have been highly visible in public settings. The increased prevalence of exterior designs during the twelfth century and later was also associated with a period of aggregation across much of the greater Cibola region (see Chapter 3; see also Kintigh 1996), perhaps suggesting that this change in the use of different design fields was associated with a transition in the social context or scale of food consumption.[1]

As the structure of settlement changed across the Pueblo III to Pueblo IV transition, so too did the nature of the designs painted on the exteriors of serving bowls. Mills (2007a) has previously shown that the sizes and boldness of exterior designs of several ceramic types produced or used in the Silver Creek area varied in relation to changes in the size and organization of public spaces through time. Specifically, during the Pueblo III period, most settlements across the greater Cibola region consisted of closely spaced clusters of room blocks characterized by a high ratio of open space to total roofed area (Mills 2007a; Potter 1998). At this time, exterior designs on bowls were typically quite large, and designs were almost always banded around the entire circumference of the bowl, making them highly visible from a distance and from almost any angle. During the early Pueblo IV period, as nucleated settlements became increasingly common, the ratio of open space to total roofed area decreased markedly as enclosed plazas became the norm (Mills 2007a; Potter 1998; see also Chapter 8). This decrease in the ratio of open to roofed space and the enclosed nature of public spaces together suggest that the average distance between participants in public gatherings decreased (see also Chamberlin 2012). As Mills (2007a) notes, this change was associated with a decrease in the size of designs painted on the exterior of vessels, as well as an increase in the frequency of unit designs that could only be viewed from certain angles.[2] From this, Mills argues that the large polychrome serving bowls produced across the greater Cibola region during the period considered in this study were likely made with a fundamental concern for visual communication.

For the purposes of this study, I collected additional data on the size of vessels and exterior designs in order to determine whether the association between the size of open spaces and the size of designs identified by Mills (2007a) for wares found in the Silver Creek area also characterizes vessels produced and recovered across the Cibola region as a whole. Following methods described in detail by Mills (2007a:221–232), I measured the height of exterior designs, as well as total vessel height, for a number of whole or partial bowls recovered from sites across the Cibola region. I included all of Mills's original data and new measurements, focusing in particular on wares not included in her study: early Zuni Glaze Wares (Heshotauthla Polychrome and Kwakina Polychrome), Tularosa White-on-red, and McDonald Painted Corrugated.

As Figure 29a illustrates, with the increased sample size and the addition of these new wares and types, the pattern of decreasing design height across the Pueblo III to Pueblo IV transition is still quite pronounced. Importantly, this

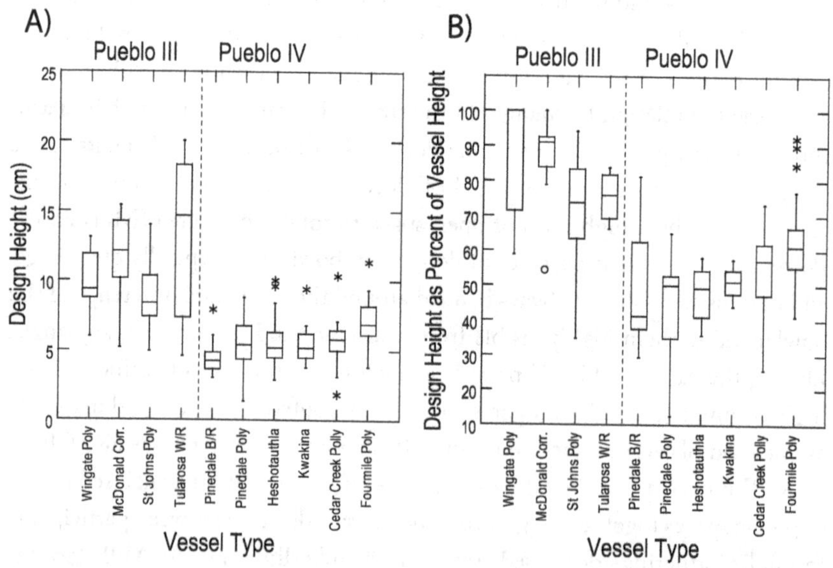


FIGURE 29. Boxplots of (A) design height in centimeters by type and (B) design height as percentage of vessel height by type.

pattern also holds when design heights are calculated as a percentage of total vessel height, demonstrating that this pattern is not the result of changes in vessel size (see Figure 29b). Together, the data presented here suggest that the red ware and polychrome serving bowls produced across the entire greater Cibola region during the Pueblo III and Pueblo IV periods were indeed produced with a fundamental concern for their visual communication potential. Thus, I argue that comparisons of the frequencies of different wares, as well as the designs on these vessels, can be used to explore patterns of shared expressions of categorical identities across the study area through time.

## CERAMIC WARE DISTRIBUTIONS AND CHANGING SCALES OF CATEGORICAL EXPRESSION

Following the patterns documented in the previous section, I argue that the relative proportions of different painted ceramic wares (in particular, red ware and polychrome ceramics) may reveal strong patterns of shared categorical identities across the study area through time. In this section, I present and describe the procedures used to produce maps showing the relative proportions of the most common polychrome ceramic wares during the Pueblo III and Pueblo IV periods, respectively. These maps demonstrate that there was a dramatic diversification of ceramics across the Pueblo III to Pueblo IV transition, as well as a major transition in the scale at which wares were shared among the inhabitants of different portions of the region.

In the analysis presented here, I focus exclusively on the painted red, orange, yellow, and polychrome wares (referred to simply as polychromes from here on out) produced and exchanged across the greater Cibola region. I do not include Cibola White Ware both because it was widely produced across almost the entire region and because frequencies of white ware declined through time across the region as a whole. Furthermore, unlike the white ware, polychromes are overwhelmingly bowls (>80 percent of vessels in many cases), usually with designs painted on their exteriors. Thus, the relative proportions of different polychrome wares, consisting primarily of bowls that were likely produced with a concern for visual communication, can be used as a proxy for patterns of active expressions of shared categorical commonality at a regional scale.

The ceramic ware proportions presented here were compiled for each time period by apportioning ceramics into the Pueblo III and Pueblo IV period using a procedure developed by John M. Roberts Jr. and colleagues (2012). For example, early Pueblo IV sites often have relatively high proportions of Early White Mountain Red Ware (St. Johns Polychrome and Springerville Polychrome) along with later Zuni Glaze Ware types. If Early White Mountain Red Ware types were included in the Pueblo IV period map, there would be substantial differences among Pueblo IV sites that are largely a product of time (i.e., sites initially constructed in the 1270s vs. the 1290s). The procedure for apportioning ceramics by period used here allows for comparisons of ceramic ware frequencies by period while limiting the effects of differences in occupation spans of sites within each period. This apportioning procedure has the effect of essentially discounting the relatively high diversity of ceramics across the Pueblo III to Pueblo IV transition (Hegmon et al. 2016) but makes these maps more useful for demonstrating major differences between the two periods.

## THE PUEBLO III PERIOD

Figure 30 shows redware and polychrome ware proportions for the Pueblo III period. As this map illustrates, most of the Cibola region was characterized by a single polychrome ware (Early White Mountain Red Ware). Beyond this, many areas where other wares are present are still dominated by Early White Mountain Red Ware. The exceptions to this broad pattern are found primarily along the southern and western edges of the study area. In the Mogollon Highlands, several sites have substantial amounts of Tularosa White-on-red. As described briefly above, Tularosa White-on-red is locally produced in the Mogollon Mountains (whereas Early White Mountain Red Ware is not) and is quite similar in design style to the imported types. To the west along the Arizona Mountains and the Silver Creek area, painted assemblages also include substantial amounts of Puerco Valley Red Ware and McDonald Painted Corrugated, both of which were likely locally produced. Like the Early White Mountain Red Ware types, McDonald Painted Corrugated is characterized by bold banded geometric designs in white on the exteriors of bowls.

In general, Figure 30 illustrates that polychrome ware distributions during the Pueblo III period were quite homogeneous. Almost the entire region was dominated by a single ware, and other wares show striking similarities in their application of geometric white designs to the exteriors of bowls. This suggests that the inhabitants of much of the greater Cibola region shared some common notion of categorical identity that was expressed in the context of public

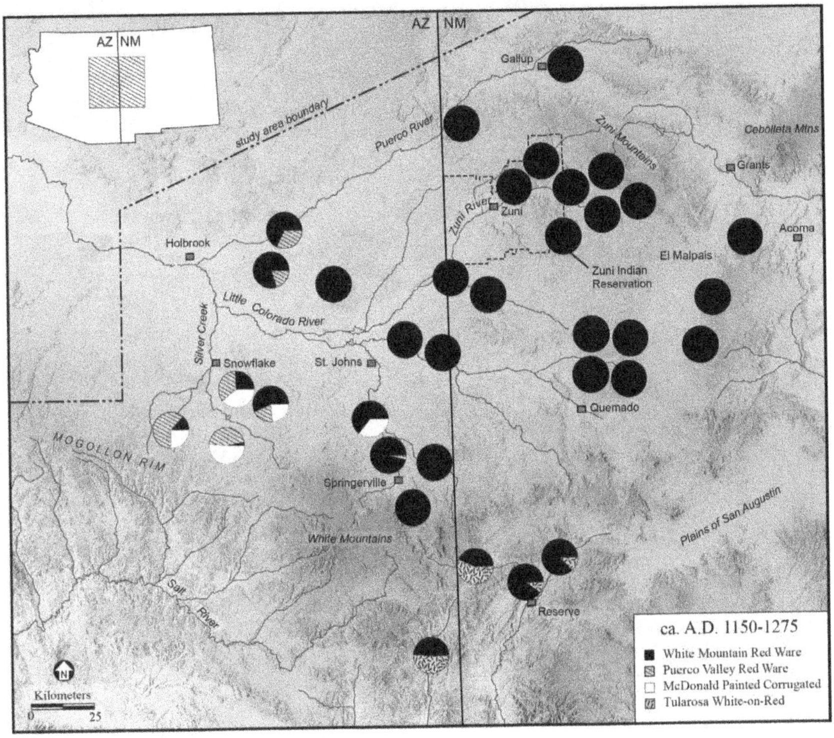


FIGURE 30. Distribution of polychrome ceramic wares for the Pueblo III period.

gatherings through the use of these similar ceramics. The application of bold white designs on the exterior of bowls used in public settings was a design convention that was likely similarly understood across the region as a whole. At the same time, the inhabitants of some areas along the edges of the Cibola region chose to produce their own visually distinct versions of vessels within this widespread design convention, perhaps suggesting the maintenance of social distinctions between the eastern and western Cibola regions at this time (see also Mills 2007b).

## THE PUEBLO IV PERIOD

Figure 31 shows the proportion of polychrome wares for the Pueblo IV period. At a glance, this map illustrates that patterns of shared ceramic wares differed markedly between the Pueblo III and Pueblo IV periods. Many more distinct

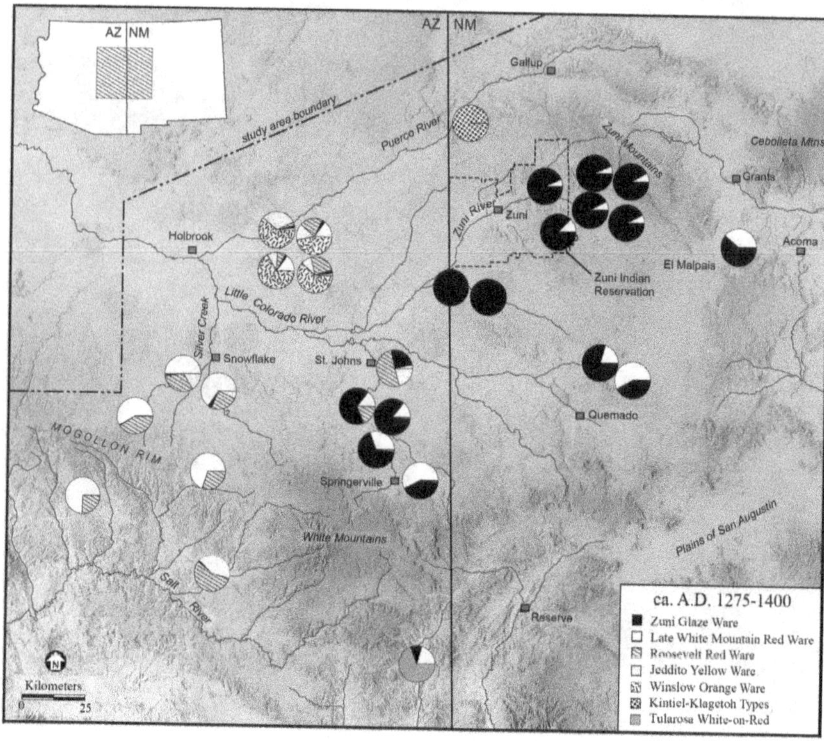


FIGURE 31. Distribution of polychrome ceramic wares for the Pueblo IV period.

wares were produced during the Pueblo IV period, and, as described earlier, the visual differences among these wares were considerably greater than during the Pueblo III period. Some areas that have traditionally been considered discrete settlement clusters are characterized by considerable ceramic ware diversity (e.g., the Upper Little Colorado, Silver Creek, and Arizona Mountains), whereas the central Zuni area (including the Pescado Basin, El Morro Valley, and West Zuni subregions) is quite homogeneous. This important point was first discussed in detail by Andrew Duff (2000, 2002), who argued that differences in ceramic diversity may have been driven in large part by demographic differences among settlement clusters across the Western Pueblo world. Duff drew on sociological theory focused on group size and interaction (e.g., Blau 1977) and argued that small populations tend to both allow and facilitate diverse interactions or expressions of identity, whereas larger social groups are typically more internally focused, often with restrictions on intergroup interactions and pressures to conform. As Duff (2000, 2002:80–84) demonstrates, the diversity of ceramic wares produced and obtained by the inhabitants of various portions of the Western Pueblo world is largely inversely related to the size of populations in those areas (see also Nelson et al. 2011). The relationship between population size and diversity is not necessarily simply a structural property of groups, however, as many areas with lower population densities were destinations for migrants across the Pueblo III to Pueblo IV transition (see Chapter 3). Thus, differences in the diversity of ceramic wares may suggest differences both in the diversity of categorical social identities expressed in the context of public gatherings and in the trajectories of population movement through time (see also Hegmon et al. 2016).

There is a strong east–west dichotomy in the distribution of ceramic wares across the study area. As noted above, sites in the Zuni area are dominated almost exclusively by Zuni Glaze Ware, with smaller amounts of Late White Mountain Red Ware (Pinedale Black-on-red and Polychrome). The Mariana Mesa and Cebolleta Mesa areas are characterized by the same two wares, but the total proportions of each ware varies considerably more, perhaps suggesting greater diversity in the expression of categorical identities in those areas. To the west along the Upper Little Colorado, there is even greater diversity. Sites in the central and northern portion of this subregion have substantial amounts of Roosevelt Red Ware and Jeddito Yellow Ware (probably not until after A.D. 1300, however) in addition to Zuni Glaze Ware and Late White Mountain Red Ware. With the exception of Jeddito Yellow Ware, all of these other wares were, at least in part, locally produced (see Duff 2002). This suggests that the Upper Little Colorado subregion was essentially the edge of the primary distribution of Zuni Glaze Ware, Roosevelt Red Ware, and Jeddito Yellow Ware. Notably, Zuni Glaze Ware is most common in the areas where Early White Mountain Red Ware was produced during the Pueblo III period.

Sites in the southern and western portions of the greater Cibola region along Silver Creek and in the Arizona Mountains are dominated almost exclusively by Roosevelt Red Ware and Late White Mountain Red Ware. This suggests that these areas were largely involved in a sphere of ceramic production and exchange distinct from the communities in the Zuni area (a suggestion further evidenced by patterns of ceramic circulation documented in Chapter 4). The dramatic differences in ware distributions further support the argument that there was a categorical distinction or social boundary between sites in the mountainous western Cibola region and the Zuni area to the east by the

Pueblo IV period. The few data available from the Mogollon Highlands area suggest that locally produced Tularosa White-on-red ceramics dominated early Pueblo IV period painted assemblages, perhaps suggesting an increasing local focus for the fourteenth-century inhabitants of this area or a lack of access to nonlocal ceramics. Along the Puerco of the West, the Petrified Forest area is dominated by varieties of Winslow Orange Ware pottery that were likely locally produced (Schachner et al. 2016) along with smaller amounts of all other common wares. Finally, the Kintiel and Manuelito Canyon areas are dominated almost exclusively by locally produced orange and yellow ware types that likely developed out of earlier White Mountain Red Ware varieties (Fowler et al. 1987; Hays-Gilpin and van Hartesveldt 1998).

Overall, the data presented here illustrate that the Pueblo III to Pueblo IV transition saw a massive diversification of ceramic wares across the Cibola region and an increasing localization of ceramic distinctions. This localization suggests that the spatial scale at which shared categorical identities were expressed through ceramics was dramatically reduced across the late thirteenth century. Most portions of the study area saw an increase in diversity at a local level across the Pueblo III to Pueblo IV transition. However, ceramics in the Zuni area and the El Morro Valley suggest that this portion of the study area remained both homogeneous and relatively discrete. It appears that by the early Pueblo IV period, the Zuni area resembled traditional anthropological notions of a well-bounded and discrete region characterized by a high degree of homogeneity, suggesting active efforts toward maintaining conformity.

## DESIGN STYLE AND SHARED CATEGORICAL IDENTITIES

In order to further explore the similarities and differences among painted vessels produced across the Cibola region, I compiled a large database of whole and partial vessel images both by photographing museum collections and by compiling other available published and unpublished photographs. Using this image database, I conducted two related analyses focused specifically on the designs painted on the exteriors of serving bowls. The first analysis consists of a quantitative comparison of common elements and design treatments found on Pueblo III period bowls recovered from sites throughout the core study area. The second analysis consists of a comparison of the nature and frequency of

TABLE 13. Whole and partial vessel photographs used in this study

| SITE/AREA | SUBREGION | EARLY WMRW | TULAROSA W/R | LATE WMRW | ZUNI GW | LOCATION / IMAGE SOURCE |
|---|---|---|---|---|---|---|
| Atsinna | EMV | | | 2 | 8 | ASU, ELMO |
| AZ W:10:50 (ASM) | AM | | | 13 | 2 | ASM |
| Casa Malpais | ULC | | | 3 | 1 | CMAP |
| Cienega | EMV | 3 | | | 3 | ASU |
| Cosper Cliff Dwelling | MH | | 1 | | | CFM |
| Coyote Creek | ULC | 9 | | 2 | | MNA |
| Foote Canyon | MH | 6 | 10 | 3 | | CFM |
| Fourmile Ruin | SC | | | 16 | | SMTH |
| Grasshopper Pueblo | AM | | | 27 | | GH |
| Greenwood Pueblo | ULC | 2 | | 1 | 1 | Kintigh unpublished photos 1996 |
| Greer, AZ | ULC | 1 | | | | Carlson 1970 |
| Halona:wa | ZUNI | | | | 12 | PMAA |
| Heshotauthla | PB | | | | 4 | PMAA |
| Higgins Flat | MH | 2 | 3 | | | CFM |
| Hooper Ranch | ULC | 3 | | 2 | | CFM |
| Horse Camp Mill | MM | 14 | | 1 | | PMAA |
| Kinishba | AM | | | 4 | 1 | ASM |
| Los Gigantes | EMV | 2 | | | | ASU |
| Mirabal | EMV | 9 | | | 2 | ASU |
| Nutria Road Sites | PB | 4 | | | | Zier 1976 |
| Ojo Bonito | WZ | | | | 2 | CFM |
| Ojo Caliente, NM | WZ | | | | 3 | CFM |

(*continued*)

TABLE 13. (continued)

| SITE/AREA | SUBREGION | EARLY WMRW | TULAROSA W/R | LATE WMRW | ZUNI GW | LOCATION / IMAGE SOURCE |
|---|---|---|---|---|---|---|
| Pinedale Ruin | SC | | | 3 | | SMTH |
| Pueblo de los Muertos | EMV | | | 2 | 26 | ASU |
| Rattlesnake Point | ULC | | | | 2 | ASU |
| Rudd Creek Pueblo | ULC | | | | 2 | ASU |
| Scribe S Pueblo | EMV | 22 | | | | ASU |
| Springerville, AZ | ULC | 2 | | | | Carlson 1970 |
| St. Johns 11:1 | ULC | 7 | | | | Carlson 1970 |
| St. Johns 12:1 | ULC | 1 | | | | Carlson 1970 |
| St. Johns 16:15 | ULC | 1 | | | | Carlson 1970 |
| St. Johns 16:5 | ULC | 2 | | | | Carlson 1970 |
| St. Johns 4:1 | WZ | 14 | | | | Carlson 1970 |
| St. Johns 6:1 | ULC | 1 | | | | Carlson 1970 |
| St. Johns 7:2 | CW | 7 | | | | Carlson 1970 |
| Techado Spring | MM | 19 | | 8 | 3 | TCAS |
| Tinaja | EMV | 1 | | | | ASU |
| UG481 | MM | 2 | | | | PMAA |
| Other/Unprovenienced | N/A | 28 | | 113 | 7 | multiple |
| ***TOTAL (N = 455)*** | | ***162*** | ***14*** | ***200*** | ***79*** | |

*Note*: AM = Arizona Mountains, CW = Carrizo Wash, EMV = El Morro Valley, MH = Mogollon Highlands, MM = Mariana Mesa, PB = Pescado Basin, SC = Silver Creek, ULC = Upper Little Colorado, WZ = West Zuni, ZUNI = Zuni Pueblo.

repeated design configurations found on the exteriors of early Pueblo IV period Zuni Glaze Ware and Late White Mountain Red Ware bowls. As will become apparent in the discussion below, Pueblo III and Pueblo IV period types were analyzed using different methods because they differed so greatly that they confounded efforts to place them within a single analytical scheme.

## DESIGN ELEMENT ANALYSIS

During the Pueblo III period, ceramic ware distributions were quite homogeneous across the study area. The purpose of the element analysis presented here is to further characterize patterns of shared categorical expression by determining to what degree specific designs or design applications may have varied on vessels of the same ware recovered from different portions of the Cibola region. The majority of previous stylistic analyses in the study area have focused on jars or the interior painted designs on bowls (e.g., Carlson 1970; Kintigh 1985b; LeBlanc 1975; but see Kelly 2006). In this study, I follow work by Summer Moore (2006) to conduct a hierarchical analysis of the simple exterior design elements found on Early White Mountain Red Ware bowls. This hierarchical approach is used to independently explore similarities and differences in primary design elements, secondary appended elements, and specific design treatments such as fills and line interactions (see also Friedrich 1970; Hegmon 1995; Plog 1980). My expectation is that, if the producers of Early White Mountain Red Ware vessels across different portions of the Cibola region shared common categorical identities, there should be a high degree of similarity in the specific decorative elements and design treatments considered here.

The first step in this analysis was to identify primary design elements that commonly occurred on the exteriors of bowls across the entire sample. In order to do this, my research assistant Garrett Trask and I independently sorted images into major design categories. Our initial groupings overlapped considerably and suggested that nine common design elements accounted for the vast majority of exterior painted designs within the image corpus. Each of these nine elements occurred more than six times across all recorded vessels. Eight of the nine common primary elements also coincided with those identified by Moore (2006) in her more detailed study of Early White Mountain Red Ware vessels from the Pettit site in the El Morro Valley, further verifying our identifications.

After primary elements were identified, each vessel photo was coded for as many variables as was possible. Primary elements were coded as one of the nine major categories described above or as "other" and described in the notes. Next, the specific details of primary elements were further characterized by coding the type of fill used for closed polygons and by noting the type of interaction between design elements. In a few cases, where primary design elements were elaborated with additional features either appended to the primary designs or placed within them, these features were coded as secondary elements. Finally, designs were characterized by documenting whether they occurred as an isolated unit or in a continuous band around each vessel and by noting the presence or absence of bounding lines around the painted design. Table 14 and Figure 32 provide examples used to code each of these variables.

In order to determine whether there were significant differences among the Early White Mountain Red Ware vessels recovered from different portions of the study area, I conducted a series of $X^2$ tests for each of the variables described above. However, because sample sizes for some subregions are small, it was necessary to combine samples from adjacent areas. In the analyses below, vessels from the Carrizo Wash and West Zuni area were considered together, as

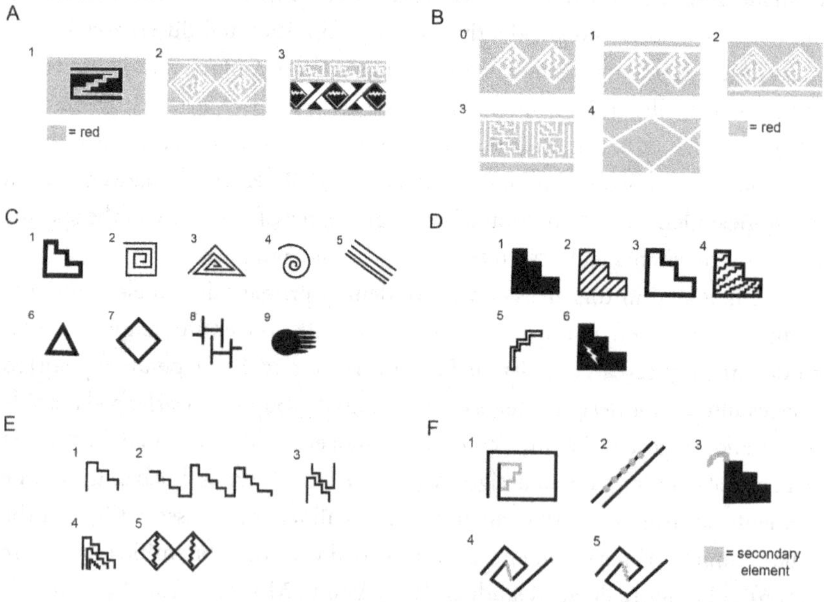


FIGURE 32. Coding examples for (A) design placement, (B) bounding lines, (C) primary design elements, (D) element fill, (E) element interaction, and (F) secondary design elements.

TABLE 14. Variables and codes used in design element analysis

| VESSEL LEVEL DESIGNATIONS | | | |
|---|---|---|---|
| | | DESIGN PLACEMENT | BOUNDING LINES |
| EXTERIOR COLOR | INTERIOR COLOR | FIGURE 32A | FIGURE 32B |
| 1. White–on-red | 1. White–on-red | 1. unit | 0. none |
| 2. Black-on-red | 2. Black-on-red | 2. single band | 1. top only |
| 3. White and black-on-red | 3. White and black-on-red | 3. multilevel band | 2. bottom only |
| 4. Black with white outlines | 4. Black with white outlines | 99. other | 3. top/bottom |
| 5. White with black outlines | 5. White with black outlines | | 4. sectioned |
| 6. Black-on-white-on-red (white band over red with black paint on top) | 6. Black-on-white-on-red (white band over red with black paint on top) | | 99. other |
| 7. B/W | 7. B/W | | |
| 99. other | 99. other | | |

| ELEMENT LEVEL DESIGNATIONS | | | |
|---|---|---|---|
| PRIMARY ELEMENT | ELEMENT FILL | ELEMENT INTERACTION | SECONDARY ELEMENT |
| FIGURE 32C | FIGURE 32D | FIGURE 32E | FIGURE 32F |
| 1. terrace/step | 1. solid | 1. isolated | 1. terrace/step |
| 2. rectangular scroll | 2. hatched | 2. running | 2. dots |
| 3. triangular scroll | 3. hollow | 3. interlocking | 3. hook |
| 4. circular scroll | 4. corbelled | 4. nested | 4. linking line |
| 5. simple lines | 5. line outlined | 5. attached | 5. linking corbel |
| 6. triangle/zigzag | 6. complex | 99. other | 99. other |
| 7. rectangular/diamond | 99. other | | |
| 8. interlocking bracket | | | |
| 9. hand/paw | | | |

were vessels from the El Morro Valley and Pescado Basin. These groupings are warranted because of the similarities in the proportions of different production sources in these sets of subregions (see Chapter 4). Beyond this, as many of the tables were relatively sparse (many cells <5), probabilities associated with the $X^2$ tests were simulated rather than calculated based on the $X^2$ distribution. Specifically, each table was randomized 10,000,000 times, and the $X^2$ statistic was calculated for each random table. Probabilities were estimated as the proportion of randomized $X^2$ values greater than or equal to the actual $X^2$ statistic. This is a common approach for such sparse tables and produces more reliable estimates of probability.

As Table 15 illustrates, there are no statistically significant differences ($\alpha$ = 0.05) by region of recovery for the coded Early White Mountain Red Ware bowls in terms of primary design elements, primary element fills, primary element interactions, or design placement, indicating that the designs painted on vessels produced and circulated across different portions of the study area were broadly similar. Put another way, the lack of statistically significant differences for these variables suggests that Early White Mountain Red Ware vessels recovered across the Cibola region were painted by people drawing on the same basic repertoire of elements, perhaps suggesting that they were expressing similar categorical identities. Interestingly, additional analyses not described in detail here further suggest that even distinct ceramic wares (including Tularosa White-on-red) were also painted using the same basic set of simple geometric elements and layouts (Peeples 2011:299). Significant differences by region were observed, however, in terms of the secondary elements and the presence or absence of bounding lines. These differences suggest that the elaboration of designs and aspects of execution did differ somewhat across the study area.

A more detailed consideration of secondary elements and bounding lines further suggests that the differences observed here were most pronounced between the Upper Little Colorado and other regions. As Table 15 shows, the diversity of secondary elements is greater, and designs lacking bounding lines are more common for vessels from both the Upper Little Colorado and, to a lesser extent, the Mogollon Highlands (where these ceramics were imported largely from the Upper Little Colorado; see Chapter 4) than other regions to the north and east. Interestingly, as the NAA study presented in Chapter 4 illustrates, the Upper Little Colorado area was largely separate from the sphere of ceramic circulation characterizing much of the Cibola region during the Pueblo III period, perhaps suggesting that direct interaction with potters to

TABLE 15. $X^2$ tables and associated probabilities for each of the five measured variables

| | EMV/PB | CW/WZ | MM | ULC | MH |
|---|---|---|---|---|---|
| Primary Element | | | | | |
| Circular scroll | 3 | 3 | 1 | 0 | 1 |
| Hand | 1 | 2 | 2 | 1 | 1 |
| Interlocking brackets | 0 | 1 | 1 | 2 | 1 |
| Lines | 2 | 3 | 2 | 0 | 0 |
| Diamond/rectangle | 1 | 0 | 7 | 1 | 0 |
| Rectangular scroll | 12 | 6 | 12 | 12 | 0 |
| Step/terrace | 13 | 4 | 12 | 5 | 5 |
| Triangle/zigzag | 8 | 4 | 7 | 4 | 1 |
| Triangular scroll | 5 | 0 | 2 | 2 | 1 |
| $X^2 = 40.0994$ | $p = 0.1518$ | | | | |
| Element Fill | | | | | |
| Solid | 2 | 2 | 1 | 2 | 1 |
| Hatched | 1 | 0 | 0 | 0 | 0 |
| Hollow | 18 | 8 | 17 | 10 | 6 |
| Corbelled | 3 | 0 | 2 | 1 | 0 |
| Line outlined | 1 | 0 | 0 | 1 | 0 |
| Complex | 0 | 0 | 3 | 0 | 0 |
| $X^2 = 16.2253$ | $p = 0.7301$ | | | | |
| Element Interaction | | | | | |
| Isolated | 6 | 6 | 13 | 6 | 4 |
| Running | 1 | 3 | 4 | 5 | 2 |
| Interlocking | 14 | 7 | 14 | 13 | 1 |
| Nested | 9 | 3 | 5 | 2 | 1 |
| Attached | 7 | 3 | 2 | 1 | 0 |
| $X^2 = 20.9792$ | $p = 0.1874$ | | | | |
| Secondary Element | | | | | |
| Step/terrace | 12 | 4 | 7 | 8 | 1 |
| Dots | 0 | 0 | 1 | 1 | 0 |
| Hook | 0 | 0 | 0 | 4 | 2 |
| Linking line | 0 | 2 | 2 | 1 | 0 |
| Linking corbel | 4 | 0 | 1 | 4 | 0 |
| $X^2 = 27.3277$ | $p = 0.03840$ | | | | |
| Design Placement | | | | | |
| Band | 34 | 19 | 25 | 23 | 6 |
| Unit | 2 | 2 | 8 | 5 | 2 |
| $X^2 = 6.0034$ | $p = 0.1961$ | | | | |
| Bounding Lines | | | | | |
| Absent | 16 | 11 | 16 | 22 | 5 |
| Present | 20 | 8 | 17 | 5 | 2 |
| $X^2 = 10.5109$ | $p = 0.03198$ | | | | |

*Note*: Statistically significant probabilities are highlighted.

the east was somewhat limited. Thus, although potters across the Cibola region apparently drew on a common suite of decorative elements, suggesting some level of shared categorical identity, differences in the details of execution suggest that the learning frameworks of potters were somewhat more local in nature.

## IDENTIFYING REPEATING DESIGN CONFIGURATIONS

The Pueblo III to Pueblo IV transition saw a major change in the ceramic designs that individuals chose to paint on vessels in the Cibola region. The simple geometric exterior designs of Early White Mountain Red Ware bowls and similar types were replaced by complex unit designs on Late White Mountain Red Ware vessels, and although geometric figures were still common, designs on Zuni Glaze Ware bowls were considerably more discrete and complex. After numerous attempts to code exterior designs on these Pueblo IV period ceramics within the same design element analysis described above, I concluded that the differences were too great to produce meaningful results. Thus, I conducted a separate analysis focused instead on identifying the frequency with which repeated design configurations appeared on these Pueblo IV bowls in order to characterize similarities and differences across the study area. The analysis presented below reveals that the scale at which common design configurations were shared varied considerably between Zuni Glaze Ware and Late White Mountain Red Ware bowls. These differences suggest that the scales at which strong categorical identities were shared and expressed likely also differed between areas dominated by each of these wares.

The analysis presented in this section, which Garrett Trask and I (2011) previously presented, is modeled after a similar study conducted by Steven LeBlanc and Lucia Henderson (2009) focused on characterizing exterior designs on Jeddito Yellow Ware vessels. In their study, LeBlanc and Henderson note that certain iconic designs painted on the exteriors of Jeddito bowls appear on multiple vessels, perhaps suggesting that these designs were used to signal aspects of social identity to those who viewed them. Through a detailed analysis of the specific attributes of these exterior designs and details of their execution, the authors convincingly argue that the complex repeated designs in Jeddito Yellow Ware may have been used as signatures, marking the work of specific artists or groups of artists. They also identified some groups of designs that were generally similar but that varied substantially in detail and in quality of execution. LeBlanc and Henderson (2009:36) define these groups of vessels as "loose sets"

FIGURE 33. Examples of one design set defined by LeBlanc and Henderson in their study of Jeddito Yellow Ware bowls (drawn based on LeBlanc and Henderson 2009:Figure 4.1).

and suggest that such similarities may indicate attempts by artists to signal membership in somewhat broader social groups. They also note the similarities between exterior designs on Jeddito vessels and those produced in the Cibola region and suggest that a consideration of repeated design configurations may produce similar results (Leblanc and Henderson 2009:21–23).

In this study, I employed the heuristics for identifying and verifying repeating design sets described by LeBlanc and Henderson (2009:25–33) to analyze a sample of Zuni Glaze Ware (Heshotauthla and Kwakina Polychrome) and Late White Mountain Red Ware (Pinedale Black-on-red and Pinedale Polychrome) bowls. The creation of design sets through this analysis was an iterative process. All provenience information was stripped from the whole vessel photographs, and they were sorted independently by me and by Garrett Trask. We first attempted to identify vessels that shared designs representing the level of similarity in details noted in the Jeddito Yellow Ware study. We also placed groups of vessels in what we called "design families" when designs were generally similar but differed substantially in detail and execution. These design families are similar to the "loose sets" described above but allow for somewhat more variation. We then compared groups created by both analysts. We considered the strongest design groupings to be those identified by both analysts

FIGURE 34. Examples of design families found on Zuni Glaze Ware bowls.

independently. Remaining unassigned vessels were then reevaluated in relation to the groups created by both analysts until relatively discrete groupings had been established.

The analyses described above did not reveal many "tight sets" of exterior designs that were as discrete or had so little variation in detail as those identified by LeBlanc and Henderson (2009). The sample considered in this analysis was considerably smaller than that used by LeBlanc and Henderson, so it is certainly possible that tight sets of designs would be present in a larger image corpus.

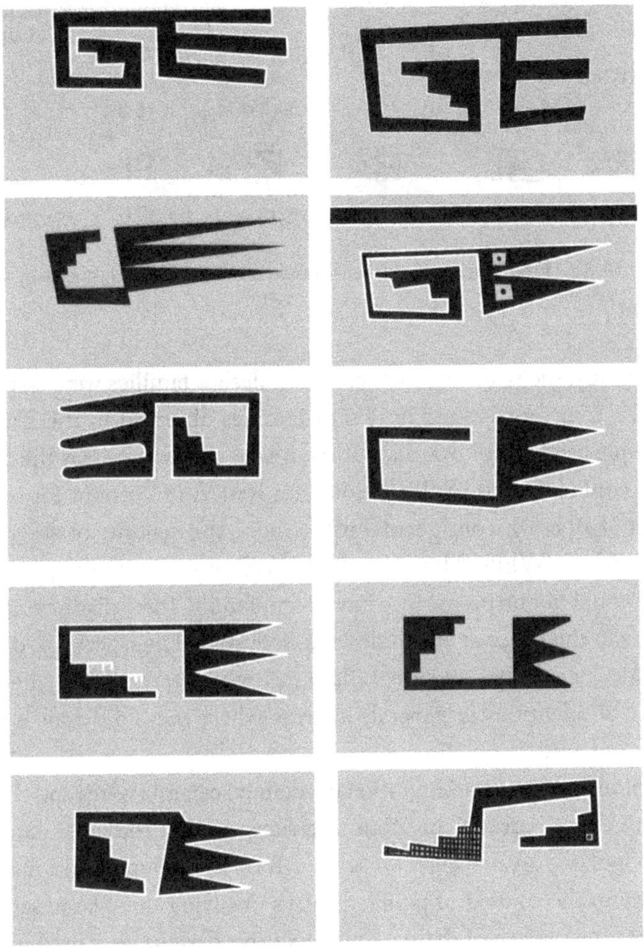

FIGURE 35. Examples of the most common design family found on Late White Mountain Red Ware (Pinedale Polychrome) bowls.

It is very likely, however, that strong design sets are much less common in the Cibola region, as nearly half of the Jeddito Yellow Ware bowls could be placed in a design set (LeBlanc and Henderson 2009:32). We were able to identify several design families. These design families likely do not represent the work of a single artist group and instead suggest common adherence to broadly shared conventions of design, perhaps further suggesting efforts at signaling shared categorical identities.

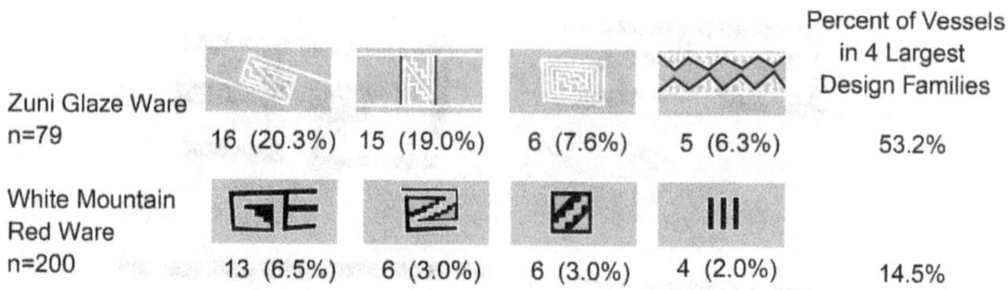


FIGURE 36. Frequencies of the four most common design families by ware.

Importantly, the scale at which common design families were shared varies widely. The four most common design families observed in the Zuni Glaze Ware sample account for over half of the image corpus, whereas the four most common families in Late White Mountain Red Ware account for only about 14 percent of all bowls considered. Furthermore, the majority of designs on the exteriors of Late White Mountain Red Ware vessels were unique (68.5 percent) and could not be placed into any design family. These distinctions suggest differences in the scales at which designs were shared and, perhaps, differences in the scales at which categorical identities were expressed (or the strength of categorical identities in general) in areas where these different wares were produced and used.

The homogeneity of both traditionally defined ceramic wares and the designs painted on those wares in the Zuni area suggests that the inhabitants of this densely populated area engaged in active efforts at producing and maintaining conformity in the context of public displays involving these large serving vessels. Interestingly, some of these highly repetitive designs were used in multiple media like wall carvings and murals (e.g., Woodbury and Woodbury 1956) and may fit the definition of "pervasive styles" described by Warren DeBoer (1991). Conformity in the realm of designs found on vessels that were used in public events may have helped to promote cooperation among the formerly distinct groups that came together to build the large towns in the Zuni area across the Pueblo III to Pueblo IV transition (sensu Kohler et al. 2004). In contrast, the diversity of designs on Late White Mountain Redware vessels may reflect the diverse origins of the small social groups that gradually consolidated to form the large villages in the western portion of the Cibola region.

Spielmann (2004) has previously noted an even broader division between Pueblo IV village clusters characterized by considerable diversity (emergent clusters) and those marked by homogeneity in material culture (integrated clusters) across the entire Southwest. Spielmann argues that the inhabitants of emergent village clusters often chose to signal certain aspects of social coherence but also maintained and expressed distinctions likely tied to their diverse histories and past affiliations. This pattern fits well with the ware distribution and stylistic information from the western and southern Cibola region described here. Within integrated clusters, like the Zuni area, the historical processes leading up to aggregation and nucleation often had a longer history locally (see also Huntley and Kintigh 2004). Material differences are often muted within integrated settlement clusters, perhaps suggesting a more coherent sense of shared (categorical) identity at the level of the settlement cluster.

## CERAMIC DESIGN AND CATEGORICAL IDENTITIES

The analyses presented above illustrate through several lines of evidence that patterns of similarity in painted ceramic vessels in the Cibola region can be used to characterize patterns of shared categorical identities at a regional scale. The size and boldness of designs painted on the exteriors of bowls varied in relation to the size and configuration of public spaces through time (see also Mills 2007a). This suggests that polychrome bowls across the Cibola region were produced with a concern for their visual communication potential. This can further be used to argue that these polychrome vessels were likely vehicles for the active expression of categorical identities in the context of public gatherings where they were used and exchanged (see Chapter 4).

In general, during the Pueblo III period, painted ceramic ware distributions were relatively homogeneous across the Cibola region. In the few areas along the southern and western edges of the study area where frequencies of wares varied somewhat, locally produced wares incorporated design configurations similar to those found on vessels produced in the central Cibola region, including bold geometric white-lined designs painted on a red-slipped surface. Furthermore, the specific design elements painted on the exteriors of bowls recovered from settlements located across the study area were also quite homogeneous, though differing in some details of execution. Together, the data presented above suggest that during the Pueblo III period highly visible conventions of design used on painted ceramics were broadly shared across most of the Cibola region. This suggests that the inhabitants of the entire region likely also shared some level of categorical identity that was regularly and publicly expressed through events involving painted ceramics. Importantly, the broad similarities and shared categorical expressions noted above spanned multiple distinct wares and even areas characterized by distinct spheres of ceramic circulation.

Patterns of similarity in ceramic designs changed quite dramatically across the Pueblo III to Pueblo IV transition. There was a massive diversification of ceramic wares in the last quarter of the thirteenth century along with an increasing localization of specific wares. Local diversity increased quite markedly in many portions of the Cibola region (see also Hegmon et al. 2016). At the same time, within the Zuni area (including the West Zuni, Pescado Basin, and El Morro Valley subregions), a strong pattern of homogeneity in ceramic wares persisted. This homogeneity was even more pronounced than in earlier periods, as the designs painted on the exteriors of Zuni Glaze Ware bowls were extremely repetitive and even appeared on multiple media. The data presented above suggest that the spatial scale (and presumably social scale) at which shared categorical identities were expressed declined across the Pueblo III to Pueblo IV transition. Within the Zuni area, people chose to express increasingly homogeneous identities in public settings, suggesting a strengthening or consolidation of categorical identities across the late thirteenth-century social transformation. In the areas to the west and south, such expressions were considerably more diverse, likely reflecting the diverse histories and past affiliations of the inhabitants of those areas.

# 8

# PUBLIC ARCHITECTURE AND PUBLIC EXPRESSIONS OF CATEGORICAL IDENTITY

PUBLIC ARCHITECTURE is defined here as highly visible built spaces with evidence for use by large numbers of individuals simultaneously. Public structures provide formal spaces for individuals to interact with those outside of their own kin or residential groups. Cross-culturally, the largest forms of architecture are often associated with public ritual or other specialized community-level activities (Adler 1989; Adler and Wilshusen 1990; Hegmon 1989:7–9; Rapoport 1982:29–30). As gathering places or focal points, public spaces are contexts where social norms and ideologies can continually be reinforced or contested. Such structures often become powerful symbols of interaction and interdependence among segments of a society (Hegmon 1989; Lipe and Hegmon 1989; Low 1996; Varien 1999:22–23). Thus, public architecture can often be conceptualized as both a venue for interaction at a large social scale and a symbol of the shared traditions that are enacted in those spaces.

I argue that communities with similar public structures were likely engaged in similar, perhaps overlapping, spheres of public ceremonialism (see also Adams 1991; Herr 2001:30–31). Furthermore, the scale of these spaces in the Cibola region suggests that public architectural features may have provided formal contexts for the active expression of identities in gatherings above the scale of coresiding units (e.g., Kintigh et al. 1996; Mills 2007a; Potter 2000). In the context of such gatherings, public buildings may have served as important "mnemonics" for shared membership in social groups and social expectations among participants with diverse origins (Hegmon 1989:7; see also Kus 1982:54). In this vein, patterns of shared public architectural features can be interpreted as one indication of shared categorical identities among the inhabitants of communities across the Cibola region.

## FORMS OF PUBLIC ARCHITECTURE IN THE CIBOLA REGION

There are a variety of common architectural features in the Cibola region that fit the broad definition of public architecture provided above, often with multiple types constructed at single settlements. Unfortunately, not all forms of public architectural spaces can be easily characterized without extensive excavation or documentation. The approach I take in this chapter is to concentrate primarily on the dimensions of variation in public structures that can be compared based largely on surface remains. Specifically, I focus on three types of features found across the Cibola region ca. A.D. 1000–1400: great kivas, great houses, and plazas. Following this, I provide a brief discussion of the limited evidence available for other public architectural features. The period considered in this chapter begins more than a century earlier and extends later in time than the interval considered in the bulk of this book. This is because many of the strongest patterns in the distribution of public architectural spaces were in place at least by the eleventh century and continued to structure regional patterns throughout the prehispanic period.

### GREAT KIVAS

Although the label "great kiva" has been applied to a wide variety of structures at different times in different places across the Southwest (see Anyon and LeBlanc 1980; Haury 1985; Herr 1994; Martin et al. 1964:55–58; Roberts 1929:73–81; Vivian and Reiter 1960), the term is usually reserved for large subterranean or semisubterranean structures that include a specific set of internal features and are inferred to have served a ritual purpose. The earliest structures traditionally accepted as great kivas date to about A.D. 300 (Martin et al. 1957:200–203; Roberts 1929; Vivian 1990; Wheat 1955). These early great kivas resemble contemporaneous residential pithouses, but they are larger and have formal features not typically found in habitation structures. Great kivas increase in formality

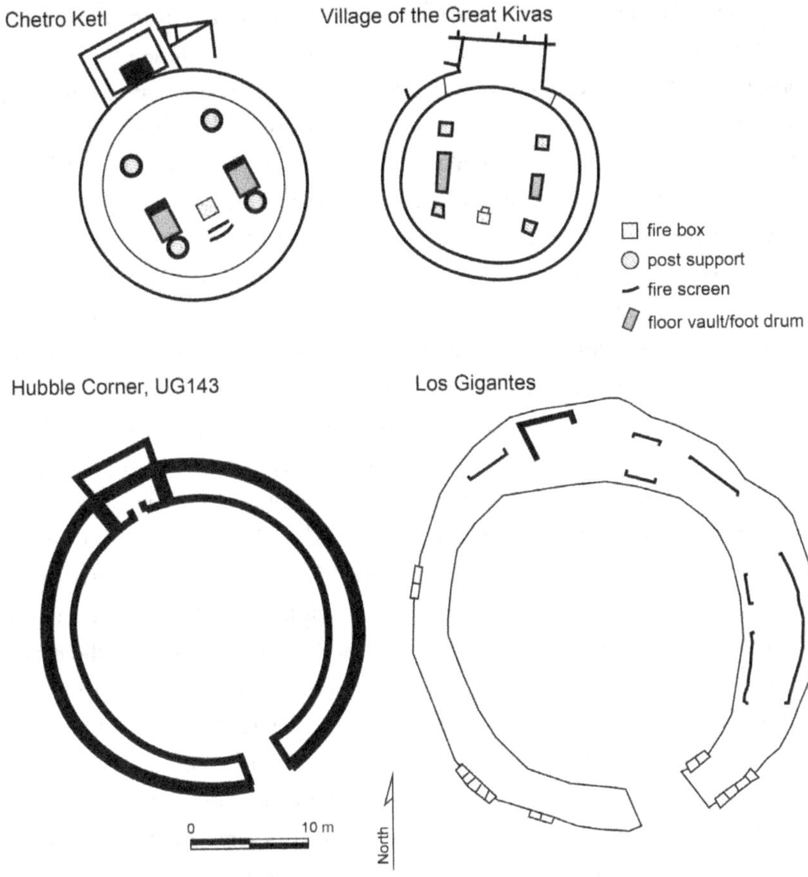


FIGURE 37. Examples of Chacoan era circular great kivas from Chaco Canyon (*top left*) and the Cibola region (*top right*) and post-Chacoan unroofed oversized great kivas from the Cibola region (*bottom row*).

and frequency through time, peaking between about A.D. 900 and 1200 (Herr 1994). The specific forms of great kivas vary at a regional scale in ways that are often identifiable based on surface remains alone.

Great kivas on the Colorado Plateau are typically circular in plan. The earliest examples are little more than oversized pithouses with earthen walls and relatively little internal embellishment. Beginning in the tenth century and escalating dramatically by the mid-eleventh century, a number of highly elaborate masonry great kivas were constructed in Chaco Canyon in the central San

Juan Basin (Van Dyke 2007:94–95). These structures range from 12 to about 22 meters in diameter and have intramural features that include massive roof support posts, formal hearth complexes, benches lining the walls, antechambers, and floor vaults that may have been used as foot drums (Lekson 2007:20–21; Van Dyke 2007; Vivian and Reiter 1960). Chacoan-style masonry great kivas were also constructed across many portions of the Cibola region at this time (Roberts 1932). Not all circular great kivas share all of the formal features of the Chacoan great kivas, but Sarah Herr (2001:30–33) argues that after the fluorescence of great kiva construction in Chaco Canyon, circular great kivas of varying degrees of formality were likely symbolically associated with Chacoan developments (see also Fowler et al. 1987:72–74; Haury 1985:386–388).

In the Cibola region there is another class of feature typically called oversized unroofed great kivas. These structures range from 25 to 35 meters in diameter and consist of an outer wall and a lower bench or inner wall, usually without any permanent internal features (Fowler et al. 1987; Kintigh et al. 1996; McGimsey 1980; Schachner 2007). Large unroofed great kivas are often associated with thirteenth-century post-Chacoan great house complexes or other post-Chacoan era communities. Unroofed great kivas are also found near some of the earliest and largest nucleated pueblos in the Zuni and El Morro Valley areas but were likely no longer constructed after the mid-thirteenth century (Duff and Schachner 2007). Oversized great kivas have been interpreted as late manifestations of Chacoan-style great kiva architecture in the Cibola region (Fowler et al. 1987:86–87). Interestingly, however, as these structures are unroofed, they may have been designed to be more inclusive than earlier roofed Chacoan era structures. Kintigh and colleagues (1996; Kintigh 1994) argue that the increased size and openness of these structures suggest that the scale of participation in communal ritual may have expanded somewhat during the Pueblo III period.

In contrast to the circular Chacoan-style great kivas found across a large portion of the Colorado Plateau, in the mountainous areas to the south, great kivas were usually square or rectangular in form during the period considered here (Hough 1907; Martin et al. 1956; Olson 1960; Rinaldo 1962; Zamora and Oakes 1999; see also Dungan 2015).[1] They typically consist of large semisubterranean masonry- or earthen-walled structures with a ramp entryway facing east or southeast, a small informal fire pit, post roof supports, floor grooves that may have been similar to Chacoan floor vaults, and masonry-lined benches in many later examples. These rectangular structures have many features in common with large Three Circle phase (post–A.D. 900) masonry-lined pithouses of the

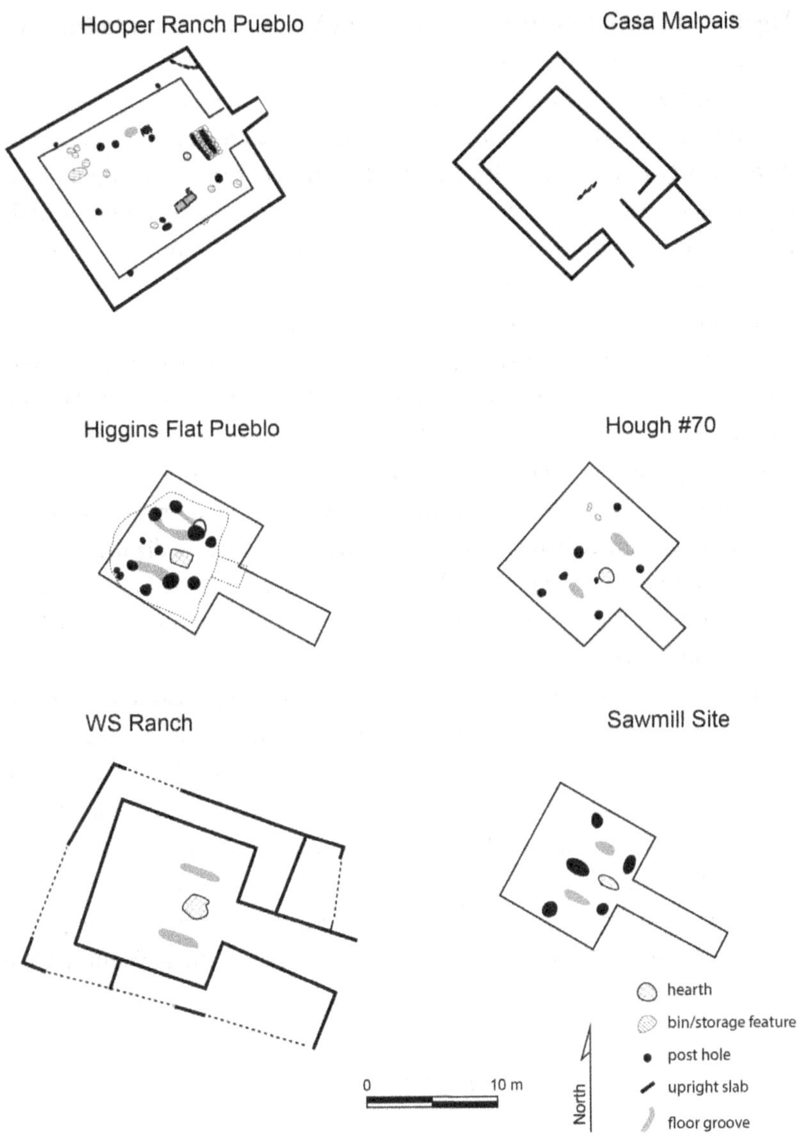


FIGURE 38. Examples of rectangular great kivas from the Upper Little Colorado (*top row*) and Mogollon Highlands (*bottom two rows*).

Mogollon Highlands and the Mimbres areas (Anyon and LeBlanc 1980; Bluhm 1957:25–27; Danson 1957:81–82).

During the tenth through twelfth century, rectangular great kivas were typically separate structures located near large pueblos or clusters of small settlements (Bluhm 1957; Olson 1960). In later centuries, rectangular great kivas were sometimes attached to masonry pueblos (e.g., Danson and Malde 1950; DeGarmo 1975; Dungan 2015; Martin et al. 1962), and some of the latest examples consist of plaza spaces converted into roofed great kivas (e.g., Riggs 2001:107–111). These plaza features are perhaps the latest great kivas constructed in the greater Cibola region (ca. A.D. 1325) and may have continued to be used throughout the fourteenth century (Riggs 2005:338–340). Although there are obvious formal similarities between circular Chacoan great kivas and rectangular great kivas (i.e., benches, overall size, floor grooves, etc.), due to the long-term persistence of their shape, entryway orientation, and distinctive floor features, many researchers see rectangular great kivas as distinct architectural developments related to a different ceremonial tradition (see discussions in Gregory and Wilcox 2007; Haury 1985:47–52; Oakes 1999; Olson 1960; Riggs 2005; Rinaldo 1964).

The long-term maintenance of distinct traditions of great kiva form and construction described above suggests that these circular and rectangular structures were used in different kinds of public ritual activities (Gregory and Wilcox 2007; Herr 2001; Whittlesey 2010). Thus, the distribution of circular and rectangular great kivas across the Cibola region may provide one indication of patterns of shared ritual expression, or categorical identities, at a broad social scale. As the distributions of various forms of great kivas across the region are closely tied to the distribution of great house architecture, these features will be discussed together in a subsequent section.

## GREAT HOUSES

Great houses are prominent and massively constructed pueblos showing strong similarities to the large structures built in Chaco Canyon between the late A.D. 800s and the early 1100s. Great houses are characterized by the presence of some number of a set of distinctive architectural features, including core and veneer masonry walls, blocked-in kivas, oversized rooms, multistory construction / massive single-story construction, or distinctive architectural layouts (Fowler and Stein 1992; Kantner and Kintigh 2006:155; Lekson 1991:31–36; Lekson 2007;

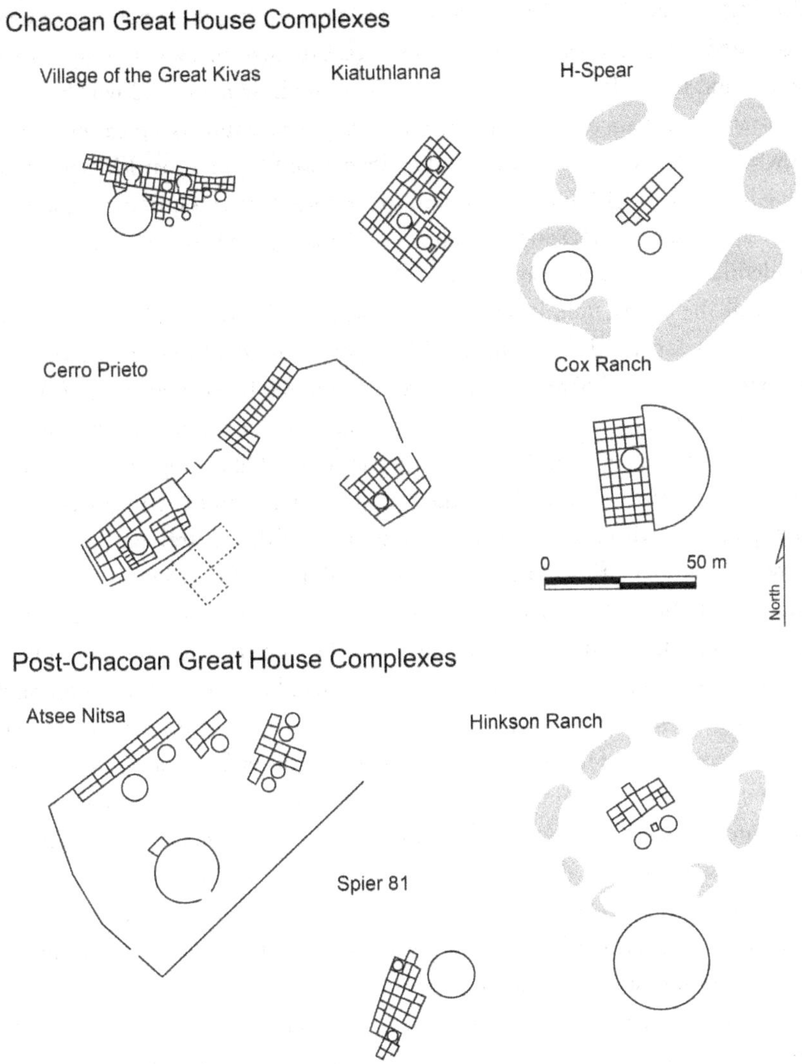


FIGURE 39. Examples of Chacoan era great house complexes (*top*) and post-Chacoan era great house complexes (*bottom*).

Van Dyke 1998). Many great houses are part of larger architectural complexes associated with features such as great kivas (see discussion above), large earthen berms, and roads. Researchers disagree regarding how many and which architectural features are essential for characterizing a structure as a great house (cf. Fowler and Stein 1992; Fowler et al. 1987:78–80; Gilpin 2003; Kintigh 2003; Marshall et al. 1979), but at a minimum, great houses are recognized as relatively large and elaborate masonry structures when compared to contemporaneous residential buildings (Lekson 1991:31–36).

Until the 1980s, definitions of the great house were usually restricted to buildings constructed during the Pueblo II period (ca. A.D. 900–1150), coinciding with the interval of great house construction in Chaco Canyon itself. More recently, however, a number of researchers have documented the continuation of many elements of great house architecture in the Cibola region at least into the late thirteenth century (ca. A.D. 1150–1275), well after the major declines in populations within Chaco Canyon and much of the central San Juan Basin (Fowler et al. 1987; Kintigh 1994; Kintigh et al. 1996). Great house complexes built during the post-Chacoan era continued to reference Chacoan architecture (massive construction, blocked-in kivas, earthen berms, etc.) but also added new elements to the architectural repertoire, including the oversized unroofed great kivas described above (Kintigh et al. 1996). Several post-Chacoan great houses may also have been symbolically linked to earlier Chacoan era structures by landscape modifications, including roads connecting noncontemporaneous structures, which some have termed "time bridges" (Fowler and Stein 1992:116–118; see also Fowler et al. 1987; Stein and Lekson 1992). The continued use of Chacoan architectural symbolism after the decline of Chaco as a regional center emphasizes the local importance of great house architectural complexes in the Cibola region (Cameron and Duff 2008).

Although a few post-Chacoan great houses persisted in some fashion into the early fourteenth century (as suggested by ceramics present; e.g., Beeson 1966:286; Hagopian et al. 2004:1034–1035; Weaver 1978:Appendix B), this specific form of architecture was no longer the focus of settlements intensively occupied after about A.D. 1275 (Duff and Schachner 2007). Across most of the Cibola region at this time, aggregated site clusters and great house sites were replaced by large nucleated pueblos (Duff 2002; Kintigh 1985a; Kintigh et al. 2004). Some of these nucleated pueblos retained certain features of Chacoan architecture (Fowler et al. 1987:93–101), but the transition to nucleated settlement represented a fundamental shift in the organization of communities and architectural space across the region as a whole and an apparent decline in the importance of Chaco Canyon as an architectural referent (Duff and Schachner 2007; Kintigh et al. 2004).

Few Chacoan or post-Chacoan great houses in the Cibola region have been extensively excavated or documented (but see Burton 1993; Fowler et al. 1987; Kintigh et al. 1996; Mahoney et al. 1995; McGimsey 1980; Roberts 1932, 1939; Schachner and Kintigh 2004; Warburton and Graves 1992). Due to their size and formal construction, however, great houses can often be identified based on surface remains alone. As discussed above, the long history of great house construction in the Cibola region suggests that these structures were powerful architectural symbols that provided contexts for communal activities in the region for nearly three centuries. I interpret the presence of great house architecture as indicative of participation in some form of shared ritual practice and shared categorical identities among the inhabitants of great house communities across the Cibola region.

## THE DISTRIBUTION OF GREAT KIVAS AND GREAT HOUSES

In order to explore the distribution of the most common public architectural features found across the Cibola region, I have compiled available locational and chronological information on all relatively well-documented great kivas and great houses throughout the study area.[2] These data were used to create a series of maps to show changes in the distribution of public architectural features through time in three temporal intervals: ca. A.D. 1000–1150, A.D. 1150–1275, and A.D. 1275–1400. These maps reveal regional-scale patterns in the distribution of the most common public structures, which I argue indicate strong patterns of shared categorical identities across the study area.

As Figure 40 shows, during the late Pueblo II period (ca. A.D. 1000–1150), Chacoan great houses and circular great kivas were common in the northern and eastern portions of the study area, including the Zuni area, the Carrizo Wash and Mariana Mesa areas, near Cebolleta Mesa, the Puerco Valley, and the Red Mesa Valley along the edges of the Cibola region. Although both circular and rectangular great kivas have been documented in the western portion of the study area between the Silver Creek and Vernon areas, there are no great houses in those areas. This pattern will be explored further below. Rectangular great kivas dating to this interval have also been documented in the Mogollon Highlands and along the edges of the Arizona Mountains.[3] Although the

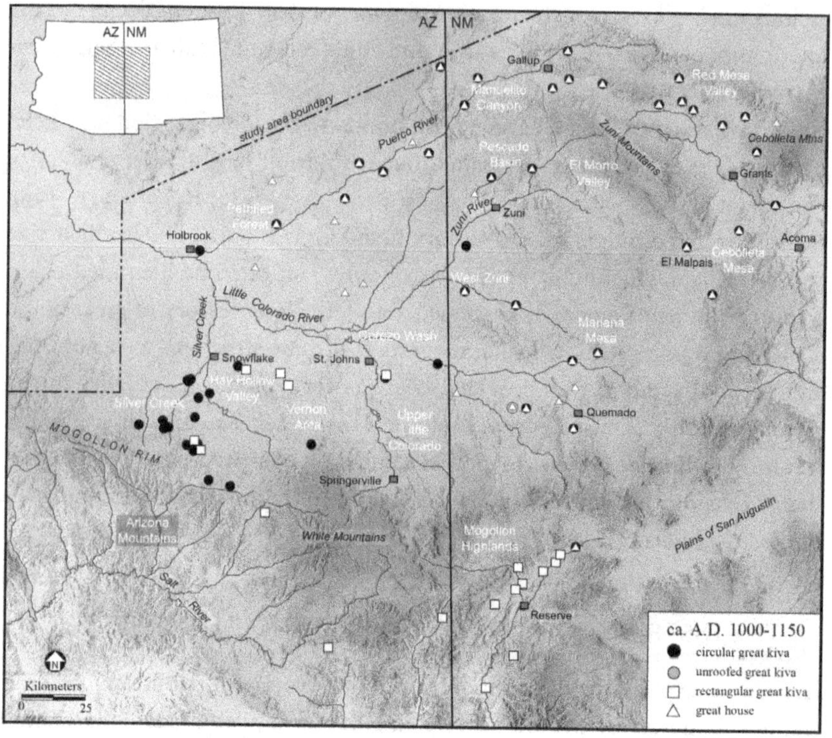


FIGURE 40. Map showing the locations of great houses and great kivas during the late Pueblo II period.

specific locations and architectural details are not known, Edward Bridge Danson (1957:61–62) noted rectangular great kivas and possible circular great kivas in the upper reaches of the Little Colorado River near the White Mountains (see also Duff 2002:69–71). Overall, despite a few intriguing but poorly known possible exceptions, the available data suggest that the distributions of great houses with circular great kivas and other communities with rectangular great kivas were fairly distinct during the late Pueblo II period.[4]

The distribution of great houses during the Pueblo III period (ca. A.D. 1150–1275) was generally similar to that documented for the previous interval, except that post-Chacoan great houses were fewer in number and more heavily concentrated in the central portion of the region near Zuni and the El Morro Valley. Notably, the Red Mesa Valley in the northeastern portion of the study area was largely depopulated by the post-Chacoan era. A few great houses and

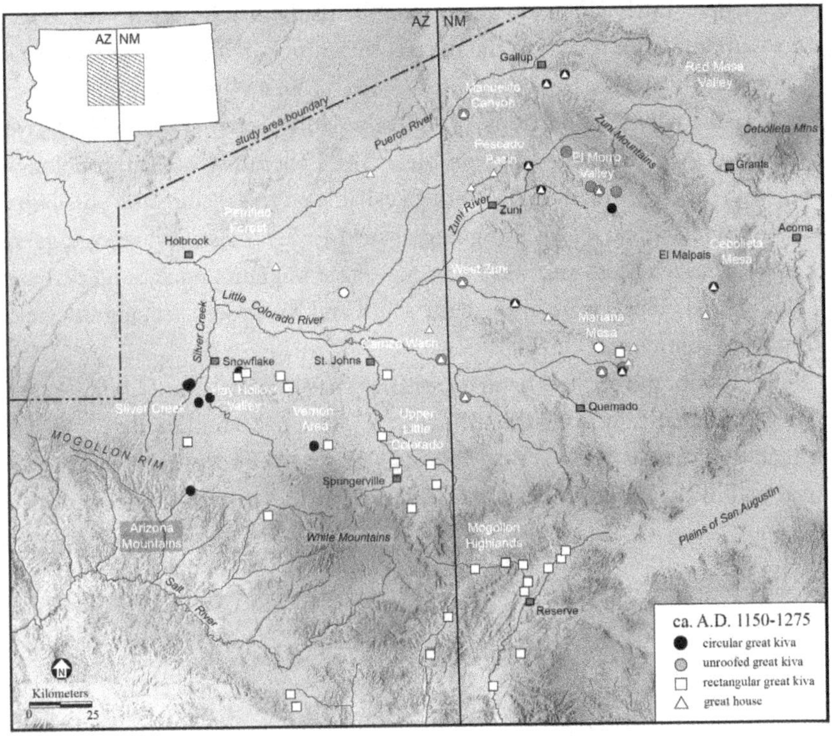


FIGURE 41. Map showing the locations of great houses and great kivas during the Pueblo III period.

circular great kivas first established during the Chacoan era probably persisted into the early thirteenth century, but absolute dates are currently unavailable. There are also a few probable examples of roofed great kivas associated with post-Chacoan great houses or other Pueblo III communities in the Zuni and Cebolleta Mesa areas (e.g., Spier 81 [Kintigh et al. 2004]; Casa Mosca [Wozniak and Marshall 1991]; LA 1584 [Schachner 2007:236]), but most newly built circular great kivas during this interval were extremely large and almost certainly unroofed. There are also at least three oversized unroofed great kivas associated with some of the earliest nucleated pueblos in the El Morro Valley and along the Upper Nutria River, but it is likely that these features were no longer in use after A.D. 1275 (see Schachner 2007:236–237, 245; Duff and Schachner 2007).[5]

The distribution of rectangular great kivas during the Pueblo III period is also similar to that for the late Pueblo II period, but the frequency of great kivas in the Upper Little Colorado area, especially in the south near Springerville, increased dramatically during the thirteenth century. In addition, one possible rectangular great kiva has been documented by an amateur archaeologist in the Mariana Mesa region from a site likely dating between about A.D. 1150 and 1250 (LA 10982; field notes on file at the Laboratory of Anthropology). Although little information is currently available on this feature, the possibility of a rectangular great kiva is intriguing, as many other lines of evidence suggest that the Mariana Mesa area was a destination for migrant populations, perhaps including individuals from areas to the south and west where rectangular great kivas were common.

The distribution of public architectural spaces across the Cibola region changed dramatically after about A.D. 1275. Although absolute dates are not available in most cases, existing data suggest that the vast majority of great kivas and likely all great houses in the Cibola region were no longer occupied

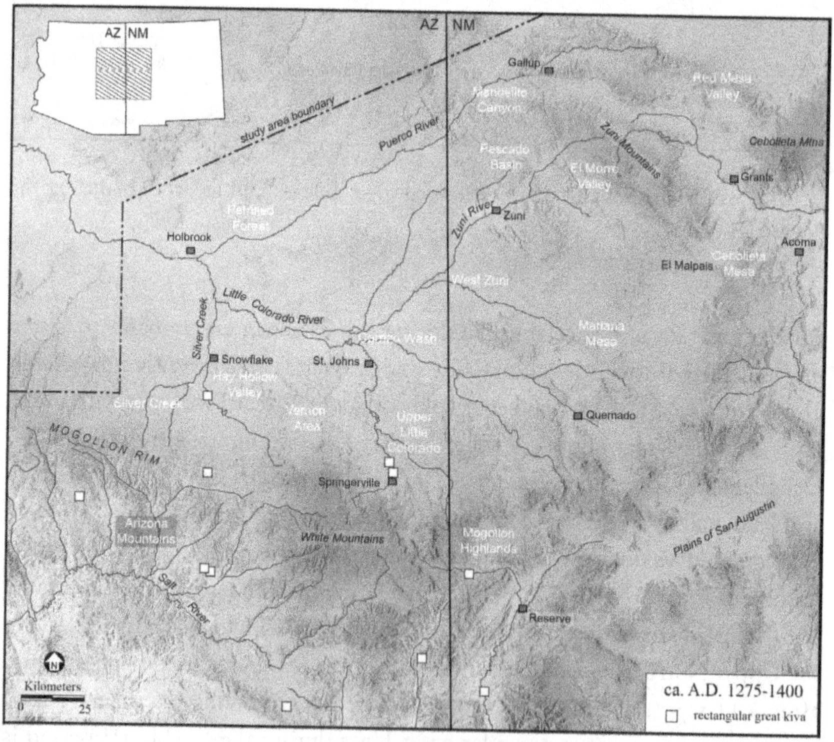


FIGURE 42. Map showing the locations of great kivas during the Pueblo IV period.

or intensively used by or around A.D. 1275. There are, however, several exceptions to this general pattern in the southern and western portions of the region. The rectangular great kivas at Hooper Ranch Pueblo (Martin et al. 1962) and Casa Malpais (Duff 1999:Appendix A) in the Upper Little Colorado area were built during the thirteenth century, but there is evidence for their continued use into the mid-fourteenth century. Some thirteenth-century rectangular great kivas in the Mogollon Highlands area, including the structures at Foote Canyon Pueblo (Rinaldo 1959), Hough's site 70 (Zamora and Oakes 1999), and WS Ranch (Tomka 1988), as well as possible rectangular great kivas at Shumway Ruin (Van Keuran 2006) and Tundastusa (Hough 1903:290) in the Silver Creek area, may have continued to be used into the fourteenth century. In the Arizona Mountains, rectangular great kivas were newly constructed at Grasshopper Pueblo and Kinishba and were substantially remodeled at Point of Pines Pueblo (AZ W:10:50 [ASM]) during the fourteenth century (ca. A.D. 1325; Riggs 2005:338–340).[6] These fourteenth-century structures consist of plazas converted into roofed areas with orientations and floor features similar to those of earlier great kivas. Interestingly, the available data suggest a divergence between the northeastern and southwestern portions of the study area, as rectangular great kivas were constructed well after circular great kivas fell out of use across the region as a whole.

One strong pattern that is apparent across all of the maps presented here is that great houses are exclusively associated with circular great kivas, both roofed and unroofed. Further, there are relatively few areas where the distributions of rectangular and circular great kivas overlap. The consistent dichotomy between areas characterized by great houses with circular great kivas and areas characterized by aggregated or clustered settlements with rectangular great kivas illustrates the long-term maintenance of regional differences in public architectural spaces across the study area. This further supports the idea that these different forms of public architecture likely related to distinct spheres of public ceremonialism and distinct contexts for categorical expression (see Riggs 2005; Whittlesey 2010). However, there are a few areas where this consistent regional pattern appears to break down to some degree.

The distribution of great kivas and great houses in the western portion of the study area, especially in the Silver Creek area, is particularly interesting in light of the general patterns described above. This western area has the highest density of circular great kivas in the study area between about A.D. 1000 and 1150 but relatively low population levels throughout the eleventh through the thirteenth century. At the same time, there are no great houses in this portion of the study area. This same general pattern of circular great kivas without great houses holds for nearby areas, including the Forestdale Valley, the Hay Hollow Valley, and the Vernon area, as well as the Chevelon Creek and Hopi Buttes areas just west of the current study area (see Burton 1993; Haury 1985:Appendix A; Herr 2001; Rinaldo 1964:55–58; Solometo 2004). Although excavated circular great kivas in these areas are similar to Chacoan-style great kivas in many ways, there are also notable differences. Specifically, these western circular great kivas are often shallow and possibly only partially roofed, the orientation is often different from that of most Chacoan great kivas, and internal features are not consistently present or as highly formalized (Burton 1993; Herr 2001:42–59; Haury 1985:415–422; Martin et al. 1961; Rinaldo 1959).

Herr (2001) argues that circular great kivas along this western edge of the study area fell along a frontier zone beyond Chaco and between other major population centers. Circular great kivas in the Silver Creek drainage and surrounding areas may have been constructed in part by migrant populations from the southern edge of the Chacoan world, including the Puerco Valley to the north (see Gregory and Wilcox 2007:140 for an alternate perspective). In this resource-rich but labor-poor western frontier, architectural symbols associated with Chacoan developments may have provided a means to integrate dispersed migrant and local households across the landscape and a context for

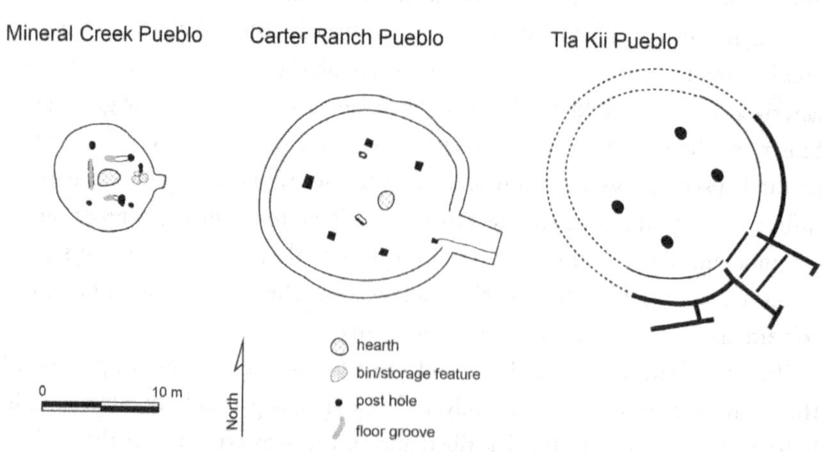


FIGURE 43. Examples of circular great kivas from the Vernon area (*left*), the Hay Hollow Valley (*center*), and the Forestdale Valley (*right*).

the coordination of social and economic activities (Herr 2001:91–94). Because population levels were low, however, the labor may not have been available to construct more formal great kivas or massive great houses.

The same general areas described above (Silver Creek, the Hay Hollow Valley, the Forestdale Valley, and the Vernon area) are essentially the only areas in the Cibola region where circular and rectangular great kivas overlap substantially in distribution. Unfortunately, little is known about the specific form and date ranges of the early rectangular great kivas in this zone, as most examples are known exclusively through surface information. Because only general descriptions are usually available, it is often difficult to distinguish between the ramp entry rectangular great kivas described above and smaller rectangular platform kivas, which are also found in this area (these features are described in detail below). Further, it is possible that some of the overlap is due in part to the lack of chronological resolution. Almost all of the circular great kivas present in this western zone during the Pueblo III period were likely initially constructed during the eleventh or early twelfth century but continued to be used through the end of the twelfth century and perhaps somewhat later (e.g., Lightfoot 1981; Martin et al. 1964). Where good chronological data are available, rectangular great kivas appear to be most common in this area in the thirteenth century (Herr 2001:24–25). The apparent architectural variability within this western zone may be a product of the diverse populations inhabiting this frontier or changing external relationships through time. Additional site recording and excavations in this area could potentially provide the data necessary to evaluate these possibilities.

## PLAZAS

For the purposes of this study, plazas are defined as open areas enclosed within the boundaries of other architectural features. In contemporary Puebloan communities, plazas are important spaces for both routine daily activities and periodic ceremonial gatherings (Adams 1991:81–86; Bunzel 1932:896–897; Dozier 1958; Parsons 1939:309; Triadan 2006). Several researchers have suggested that changes in the specific forms and sizes of the plazas through time may indicate changes in the kinds of ritual or the scale of activities occurring within those spaces (Adams 1991; Chamberlin 2008:121–158, 2012; Mills 2007a; Potter 1998). Thus, I argue that patterns of shared ritual practices and categorical identities can be explored through an examination of patterns of similarities and differences in plaza spaces across the Cibola region.

Several of the largest sites in the Cibola region have been mapped in ways that allow for the consideration of overall site plans and the nature of plaza spaces, but most have not been so thoroughly documented. Thus, the approach I take in this section is to describe general trends in the use of plaza spaces across the Cibola region through time rather than attempting to map the distributions of specific forms. This discussion necessarily reduces much of the variability present in plaza architecture across the region as a whole, but some broad-scale patterns are still identifiable.

Although enclosed plazas are known from a few eleventh- and twelfth-century great houses across the Cibola region and elsewhere (Fowler et al. 1987:80–81; see plan maps in Fowler et al. 1987; Marshall et al. 1979; Van Dyke 1998; Warburton and Graves 1992), formal plaza spaces are relatively rare across the Cibola region until the thirteenth century.[7] Schachner (2012) recently documented several partially enclosed plazas in the El Morro Valley dating from about A.D. 1225–1275. These plaza pueblos consist of L- or C-shaped masonry structures partially encircling large open spaces, some of which have evidence for being cleared down to bedrock. Similar partially enclosed L- or C-shaped plaza pueblos have also been mapped along the Zuni River Valley to the west (Kintigh 1985a:Figure 4.39), in the Cebolleta Mesa area to the east (Roney 1996), and in the Mariana Mesa district to the south. Some of these partially enclosed plazas are located near mesa edges that may have served to further bound portions of the open space, while other settlements have low walls encircling the open area. The specific nature of the open spaces at these sites and how they might have been used are not currently well understood, but these partially enclosed open spaces bounded by planned constructions may have been predecessors to the fully enclosed plazas that characterized late thirteenth-century sites in these same areas. At sites dating to about the same period in the southern portion of the study area, including the Upper Little Colorado, the Mogollon Highlands, and the Silver Creek and Arizona Mountains areas, open areas partially surrounded by loose clusters of room blocks have sometimes also been called plazas (Danson 1957:82–83), but these spaces do not appear to have been as formally bounded as those at contemporaneous settlements on the Colorado Plateau.[8]

The mid- to late thirteenth century also saw the construction of the first true plaza-oriented communities in the Cibola region. Plaza-oriented communities consist of large nucleated pueblos constructed around one or more well-defined open areas. Unlike many post-Chacoan era communities with

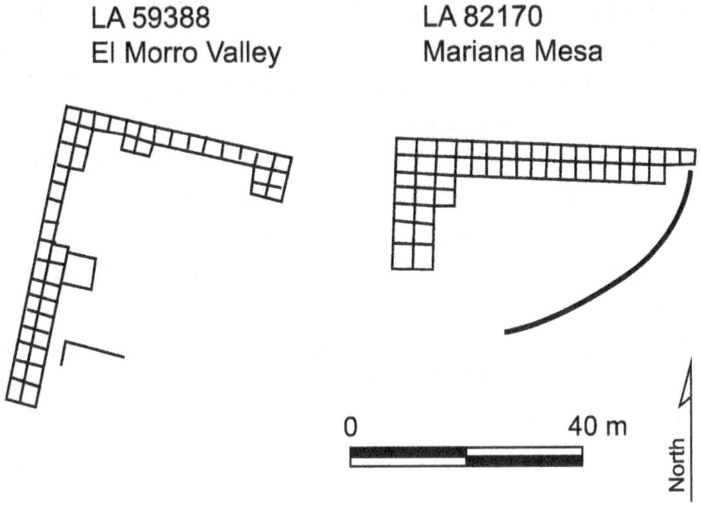


FIGURE 44. Examples of late Pueblo III period partially enclosed plaza pueblos.

numerous dispersed small room blocks, nucleated communities were entirely encompassed within one or a few closely spaced structures. By about A.D. 1275, these plaza-oriented nucleated communities had become the dominant pattern across the El Morro Valley and Zuni area and, by A.D. 1300, across most of the Cibola region and the Colorado Plateau in general (Adams 1991; Adams and Duff 2004).[9] The specific form of plaza-oriented communities varied, however, from place to place across the study area, perhaps suggesting differences in the use of space or in the scale and organization of construction.

In most of the areas where Chacoan architectural complexes are known, including the Puerco Valley, areas along the Zuni River, and the El Morro Valley, as well as in the Mariana Mesa and Cebolleta Mesa areas, thirteenth- and early fourteenth-century plaza-oriented pueblos consist of massive planned constructions, many with distinctive rectangular and circular layouts. These nucleated pueblos were some of the largest prehistoric constructions anywhere in the Southwest at this time, some with more than 1,400 rooms.

Available ceramic data suggest that the earliest nucleated pueblos in this area were likely constructed around A.D. 1225 or 1250 (Kintigh 1985a; Schachner 2012). Some of the first nucleated structures may not have been truly plaza oriented, as interior spaces may have been almost entirely filled with single-story rooms and possibly smaller plazas or courtyards (Duff and Schachner 2007:193–194). By A.D. 1275 or shortly thereafter, however, virtually the entire population of this northern portion of the study area was residing in one of these nucleated towns, and most were constructed around one or more large formal plazas (Kintigh 1985a; Watson et al. 1980). Although there is certainly variation across the study area, these plaza-oriented pueblos are similar in that they were apparently planned and rapidly constructed, and they consisted of long linear room blocks built by ladder construction around large open plazas.

Variation in the shapes of nucleated pueblos in the El Morro Valley and along the Zuni River may highlight somewhat smaller-scale social distinctions among the inhabitants of different communities in this area. As mentioned above, nucleated towns in these areas are typically either circular or rectangular, or they are composites combining both shapes. There are several interesting distinctions between circular and rectangular towns, including differences in the frequencies of ritual fauna (Potter 1997:223–226) and differences in the frequencies of certain Zuni Glaze Ware types (Huntley and Kintigh 2004:70–71). It is possible that these subtle differences indicate variation in religious practice or perhaps categorical identities among the inhabitants of different communities in the Zuni area. James Potter (1997, 2000) argues that the duality of community forms suggests that circular and rectangular pueblos may have played complementary roles in regional spheres of religious practices. Interestingly, some of the earliest nucleated towns in the Zuni area combined circular and rectangular structures, suggesting that such distinctions may have originally emerged from intracommunity relationships (Potter 1997:224).

Plaza-oriented pueblos are also known in the southern portions of the study area, including the Silver Creek area, along the Arizona Mountains, in the Upper Little Colorado, and perhaps in the Mogollon Highlands. Although there are a few exceptions, plaza-oriented pueblos in this southern Cibola region tend to date primarily to the latter half of the thirteenth century (Kaldahl et al. 2004; Lowell 1991; Reid 1989). Further, where good data are available, most Pueblo IV period plaza-oriented pueblos in the southern Cibola region appear to have grown accretionally rather than being planned and rapidly constructed around a plaza (Duff and Lekson 2006:330; Lowell 2001; Mills 1998:67; Riggs 2001:106–107). Due to this accretional construction, plaza-oriented pueblos in the southern Cibola region tend to have agglomerative layouts consisting of massed clusters of rooms with no overall settlement plan (see Figure 45). In the Mogollon Highlands, as I have defined the area for the purposes of this study, no unambiguous examples of fully enclosed plazas have been documented (Lekson 1996:170–171). At Foote Canyon Pueblo on the Blue River, there is a large area enclosed by a series of rooms that has been called a plaza, but this area was apparently roofed (Rinaldo 1959:181) and perhaps is more similar to the converted plaza / great kivas in the Arizona Mountains. Although Walter Hough (1907) mapped plazas and courtyards at several sites along the San Francisco and Blue River Valleys, subsequent investigations have not been able to definitively identify these features (see Zamora and Oakes 1999). Overall, what can be said is that in the southern Cibola region enclosed plazas were most frequently products of the accretional growth of large villages rather than planned constructions and that plazas were far less formal at settlements in the Mogollon Highlands.

The nucleated, plaza-oriented settlement layout characterized virtually the entire Cibola region, as well as much of the northern Southwest, after about A.D. 1275–1300. This suggests broad similarities in public ritual practices across the entire Cibola region. Indeed, Adams (1991) argues that the rapid spread of plazas and plaza-oriented pueblos across the Southwest was likely associated with the spread of the Katsina religion at this time. At the same time, there are apparently differences in how nucleated communities and plaza spaces were constructed across the study area. In the northern and eastern portions of the study area, plazas appear to have been quite large planned constructions, whereas in the south, plazas appear to have typically been smaller and developed somewhat more slowly as villages grew. Overall, this suggests that the scale at which construction was organized may have been greater in the northeastern portions of the study area than in the southern portions. It is interesting that the massive *planned* nucleated pueblos are found primarily in areas where earlier Chacoan complexes are known. This pattern perhaps suggests that labor coordination for construction was in part a legacy of Chacoan influence in the region (see also Fowler and Stein 1992; Fowler et al. 1987). Additionally, the differences in plaza form and village form between the northern and eastern portions of the study area and areas to the south and west may suggest differences in the activities occurring in those spaces and perhaps the emergence of a categorical distinction between these broad areas during the Pueblo IV period.

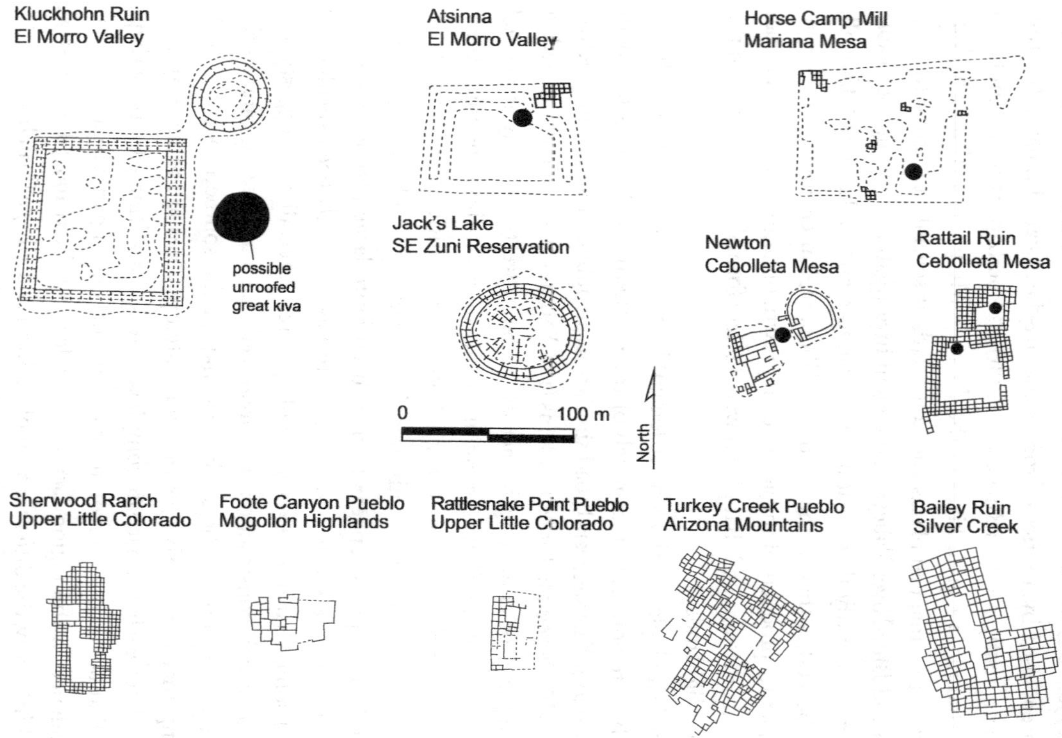


FIGURE 45. Examples of Pueblo IV period plaza pueblos in the northern Cibola region (*top*) and southern Cibola region (*bottom*).

## OTHER ARCHITECTURAL FEATURES

In addition to the large public spaces described above, there are other smaller architectural features found at many settlements in the Cibola region that may have also served a public or ceremonial purpose. In particular, oversized kivas and rectangular room block kivas may also have been used as ceremonial spaces. Although these structures may be too small to have enclosed events that included all or even most members of a community, specific aspects of these features suggest that the activities conducted within them differed from the activities conducted in common domestic spaces (see Lipe 2002:220–221 on public structures as exclusive spaces). In this section, I briefly describe the limited evidence available for these smaller, potentially ceremonial spaces.

During the period considered in this study, typical kivas in the Cibola region consisted of circular, D-shaped, or rectangular subterranean or semisubterranean structures, usually 3–4 meters across, with masonry-lined benches, vent complexes, and sometimes floor vaults, sipapus, or other specialized floor features (see plan maps in Dittert 1959; Martin et al. 1964; McGimsey 1980; Roberts 1939; Ruppé 1990; Varien 2000; Zier 1976; see also Smith 1972:127; Smiley 1952:11–12). Although there is some indication that small subterranean kivas were somewhat less common in the Cibola region than in much of the rest of the northern Southwest (Kintigh et al. 2004:445), where excavation data are available, small kivas appear to be present at most sites on the Colorado Plateau and somewhat less frequently at sites in the Upper Little Colorado and below the Mogollon Rim after about A.D. 1150. Kivas are sometimes associated with evidence for certain specialized activities such as weaving (see Varien 1990:65), but these features are not typically interpreted as public or ceremonial spaces in the Cibola region (cf. Kintigh et al. 2004:445). In some portions of the study area, however, there appears to have been a class of structures intermediate in size between typical small kivas described above and the much larger great kivas. It is possible that these features were also intermediate in terms of their ceremonial importance (as has been suggested for Pueblo I period pit structures in the Dolores area; see Schachner 2001; Wilshusen 1989). For the purposes of this chapter, I refer to these intermediate structures as oversized kivas.

Oversized kivas ranging from about 8–10 meters in diameter have been documented at several settlements across the Cibola region, and large depressions that may represent similar features have been recorded at many others. In the few contexts where these structures have been excavated enough to determine their form, oversized kivas appear to be D shaped in plan, sometimes with subterranean walls and sometimes incorporated into room block architecture. Probable examples of oversized kivas have been partially excavated associated with post-Chacoan great houses in the Mariana Mesa area (Jimmy Smith, personal communication 2010) and the El Morro Valley (Schachner and Kintigh 2004). In addition to this, depressions that may represent similar oversized kivas have been recorded at the post-Chacoan great house of Atsee Nitsa along the Puerco Valley (Fowler et al. 1987:87), two post-Chacoan great houses in the Cebolleta Mesa region (Peeples, personal observation 2015), and contemporaneous non–great house sites in the El Morro Valley (CS195, Pettit; Schachner 2007:235).

Oversized kivas have also been recorded in association with nucleated sites dating to the Pueblo IV period, including the excavated structures at Atsinna (Woodbury 1954) and Mirabal (Watson et al. 1980:Figure 6) in the El Morro Valley, at Techado Spring (Smith et al. 2009:Figure 12) and Horse Camp Mill (McGimsey 1980:Figure 40) in the Mariana Mesa area, at Big House along the Rio Puerco (Fowler et al. 1987:96), and at Los Pilares (Ruppé 1990:Figure 14) in the Cebolleta Mesa area. Some of these features have sometime been referred to as great kivas in the literature (Danson 1957:Table 16; Smith et al. 2010:25; Watson et al. 1980:211–212), but they are smaller than typical Chacoan or post-Chacoan era great kivas and lack many of the formal features found in great kivas. Little can currently be said about the regional distribution of oversized kivas, but these features appear to be associated primarily with post-Chacoan era communities and Pueblo IV period nucleated towns in the northern Cibola region along the Zuni and Puerco Rivers, as well as in the Mariana Mesa and Cebolleta Mesa districts (i.e., areas characterized by substantial Chacoan influence).

Rectangular room block kivas (or platform kivas) are relatively large rooms incorporated into room blocks, often with flagstone-lined floors, elaborate masonry walls, wall niches, formal hearths, ventilator complexes, and sometimes benches or raised platforms along one or more walls in the latest examples (Adams 1991:103–110). Unlike rectangular great kivas, these rooms typically lack floor grooves and ramped entries. In the Cibola region, rectangular room block kivas are similar in many ways to the well-documented fourteenth-century and later rectangular kivas of the Hopi Mesas (Smith 1972). Some have argued that rectangular room block kivas combine features of northern small kivas from the Colorado Plateau and the rectangular great kivas of areas south of the Mogollon Rim, while others see the origins of the rectangular kivas in earlier subterranean structures from northern Arizona (cf. Adams 1991:103–110; Gumerman and Skinner 1968; Lyons 2001:Chapter 9). Wherever these features originated, they become common across the Cibola region and in many other areas around the mid- to late thirteenth century (ca. A.D. 1275), in particular at nucleated pueblos built around open plazas (Adams 1991:Figure 5.8). Adams argues that, like enclosed plazas, rectangular room block kivas are associated with the spread of the Katsina religion across much of the Southwest at this time. Indeed,

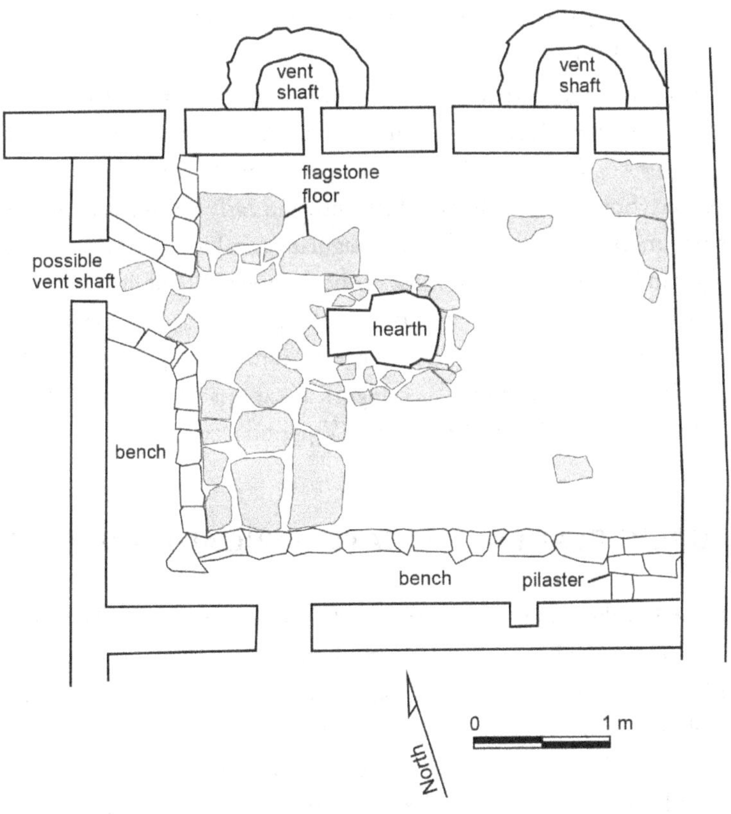


FIGURE 46. Rectangular room block kiva from Pueblo de los Muertos in the El Morro Valley.

rectangular room block kivas are essentially the only structures where murals depicting Katsinas have been documented (Adams 1991:84).

Rectangular room block kivas fitting the description above have been documented in contexts dating to about A.D. 1275 or later in almost every portion of the Cibola region study area where excavation data are available. Although rectangular room block kivas with raised platforms are known from Point of Pines (Adams 1991:109), they are not known from any other extensively excavated sites along the Arizona Mountains (see Adams 1991:108–109; Lyons 1999:Appendix BB). In the Mogollon Highlands, although there are some rooms that show similarities to rectangular room block kivas (Martin et al. 1956:44–46), there are no unambiguous examples.[10] In general, available data suggest that rectangular room block kivas were present across most of the Cibola region, in particular after A.D. 1300, but primarily limited to areas above the Mogollon Rim.

Adams (1991) argues that the relatively rapid and widespread appearance of rectangular room block kivas across much of the Cibola region and beyond may suggest some degree of shared ritual practice among the inhabitants of much of the northern Southwest in the late thirteenth and early fourteenth centuries. At the same time, the apparent lack of rectangular room block kivas in the Mogollon Highlands and throughout most of the Arizona Mountains, as well as the continued use and construction of rectangular great kivas in these areas, could be used to argue for broad-scale differences in ceremonial practice and distinctions in the common contexts of categorical expressions in areas above and below the Mogollon Rim by the Pueblo IV period (see also Whittlesey 2010).

## PUBLIC PLACES AND CATEGORICAL IDENTITIES

The discussion above illustrates that the Cibola region was marked by numerous distinct forms of public architecture throughout the period considered here. Some features, such as enclosed plazas and rectangular room block kivas, had extremely broad distributions encompassing most of the Cibola region and beyond, although the specific forms and perhaps uses may have differed from place to place. Such widespread features suggest some level of similarity in ceremonial practice and perhaps categorical identity across most of the Cibola region at least during the Pueblo IV period (e.g., Adams 1991). Other features, such as great houses and circular or rectangular great kivas, appear to have had limited distributions, suggesting distinct patterns of categorical expression among the inhabitants of somewhat smaller areas through time.

In general, based on the patterns documented above, the Cibola region can be divided into two broad geographic areas characterized by similar public architectural features through time. First, the northern portions of the study area, including the entire Zuni River Valley, the El Morro Valley, the Mariana Mesa area, the Puerco Valley, and the Cebolleta Mesa area, are characterized by great houses, circular great kivas, and, by the late thirteenth century, planned nucleated plaza pueblos, many of distinctive shapes. The southern portions of the region, including the Upper Little Colorado area, the Arizona Mountains, and the Mogollon Highlands, are characterized by a lack of great houses, rectangular great kivas, and, across most of this area, agglomerative settlements focused around one or more less formal plazas after the mid- to late thirteenth century. The western portions of the study area, from the Vernon area to Silver Creek, are marked by circular great kivas without great houses, rectangular great kivas perhaps later in time, and agglomerative plaza-oriented pueblos by the late thirteenth century. The diversity of features along this western frontier may suggest the presence of populations with diverse origins or changing patterns of regional interaction through time.

The consistent and relatively distinct distributions of the suites of public architectural features described above suggest that there were likely substantial differences in the common contexts for ceremonial activity across different portions of the Cibola region that were maintained for centuries. Different portions of the study area also appear to have been marked by somewhat different trajectories of change in public spaces through time. Across the northern Cibola region as it is defined in this chapter, great kivas generally increase in size from the late Pueblo II to the Pueblo III period. The latest examples lack roofs, perhaps suggesting that these structures were becoming more inclusive spaces through time. By about A.D. 1275 circular great kivas in the northern Cibola region appear to have declined dramatically or fallen out of use altogether and were replaced by massive enclosed plazas. In the southern portion of the Cibola region, rectangular great kivas were never fully replaced by enclosed plazas during the period considered here, and, indeed, rectangular great kivas were newly constructed within plaza spaces as late as the first quarter of the fourteenth century. There was a great deal of diversity in the forms of public spaces found at many settlements in the western and southern portions of the region during the Pueblo IV period (Mills 1998). Similar patterns of change through time have been documented in the Mogollon Highlands areas, but fully enclosed plazas were apparently absent or never as formal as in other portions of the southern Cibola region. These differences in the trajectories of change in public features through time further suggest that these different portions of the Cibola region may have been involved in distinct and largely separate spheres of public ceremonialism, further suggesting the maintenance of distinct categorical identities. Intriguingly, the distribution of Chacoan architecture during the eleventh century presages most of the patterns of similarity in architectural features across the subsequent 400 years.

# 9

# SOCIAL IDENTITY AND SOCIAL CHANGE IN THE CIBOLA WORLD AND BEYOND

I BEGAN THIS book by recounting one of many encounters I have had with members of the public asking "Who were the people who lived here?" Identity is a complex concept in the contemporary world and perhaps even more so when we must examine it through the lens of material remains alone. As I hope I have illustrated throughout the preceding chapters, despite considerable analytical and theoretical challenges, it is possible to craft a nuanced and satisfying answer to the "who" question somewhere between a reliance on static archaeological cultures on the one hand and the seemingly endless complexity of individual and cross-cutting group identities on the other. Beyond this, I argue that explorations of the *processes* involved in social identification such as those presented in this book are essential to understanding the organization and trajectory of widespread social change more generally.

One of the primary tensions in archaeological and anthropological investigations of identity, especially when considering very large geographic and demographic scales, is the notion that group identities are both constantly in flux while also remaining persistent enough that we can often recognize discrete social groups across huge spans of time (see Bentley 1987:24–27; Jenkins 2000; Jones 1997:84–105). Individuals can and do strategically manipulate their expressions of identity and group membership through material culture in ways that complicate our ability to identify and track social groups through archaeological data (e.g., Dietler and Herbich 1998; Fennell 2000; Hodder 1982). At the same time, even the staunchest opponent of traditional culture historical models would concede that there are *some* contexts where the material patterns we observe in the archaeological record show a great deal of parity across multiple lines of evidence. In some cases, such patterns even suggest strong historical relationships with contemporary ethnolinguistic groups and social boundaries. The Pueblo Southwest is certainly ripe with such situations at various spatial and temporal scales (see Ware 2015). If we limit ourselves to searching only for such tight correspondences across all the available evidence, however, we are bound to be disappointed more often than not. At the same time, I argue that it would also be a mistake to write off apparent mismatches across different lines of material evidence for shared identities at any scale as simply analytical noise or *short-lived* situations created by interactions among distinct social groups (cf. Jones 1997:122–127; Gosselain 2000; MacEachern 1998; Sætersdal 1999).

In this book, I have attempted to find a new way of conceptualizing social identity at large scales through archaeological evidence. This work builds on a large body of comparative social science research focused on the processes through which both collective identities and coordinated action emerge. The framework that I develop in the beginning of this book suggests that social identity and social change are intrinsically linked and that different configurations of shared *relational connections* and *categorical distinctions* can variously hamper or promote large-scale cooperation (Nexon 2009; Tilly 1978, 2001; White 2008a). Further, this work suggests that the social and spatial scales at which relations and categories intersect (i.e., the scale at which catnets emerge) are often the scales at which truly transformative collective action takes hold. In this final chapter, I draw together the various lines of evidence presented throughout this study to paint a synthetic picture of how patterns of relational and categorical social identification changed at regional scales. This synthesis further allows me to assess the Pueblo III to Pueblo IV transition in the Cibola region in light of models of social transformation typically applied only to contemporary or recent historic settings.

In Chapter 2 I set out a few key principles and expectations for evaluating the relationship between different modes of social identification and social transformation. To briefly recount, I argue that the process of social identification among large groups of people can be profitably investigated by considering both its relational and its categorical dimensions and that parsing identity in this way can provide new insights into the nature and scale of social change. Empirical research in many contemporary and recent historic contexts suggests that truly transformative social change occurs most frequently among catnets: groups of people who share *both* strong relational connections and a high degree of categorical homogeneity. At the same time, this work suggests that strong relational connections often precede the establishment of new formal categorical distinctions at a given scale. Thus, we may expect to see a trajectory of change through time marked by changes in the geographic and social scale of correspondence between relations and categories. I revisit these general points below to explore the complex relationships between identity and social change in the Cibola region and to further consider what this case study has to say about the process of social transformation more generally.

## TRACKING RELATIONS AND CATEGORIES IN THE CIBOLA REGION

In contrast to assumptions pervasive in many traditional archaeological explorations of social identity, relations and categories (i.e., tight-knit networks of interaction and formally recognized and expressed social groups) are not necessarily coterminous. I suggest that a more explicit recognition of this very basic point can facilitate new insights into the processes involved in social identification in archaeological contexts and new ways to think about how social identities change through time. In this section, I briefly summarize the various lines of evidence used to track both relational connections and categorical distinctions and, finally, how they intersect or diverge through time.

The discussion below is guided by a series of maps shown in Figures 47 and 48 that provide a distillation of the complex spatial and temporal patterns of relations and categories across the numerous material proxies described in the previous chapters. The visualization of patterns across these different lines of material evidence is complicated, in part because the spatial extent of data availability for each analysis differs (i.e., some analyses are limited only to the core subregions, while others include data from sites in the complementary subregions). Thus, these maps should not be interpreted as providing clearly defined distributions and boundaries of relations and categories across the study area through time. Instead, these maps are best viewed as simply interpretations and summary assessments of the most robust trajectories of changing similarity and difference across space and through time. As the discussion below will highlight, although there is a high degree of parity across multiple measures

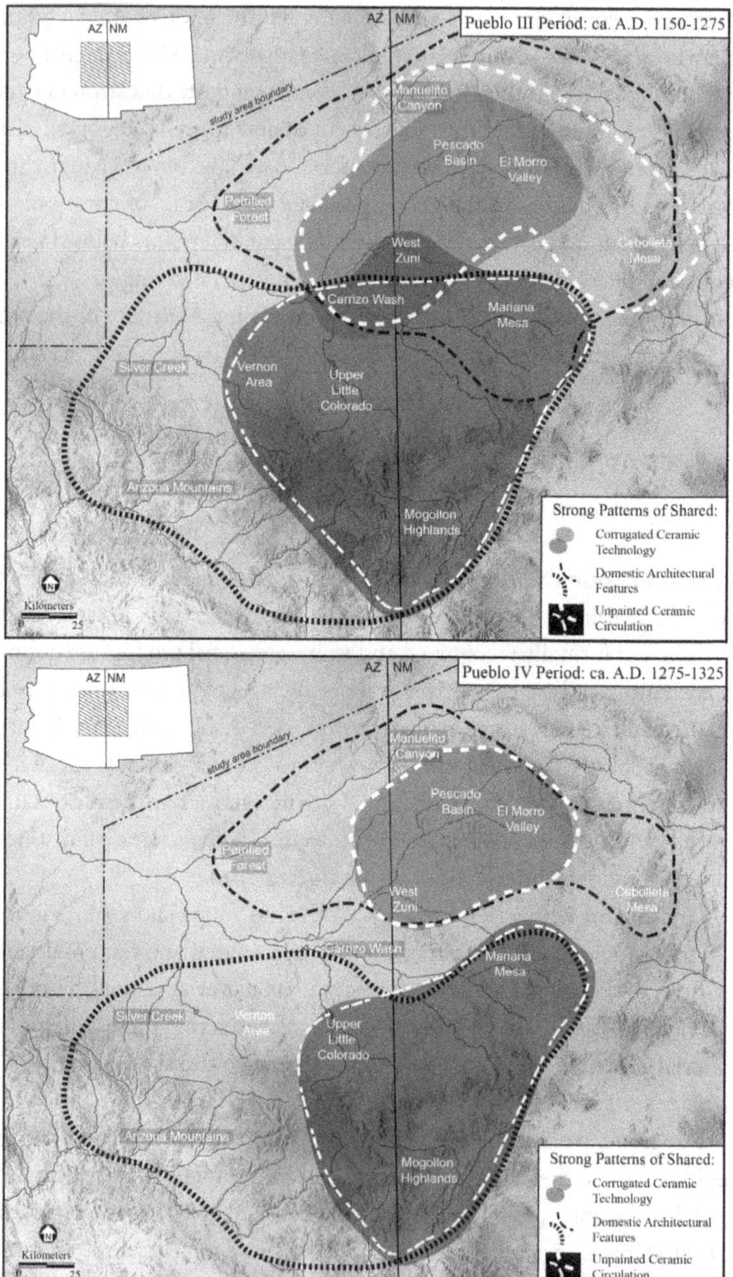


FIGURE 47. Maps showing the portions of the study area marked by strong similarities in terms of each material proxy for relational connections for the Pueblo III (*top*) and Pueblo IV (*bottom*) periods.

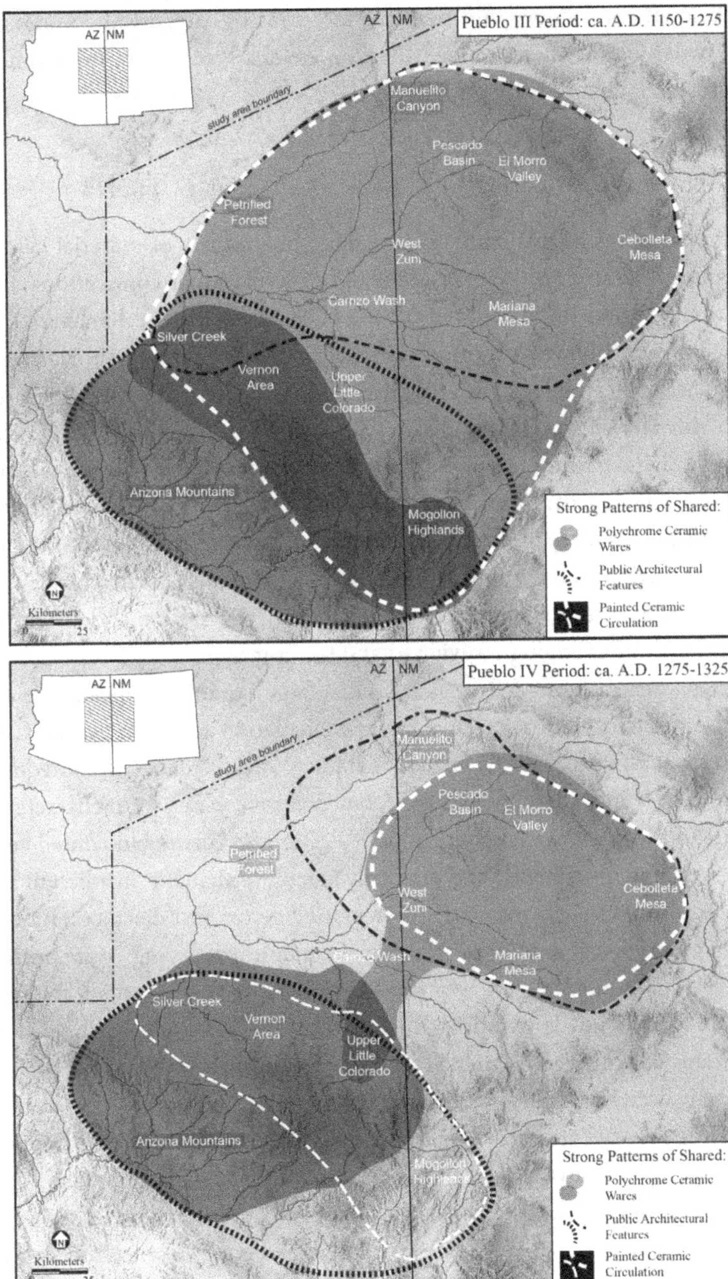


FIGURE 48. Maps showing the portions of the study area marked by strong similarities in terms of each material proxy for categorical commonality for the Pueblo III (*top*) and Pueblo IV (*bottom*) periods.

of relational connections and multiple measures of categorical commonality, these two different modes of identification are characterized by quite different trajectories of change through time.

## EVIDENCE FOR RELATIONAL CONNECTIONS

For the purposes of this study, I used three major lines of material evidence to explore the strength and directionality of relational connections across the Cibola region through time: (1) ceramic compositional characterizations focused on identifying patterns of ceramic circulation (for unpainted vessels in particular), (2) technological characterizations of unpainted pottery focused on identifying shared production methods and learning frameworks, and (3) technological characterizations of domestic architectural spaces and features focused on characterizing common household building practices. Remarkably, the strongest patterns of similarity across each of these distinct lines of material evidence overlap considerably, suggesting that the material patterns identified through each relate to similar vectors of frequent interaction and strong relational connections among individuals and larger groups.

In Chapter 4 I presented an analysis of a large ceramic compositional database in order to explore patterns of ceramic circulation across the greater Cibola region through time. As this analysis demonstrated, ceramics were frequently transported across the Cibola region, but different wares were characterized by different intensities and geographic scales of movement. Unpainted vessels were circulated infrequently and primarily among settlements in adjacent areas, whereas painted vessels were often transported across vast distances. Based on ethnoarchaeological studies of traditional ceramic-producing communities, I argue that unpainted vessels are most likely to be circulated among frequently interacting individuals within tight-knit relational networks, such as among kin groups or marriage partners. Painted vessels, on the other hand, are more frequently used and exchanged in contexts of public gatherings as a means for solidifying somewhat more distant relational connections (i.e., less frequently activated) among participants. Thus, these compositional data provide evidence for different kinds of connections at different geographic and social scales. As I describe in greater detail in Chapter 7, painted vessels are closely associated with the active expression of identities, suggesting that the circulation of painted vessels may also provide evidence of *categorical expressions* across the Cibola region. In other words, settlements and areas that were involved in common spheres of painted ceramic circulation were also likely involved in common spheres of public ceremonialism, providing a context for expressing and contesting categorical commonality. Thus, following this line of argument, as outlined in Chapter 4, I discuss the circulation of painted ceramics along with other lines of evidence for categorical commonality below.

Most unpainted vessels were discarded in the general areas where they were produced, but small numbers were also sometimes transported across the Cibola region, primarily within two overarching spheres roughly conforming to the northern (El Morro Valley, Pescado Basin, West Zuni, Carrizo Wash, and Cebolleta Mesa) and southern (Upper Little Colorado, Mariana Mesa, and Mogollon Highlands) portions of the core study area (Figure 47). These northern and southern spheres of ceramic circulation were quite consistent across the Pueblo III to Pueblo IV transition despite the depopulation of several areas and massive population movements into others. These two broad zones were not entirely discrete, however, as settlements along the edges of each area (in the Carrizo Wash area in particular) were characterized by some evidence for interaction in both directions. Overall, this suggests that the relational networks through which unpainted ceramics circulated were relatively local in nature and somewhat permeable but that there was also a strong tendency for the segmentation of regional networks of exchange that increased through time as areas along the edges of these two spheres of circulation were depopulated.

Throughout this study, I argue that examinations of patterns of similarity in aspects of technology that were learned in the context of frequent and direct interaction can provide a good proxy for patterns of strong relational connections and historical ties among individuals and larger groups across the study area. In Chapter 5 I presented a detailed technological analysis focused on the production of unpainted ceramic vessels using formal methods for social network analysis across the core subregions of the study area. The basic premise of this analysis is that patterns of similarity in the methods used to produce these household goods provide indications of the strongest patterns of frequent interaction and social learning and, by extension, strong relational connections among the inhabitants of the study area. One of the major results of this analysis was that the patterns of similarity in the methods used to produce unpainted vessels were closely related to the spatial distance between settlements. This spatial relationship was pronounced during both the Pueblo III and Pueblo IV periods and, importantly, also in comparisons between periods. The consistency in this spatial pattern through time suggests that the Pueblo III to Pueblo IV transition was largely organized among groups of people that were *already interacting on a regular basis prior to the late thirteenth-century social transformation.* The few exceptions to this general pattern, primarily involving settlements in the Mariana Mesa area, provide evidence for patterns of long-distance population movement across the Cibola region through time.

Based on the ceramic technological data, it is again possible to divide the study area into two zones that were characterized by strongly overlapping internal social ties, with relatively few external ties. Interestingly, these tight-knit networks of settlements once again largely conform to the northern (El Morro Valley, Pescado Basin, West Zuni, and Carrizo Wash) and southern (Upper Little Colorado, Vernon Area, Mariana Mesa, and Mogollon Highlands) portions of the study area through time (Figure 47). As was the case with the circulation of unpainted vessels, settlements along the edges of these two overarching groups (particularly during the Pueblo III period) showed some similarities to settlements in both the northern and southern portions of the study area. A few settlements along the edges of these two groups may have even produced pottery that was technologically transitional between the dominant technologies characterizing areas to the north and south. The technological divide between the north and the south became more pronounced across the Pueblo III to Pueblo IV transition, at least in part due to the depopulation of some areas along the edges of these two overarching zones. Overall, this suggests that the patterns of interaction through which pottery production was learned were likely local in nature, characterized to some degree by a north vs. south dichotomy, but that any boundaries to interaction were also likely quite permeable.

Finally, in Chapter 6 I characterized the technology of domestic architectural construction across the Cibola region as a complement to the more detailed technological analysis of unpainted pottery described above. As the architectural sample was defined by the extent of existing excavation data, the level at which comparisons could be made was somewhat coarser than with other analyses, but at the same time, data were available across a broader geographic area. The available evidence suggests similar patterns of technological similarity to those described above. Specifically, patterns of domestic feature style (hearths and mealing bins), as well as their size and placement within rooms, once again suggest a division of the study area into a northern (El Morro Valley, Pescado Basin, West Zuni, and Carrizo Wash, as well as nearby areas, including the Hardscrabble Wash, Cebolleta Mesa, Mount Taylor, Manuelito Canyon, and Petrified Forest) and a southern (Upper Little Colorado, Mariana Mesa, and

Mogollon Highlands, as well as areas in Silver Creek, Hay Hollow Valley, and the Arizona Mountains) zone characterized by consistently overlapping patterns of feature styles and arrangements. Although the nature of the sample did not allow for quantitative comparisons of change through time, the strongest patterns of similarity persist across the Pueblo III to Pueblo IV transition where data from both periods are available (though the distribution of settlement contracts during the Pueblo IV period).

The multiple lines of evidence used to track the strength, scale, and direction of relational connections across the Cibola region through time provide complementary results. Specifically, evidence for the strongest relational connections across the region suggests that the most frequent vectors of interaction were largely local in nature and, furthermore, that there was a strong tendency toward segmentation of regional relational networks between the northern and southern portions of the study area. The strongest patterns of relational social ties were consistent across the Pueblo III to Pueblo IV social transformation despite the fundamental reorganization of settlement structure and location across this transition. Interestingly, the northern and southern portions of the study area, which are characterized by increasingly distinct relational networks of interaction through time, roughly conform to areas traditionally placed within the Anasazi and Mogollon archaeological culture areas, respectively, a topic I return to in more detail below.

## EVIDENCE FOR SHARED CATEGORICAL IDENTITIES

As described in detail in Chapter 2, categorical identification refers to the process through which individuals identify themselves and others as members of larger collectives based on similarities in socially defined roles or groups to which individuals can belong. In contrast to relational identification, categorical identification occurs through an active and conscious process of boundary marking and symbolization rather than through frequent interaction and/or historical connections alone. In this study, I have relied on three primary lines of evidence for documenting patterns of categorical commonality across the study area through time: evidence for the active expression of identities through (1) highly visible designs painted on polychrome ceramics and (2) shared forms of public architectural spaces across the region, and evidence for participation in (3) shared spheres of painted ceramic circulation, suggesting common contexts of public ceremonialism. Patterns of similarity along all these lines of evidence overlap to a considerable degree, but importantly, these patterns also differ in several respects from the strongest patterns of relational connections outlined above.

Categorical identities must be symbolized in order to facilitate recognition among members and nonmembers of a social group. Thus, patterns of similarity in highly visible and public aspects of style can provide indications of shared categorical expressions and identities at a regional scale. In Chapter 7 I characterized patterns of stylistic similarity and difference in the designs found on painted ceramics, focusing in particular on designs painted on the exteriors of large polychrome serving bowls across the Cibola region. Based on contextual data relating changes in design size and boldness through time to the organization of public space, I argue that these vessels were produced with a fundamental concern for visual communication and thus are good candidates for active and intentional signals of categorical social identities (see also Mills 2007a).

During the Pueblo III period, although there was considerable variation in the surface treatments characterizing vessels across the study area, the inhabitants of much of the greater Cibola region produced or obtained vessels characterized by similar simple, geometric, and circumferential designs painted in bold white lines on a red or reddish-brown surface. Beyond this, the most commonly used design elements were similar for vessels recovered across the study area, even between areas characterized by relatively little direct exchange. This suggests that vessels produced and used across the Cibola region at this time were made by individuals employing similar design conventions, indicating perhaps some degree of shared categorical identity across much of the region.

Across the Pueblo III to Pueblo IV transition, however, patterns of stylistic similarity in bowl exterior designs broke down. The Zuni area to the east and the western and southern (Upper Little Colorado, Mariana Mesa, Mogollon Highlands, Silver Creek, and Arizona Mountains) portions of the region diverged and began to produce vessels that differed in terms of design color and the structure of exterior designs. In the most populous areas near the Zuni River Valley after about A.D. 1275, potters began to produce vessels that archaeologists have designated as Zuni Glaze Wares. These Zuni Glaze Ware vessels were characterized by exterior designs that were simple, geometric, and circumferential, much like earlier polychrome pottery across the region. However, specific designs were repeated with a much greater frequency and even across other media such as wall murals. This repetition and homogeneity suggest active efforts toward maintaining conformity by potters in the Zuni area. To the west at about the same time (A.D. 1275), potters began producing vessels that archaeologists have designated as Early White Mountain Red Ware (Pinedale Polychrome) types. On the exteriors of these White Mountain Red Ware bowls, the simple geometric designs of earlier polychrome bowls were largely replaced by intricate unit designs, often consisting of animals or other recognizable forms. The broad differences between vessels produced in the eastern and western portions of the Cibola region suggest the emergence of a categorical social boundary between these areas across the Pueblo III to Pueblo IV transition. Interestingly, settlements between the primary production areas of these two distinct ceramic traditions, in particular in the Upper Little Colorado region, were characterized by a mixture of both Zuni Glaze Ware and Late White Mountain Red Ware vessels, both locally produced and imported (along with other wares after A.D. 1325). This may suggest that these areas were inhabited by diverse populations or that the inhabitants of these areas were making active efforts to signal multiple categorical identities.

As expressions of categorical identity often take place in public settings, patterns of similarity in public spaces may provide indications of shared categorical identities at a regional scale. In Chapter 8 I explored patterns of similarity in the distribution and form of public architectural spaces across the Cibola region through time. There are a number of distinct varieties of public architectural features found across the study area, often with multiple features constructed at single communities. Although there is a great deal of change through time in the specific forms of public structures, many of the strongest patterns of similarity and difference across the region are relatively consistent across the late thirteenth-century social transformation. In general, the northern and eastern portions of the study area (El Morro Valley, Pescado Basin, West Zuni, Carrizo Wash, Cebolleta Mesa, Puerco Valley, and Mariana Mesa) were characterized by great houses, circular great kivas, and, after the Pueblo III to Pueblo IV transition, nucleated pueblos, many of distinctive shapes. The southern portions of the study area (Upper Little Colorado, Mogollon Highlands, and Arizona Mountains) were characterized by a lack of great houses, rectangular great kivas, and agglomerative villages constructed around one or more plazas after the Pueblo III to Pueblo IV transition. A few areas along the western portions of the study area from the Vernon area to Silver Creek were marked by circular great kivas without great houses during the eleventh and early twelfth centuries, rectangular great kivas perhaps later in time, and agglomerative plaza-oriented pueblos by the Pueblo IV period. The diversity of features along this western frontier of the Cibola region suggests the presence of populations with diverse historical origins (Herr 2001). The consistent patterns of similarity in suites of public architectural spaces documented in this study suggest that the eastern and western portions of the study area may have been characterized by distinct forms and contexts for ceremonial activities that were maintained for centuries. Certain widespread features were shared across the entire region both before and after the thirteenth-century social transformation (e.g., plazas, great kivas), but the specific forms of these features and trajectories of change across the period considered here differed considerably from place to place.

Patterns of painted ceramic circulation provide some additional insights into the patterns described above. I suggest that the participation in shared spheres of circulation of painted vessels provides an indication of the scales of shared participation in public ceremonialism, which may further provide insight into the scales at which *categorical identities* were expressed. The circulation of painted vessels was considerably more frequent and geographically expansive than that of unpainted vessels. During the Pueblo III period, most of the Cibola region was involved in a widespread sphere of ceramic circulation that appears to have centered on the Pescado Basin in the Zuni area (though little information is currently available for the Pueblo III period in the Arizona Mountains). Communities spread far and wide across the region were linked through the exchange of painted ceramics, probably occurring in the context of periodic public gatherings. This suggests that the inhabitants of much of the Cibola region shared broad social ties based on their common participation in such gatherings. Interestingly, the Upper Little Colorado area appears to have been isolated from this widespread sphere of ceramic circulation, perhaps suggesting the emergence of a social boundary or some kind of hindrance to certain kinds of interaction between the eastern and western portions of the Cibola region at least by the Pueblo III period.

After the Pueblo III to Pueblo IV transition, the circulation of painted vessels was increasingly localized and limited within the central Zuni area (Pescado Basin, El Morro Valley, and Upper Nutria in particular), while long-distance exchange was more common among settlements to the west, at least by the late Pueblo IV period. This transition in the dominant patterns of exchange was associated with the increased local production of polychrome vessels in the western Cibola region. These data suggest that the inhabitants of the eastern and western portions of the study area were increasingly involved in distinct spheres of painted ceramic exchange and public ceremonialism, likely indicating an increasing consolidation of distinct categorical identities across the late thirteenth-century social transformation.

Overall, the material evidence for patterns of shared categorical expressions across the Cibola region documented in this study suggests that there was an increasing regional divergence and localization of categorical expressions across the Pueblo III to Pueblo IV transition and a broadening divide between the east and west in particular. Within the Zuni area, including all of the lands along the Zuni River Valley and the El Morro Valley, the Pueblo III to Pueblo IV transition was marked by an increasing homogenization of ceramic design and the creation of new forms of public architecture and communities that differed from those found across the rest of the study area. In areas to the south and west, evidence for categorical expressions in terms of ceramics and public features instead became somewhat more diverse through time. These differences may relate to patterns of regional population movement across the Cibola region. Specifically, in the southern and western Cibola region, there is evidence for the arrival of migrants from outside the region across the Pueblo III to Pueblo IV transition, whereas population movement in the Zuni area was likely local in nature. Importantly, although changes in the expression of categorical identities through different lines of material evidence do overlap to a considerable degree, these patterns do not map onto the strongest patterns of relational connections described above.

## RECONNECTING RELATIONS AND CATEGORIES

As this very brief overview illustrates, the strongest patterns of relational connections are remarkably similar across several lines of material evidence, as are the strongest patterns of categorical distinctions. There are, however, substantial disparities *between* these two dimensions of identification that merit further consideration. The lack of a consistent fit between the strongest patterns of relations and categories is intriguing but not entirely surprising in light of the theoretical perspective considered in this study. Although shared relations and categorical identities often overlap to a degree in many social settings, they can and do sometimes also vary independently (see Stokke and Tjomsland 1996; Tilly 1978). In many archaeological studies, mismatches between material evidence for relational connections (i.e., interaction) and categorical identities (i.e., active expressions of similarity/difference) have often been seen primarily as simply hindrances to identifying social groups using archaeological data (e.g., Jones 1997:122–127; MacEachern 1998; Sætersdal 1999). The theoretical model used in this study suggests instead that such mismatches may also indicate particular social configurations that would have influenced the potential for and trajectory of coordinated social action and social transformation among large groups of people.

The Mariana Mesa area represents a particularly good example of an area marked by a mismatch of relational social ties and expressions of categorical identity. Specifically, the inhabitants of this area appear to have had strong relational social ties, suggesting frequent interaction and/or common historical origins with communities in the southern and western Cibola region, including areas below the Mogollon Rim. As I suggest in several of the previous chapters, such relational connections were likely forged in part through long-term patterns of immigration into the Mariana Mesa region from the western and southern Cibola region or perhaps even farther afield. At the same time, the residents of this area produced and obtained painted vessels similar to those made by the inhabitants of the northern Cibola region and constructed massive great houses, circular great kivas, and walled villages very similar to those to the north. Overall, the varying lines of material evidence combined in this study suggest that the inhabitants of the Mariana Mesa area made active efforts toward signaling shared categorical commonalities with populations in the Zuni area in particular, despite their strong relational and historical connections with populations primarily to the west and south of the Colorado Plateau.

The mismatch between strong patterned relations and categorical expressions in the Mariana Mesa area during the Pueblo III and early Pueblo IV periods (ca. A.D. 1150–1325) considered in this study has an even deeper history than the period considered in this study. In a series of recent analyses, Andrew Duff and several of his students (Clark 2010; Duff 2005; Duff and Nauman 2010; Elkins 2007; Nauman 2007; Wichlacz 2009) have documented a similar pattern of painted ceramics and public architectural traditions associated with Chacoan settlements to the north along with unpainted ceramic assemblages dominated by a southern technological tradition at several eleventh-century great house and non–great house communities along the southern edge of the Colorado Plateau west of Mariana Mesa. Duff and colleagues argue that these communities, sitting along the traditional boundary between the Ancestral Pueblo and Mogollon archaeological culture areas, were likely constructed and occupied by a diverse, possibly multiethnic population, primarily comprised of people with social ties and origins south of the plateau.[1]

As the previous chapters have demonstrated, there was certainly some degree of interaction between the inhabitants of the Mariana Mesa area and the northern Cibola region near Zuni and the El Morro Valley. Small numbers of unpainted vessels produced in the Zuni area did find their way to settlements in the Mariana Mesa region during the period considered here, suggesting that some segment of the population of this area may have had close social ties to communities along the Zuni River and the El Morro Valley. Perhaps more importantly, the inhabitants of the Mariana Mesa area also obtained substantial numbers of painted vessels (in particular polychrome bowls) produced in the Zuni area to the north. Indeed, during the Pueblo III period, St. Johns Polychrome bowls produced in the Pescado Basin were common at the sampled Mariana Mesa settlements. The movement of large numbers of painted vessels suggests that communities in the Mariana Mesa area may have been hosting or participating in periodic public gatherings, likely including people from the Zuni area to the north, where these painted vessels were exchanged. The common participation in such gatherings perhaps suggests "weak" relational ties between Mariana Mesa and the inhabitants of areas to the north. However, the movement of vessels from the Zuni area to the Mariana Mesa settlements was not reciprocal. This suggests that the Mariana Mesa settlements were likely somewhat peripheral to the sphere of exchange and public ceremonialism that characterized settlements along the Zuni River and the El Morro Valley during the period considered in this study. Interestingly, this also suggests that categorical expressions of similarity may have been mediated through relatively ephemeral and infrequent relational interactions. This last point fits squarely within Charles Tilly's (1978) suggestion that strong categorical distinctions often emerge out of less frequently activated networks of relational interaction (see also Mische 2011:86).

The question that arises from the discussion above is, why did people in the Mariana Mesa region choose to express shared categorical identities (through the construction of great houses, great kivas, and painted ceramics) with populations in the northern Cibola region despite their strong social ties, historical connections, and frequent interactions with areas to the south of the Colorado Plateau? At a very basic level, the construction of Chacoan-inspired architectural complexes suggests an awareness of developments in Chaco Canyon and the political and social power of Chaco itself. It is possible that the leaders of local communities in the Mariana Mesa region used Chacoan-inspired architectural symbolism to exploit the political and social resources associated with Chaco (and later post-Chacoan developments) to their own advantages (see Cameron and Duff 2008; Duff 2005). The construction of similar public architectural features, representing common contexts for public ceremonialism, suggests some degree of participation or ideological buy-in to widely held cosmological principles associated with Chaco and later developments (e.g., Fowler and Stein 1992; Fowler et al. 1987; Lekson 2006; Stein and Lekson 1992). Indeed, it is even possible that some segments of the population residing in this area had historical connections or other strong direct ties to Chaco itself. Importantly, as the evidence presented in this study suggests, such an ideological buy-in does not necessarily indicate a high degree of direct and frequent interaction.

I am, of course, not the first to point out that strong patterns of interaction and active expressions of identity are not necessarily isomorphic. For example, Sîan Jones (1997:122–127; see also Eckert 2008:2–3) notes that the extent to which a shared enculturative milieu does or does not overlap with the boundaries of ethnic groups and how such groups are symbolized through material culture can vary considerably. From this, Jones suggests that certain contexts may be more or less amenable for considerations of social identity, specifically ethnicity, through archaeological remains. In other words, where practice and ethnicity do not overlap, it may be difficult to identify discrete social groups through material culture without some other line of independent evidence. While it is true that we must be careful not to assume that all social differences will be expressed through material culture and, conversely, that not all material culture differences indicate social distinctions, through careful contextualization it is often possible to identify the most robust social boundaries (categorical distinctions) and patterns of interaction (relational connections). From this, I argue that mismatches in the strongest evidence for frequent interaction and active expressions of social identities do not simply influence our ability to identify discrete social groups in the past but may also suggest particular configurations of social relationships that would have influenced the organization of cooperation and collective actions among populations at large social and spatial scales.

## SOCIAL IDENTITY AND SOCIAL CHANGE IN THE CIBOLA WORLD

The complex interrelationships between relational and categorical identities described above play a foundational role in the creation of contexts where lasting collective action is likely to occur. Furthermore, the relationships between these modes of identity also influence potential long-term success of such sustained collective actions. Collective actions that are truly transformative are most frequent among groups of individuals characterized by both strong relational connections and a high degree of categorical homogeneity, in other words, catnets. Importantly, many widespread social transformations involve the creation of a social setting resembling a catnet at a new geographic or demographic scale out of some other combination of relations and categories.

Building on this perspective, I argue that the patterns of frequent interaction representing strong relational connections prior to a period of transformation (i.e., prior to the Pueblo III to Pueblo IV transition) should provide an indication of the lines along which increasingly dense relational networks and new categorical identities are most likely to form or solidify across that transformation. Put another way, if the Pueblo III to Pueblo IV transition follows the typical trajectory of social transformation processes documented in many contemporary and recent historical settings (see Diani 2003; McAdam 2003; McAdam et al. 2001; Tilly 1978), we should expect a trajectory of change through time marked by an increasing consolidation of groups sharing strong relational connections, followed by the creation of new and more distinct categorical identities. In this section, I demonstrate that such a pattern of change through time is well supported for the Cibola region.

Although it is difficult to identify the specific actions and events involved in the process of social transformation through archaeological remains alone, it may be possible to demonstrate general similarities in the trajectories of change through time between archaeological cases and other well-studied contemporary contexts. Such similarities further suggest underlying structural correspondence in the mechanisms involved in widespread social change among vastly different social settings. This general comparison is not meant to provide a causal explanation for social transformation; instead, it provides a mechanical one. As Doug McAdam and others put it, such mechanisms represent "a delimited class of events that alter relations among specified elements in identical or closely similar ways over a variety of situations" (2001:11; see also Tilly 2001:24–26). If the social transformation in the Cibola region is governed by mechanisms that are similar to the transformations in contemporary and recent historic contexts (i.e., state-level and commercial societies), it would suggest that the traditional scope of comparative research focused on social transformation has been far too narrow. Demonstrating that such similarities exist is particularly important, as scholars studying the interrelationships between identity and social change in contemporary and recent historical settings often assume that premodern and nonstate societies operated primarily in terms of relations (kinship in particular) and therefore were typically not subject to the dynamics of social transformation described throughout this study (e.g., Calhoun 1997:42–48).

As summarized in the previous section, the various lines of material evidence for the strongest patterns of relational connections across the Cibola region considered in this study were remarkably consistent across the Pueblo III to Pueblo IV transition. At one level, this suggests that the establishment of nucleated settlements was largely organized among groups of individuals who were already interacting on a regular basis prior to the late thirteenth-century transformation (see also Kintigh 2007; Kintigh et al. 2004). At the same time, there were also important changes in the nature and scale of relational networks across this transition that may have influenced the organization and scale of coordinated social change at this time. The framework used in this study suggests that we might expect the relative density of subgroups within a network (the proportion of total possible social ties that are active) to vary in relation to the potential for collective action at a particular scale (see Kim and Bearman 1997; Siegel 2008; Tilly 1978; White 2008a). As the number and strength of internal connections for a given subgroup within a larger network increase relative to the overall network, the importance of that subgroup as a center of collective mobilization is also likely to increase (see Nexon 2009:52–61).

As described above, during both the Pueblo III and Pueblo IV periods there was a strong tendency toward segmentation into two subgroups of settlements characterizing the northern and southern portions of the study area, respectively, but the degree of segmentation increased through time. The formal networks defined based on ceramic technological similarity in Chapter 5 illustrate this point well. During the Pueblo III period the northern and southern portions of the study area represent a single component connected through a few sites located along the transition from the north to the south. By the Pueblo IV period, the ceramic technological network is clearly divided into distinct components for the north and south, with strong internal connections for each subgroup and only weak similarities across these subgroups. This same pattern is also reflected in the dramatically increased segmentation of networks of ceramic circulation during the Pueblo IV period, as the northern Cibola region in particular is increasingly characterized largely by local ceramic circulation. This trend toward segmentation across multiple lines of evidence suggests that across the Pueblo III to Pueblo IV transition, somewhat smaller areas within the larger Cibola region became the more likely scales of collective mobilization and social transformation rather than the region as a whole.

Importantly, the Pueblo III to Pueblo IV transition did not only entail a consolidation and segmentation of regional networks of interaction. This transition also saw the creation of new and more discrete categorical identities. During the last years of the thirteenth century, the Cibola region was marked by an increasing localization of distinctions in highly visible expressions of categorical identity, including polychrome ceramics and public architectural spaces. As I argue above, the public nature of these new categorical expressions suggests that people were making active and unprecedented efforts toward marking social similarities, boundaries, and shared categorical identities during the Pueblo IV period. Within the Zuni area there was a widespread homogenization of such public categorical expressions, which perhaps further suggests active efforts toward maintaining social conformity (see Hegmon et al. 2016). Conversely, along the edges of the Cibola region, the Pueblo III to Pueblo IV transition was marked by a pattern of increasing diversity in categorical expressions through time, in particular in terms of painted ceramics. These different portions of the Cibola region were characterized by different scales of population movement in the late thirteenth century. Specifically, the western and southern portions of the Cibola region likely saw the arrival of migrants from northeastern Arizona or other areas during the late thirteenth century, whereas population movement into the Zuni area was likely more local in nature.

As the brief discussion above illustrates, the Pueblo III to Pueblo IV transition in the Cibola region was marked by a consolidation of relational networks of interaction followed by the creation and spread of new and more distinct categorical identities. The scale at which new categorical expressions of identity were shared differed across the region, perhaps largely as a result of the differing population histories of specific areas. However, across the Pueblo III to Pueblo IV transition, the Zuni area in particular increasingly resembled the idealized description of a catnet described above as a social context marked by strongly overlapping relational connections and shared and homogeneous categorical identities. The trajectory of change through time documented here suggests that the late thirteenth-century social transformation in the Cibola region was characterized by processes that might be expected based on characterizations of contemporary instances of collective mobilization and social transformation described in Chapter 2. This further suggests that the historical ubiquity of social transformation processes, which have traditionally been seen as limited to state-level societies, needs to be reevaluated.

In many ways, the picture of increasingly homogeneous relations and categories in the Zuni area described above is similar to the model of regional-scale interaction in the later Pueblo IV period previously presented by Duff (2002). Relying primarily on data relating to the production and exchange of ceramics, Duff (2002:187–192) argues that the broader Western Pueblo region (a somewhat larger unit than the greater Cibola region considered in this study) is marked by a dichotomy between high-density population areas characterized by material homogeneity (Zuni and Hopi) and low-density population areas characterized by greater material diversity. Duff argues that the differences in the degree of material homogeneity among various portions of the Western Pueblo world are tied to the structural constraints of different demographic configurations. Specifically, he argues that smaller populations likely would have allowed for and even facilitated diverse expressions of identity, whereas such expressions are more likely to have been suppressed in higher-density population areas. From this, he further argues that explorations of social identity in archaeology should be conducted through a consideration of social interactions in relation to demographic conditions "without regard to outward expression of identity in material culture itself" (Duff 2002:187). While I do not disagree that there is a reasonably strong negative relationship between population density and material diversity (see also Nelson et al. 2011), the results presented in this study suggest that this relationship is not strictly structurally determined. Instead, I argue that changing patterns of interactions (relations) and active expressions of identity (categories) through material culture can and do vary independently; further, the varying relationship between these different dimensions and expressions of identity can create contexts more or less ripe for social change.

## RELATIONS, CATEGORIES, AND THE ARCHAEOLOGY OF IDENTITY

The research presented here provides a new perspective for understanding archaeologically observed social transformations by relating the mechanisms involved in the process of social change to the nature and scale of social identities more generally. This perspective relies on a set of concepts and expectations derived from relational sociology that have not been previously applied to archaeological analyses. This study has also presented a number of new methods for operationalizing this model and new insights into how to address regional-scale social processes through archaeological data. The theoretical framework employed in this study has previously only been applied to (and argued to only be relevant for) contemporary and recent historical settings, in particular focused on state-level, commercial, and democratic societies. By demonstrating the applicability of this framework to the Cibola region, this study also provides a case study for comparing the relationships between social transformation and collective identity across a broader array of historical and political contexts. Furthermore, this research also provides theoretical tools for exploring scales of social organization that have often been overlooked or taken for granted in the past.

At the most basic level, this work is fundamentally concerned with issues of identity and how we can study it through material culture. This is a topic of broad theoretical relevance to archaeology in general, but in North America, it is also one with quite concrete ramifications. Considerations of identity have taken on a new importance over the last twenty years due in large part to the passage of the Native American Graves Protection and Repatriation Act of 1990 (NAGPRA; 25 U.S.C. 3001). Among other provisions, NAGPRA mandates a process through which certain cultural items (human remains, funerary objects, sacred objects, and objects of cultural patrimony) held by museums and federal agencies may be repatriated to lineal descendants or Native American tribes deemed culturally affiliated with those objects. Cultural affiliation is defined as "a relationship of shared group identity which can be reasonably traced historically or prehistorically between a present day Indian tribe or Native Hawaiian organization and an identifiable earlier group" (25 U.S.C. 3001). Relationships of cultural affiliation are assessed based on a preponderance of evidence, including archaeological information.

NAGPRA has often been interpreted as requiring the identification of a bounded social group (a cultural entity) in the past and tracking its connections with a modern tribal organization (a political entity). Seen in this way, cultural affiliation is often assessed in terms of archaeological cultures, reified as bounded social groups (see Todd 2005). This approach has been criticized by many as homogenizing both the archaeological record and contemporary Native American groups (e.g., Bernardini 2005; Dongoske et al. 1997).

How, then, does the multidimensional model of social identity used in this study relate to concepts of cultural affiliation as they are applied in NAGPRA and traditional cultural taxonomies in general? As noted in several of the previous chapters, patterns of relational and categorical connections do, at different times and places, *sometimes* show a strong correspondence with archaeological cultures as they have been traditionally defined (i.e., archaeological constructs such as Anasazi and Mogollon). For example, the strongest patterns of technological similarity in terms of unpainted pottery production and domestic architecture are strongly bifurcated along the traditional boundary between areas traditionally defined as Anasazi and Mogollon territory, respectively. This suggests, not surprisingly, that the archaeological cultural designations defined so long ago by the first generation of cultural historians in the Southwest likely do capture certain aspects of interaction (relations) and active expressions of identity (categories) among people at regional scales. At the same time, the analyses presented in this study suggest that such rigid taxonomies also mask a considerable amount of variation and, perhaps most importantly, are not particularly amenable to considerations of change through time. Beyond this, traditional cultural taxonomic classifications are based on the assumption that patterns of interaction and identity should consistently overlap at some scale, an assumption explicitly rejected in this study. Indeed, I would argue that many (perhaps most) cultural historical debates in archaeology (e.g., the Mogollon controversy; see Reid and Whittlesey 2010) boil down to differences between scholars emphasizing either relational connections or categorical distinctions independently, without considering the interplay between them.

The approach to social identity advocated in this study not only allows patterned relations and categorical distinctions to vary independently but actually focuses on the relationship between these dimensions of identity. Although assessments of cultural affiliation based on such complex notions of identity as multiple and fluid are considerably more difficult than assessments that emphasize traditional cultural taxonomies or geography, such efforts have been successful in the recent past (see Beisaw 2010). Perhaps most importantly, the multidimensional model of social identity used in this study is more in line with many traditional tribal notions of culture and identity in that it does not force Native American groups to approach affiliation through a strictly limited range of social and political organizational forms.

# NOTES

## CHAPTER 1

1. The association of social movements with contemporary politics can largely be attributed to the concentration on conflictual social movements in sociology and political science. Modern state power structures tend to engender conflictual dynamics (McAdam et al. 2001). It is likely the case that nonconflictual movements may have been more common in the past.

## CHAPTER 3

1. There is evidence for the construction and use of irrigation canals along the Zuni River Valley and the primary tributaries as early as 1000 B.C. continuing until about A.D. 1000 (Damp et al. 2002). Throughout this interval, irrigation agriculture appears to have been relatively small scale and a minor component of the regional agricultural system. With the construction of the protohistoric Zuni towns in the fourteenth century, however, irrigation agriculture may have taken on a new importance. The construction of these towns was marked by a shift in settlement from the upper reaches of the Zuni River and the El Morro Valley to the areas in and around the modern Pueblo of Zuni. Keith Kintigh (1985a) argues that this settlement shift was associated with a transition from runoff agriculture to an agricultural economy dominated by irrigation.

2. Chaco Canyon was a major center in northwestern New Mexico from the late ninth through the mid-twelfth century. It was associated with large-scale architectural complexes, including multistoried masonry pueblos, great kivas, roads, and other features. By the mid-eleventh century, Chaco-style great house complexes had been constructed in many portions of the northern Southwest, including the Cibola region. There are numerous competing theories regarding what the regional distribution of Chacoan great houses may have represented in social and political terms (see Lekson 2007), but there is little doubt that developments in Chaco Canyon reverberated across much of the northern Southwest at this time.
3. One of these unroofed great kivas is located in the area between the nucleated Mirabal and Cienega sites in the El Morro Valley. Although both of these nucleated pueblos certainly do contain components that postdate A.D. 1275, Mirabal is the only excavated nucleated village with any tree ring cutting dates prior to A.D. 1279. The very small ceramic collection obtained from the unroofed great kiva itself included no glaze-painted ceramics, providing some additional evidence that the structure likely predates A.D. 1275. Other possible unroofed great kivas have been recorded at the nucleated Box S and Kluckhohn sites in the Upper Nutria and El Morro Valley areas, respectively. Although both of these sites probably have post–A.D. 1275 components, they contain considerably less Zuni Glaze Ware than nucleated pueblos with absolute dates after A.D. 1275.

## CHAPTER 4

1. The primary compositional group formation procedure conducted for this study included a total of 2,136 sherds and archaeological clays from sites in the primary study area, as well as a much smaller number of samples from the Cebolleta Mesa, Manuelito Canyon, and Cañada Alamosa areas in the complementary portions of the study area. Additional samples from the Silver Creek drainage and the Arizona Mountains were not included in the primary compositional group formation procedures described below because fewer elements (30) were measured for these samples. These samples were later projected against groups formed within the primary compositional sample as described in the online appendix.

2. Gregson Schachner's (2012) study focused on the El Morro Valley sampled White Mountain Red Ware and Cibola Gray Ware but did not analyze any samples of Cibola White Ware. Although it was not possible to analyze enough additional samples of Cibola White Ware from the El Morro Valley to equal the site-wide proportions of this ware, the results presented here suggest that Cibola White Ware was compositionally similar to existing samples from the El Morro Valley and that this ware circulated along similar lines to the much larger White Mountain Red Ware sample.
3. Within the Upper Little Colorado region, it is possible to track the movement of vessels between the northern, central, and southern portions of the drainage. Duff (2002) describes evidence for the differential movement of vessels within the Upper Little Colorado area during the Pueblo IV period, so this topic is not discussed in detail here. During the Pueblo III period, there was little occupation of the central and northern Upper Little Colorado area, which fits with the virtual absence of compositional groups attributed to those areas at Pueblo III settlements across the region as a whole.

## CHAPTER 5

1. Variables were defined based on the observed variation in corrugated ceramics noted during a pilot study focused on a large sample of ceramic whole vessels and sherds from the El Morro Valley and the Upper Little Colorado subregions. The coding system was further refined through experimental reproductions of corrugated pottery directed at identifying the specific techniques that may have produced a particular attribute in a finished vessel. Observations of corrugated pottery production by John Olsen at the 2009 Leupp Kiln Conference were particularly helpful in refining the coding scheme used here.
2. The clustering level chosen here was selected after numerous trials as a compromise between consistency and interpretability. The general patterns of similarity across the region discussed in this chapter are not, however, severely impacted by the cluster level selected.
3. When only comparisons involving settlements in the Mariana Mesa area are considered, there is actually a weak positive correlation between spatial distance and ceramic technological similarity (Pearson's $r = 0.53$).

4. The Fruchterman-Reingold force-directed algorithm was selected for this analysis.
5. Possible exceptions to the general spatial pattern of relationships noted above include Baca Pueblo in the Upper Little Colorado subregion and WS Ranch in the Mogollon Highlands area. Baca Pueblo is not strongly similar to other sites in the Upper Little Colorado area and shares only a single tie with Ojo Bonito in the West Zuni subregion. Interestingly, Baca Pueblo is the only site in the sample with substantial amounts of Roosevelt Red Ware (ULCPP field notes), a painted ware that some have suggested may have been first produced primarily by migrants from the Kayenta area in northeastern Arizona (Lyons 2003; see also Crown 1994). Roosevelt Red Ware at Baca Pueblo is primarily limited to floor contexts and was likely only present during the latest occupation of the site (see Duff 1999:5.32). As many of the measured sherds also came from floor contexts, the sample may be heavily weighted toward this latest occupation. The presence of migrants from outside the Cibola region could potentially explain the relatively weak similarities between Baca Pueblo and all other sites considered in this study. In addition to this, the WS Ranch site, near Glenwood, New Mexico, in the far southern reaches of the study area, does not show particularly strong similarities to any other site in the sample considered here. The WS Ranch site has a somewhat longer occupation than most other sites included in this study (ca. A.D. 900–1350; see Robinson 1992). Although efforts were made to limit the ceramic sample to vessels from late thirteenth- and early fourteenth-century contexts, it is possible that some of the variation in this sample is due to the inadvertent inclusion of vessels produced in earlier periods.

## CHAPTER 6

1. This pattern may change through time, however. Barbara Mills (1998) notes that prior to about A.D. 1325, settlements in the Silver Creek area were characterized by agglomerative construction, whereas during the later fourteenth century, ladder construction was more common. In the primary portion of the study area considered here, the distinction between areas dominated by ladder-type construction and areas dominated by sites with agglomerative layouts appears to have been in place throughout the period considered in this study.

2. Hearths were categorized as "along a wall" if either one side of the hearth was formed by the wall of the room itself or if the hearth was less than approximately 20 cm from the wall. Hearths were defined as being in a "room corner" when two sides of the hearth were either formed by the wall of the room or less than 20 cm from two walls. Hearths were defined as "room interior" when they did not fit into the categories described above. The vast majority of room interior hearths were roughly centrally located.
3. Patterns of hearth placement change dramatically across the Protohistoric transition in the Zuni region (ca. A.D. 1450), with the vast majority of hearths at Hawikku located in room centers. Interestingly, the Protohistoric transition at Zuni has often been associated, based on several different lines of evidence, with the arrival of migrants from many of the areas to the south (Mills 2007b; Peeples 2014; Schachner 2006), where central hearth placement was the dominant pattern.
4. It is also possible that lower frequency of grinding facilities in the El Morro Valley and Pescado Basin areas may be due to a greater frequency of extramural grinding areas. Although such features are known from the Homol'ovi area (Ortman 1998:179), there is currently little evidence for permanent outdoor grinding facilities in the Cibola region.
5. Coursed adobe construction appears to have also been common at sites dominated by Socorro Black-on-white just east of the Acoma/Cebolleta area (Wozniak and Marshall 1991:6.40–6.42; Wendorf 1956).

## CHAPTER 7

1. Interestingly, there is even evidence in some portions of the Cibola region that settlements with certain architectural features (kivas and great kivas) had higher relative frequencies of polychrome bowls, perhaps suggesting that public food consumption and serving occurred more often in association with certain architectural features.
2. Mills (2007a) also notes that during the late Pueblo IV period (ca. A.D. 1325–1400), as the average size of plaza spaces increased, the height of designs and the frequency of banded designs once again increased. Such a transition was not noted in the Zuni area; however, the average size of plaza spaces did not differ substantially between the early and late Pueblo IV periods (see Chapter 8).

## CHAPTER 8

1. Prior to about A.D. 900, most great kivas in the mountains and to the south were typically circular or bean shaped in form (Anyon and LeBlanc 1980; Haury 1985), though they were also distinct in several features from Chacoan-style great kivas on the Colorado Plateau to the north. Haury (1985) documented a long sequence of circular great kiva construction in the Forestdale Valley that extended into the period considered in this study. Herr (2001) argues, however, that although they share many similarities with earlier southern great kivas, post–A.D. 1000 circular great kivas in the Forestdale Valley and in the Silver Creek area were likely related to and referencing Chacoan developments.
2. For the purposes of this study, I limit the distribution of great houses to those with relatively uncontroversial great house status. There are a number of other structures, especially in areas within the Mogollon Highlands, that have been put forth as possible great houses (Fowler et al. 1987:213–214; Lekson 1991:Figure 3.10, 1999). These potential great house sites generally have fewer features in common with Chacoan constructions than with great houses farther north, but they do meet the criterion of being large in relation to other contemporaneous habitations. Potential examples of great houses in these areas need to be documented in more detail in order to assess their historical or social connections with the rest of the Chacoan/post-Chacoan world.
3. The specific date range of many great kivas in the Mogollon Highlands area is unknown, as most of these sites have not been intensively investigated. Where no additional information was available, great kivas were assumed to span the entire estimated occupation of the sites where they were located.
4. Interestingly, there is also at least one possible great house and an associated circular great kiva in the Mogollon Highlands along Apache Creek near the town of Aragon, New Mexico. This site was first recorded by Hough in 1905 as No. 111 and is also sometimes known as the Aragon site (Hough 1907). The Aragon site is a relatively poorly known C-shaped pueblo of about 70 rooms with massive coursed stone walls, multiple stories, and a large circular depression which may represent a great kiva (Hough 1907; Schroeder and Wendorf 1954). Unfortunately, this site was largely destroyed by highway construction in the 1950s and completely bulldozed in the 1980s. Hough (1907:Plate VIII) published two photographs of the walls and possible great kiva depression at Aragon. Although only limited information is available for the Aragon site,

it potentially represents the southernmost great house in the region (see also Lekson 1999:42–44). Overall, however, despite intriguing possible exceptions such as the Aragon site, the available data suggest that the distributions of great houses with circular great kivas and other communities with rectangular great kivas were fairly distinct during the late Pueblo II period.

5. Ceramic seriation of collections from nucleated pueblos associated with unroofed great kivas suggests that these sites primarily date to the mid- to late thirteenth century (Huntley 2004; Kintigh 1985; Schachner 2007). One unroofed great kiva (CS189) in the El Morro Valley may be an exception to this general pattern. This isolated structure is located between two large nucleated pueblos (Cienega and Mirabal). Although both of these nucleated sites have thirteenth-century occupations, they also both continued to be occupied into the fourteenth century. It is possible that the unroofed great kiva continued to be used into the fourteenth century as well. However, the small ceramic collection available from the area in and around the great kiva itself contains no glaze-painted ceramics, suggesting a pre–A.D. 1275 date.

6. The thirteenth-century pueblo of Turkey Creek in the Point of Pines area included a plaza space that was converted into a great kiva during the thirteenth century (Lowell 1991). In addition to this, the roofed plaza area excavated at Foote Canyon Pueblo along the Blue River may have been a similar structure, although internal floor features other than post holes were not documented (Rinaldo 1959:181).

7. The earliest formal plazas in the Cibola region are associated with eleventh-century Chacoan great houses. These spaces typically consist of bounded areas lined by room blocks or an enclosing wall, often also containing other internal features such as subterranean kivas, hearths, and low masonry walls. Many examples are slightly elevated above the ground surface outside the plaza. In general, enclosed formal plaza areas of this kind are relatively rare in the Cibola region but have been documented at a few Chacoan and post-Chacoan great houses throughout their entire regional distribution. Several great house plazas include elaborate masonry features that have been interpreted as offering boxes, perhaps hinting at the ceremonial activities occurring within these spaces (Fowler et al. 1987:80–81; Marshall et al. 1979:202).

8. Broken K Pueblo in the Hay Hollow Valley may also represent an early example of a partially enclosed plaza pueblo (Hill 1970), although this settlement may have grown into this form rather than being initially planned and constructed around a plaza. There are also possible formal plazas in the Mogollon

Highlands area that have been recorded by Hough, but little information is available on these spaces.

9. Adams (1991:101–103, 125) argues that enclosed plazas north of the Mogollon Rim may have had their origins in the coursed adobe pueblos south of the Gila River down into the Casas Grandes area. Interestingly, however, the site plans examined for this study suggest that partially and fully enclosed plaza spaces were already common in the northern Cibola along the Zuni and Puerco Rivers by the mid-thirteenth century and perhaps somewhat earlier. The massive perimeter walls of many thirteenth-century and later nucleated plaza-oriented pueblos may have developed out of earlier Chacoan architectural forms rather than the southern plaza pueblos (Fowler et al. 1987:97).

10. In addition to the well-dated rectangular and platform kivas documented by Lyons (2001:Chapter 9), other examples have been documented at large sites in the El Morro Valley, including Pueblo de los Muertos and Atsinna (Cibola Archaeological Research Project notes), in the Manuelito Canyon area at Naat'a'anii Bikin (Fowler et al. 1987:97), in the Mariana Mesa area at Horse Camp Mill (McGimsey et al. 1980; Peeples, field notes 2011) and Techado Spring pueblo (Smith et al. 2009), possibly in the Cebolleta Mesa area at the site of Los Pilares (Forrester 1964), and at the Protohistoric and Historic Zuni villages of Hawikuh (Smith et al. 1966) and Kechiba:wa (Cambridge University, field notes 1919).

## CHAPTER 9

1. Even earlier in time (ca. A.D. 600–900), a number of sites along the southern edge of the Colorado Plateau have been recorded that include ceramics associated with both the Anasazi (e.g., Lino Gray, Kana'a Gray, Cibola White Ware, etc.) and Mogollon (Alma Brown Ware, Forestdale Brown Ware, Mogollon Red-on-brown, etc.) areas in varying proportions (Danson 1957:71). William Wasley (1959) argues that, at the Cerro Colorado site near Quemado, both Anasazi and Mogollon ceramic wares were locally produced.

# REFERENCES CITED


Abbott, David R. 2000. *Ceramics and Community Organization among the Hohokam.* University of Arizona Press, Tucson.

Accola, Richard M. 1981. Mogollon Settlement Patterns in the Middle San Francisco River Drainage, West-Central New Mexico. *Kiva* 46(3): 155–168.

Adams, E. Charles. 1991. *The Origin and Development of the Pueblo Katsina Cult.* University of Arizona Press, Tucson.

———. 1993. Toward Understanding the Technological Development of Manos and Metates. *Kiva* 58:331–344.

Adams, E. Charles, and Andrew I. Duff (editors). 2004. *The Protohistoric Pueblo World, A.D. 1275–1600.* University of Arizona Press, Tucson.

Adler, Michael A. 1989. Ritual Facilities and Social Integration in Nonranked Societies. In *The Architecture of Social Integration in Prehistoric Pueblos*, edited by W. D. Lipe and M. Hegmon, pp. 35–52. Occasional Paper No. 1. Crow Canyon Archaeological Center, Cortez, Colorado.

——— (editor). 1996. *The Prehistoric Pueblo World: A.D. 1150–1350.* University of Arizona Press, Tucson.

Adler, Michael A., and Richard H. Wilshusen. 1990. Large-Scale Integrative Facilities in Tribal Societies: Cross-Cultural and Southwestern U.S. Examples. *World Archaeology* 22(2): 133–144.

Anyon, Roger. 1984. *Test Excavations at Seven Prehistoric Sites on the Clo-Chin-Toh Land Exchange near Ramah, McKinley County, New Mexico.* University of New Mexico, Office of Contract Archaeology. Submitted to Cibola National Forest.

Anyon, Roger, Susan M. Collins, and Kathryn H. Bennet. 1983. *Archaeological Investigations between Manuelito Canyon and Whitewater Arroyo, Northwest New Mexico.* Zuni Cultural Resource Enterprise Report No. 185. Zuni Cultural Resource Enterprise, Pueblo of Zuni.

Anyon, Roger, and Steven A. LeBlanc. 1980. The Architectural Evolution of Mogollon-Mimbres Communal Structures. *Kiva* 45:252–277.

Arnold, Dean E., Hector Neff, and Ronald L. Bishop. 1991. Compositional Analysis and "Sources" of Pottery: An Ethnoarchaeological Approach. *American Anthropologist* 93:70–90.

Arnold, Dean E., Hector Neff, and Michael D. Glascock. 2000. Testing Assumptions of Neutron Activation Analysis: Communities, Workshops and Paste Preparation in Yucatán, Mexico. *Archaeometry* 42:301–316.

Asouti, Eleni. 2006. Beyond the Pre-pottery Neolithic B Interaction Sphere. *Journal of World Prehistory* 20(2–4): 87–126.

Aunio, Anna-Liisa, and Suzanne Staggenborg. 2011. Transnational Linkages and Movement Communities. *Sociology Compass* 5(5): 364–375.

Baldassarri, Delia S. 2009. Collective Action. In *The Oxford Handbook of Analytical Sociology*, edited by P. Hedström and P. S. Bearman, pp. 391–418. Oxford University Press, Oxford.

Bannister, Bryant, John W. Hannah, and William J. Robison. 1970. *Tree-Ring Dates from New Mexico: M–N, S, Z: Southwestern New Mexico.* Laboratory of Tree-Ring Research, University of Arizona, Tucson.

Barnett, Franklin. 1974. *Sandstone Hill Pueblo Ruin: Cibola Culture in Catron County, New Mexico.* Albuquerque Archaeological Society, Albuquerque, New Mexico.

Barth, Frederick (editor). 1969. *Ethnic Groups and Boundaries.* Waveland Press, Prospect Heights, Illinois.

Baxter, Sylvester. 1882. The Father of the Pueblos. *Harper's New Monthly Magazine* 65:72–91.

Beeson, William Jean. 1966. Archaeological Survey near St. Johns, Arizona: A Methodological Study. Unpublished Ph.D. dissertation, University of Arizona.

Beisaw, April M. 2010. Memory, Identity, and NAGPRA in the Northeastern United States. *American Anthropologist* 112(2): 244–256.

Bentley, G. Carter. 1987. Ethnicity and Practice. *Comparative Studies in Society and History* 29(1): 24–55.

———. 1991. Response to Yelvington. *Comparative Studies in Society and History* 33(1): 169–175.

Bernardini, Wesley. 1998. Conflict, Migration, and the Social Environment: Interpreting Architectural Changes in Early and Late Pueblo IV Aggregations. In *Migra-*

*tion and Reorganization: The Pueblo IV Period in the American Southwest*, edited by K. A. Spielmann, pp. 91–114. Anthropological Papers No. 51. Arizona State University, Tempe.

———. 2005. *Hopi Oral Tradition and the Archaeology of Identity*. University of Arizona Press, Tucson.

Bernardini, Wesley, and Matthew A. Peeples. 2015. Sight Communities: The Social Significance of Shared Visual Landmarks. *American Antiquity* 80(2): 215–235.

Bice, Richard A. 2004. The AS-6 Pueblo and Pithouse Site (LA12133) North of Quemado, New Mexico. In *Ever Westward: Papers in Honor of Elizabeth Kelley*, edited by R. N. Wiseman, T. C. O'Laughlin, and C. T. Snow, pp. 11–30. Papers of the Archaeological Society of New Mexico No. 30. Archaeological Society of New Mexico, Albuquerque.

Binford, Lewis R. 1962. Archaeology as Anthropology. *American Antiquity* 28:217–225.

———. 1965. Archaeological Systematics and the Study of Cultural Process. *American Antiquity* 31:203–210.

Bishop, Ronald L., Robert L. Rands, and George R. Holley. 1982. Ceramic Compositional Analysis in Archaeological Perspective. In *Advances in Archaeological Method and Theory*, Vol. 5, edited by M. B. Schiffer, pp. 275–330. Academic Press, New York.

Blake, Emma. 2014. *Social Networks and Regional Identity in Bronze Age Italy*. Cambridge University Press, Cambridge.

Blanton, Richard. 2010. Collective Action and Adaptive Socioecological Cycles in Premodern States. *Cross-Cultural Research* 44:41–59.

———. 2011. Cultural Transformation, Art, and Collective Action in Polity Building. *Cross-Cultural Research* 45:106–127.

Blanton, Richard, and Lane F. Fargher. 2008. *Collective Action in the Formation of Premodern States*. Springer, New York.

———. 2009. Collective Action in the Evolution of Pre-modern States. *Social Evolution and History* 8(2): 133–166.

Blau, Peter M. 1977. *Inequality and Heterogeneity*. Free Press, New York.

Blinman, Eric. 1989. Potluck in the Protokiva: Ceramics and Ceremonialism in Pueblo I Villages. In *The Architecture of Social Integration in Prehistoric Pueblos*, edited by W. D. Lipe and M. Hegmon, pp. 113–124. Occasional Paper No. 1. Crow Canyon Archaeological Center, Cortez, Colorado.

Blitz, John. 1993. Big Pots for Big Shots: Feasting and Storage in a Mississippian Community. *American Antiquity* 58(1): 80–96.

Bluhm, Elaine A. 1957. *The Sawmill Site: A Reserve Phase Village, Pine Lawn Valley, Western New Mexico*. Fieldiana: Anthropology Vol. 47, No. 1. Chicago Natural History Museum, Chicago.

Borck, Lewis. 2016. Lost Voices Found: An Archaeology of Contentious Politics in the Greater Southwest, A.D. 1100–1450. Unpublished Ph.D. dissertation, University of Arizona.

Borck, Lewis, Barbara J. Mills, Matthew A. Peeples, and Jeffery J. Clark. 2015. Are Social Networks Survival Networks? An Example from the Late Prehispanic Southwest. *Journal of Archaeological Method and Theory* 22(1): 33–57.

Bordes, François. 1973. On the Chronology and Contemporaneity of Different Paleolithic Cultures in France. In *The Explanation of Culture Change: Models in Prehistory*, edited by C. Renfrew, pp. 217–226. Duckworth, London.

Borgatti, Stephen P., and Daniel S. Halgin. 2011. On Network Theory. *Organization Science* 22(5): 1168–1181.

Bourdieu, Pierre. 1977. *Outline of a Theory of Practice*. Translated by R. Nice. Cambridge University Press, Cambridge.

Bowser, Brenda J. 2000. From Pottery to Politics: An Ethnoarchaeological Study of Political Factionalism, Ethnicity, and Domestic Pottery Style in the Ecuadorian Amazon. *Journal of Archaeological Method and Theory* 7(3): 219–248.

Bradley, Bruce A. 1996. Pitchers to Mugs: Chacoan Revival at Sand Canyon Pueblo. *Kiva* 61(3): 241–255.

Brainerd, George W. 1951. The Place of Chronological Ordering in Archaeological Analysis. *American Antiquity* 16(4): 301–313.

Brandt, Elizabeth A. 1994. Egalitarianism, Hierarchy, and Centralization in the Pueblos. In *The Ancient Southwestern Community: Models and Methods for the Study of Social Organization*, edited by W. H. Wills and R. D. Leonard, pp. 9–23. University of New Mexico Press, Albuquerque.

Braun, David P., and Stephen Plog. 1982. Evolution of "Tribal" Social Networks: Theory and Prehistoric North American Evidence. *American Antiquity* 47:504–525.

Bronitsky, Gordon, and Robert Hamer. 1986. Experiments in Ceramic Technology: The Effects of Various Tempering Materials on Impact and Thermal-Shock Resistance. *American Antiquity* 51(1): 89–101.

Brubaker, Rogers, and Frederick Cooper. 2000. Beyond "Identity." *Theory and Society* 29(1): 1–47.

Brughmans, Tom. 2010. Connecting the Dots: Towards Archaeological Network Analysis. *Oxford Journal of Archaeology* 29(3): 277–303.

———. 2013. Thinking through Networks: A Review of Formal Network Methods in Archaeology. *Journal of Archaeological Method and Theory* 20:623–662.

Brumfiel, Elizabeth, and John Fox. 1994. *Factional Competition and Political Development in the New World*. Cambridge University Press, Cambridge.

Brunson, Judy L. 1985. Corrugated Ceramics as Indicators of Interaction Spheres. In *Decoding Prehistoric Ceramics*, edited by B. A. Nelson, pp. 102–127. Southern Illinois University Press, Carbondale.

Bullard, William Rotch, Jr. 1962. *The Cerro Colorado Site and Pithouse Architecture in the Southwestern United States prior to A.D. 900*. Papers of the Peabody Museum of Archaeology and Ethnology, Harvard University No. 44(2). Peabody Museum, Cambridge, Massachusetts.

Bunzel, Ruth L. 1932. Zuñi Katchinas. In *47th Annual Report of the Bureau of American Ethnology for the Years 1929–1930*, pp. 837–1086. Government Printing Office, Washington, D.C.

Burmeister, Stefan. 2000. Archaeology and Migration: Approaches to an Archaeological Proof of Migration. *Current Anthropology* 41(4): 539–567.

Burton, Jeffery F. 1990. *Archaeological Investigations at Puerco Ruin, Petrified Forest National Park, Arizona*. Publications in Anthropology No. 54. Western Archaeological and Conservation Center, National Park Service, Tucson.

———. 1993. *When Is a Great Kiva? Excavations at McCreery Pueblo, Petrified Forest National Park, Arizona*. Publications in Anthropology No. 63. Western Archaeological and Conservation Center, National Park Service, Tucson.

Calhoun, Craig. 1993. "New Social Movements" of the Early Nineteenth Century. *Social Science History* 17(3): 385–427.

———. 1994. Social Theory and the Politics of Identity. In *Social Theory and the Politics of Identity*, edited by C. Calhoun, pp. 9–36. Blackwell Publishers, Oxford.

———. 1995. *Critical Social Theory: Culture, History, and the Challenge of Difference*. Blackwell Publishers, Oxford.

———. 1997. *Nationalism*. University of Minnesota Press, St. Paul.

Cameron, Catherine M. 1998. Coursed Adobe Architecture, Style, and Social Boundaries in the American Southwest. In *The Archaeology of Social Boundaries*, edited by M. T. Stark, pp. 183–207. Smithsonian Institution Press, Washington, D.C.

———. 1999. Room Size, Organization of Construction, and Archaeological Interpretation in the Puebloan Southwest. *Journal of Anthropological Archaeology* 18:201–239.

Cameron, Catherine M., and Andrew I. Duff. 2008. History and Process in Village Formation: Context and Contrasts from the Northern Southwest. *American Antiquity* 73:29–57.

Carballo, David M. (editor). 2012. *Cooperation and Collective Action: Archaeological Perspectives*. University Press of Colorado, Boulder.

Carlson, Roy A. 1970. *White Mountain Redware: A Pottery Tradition of East-Central Arizona and Western New Mexico*. Anthropological Papers of the University of Arizona No. 19. University of Arizona Press, Tucson.

Carr, Christopher. 1995. A Unified Middle-Range Theory of Artifact Design. In *Style, Society, and Person: Archaeological and Ethnological Perspectives*, edited by C. Carr and J. E. Neitzel, pp. 171–258. Plenum Press, New York.

Chamberlain, Matthew. 2008. Evaluating the Cultural Origins of Complexity in the Ancestral Pueblo World. Unpublished Ph.D. dissertation, Arizona State University.

———. 2012. Plazas, Performance, and Symbolic Power in the Ancestral Pueblo Region. In *Religious Transformation in the Late Pre-Hispanic Pueblo World*, edited by D. M. Glowacki and S. Van Keuren, pp. 130–152. University of Arizona Press, Tucson.

Childe, V. Gordon. 1929. *The Danube in Prehistory*. Oxford University Press, Oxford.

Ciolek-Torrello, Richard. 1985. A Typology of Room Function at Grasshopper Pueblo, Arizona. *Journal of Field Archaeology* 12:41–63.

Ciolek-Torrello, Richard, and J. Jefferson Reid. 1974. Change in House Size at Grasshopper. *Kiva* 40:39–48.

Clark, Jeffrey J. 2001. *Tracking Prehistoric Migrations: Pueblo Settlers among the Tonto Basin Hohokam*. Anthropological Papers No. 65. University of Arizona Press, Tucson.

Clark, Jeffery J., and Patrick D. Lyons. 2013. *Mounds and Migrants: Late Prehistoric Archaeology of the Lower San Pedro River Valley, Arizona*. Anthropological Papers, No. 45. Archaeology Southwest, Tucson.

Clark, Tiffany C., Gregson Schachner, Suzanne L. Eckert, Todd L. Howell, and Deborah L. Huntley. 2006. Rudd Creek Pueblo: A Late Tularosa Phase Village in East Central Arizona. *Kiva* 71(4): 397–428.

Clarke, David L. 1968. *Analytical Archaeology*. Methuen, London.

Cohen, Abner (editor). 1974. *Urban Ethnicity*. University of California Press, Berkeley.

Cohen, Ronald. 1978. Ethnicity: Problem and Focus in Anthropology. *Annual Review of Anthropology* 7:379–403.

Collar, Anna, Fiona Coward, Tom Brughmans, and Barbara J. Mills. 2015. Networks in Archaeology: Phenomena, Abstraction, Representation. *Journal of Archaeological Method and Theory* 22:1–32.

Colton, Harold S. 1939. *Prehistoric Culture Units and Their Relationships in Northern Arizona*. MNA Bulletin 17. Museum of Northern Arizona, Flagstaff.

———. 1953. *Potsherds: An Introduction to the Study of Prehistoric Southwestern Ceramics and Their Use in Historic Reconstruction*. MNA Bulletin 25. Northern Arizona Society of Science and Art, Flagstaff.

Comaroff, John L., and Jean Comaroff. 1992. *Ethnography and the Historical Imagination*. Westview Press, Boulder, Colorado.

Conkey, Margaret, and Christine Hastorf (editors). 1990. *The Uses of Style in Archaeology*. Cambridge University Press, New York.

Cordell, Linda S. 1997. *Archaeology of the Southwest*. 2nd ed. Academic Press, New York.

———. 1998. *Before Pecos: Settlement Aggregation at Rowe, New Mexico*. Anthropological Papers No. 6. Maxwell Museum of Anthropology, University of New Mexico, Albuquerque.

Cordell, Linda S., and Judith A. Habicht-Mauche (editors). 2012. *Potters and Communities of Practice: Glaze Paint and Polychrome Pottery in the American Southwest, A.D. 1250–1700*. University of Arizona Press, Tucson.

Cordell, Linda S., Carla R. Van West, Jeffry S. Dean, and Deborah A. Muenchrath. 2007. Mesa Verde Settlement History and Relocation: Climate Change, Social Networks, and Ancestral Pueblo Migration. *Kiva* 72:379–406.

Croes, Dale R. 1989. Prehistoric Ethnicity on the Northwest Coast of North America: An Evaluation of Style in Basketry and Lithics. *Journal of Anthropological Archaeology* 8:101–130.

Crossley, Nick. 2011. *Towards Relational Sociology*. Routledge, New York.

Crown, Patricia L. 1981. The Ceramic Assemblage. In *Prehistory of the St. Johns Area, East-Central Arizona: The TEP St. Johns Project*, edited by D. A. Westfall, pp. 233–290. Arizona State Museum Archaeological Series No. 153. University of Arizona Press, Tucson.

———. 1994. *Ceramics and Ideology: Salado Polychrome Pottery*. University of New Mexico Press, Albuquerque.

———. 2000. Women's Role in Changing Cuisine. In *Women and Men in the Prehispanic Southwest: Labor, Power, and Prestige*, edited by P. L. Crown, pp. 221–266. School of American Research Press, Santa Fe.

Curta, Florin. 2007. Some Remarks on Ethnicity in Medieval Archaeology. *Early Medieval Europe* 15(2): 159–185.

Cushing, Frank Hamilton. 1890. Preliminary Notes on the Origin, Working Hypothesis, and Primary Researches of the Hemenway Southwestern Archaeological Expedition. Paper presented at the Seventh Congrès International des Américanistes, Berlin, 1888.

———. 1896. Outlines of Zuni Creation Myths. In *Thirteenth Annual Report of the Bureau of American Ethnology, 1891–1892*, pp. 321–447. Smithsonian Institution, Washington, D.C.

———. 1920. *Zuni Breadstuff*. Indian Notes and Monographs No. 8. Museum of the American Indian, New York.

Damp, Jonathan E., Stephen A. Hall, and Susan J. Smith. 2002. Early Irrigation on the Colorado Plateau near Zuni Pueblo, New Mexico. *American Antiquity* 67:665–676.

Danson, Edward Bridge. 1957. *An Archaeological Survey of West Central New Mexico and East Central Arizona*. Papers of the Peabody Museum 44. Harvard University Press, Cambridge, Massachusetts.

Danson, Edward Bridge, and Harold E. Malde. 1950. Casa Malpais: A Fortified Site at Springerville, Arizona. *Plateau* 22(4): 61–67.

Dean, Jeffrey S. 1988. The View from the North: An Anasazi Perspective on the Mogollon. *Kiva* 53:197–199.

DeBoer, Warren R. 1991. The Decorative Burden: Design, Medium, and Change. In *Ceramic Ethnoarchaeology*, edited by W. A. Longacre, pp. 144–161. University of Arizona Press, Tucson.

DeGarmo, Glen Dean. 1975. Coyote Creek, Site 01: A Methodological Study of a Prehistoric Pueblo Population. Unpublished Ph.D. dissertation, University of California, Los Angeles.

Della Porta, Donatella, and Mario Diani. 2006. *Social Movements: An Introduction*. Blackwell Publishing, Malden, Massachusetts.

Diani, Mario. 1992. The Concept of the Social Movement. *Sociological Review* 40(1): 1–25.

———. 2003. Networks and Social Movements: A Research Programme. In *Social Movements and Networks: Relational Approaches to Collective Action*, edited by M. Diani and D. McAdam, pp. 299–319. Oxford University Press, Oxford.

———. 2007. The Relational Element in Charles Tilly's Recent (and Not So Recent) Work. *Social Networks* 29:316–323.

———. 2013. Catnets. In *The Wiley-Blackwell Encyclopedia of Social and Political Movements*, edited by D. A. Snow, D. della Porta, B. Klandermans, and D. McAdam, pp. 170–172. Vol. 1. Wiley-Blackwell, Hoboken, New Jersey.

Diani, Mario, and Doug McAdam (editors). 2003. *Social Movements and Networks*. Oxford University Press, Oxford.

Díaz-Andreu, Margarita, Sam Lucy, Staša Babic, and David N. Edwards. 2005. *The Archaeology of Identity: Approaches to Gender, Age, Ethnicity, Status and Religion*. Routledge, New York.

Dibble, Alison C., Wesley A. Wright, Christopher S. Campbell, and Craig W. Greene. 1998. Quantitative Morphology of the *Amelanchier* Agamic Complex (Rosaceae) at a Maine Site. *Systematic Botany* 23(1): 31–41.

Dietler, Michael, and Ingrid Herbich. 1998. Habitus, Techniques, Style: An Integrated Approach to the Social Understanding of Material Culture and Boundaries. In *The Archaeology of Social Boundaries*, edited by M. T. Stark, pp. 232–263. Smithsonian Institution Press, Washington, D.C.

Dittert, Alfred E. 1959. Culture Change in the Cebolleta Mesa Region, Central Western New Mexico. Unpublished Ph.D. dissertation, University of Arizona.

Dongoske, Kurt E., Michael Yeatts, Roger Anyon, and T. J. Ferguson. 1997. Archaeological Cultures and Cultural Affiliation: Hopi and Zuni Perspectives in the American Southwest. *American Antiquity* 62(4): 600–608.

Dozier, Edward P. 1958. Cultural Matrix of Singing and Chanting in Tewa Pueblos. *International Journal of American Linguistics* 24(4): 268–272.

Duff, Andrew I. 1999. Regional Interaction and the Transformation of Western Pueblo Identities, A.D. 1275–1400. Unpublished Ph.D. dissertation, Arizona State University.

———. 2000. Scale, Interaction, and Regional Analysis in Late Pueblo Prehistory. In *The Archaeology of Regional Interaction: Religion, Warfare, and Exchange across the American Southwest*, edited by M. Hegmon, pp. 51–71. University Press of Colorado, Boulder.

———. 2002. *Western Pueblo Identities: Regional Interaction, Migration, and Transformation*. University of Arizona Press, Tucson.

———. 2004. Settlement Clustering and Village Interaction in the Upper Little Colorado Region. In *The Protohistoric Pueblo World: A.D. 1275–1600*, edited by E. C. Adams and A. I. Duff, pp. 75–84. University of Arizona Press, Tucson.

———. 2005. On the Fringe: Community Dynamics at Cox Ranch Pueblo. In *Proceedings of the 13th Mogollon Archaeology Conference (2004)*, edited by L. Ludeman, pp. 303–319. New Mexico State University, Las Cruces.

Duff, Andrew I., and Stephen H. Lekson. 2006. Notes from the South. In *The Archaeology of Chaco Canyon, an Eleventh Century Pueblo Regional Center*, edited by S. H. Lekson, pp. 315–337. School of American Research, Santa Fe.

Duff, Andrew I., and Alissa L. Nauman. 2010. Engendering the Landscape: Resource Acquisition, Artifact Manufacture, and Household Organization in a Chacoan Great House Community. In *Engendering Households in the Prehistoric Southwest*, edited by B. Roth, pp. 12–33. University of Arizona Press, Tucson.

Duff, Andrew I., and Gregson Schachner. 2007. Becoming Central. In *Hinterlands and Regional Dynamics in the Ancient Southwest*, edited by A. P. I. Sullivan and J. M. Bayman, pp. 185–200. University of Arizona Press, Tucson.

Dungan, Katherine A. 2015. Religious Architecture and Borderlands Histories: Great Kivas in the Prehispanic Southwest, 1000 to 1400 C.E. Unpublished Ph.D. dissertation, University of Arizona.

Dungan, Katherine A., and Matthew A. Peeples. n.d. Public Architecture as Performance Space in the Prehispanic Central Southwest. *Journal of Anthropological Archaeology* in review.

Eckert, Suzanne L. 1995. The Process of Aggregation in the Post-Chacoan Era: A Case Study from the Lower Zuni River Region. Unpublished M.A. thesis, Arizona State University.

———. 2006. Black-on-White to Glaze-on-Red: The Adoption of Glaze Technology in the Central Rio Grande Valley. In *The Social Life of Pots: Glaze Wares and Cultural Dynamics in the Southwest, A.D. 1250–1680*, edited by J. A. Habicht-Mauche, S. L. Eckert, and D. L. Huntley, pp. 163–178. University of Arizona Press, Tucson.

———. 2008. *Pottery and Practice: The Expression of Identity at Pottery Mound and Hummingbird Pueblo*. University of New Mexico Press, Albuquerque.

Edgar, Heather Joy Hecht. 2004. Dentitions, Distance, and Difficulty: A Comparison of Two Statistical Techniques for Dental Morphological Data. *Dental Anthropology* 17(2): 55–61.

Ekeh, Peter P. 1990. Social Anthropology and Two Contrasting Uses of Tribalism in Africa. *Comparative Studies in Society and History* 32(4): 660–700.

Elkins, Melissa Anne. 2007. Serving Up Ethnic Identity in Chacoan Frontier Communities: The Technology and Distribution of Mogollon and Puebloan Ceramic Wares in the Southern Cibola Region. Unpublished M.A. thesis, Washington State University.

Emberling, Geoff. 1997. Ethnicity in Complex Societies: Archaeological Perspectives. *Journal of Archaeological Research* 5(4): 295–344.

Emirbayer, Mustafa. 1997. Manifesto for Relational Sociology. *American Journal of Sociology* 103(2): 281–317.

Emirbayer, Mustafa, and Jeff Goodwin. 1994. Network Analysis, Culture, and the Problem of Agency. *American Journal of Sociology* 99(6): 1411–1454.

Everitt, Brian S., Sabine Landau, and Morven Leese. 2001. *Cluster Analysis*. Wiley, London.

Feinman, Gary M. 2011. Size, Complexity, and Organizational Variation: A Comparative Approach. *Cross-Cultural Research* 45:37–58.

Fenn, Thomas, Barbara J. Mills, and Maren Hopkins. 2006. The Social Contexts of Glaze Paint Ceramic Production and Consumption in the Silver Creek Area. In *The Social Life of Pots: Glaze Wares and Cultural Dynamics in the Southwest, A.D. 1250–1680*, edited by J. A. Habicht-Mauche, S. A. Eckert, and D. L. Huntley, pp. 60–85. University of Arizona Press, Tucson.

Fennell, Christopher C. 2000. Conjuring Boundaries: Inferring Past Identities from Religious Artifacts. *International Journal of Historical Archaeology* 4(4): 281–313.

Ferguson, Jeffrey R., and Michael D. Glascock. 2008. *Instrumental Neutron Activation Analysis of Pottery from Rio Alamosa and Rio Salado, Southwestern New Mexico*. Report on file, University of Missouri Research Reactor.

Ferguson, T. J. 2007. Zuni Traditional History and Cultural Geography. In *Zuni Origins: Toward a New Synthesis of Southwestern Archaeology*, edited by D. A. Gregory and D. R. Wilcox, pp. 377–403. University of Arizona Press, Tucson.

Ferguson, T. J., and E. Richard Hart. 1985. *A Zuni Atlas*. University of Oklahoma Press, Norman.

Fewkes, Jessie Walter. 1891. Reconnaissance of Ruins in or near the Zuñi Reservation. *Journal of American Ethnology and Archaeology* 1:92–132.

Flanagan, J. G. 1989. Hierarchy in "Simple" Egalitarian Societies. *Annual Review of Anthropology* 18:245–266.

Forrester, Robert E. 1964. *Archaeological Investigations at Los Pilares 2:24-D, Western Valencia County, New Mexico*. Kow-ina Cultural Research Foundation, Inc.

———. 1966. *Archaeological Investigations at Sites near Los Pilares 2:24-D, Western Valencia County, New Mexico*. Kow-ina Cultural Research Foundation, Inc.

Foster, Brian L. 1974. Ethnicity and Commerce. *American Ethnologist* 1(3): 437–448.

Fowler, Andrew P., and John R. Stein. 1992. The Anasazi Great House in Space, Time, and Paradigm. In *Anasazi Regional Organization and the Chaco System*, edited by D. E. Doyel, pp. 101–122. Anthropological Papers No. 5. Maxwell Museum of Anthropology, University of New Mexico, Albuquerque.

Fowler, Andrew P., John R. Stein, and Roger Anyon. 1987. *An Archaeological Reconnaissance of West-Central New Mexico: The Anasazi Monuments Project*. Submitted to the Office of Cultural Affairs, Historic Preservation Division, State of New Mexico.

Friedrich, Margaret Hardin. 1970. Design Structure and Social Interaction: Archaeological Implications of an Ethnographic Analysis. *American Antiquity* 35:332–343.

Frisbie, Theodore R. 1984. Zuni and the Mogollon: A New Look at an Old Question. In *Recent Research in Mogollon Archaeology*, edited by S. Upham, F. Plog, D. G. Batcho, and B. E. Kauffman, pp. 98–114. Occasional Papers No. 10. New Mexico State University Museum, Las Cruces.

Gann, Douglass W. 1996. The Use of Adobe Architecture in the Homol'ovi Region. In *River of Change: Prehistory of the Middle Little Colorado Valley, Arizona*, edited by E. C. Adams, pp. 93–106. Arizona State Museum Archaeological Series No. 195. Arizona State Museum, Tucson.

Geary, Patrick. 1983. Ethnic Identity as a Situational Construct in the Early Middle Ages. *Mitteilungen der Anthropologischen Gesellschaft in Wien* 113:15–26.

Geertz, Clifford. 1963. The Integrative Revolution: Primordial Sentiments and Civil Politics in the New States. In *Old Societies and New States: The Quest for Modernity in Asia and Africa*, edited by C. Geertz, pp. 107–113. Free Press, New York.

Gifford, James C., and Watson Smith. 1978. *Gray Corrugated Pottery from Awatovi and Other Jeddito Sites in Northeastern Arizona*. Peabody Museum of Archaeology and Ethnology, Cambridge, Massachusetts.

Gilpin, Dennis. 2003. Chaco-Era Site Clustering and the Concept of Communities. *Kiva* 69:171–205.

Gilpin, Dennis, and Jim Hasbargen. 2004. Architecture and Settlement Patterns. In *Archaeological Excavations in the Carrizo Wash Valley, East-Central Arizona: Data Recovery on the Fence Lake Mine Transportation Corridor*, edited by D. Gilpin, D. A. Phillips Jr., J. H. Ballagh, F. M. O'Hara III, L. Martin, and L. Dickerson, pp. 1081–1106. Vol. 3. SWCA, Flagstaff, Arizona.

Gladwin, Winfred, and Harold S. Gladwin. 1934. *A Method for Designation of Cultures and Their Variations*. Medallion Papers 15. Gila Pueblo, Globe, Arizona.

Glowacki, Donna M. 2011. The Role of Religion in the Depopulation of the Central Mesa Verde Region. In *Religious Transformation in the Late Pre-Hispanic Pueblo World*, edited by D. M. Glowacki and S. Van Keuren, pp. 66–85. University of Arizona Press, Tucson.

———. 2015. *Living and Leaving: A Social History of Regional Depopulation in Thirteenth-Century Mesa Verde*. University of Arizona Press, Tucson.

Glowacki, Donna M., and Hector Neff (editors). 2002. *Ceramic Production and Circulation in the Greater Southwest: Source Determination by INAA and Complementary Mineralogical Investigations*. Cotsen Institute of Archaeology at UCLA, Los Angeles.

Goetze, Christine E., and Barbara J. Mills. 1993. Classification Criteria for Wares and Types. In *Across the Colorado Plateau: Anthropological Studies along the San Juan Basin and Transwestern Mainline Expansion Pipeline Routes*, edited by B. J. Mills, C. E. Goetze, and M. N. Zedeño, pp. 21–86. Vol. 16. Office of Contract Archaeology and the Maxwell Museum of Anthropology, University of New Mexico, Albuquerque.

Golitko, Mark, and Gary M. Feinman. 2015. Procurement and Distribution of Pre-Hispanic Mesoamerican Obsidian, 900 B.C.–A.D. 1529: A Social Network Analysis. *Journal of Archaeological Method and Theory* 22(1): 206–247.

Golitko, Mark, James Meierhoff, Gary M. Feinman, and Patrick Ryan Williams. 2012. Complexities of Collapse: The Evidence of Maya Obsidian as Revealed by Social Network Graphical Analysis. *Antiquity* 86(332): 507–523.Gosselain, Olivier P. 1998. Social and Technical Identity in a Clay Crystal Ball. In *The Archaeology of Social Boundaries*, edited by M. T. Stark, pp. 78–106. Smithsonian Institution Press, Washington, D.C.

———. 2000. Materializating Identities: An African Perspective. *Journal of Archaeological Method and Theory* 7(3): 187–217.

Gould, Roger V. 1993. Collective Action and Network Structure. *American Sociological Review* 58(2): 182–196.

Gower, J. C. 1971. A General Coefficient of Similarity and Some of Its Properties. *Biometrics* 27:857–871.

Granovetter, Mark S. 1973. The Strength of Weak Ties. *American Journal of Sociology* 78(6): 1360–1380.

Graves, Michael W. 1991. Pottery Production and Distribution among the Kalinga: A Study of Household and Regional Organization and Differentiation. In *Ceramic Ethnoarchaeology*, edited by W. A. Longacre, pp. 112–143. University of Arizona Press, Tucson.

Graves, William M., and Suzanne A. Eckert. 1998. Decorated Ceramic Distributions and Ideological Developments in the Northern and Central Rio Grande Valley, New Mexico. In *Migration and Reorganization: The Pueblo IV Period in the American Southwest*, edited by K. A. Spielmann, pp. 263–283. Anthropological Papers No. 51. Arizona State University, Tempe.

Green, Jesse (editor). 1990. *Cushing at Zuni: The Correspondence and Journals of Frank Hamilton Cushing, 1879–1884*. University of New Mexico Press, Albuquerque.

Gregory, David A., and David R. Wilcox (editors). 2007. *Zuni Origins: Toward a New Synthesis of Southwestern Archaeology*. University of Arizona Press, Tucson.

Gumerman, George J., and S. Alan Skinner. 1968. A Synthesis of the Prehistory of the Central Little Colorado Valley, Arizona. *American Antiquity* 33:185–199.

Haas, Jonathan, and Winfred Creamer. 1996. The Role of Warfare in the Pueblo III Period. In *The Prehistoric Pueblo World: A.D. 1150–1350*, edited by M. A. Adler, pp. 205–213. University of Arizona Press, Tucson.

Hagopian, Janet, Kelley Hays-Gilpin, and Jim Hasbargen. 2004. Ceramic Analysis. In *Archaeological Investigations in the Carrizo Wash Valley, East-Central Arizona: Date Recovery on the Fence Lake Mine Transportation Corridor*, edited by D. Gilpin, D. A. Phillips Jr., J. H. Ballagh, F. M. O'Hara III, L. Martin, and L. Dickerson. SWCA Cultural Resources Report No. 03-265. SWCA, Flagstaff.

Hally, David J. 1986. The Identification of Vessel Function: A Case Study from Northwest Georgia. *American Antiquity* 51(2): 267–295.

Hansen, John A., and Michael B. Schiffer. 1975. The Joint Site: A Preliminary Report. In *Chapters in the Prehistory of Eastern Arizona IV*, pp. 47–91. Fieldiana: Anthropology 65. Field Museum of Natural History, Chicago.

Hart, John P., and William Engelbrecht. 2012. Northern Iroquoian Ethnic Evolution: A Social Network Analysis. *Journal of Archaeological Method and Theory* 19(2): 322–349.

Haury, Emil W. 1936. *The Mogollon Culture of Southwestern New Mexico*. Medallion Papers 20. Gila Pueblo, Globe, Arizona.

———. 1950. A Sequence of Great Kivas in the Forestdale Valley, Arizona. In *For the Dean: Essays in Anthropology in Honor of Byron Cummings*, edited by E. K. Reed and D. S. King, pp. 29–39. Hohokam Museum Association and the Southwestern Monuments Association, Tucson and Santa Fe.

———. 1985. *Mogollon Culture in the Forestdale Valley, East-Central Arizona*. University of Arizona Press, Tucson.

Hawkins, Julie A., Laura White Olascoaga, Colin E. Hughes, José-Luis R. Contreras Jiménez, and Pedro Mercado Ruardo. 1999. Investigation and Documentation of Hybridization between *Parkinsonia aculeata* and *Cercidium praecox* (Leguminosae: Caesalipinioideae). *Plant Systematics and Evolution* 216(1–2): 49–68.

Hays-Gilpin, Kelley, and Eric van Hartesveldt. 1998. *Prehistoric Ceramics of the Puerco Valley: The 1995 Chambers-Sanders Trust Lands Ceramic Conference*. Museum of Northern Arizona Ceramic Series No. 7. Museum of Northern Arizona, Flagstaff.

Hegmon, Michelle. 1989. Social Integration and Architecture. In *The Architecture of Social Integration in Prehistoric Pueblos*, edited by W. D. Lipe and M. Hegmon, pp. 5–14. Occasional Papers 1. Crow Canyon Archaeological Center, Cortez, Colorado.

———. 1992. Archaeological Research on Style. *Annual Review of Anthropology* 21: 517–536.

———. 1995. *The Social Dynamics of Pottery Style in the Early Puebloan Southwest*. Occasional Papers 4. Crow Canyon Archaeological Center, Cortez, Colorado.

———. 1998. Technology, Style, and Social Practices: Archaeological Approaches. In *The Archaeology of Social Boundaries*, edited by M. T. Stark, pp. 264–279. Smithsonian Institution Press, Washington, D.C.

———. 2000. Advances in Ceramic Ethnoarchaeology. *Journal of Archaeological Method and Theory* 7(3): 129–137.

Hegmon, Michelle, Jette Arneborg, Andrew J. Dugmore, George Hambrecht, Scott Ingram, Keith W. Kintigh, Thomas H. McGovern, Margaret C. Nelson, Matthew A. Peeples, Ian Simpson, Katherine A. Spielmann, Richard Streeter, and Orri Vesteinsson. 2014. The Human Experience of Social Change and Continuity: The Southwest and the North Atlantic in "Interesting Times" ca. 1300. In *Climates of Change: The Shifting Environments of Archaeology*, edited by L. C. Tremain and M. Sawyer, pp. 53–67. Proceedings of the 44th Annual Chacmool Conference. University of Calgary Press, Calgary.

Hegmon, Michelle, Jacob Freeman, Keith W. Kintigh, Margaret C. Nelson, Sarah Oas, Matthew A. Peeples, and Andrea Torvinen. 2016. Marking and Making Difference: Representational Diversity in the U.S. Southwest. *American Antiquity* 81(2): 253–272.

Hegmon, Michelle, Margaret C. Nelson, and Mark J. Ennes. 2000. Corrugated Pottery, Technological Style, and Population Movement in the Mimbres Region of the American Southwest. *Journal of Anthropological Research* 56(2): 217–240.

Hegmon, Michelle, Margaret C. Nelson, and Susan Ruth. 1998. Abandonment, Reorganization, and Social Change: Analyses of Pottery and Architecture from the Mimbres Region of the American Southwest. *American Anthropologist* 100:148–162.

Hegmon, Michelle, Matthew A. Peeples, Ann P. Kinzig, Stephanie Kulow, Cathryn M. Meegan, and Margaret C. Nelson. 2008. Social Transformation and Its Human Costs in the Prehispanic U.S. Southwest. *American Anthropologist* 110(3): 313–324.

Herbich, Ingrid. 1987. Learning Patterns, Potter Interaction and Ceramic Style among the Luo of Kenya. *African Archaeological Review* 5:139–204.

Herr, Sarah A. 1994. Great Kivas as Integrative Architecture in the Silver Creek Community. Unpublished M.A. thesis, University of Arizona.

———. 2001. *Beyond Chaco: Great Kiva Communities on the Mogollon Rim Frontier*. Anthropological Papers 66. University of Arizona Press, Tucson.

Hill, James N. 1968. Broken K Pueblo: Patterns of Form and Function. In *New Perspectives in Archaeology*, edited by S. R. Binford and L. R. Binford, pp. 103–142. Aldine, Chicago.

———. 1970. *Broken K Pueblo: Prehistoric Social Organization in the American Southwest*. Anthropological Papers of the University of Arizona 18. University of Arizona Press, Tucson.

Hill, J. Brett, Jeffrey J. Clark, William H. Doelle, and Patrick D. Lyons. 2004. Prehistoric Demography in the Southwest: Migration, Coalescence, and Hohokam Population Decline. *American Antiquity* 69(4): 689–716.

Hill, J. Brett, Matthew A. Peeples, Deborah L. Huntley, and H. Jane Carmack. 2015. Spatializing Social Network Analysis in the Precontact U.S. Southwest. *Advances in Archaeological Practice* 3(1): 63–77.

Hillier, Bill, and Julienne Hansen. 1984. *The Social Logic of Space*. Cambridge University Press, Cambridge.

Hodder, Ian. 1979. Social and Economic Stress and Material Culture Patterning. *American Antiquity* 44:446–454.

———. 1982. *Symbols in Action*. Ethnoarchaeological Studies of Material Culture. Cambridge University Press, Cambridge.

Hogan, Patrick. 1985. *Prehistoric Settlement Patterns in West-Central New Mexico: The Fence Lake Coal Lease Surveys*. Office of Contract Archaeology, University of New Mexico.

Homburg, Jeffrey A., Jonathan A. Sandor, and Jay B. Norton. 2005. Anthropogenic Influences on Zuni Agricultural Soils. *Geoarchaeology: An International Journal* 20(7): 661–693.

Hough, Walter. 1903. Archaeological Fieldwork in Northeastern Arizona: The Museum-Gates Expedition of 1901. In *Report of the U.S. National Museum*, pp. 279–358. U.S. Government Printing Office, Washington, D.C.

———. 1907. *Antiquities of the Upper Gila and Salt River Valleys in Arizona and New Mexico.* Bulletin 35. Bureau of American Ethnology, Smithsonian Institution, Washington, D.C.

Howell, Todd L. 2000. *The Archaeology and Ethnohistory of Oak Wash, Zuni Indian Reservation, New Mexico.* Zuni Cultural Resource Enterprise Report No. 664. Zuni Cultural Resource Enterprise, Pueblo of Zuni.

———. 2004. *Archaeological Investigations at Site LA 132353 for the Proposed New Ramah High School, Ramah, McKinley County, New Mexico.* Zuni Cultural Resource Enterprise Report No. 819. Zuni Cultural Resource Enterprise, Pueblo of Zuni.

Howell, Todd L., and Keith W. Kintigh. 1996. The Archaeological Identification of Kin Groups Using Mortuary and Biological Data: An Example from the American Southwest. *American Antiquity* 61:537–554.

Hu, Di. 2013. Approaches to the Archaeology of Ethnogenesis: Past and Emergent Perspectives. *Journal of Archaeological Research* 21:371–402.

Hunter-Anderson, Rosiland L. 1977. *An Archaeological Survey of the Yellowhouse Dam Area.* Report on file, Office of Contract Archaeology, University of New Mexico.

Huntley, Deborah L. 2004. Interaction, Boundaries, and Identities: A Multiscalar Approach to the Organizational Scale of Pueblo IV Zuni Society. Unpublished Ph.D. dissertation, Arizona State University.

———. 2006. From Recipe to Identity: Exploring Zuni Glaze Ware Communities of Practice. In *The Social Life of Pots: Glaze Wares and Cultural Dynamics in the Southwest, A.D. 1250–1680*, edited by J. A. Habicht-Mauche, S. A. Eckert, and D. L. Huntley, pp. 105–123. University of Arizona Press, Tucson.

———. 2008. *Ancestral Zuni Glaze-Decorated Pottery: Viewing Pueblo IV Regional Organization through Ceramic Production and Exchange.* Anthropological Papers No. 72. University of Arizona Press, Tucson.

Huntley, Deborah L., and Keith W. Kintigh. 2004. Archaeological Patterning and the Organizational Scale of Late Prehistoric Settlement Clusters in the Zuni Region of New Mexico. In *The Protohistoric Pueblo World: A.D. 1275–1600*, edited by E. C. Adams and A. I. Duff, pp. 62–74. University of Arizona Press, Tucson.

James, Steven R. 1994. Regional Variation in Prehistoric Pueblo Households and Social Organization: A Quantitative Approach. Unpublished Ph.D. dissertation, Arizona State University.

———. 1997. Change and Continuity in Western Pueblo Households during the Historic Period in the American Southwest. *World Archaeology* 28(3): 429–456.

Jenkins, Richard. 1997. *Rethinking Ethnicity*. Sage, London.

———. 2000. Categorization: Identity, Social Process and Epistemology. *Current Sociology* 48(3): 7–25.

———. 2004. *Social Identity*. Routledge, London.

Jennings, Calvin H. 1967. *1967 Excavations at the Puerco Site: Preliminary Report*. Report on file, Western Archaeological and Conservation Center, National Park Service.

Jones, Sîan. 1996. Discourses of Identity in the Interpretation of the Past. In *Cultural Identity in Archaeology*, edited by P. Graves-Brown, S. Jones, and C. Gable, pp. 62–80. Routledge, London.

———. 1997. *The Archaeology of Ethnicity: Constructing Identities in the Past and Present*. Routledge, London.

Jordan, Terry G., and Matti Kaups. 1987. Folk Architecture in Cultural and Ecological Context. *Geographical Review* 77:52–75.

Kaldahl, Eric J., Scott Van Keuren, and Barbara J. Mills. 2004. Migration, Factionalism, and the Trajectories of Pueblo IV Period Clusters in the Mogollon Rim Region. In *The Protohistoric Pueblo World, A.D. 1275–1600*, edited by E. C. Adams and A. I. Duff, pp. 85–94. University of Arizona Press, Tucson.

Kantner, John. 2008. The Archaeology of Regions: From Discrete Analytical Toolkit to Ubiquitous Spatial Perspective. *Journal of Archaeological Research* 16:37–81.

Kantner, John, and Keith W. Kintigh. 2006. The Chaco World. In *The Archaeology of Chaco Canyon, an Eleventh Century Pueblo Regional Center*, edited by S. H. Lekson, pp. 153–188. School of American Research, Santa Fe.

Kaufman, Leonard, and Peter J. Rousseeuw. 1990. *Finding Groups in Data: An Introduction to Cluster Analysis*. Wiley, New York.

Kaufmann, Eric P. (editor). 2004. *Rethinking Ethnicity: Majority Groups and Dominant Minorities*. Routledge, New York.

Kidder, Alfred V. 1932. *The Artifacts of Pecos*. Papers of the Phillips Academy Southwestern Expedition No. 6. New Haven, Connecticut.

Killick, David. 2004. Social Constructionist Approaches to the Study of Technology. *World Archaeology* 36(4): 571–578.

Kim, Hyojoung, and Peter S. Bearman. 1997. The Structure and Dynamics of Movement Participation. *American Sociological Review* 62(1): 70–93.

Kimes, T., C. Haselgrove, and Ian Hodder. 1982. A Method for the Identification of the Location of Regional Cultural Boundaries. *Journal of Anthropological Archaeology* 1(2): 113–131.

Kintigh, Keith W. 1980. *Archaeological Clearance Investigation of the Miller Canyon and Southeastern Boundary Fencing Projects, Zuni Indian Reservation, New Mexico*. Zuni Archaeology Program, Pueblo of Zuni.

———. 1985a. *Settlement, Subsistence, and Society in Late Zuni Prehistory*. Anthropological Papers No. 44. University of Arizona Press, Tucson.

———. 1985b. Social Structure, the Structure of Style, and Stylistic Patterns in Cibola Pottery. In *Decoding Prehistoric Ceramics*, edited by B. Nelson, pp. 35–74. Southern Illinois University Press, Carbondale.

———. 1990. Intrasite Spatial Analysis: A Commentary on Major Methods. In *Mathematics and Information Science in Archaeology: A Flexible Framework*, edited by A. Voorrips, pp. 165–200. Studies in Modern Archaeology. Holos, Bonn.

———. 1994. Chaco, Community Architecture, and Cibolan Aggregation. In *The Ancient Southwestern Community: Models for the Study of Prehistoric Social Organization*, edited by W. H. Wills and R. D. Leonard, pp. 131–140. University of New Mexico Press, Albuquerque.

———. 1996. The Cibola Region in the Post-Chacoan Era. In *The Prehistoric Pueblo World, A.D. 1150–1350*, edited by M. Adler, pp. 131–144. University of Arizona Press, Tucson.

———. 2003. Coming to Terms with the Chaco World. *Kiva* 69:93–116.

———. 2007. Late Prehistoric and Protohistoric Settlement Systems in the Zuni Area. In *Zuni Origins: Toward a New Synthesis of Southwestern Archaeology*, edited by D. A. Gregory and D. R. Wilcox, pp. 361–376. University of Arizona Press, Tucson.

Kintigh, Keith W., and Albert J. Ammerman. 1982. Heuristic Approaches to Spatial Analysis in Archaeology. *American Antiquity* 47(1): 31–63.

Kintigh, Keith W., Donna M. Glowacki, and Deborah L. Huntley. 2004. Long-Term Settlement History and the Emergence of Towns in the Zuni Area. *American Antiquity* 69(3): 432–456.

Kintigh, Keith W., Todd L. Howell, and Andrew I. Duff. 1996. Post-Chacoan Social Integration at the Hinkson Site, New Mexico. *Kiva* 61(3): 257–274.

Kleinman, Joshua J. 2010. Analysis of Corrugated Pottery from the Hopi Mesas: A Quantitative Approach. Unpublished M.A. thesis, Northern Arizona University.

Knappett, Carl, and Ray Rivers (editors). 2013. *New Approaches in Region Network Analysis*. Oxford University Press, Oxford.

Kohler, Timothy A., Stephanie VanBuskirk, and Samantha Ruscavage-Barz. 2004. Vessels and Villages: Evidence for Conformist Transmission in Early Village

Aggregations on the Pajarito Plateau, New Mexico. *Journal of Anthropological Archaeology* 23(1): 100–118.

Kollock, Peter. 1998. Social Dilemmas: The Anatomy of Cooperation. *Annual Review of Sociology* 24:183–214.

Kossinna, Gustaf. 1911. *Der Herkunft der Germanen*. Kabitzsch, Leipzig.

Kristiansen, Kristian, and Michael Rowlands (editors). 1998. *Social Transformations in Archaeology: Global and Local Perspectives*. Routledge, New York.

Kroeber, Alfred L. 1939. *Cultural and Natural Areas of Native North America*. University of California Publication in American Archaeology and Ethnology 38. University of California Press, Berkeley.

Kukelman, Kristan A., Ricky R. Lightfoot, and Debra L. Martin. 2000. Changing Patterns of Violence in the Northern San Juan Region. *Kiva* 66:147–165.

———. 2002. The Bioarchaeology and Taphonomy of Violence at Castle Rock and Sand Canyon Pueblos, Southwestern Colorado. *American Antiquity* 67:486–513.

Kuran, Timur. 1989. Sparks and Prairie Fires: A Theory of Unanticipated Political Revolution. *Public Choice* 61(1): 41–74.

Kus, Susan. 1982. Matters Material and Ideal. In *Symbolic and Structural Archaeology*, edited by I. Hodder, pp. 47–62. Cambridge University Press, Cambridge.

LeBlanc, Steven A. 1975. Micro-seriation: A Method for Fine Chronologic Differentiation. *American Antiquity* 40(1): 22–38.

———. 1989. Cibola: Shifting Cultural Boundaries. In *Dynamics of Southwest Prehistory*, edited by L. S. Cordell and G. J. Gumerman, pp. 337–370. Smithsonian Institution Press, Washington, D.C.

———. 1999. *Prehistoric Warfare in the American Southwest*. Anthropological Papers No. 1. National Park Service, U.S. Department of the Interior, Washington, D.C.

———. 2001. Warfare and Aggregation in the El Morro Valley, New Mexico. In *Deadly Landscapes: Case Studies in Prehistoric Southwestern Warfare*, edited by G. E. Rice and S. A. LeBlanc, pp. 19–50. University of Utah Press, Salt Lake City.

LeBlanc, Steven A., and Lucia R. Henderson. 2009. *Symbols in Clay: Seeking Artists' Identities in Hopi Yellow Ware Bowls*. Papers of the Peabody Museum No. 84. Peabody Museum of Ethnology and Archaeology, Cambridge, Massachusetts.

Lechtman, Heather. 1977. Style in Technology: Some Early Thoughts. In *Material Culture: Styles, Organization, and Dynamics of Technology*, edited by H. Lechtman and R. S. Merrill, pp. 3–20. West Publishing, St. Paul, Minnesota.

Lekson, Stephen H. 1991. Settlement Pattern and the Chaco Region. In *Chaco and Hohokam: Prehistoric Regional Systems in the American Southwest*, edited by P. L. Crown and W. J. Judge. School of American Research, Advanced Seminar Series. SAR Press, Santa Fe.

———. 1996. Southwestern New Mexico and Southeastern Arizona. In *The Prehistoric Pueblo World: AD 1150–1350*, edited by M. A. Adler, pp. 170–176. University of Arizona Press, Tucson.

———. 1999. *The Chaco Meridian: Centers of Political Power in the Ancient Southwest.* Altamira Press, Walnut Creek, California.

———. 2007. *The Architecture of Chaco Canyon.* University of Utah Press, Salt Lake City.

Lemonnier, Pierre. 1986. The Study of Material Culture Today: Toward an Anthropology of Technical Systems. *Journal of Anthropological Archaeology* 5(2): 147–186.

Leroi-Gourhan, André. 1964. *Le geste et la parole, tome I: Technique et langage.* Albin Michel, Paris.

Lesure, Richard G. 1998. Vessel Form and Function in an Early Formative Ceramic Assemblage from Coastal Mexico. *Journal of Field Archaeology* 25(1): 19–36.

Lewis, Martin W. 1991. Elusive Societies: A Regional-Cartographical Approach to the Study of Human Relatedness. *Annals of the Association of American Geographers* 81(4): 605–626.

Liebmann, Matthew J. 2012. *Revolt: An Archaeological History of Pueblo Resistance and Revitalization in 17th Century New Mexico.* University of Arizona Press, Tucson.

Lightfoot, Kent G. 1981. Prehistoric Political Development in the Little Colorado Region, East-Central Arizona. Unpublished Ph.D. dissertation, Arizona State University.

———. 1984. *Prehistoric Political Dynamics: A Case Study from the American Southwest.* Northern Illinois University Press, DeKalb.

Linthicum, B. Lynn. 1980. Pettit Site Masonry: A Study in Intra-site Social Integration. Unpublished M.A. thesis, Wake Forest University.

Lipe, William D. 2002. Social Power in the Central Mesa Verde Region, A.D. 1150–1290. In *Seeking the Center Place: Archaeology and Ancient Communities in the Mesa Verde Region*, edited by M. D. Varien and R. H. Wilshusen, pp. 203–232. University of Utah Press, Salt Lake City.

Lipe, William D., and Michelle Hegmon. 1989. Historical and Analytical Perspectives on Architecture and Social Integration in the Prehistoric Pueblos. In *The Architecture of Social Integration in Prehistoric Pueblos*, edited by W. D. Lipe and M. Hegmon, pp. 15–34. Occasional Paper No. 1. Crow Canyon Archaeological Center, Cortez, Colorado.

Longacre, William A. 1964. A Synthesis of Upper Little Colorado Prehistory. In *Chapters in the Prehistory of Eastern Arizona II*, edited by P. S. Martin, J. B. Rinaldo, W. A. Longacre, L. G. Freeman Jr., J. Brown, H. Hevly, and M. E. Cooley, pp. 201–215. Fieldiana: Anthropology 55. Field Museum of Natural History, Chicago.

Low, Setha M. 1996. Spatializing Culture: The Social Production and Social Construction of Public Space in Costa Rica. *American Ethnologist* 23:861–879.

Lowell, Julia C. 1991. *Prehistoric Households at Turkey Creek Pueblo, Arizona*. Anthropological Papers No. 54. University of Arizona Press, Tucson.

———. 1999. The Fires of Grasshopper: Enlightening Transformations in Subsistence Practices through Fire-Feature Analysis. *Journal of Anthropological Archaeology* 18:441–470.

Lyons, Patrick D. 2001. Winslow Orange Ware and the Ancestral Hopi Migration Horizon. Unpublished Ph.D. dissertation, University of Arizona.

———. 2003. *Ancestral Hopi Migrations*. Anthropological Paper 68. University of Arizona Press, Tucson.

Lyons, Patrick D., and Jeffrey J. Clark. 2008. Interaction, Enculturation, Social Distance and Ancient Ethnic Identities. In *Archaeology without Borders: Contact, Commerce, and Change in the U.S. Southwest and Northern Mexico*, edited by L. D. Webster and M. E. McBrinn, pp. 185–208. University Press of Colorado, Boulder.

———. 2012. A Community of Practice in Diaspora: The Rise and Demise of Roosevelt Red Ware. In *Potters and Communities of Practice: Glaze Paint and Polychrome Pottery in the American Southwest, A.D. 1250–1700*, edited by L. Cordell and J. A. Habicht-Mauche, pp. 19–33. University of Arizona Press, Tucson.

MacEachern, Scott. 1998. Scale, Style and Cultural Variation: Technological Traditions in the Northern Mandara Mountains. In *The Archaeology of Social Boundaries*, edited by M. T. Stark, pp. 107–131. Smithsonian Institution Press, Washington, D.C.

Mahoney, Nancy, Andrew I. Duff, and Keith W. Kintigh. 1995. The Role of Chacoan Outliers in Local Organization. Paper presented at the 60th Annual Meeting of the Society for American Archaeology, Minneapolis.

Marshall, Michael P., John R. Stein, Richard W. Loose, and Judith E. Novotny. 1979. *Anasazi Communities of the San Juan Basin*. Public Service Company of New Mexico and the State of New Mexico, Historic Preservation Bureau, Santa Fe.

Martin, Paul S. 1943. *The SU Site: Excavations at a Mogollon Village, Western New Mexico, 1941*. Fieldiana: Anthropology 32(2). Field Museum of Natural History, Chicago.

———. 1951. The Peoples of the Pine Lawn Valley. *Scientific American* 185(1): 46–51.

———. 1961. *Mineral Creek Site and Hooper Ranch Pueblo, Eastern Arizona*. Fieldiana: Anthropology 52. Chicago Natural History Museum, Chicago.

Martin, Paul S., William A. Longacre, and James N. Hill. 1967. *Chapters in the Prehistory of Eastern Arizona, III*. Fieldiana: Anthropology 57. Field Museum of Natural History, Chicago.

Martin, Paul S., and John B. Rinaldo. 1950. *Sites of the Reserve Phase, Pine Lawn Valley, Western New Mexico.* Fieldiana: Anthropology 38. Chicago Natural History Museum, Chicago.

———. 1960. *Table Rock Pueblo, Arizona.* Fieldiana: Anthropology 51(2). Chicago Natural History Museum, Chicago.

Martin, Paul S., John B. Rinaldo, and Eloise R. Barter. 1957. *Late Mogollon Communities: Four Sites of the Tularosa Phase, Western New Mexico.* Fieldiana: Anthropology 49(1). Chicago Natural History Museum, Chicago.

Martin, Paul S., John B. Rinaldo, John B. Bluhm, and Hugh C. Cutler. 1956. *Higgins Flat Pueblo, Western New Mexico.* Fieldiana: Anthropology 45. Chicago Natural History Museum, Chicago.

Martin, Paul S., John B. Rinaldo, John B. Bluhm, Hugh C. Cutler, and Roger Grange Jr. 1952. *Mogollon Cultural Continuity and Change: The Stratigraphic Analysis of Tularosa and Cordova Caves.* Fieldiana: Anthropology 40. Chicago Natural History Museum, Chicago.

Martin, Paul S., John B. Rinaldo, and William A. Longacre. 1961. *Mineral Creek Site and Hooper Ranch Pueblo: Eastern Arizona.* Fieldiana: Anthropology 52. Chicago Natural History Museum, Chicago.

Martin, Paul S., John B. Rinaldo, William A. Longacre, Constance Cronin, Leslie G. Freeman Jr., and James Schoenwetter. 1962. *Chapters in the Prehistory of Eastern Arizona, I.* Fieldiana: Anthropology 53. Chicago Natural History Museum, Chicago.

Martin, Paul S., John B. Rinaldo, William A. Longacre, Leslie G. Freeman Jr., James A. Brown, Richard H. Hevly, and M. E. Cooley. 1964. *Chapters in the Prehistory of Eastern Arizona, II.* Fieldiana: Anthropology 55. Field Museum of Natural History, Chicago.

McAdam, Doug. 1999. *Political Process and the Development of Black Insurgency, 1930–1970.* University of Chicago Press, Chicago.

———. 2003. Beyond Structural Analysis: Toward a More Dynamic Understanding of Social Movements. In *Social Movements and Networks: Relational Approaches to Collective Action*, edited by M. Diani and D. McAdam, pp. 281–298. Oxford University Press, Oxford.

McAdam, Doug, and Ronnelle Paulson. 1993. Specifying the Relationship between Social Ties and Activism. *American Journal of Sociology* 99(3): 640–667.

McAdam, Doug, Sidney Tarrow, and Charles Tilly. 2001. *Dynamics of Contention.* Cambridge University Press, Cambridge.

———. 2008. Methods for Measuring Mechanisms of Contention. *Qualitative Sociology* 31:307–331.

McCarthy, John D., and Mark Wolfson. 1992. Consensus Movements, Conflict Movements, and the Cooperation of Civic and State Infrastructures. In *Frontiers in Social Movement Research*, edited by A. D. Morris and C. McClurg Mueller, pp. 273–300. Yale University Press, New Haven, Connecticut.

McGary, Thomas E. 1975. Cibola Corrugated: A Proposed New Pottery Type from the Southwest. Unpublished M.A. thesis, Wichita State University.

McGimsey, Charles R., III. 1980. *Mariana Mesa: Seven Prehistoric Settlements in West-Central New Mexico*. Papers of the Peabody Museum of Archaeology and Ethnology 72. Harvard University, Cambridge, Massachusetts.

McGuire, Randall H. 1989. The Greater Southwest as a Periphery of Mesoamerica. In *Centre and Periphery: Comparative Studies in Archaeology*, edited by T. C. Champion, pp. 40–66. Unwin and Hyman, London.

McGuire, Randall H., and Dean J. Saitta. 1996. Although They Have Petty Captains, They Obey Them Badly: The Dialectics of Prehispanic Western Pueblo Social Organization. *American Antiquity* 61(2): 197–216.

McKay, James M. 1982. An Exploratory Synthesis of Primordial and Mobilizationist Approaches to Ethnic Phenomena. *Ethnic and Racial Studies* 5(4): 395–420.

McPherson, Miller, Lynn Smith-Lovin, and James M. Cook. 2001. Birds of a Feather: Homophily in Social Networks. *Annual Review of Sociology* 27:415–444.

Meanwell, Jennifer L. 2015. Technical Requirements and Technical Choices in Pottery Production: A View from the Middle Balsas Region of Guerrero, Mexico. *American Antiquity* 80(2): 312–331.

Meinander, Carl F. 1981. The Concept of Culture in European Archaeological Literature. In *Towards a History of Archaeology*, edited by G. Daniel, pp. 100–111. Thames and Hudson, London.

Michaelson, Marc. 1994. Wangari Maathai and Kenya's Green Belt Movement: Exploring the Evolution and Potentialities of Consensus Movement Mobilization. *Social Problems* 41(4): 540–561.

Michaelson, Robert S. 1977. Enigmas in Interpreting Mormonism. *Sociological Analysis* 38(2): 145–153.Mills, Barbara J. 1995. The Organization of Protohistoric Zuni Ceramic Production. In *Ceramic Production in the American Southwest*, edited by B. J. Mills and P. L. Crown, pp. 200–230. University of Arizona Press, Tucson.

———. 1998. Migration and Pueblo IV Community Reorganization in the Silver Creek Area, East-Central Arizona. In *Migration and Community Reorganization: The Pueblo IV Period in the American Southwest*, edited by K. A. Spielmann, pp. 65–80. Anthropological Research Papers 51. Arizona State University, Tempe.

———. 2007a. A Regional Perspective on Ceramics and Zuni Identity, A.D. 200–1630. In *Zuni Origins: Toward a New Synthesis of Southwestern Archaeology*, edited by D. A. Gregory and D. R. Wilcox, pp. 210–238. University of Arizona Press, Tucson.

———. 2007b. Performing the Feast: Visual Display and Suprahousehold Commensalism in the Puebloan Southwest. *American Antiquity* 72(2): 210–240.

———. 2016. Communities of Consumption: Cuisines as Networks of Situated Practice. In *Learning and Doing: Communities of Practice in Scalar Perspective*, edited by A. B. Stahl and A. Roddick. University of Arizona Press, Tucson.

Mills, Barbara J., Jeffery J. Clark, Matthew A. Peeples, W. Randall Haas Jr., John M. Roberts Jr., J. Brett Hill, Deborah L. Huntley, Lewis Borck, Ronald L. Breiger, Aaron Clauset, and M. Steven Shackley. 2013. The Transformation of Social Networks in the Late Prehispanic U.S. Southwest. *Proceedings of the National Academy of Sciences* 110:5785–5790.

Mills, Barbara J., Sarah A. Herr, and Scott Van Keuren. 1999. *Living on the Edge of the Rim: Excavations and Analysis of the Silver Creek Archaeological Research Project, 1993–1998*. Arizona State Museum Archaeological Series No. 192. University of Arizona, Tucson.

Mills, Barbara J., Matthew A. Peeples, W. Randall Haas Jr., Lewis Borck, Jeffery J. Clark, and John M. Roberts Jr. 2015. Multiscaler Perspectives on Social Networks in the Late Prehispanic Southwest. *American Antiquity* 80(1): 3–24.

Mills, Barbara J., John M. Roberts Jr., Jeffery J. Clark, William R. Haas Jr., Deborah L. Huntley, Matthew A. Peeples, Lewis Borck, Susan C. Ryan, Meaghan A. Trowbridge, and Ronald L. Breiger. 2013. The Dynamics of Social Networks in the Late Prehispanic U.S. Southwest. In *New Approaches in Regional Network Analysis*, edited by C. Knappett and R. Rivers, pp. 185–206. Oxford University Press, Oxford.

Mindeleff, Victor. 1891. *A Study of Pueblo Architecture in Tusayan and Cibola*. Eighth Annual Report of the Bureau of American Ethnology. Smithsonian Institution, Washington, D.C.

Mische, Ann. 2009. *Partisan Publics: Communication and Contention across Brazilian Youth Activist Networks*. Princeton University Press, Princeton, New Jersey.

———. 2011. Relational Sociology, Culture, and Agency. In *The SAGE Handbook of Social Network Analysis*, edited by J. P. Scott and P. Carrington, pp. 80–97. SAGE Publications, London.

Moeller, D. A., and B. A. Schaal. 1999. Genetic Relationships among Native American Maize Accessions of the Great Plains Assessed by RAPDs. *Theoretical and Applied Genetics* 99:1061–1067.

Moerman, Michael. 1965. Ethnic Identification in a Complex Civilization: Who Are the Lue? *American Anthropologist* 67(5): 1215–1230.

Moore, Summer. 2006. White Mountain Redware at the Pettit Site: A Study of Intra-community Social Organization in West-Central New Mexico. Unpublished M.A. thesis, University of Denver.

Muenchrath, Deborah A., Maya Kuratomi, Jonathan A. Sandor, and Jeffrey A. Homburg. 2002. Observational Study of Maize Production Systems of Zuni Farmers in Semiarid New Mexico. *Journal of Ethnobiology* 22(1): 1–33.

Narroll, Raoul. 1964. Ethnic Unit Classification. *Current Anthropology* 5:283–314.

Nauman, Alissa L. 2007. Learning Frameworks and Technological Traditions: Pottery Manufacture in a Chaco Period Great House Community on the Southern Colorado Plateau. Unpublished M.A. thesis, Washington State University.

Neff, Hector. 2002. Quantitative Techniques for Analyzing Ceramic Compositional Data. In *Ceramic Production and Circulation in the Greater Southwest: Source Determination by INAA and Complementary Mineralogical Investigations*, edited by D. M. Glowacki and H. Neff, pp. 15–36. Cotsen Institute of Archaeology Monograph 44. Cotsen Institute of Archaeology at UCLA, Los Angeles.

Neff, Hector, James W. Cogswell, and Louis M. Ross Jr. 2003. Supplementing Bulk Chemistry in Archaeological Ceramic Provenance Investigations. In *Patterns and Process: A Festschrift in Honor of Dr. Edward V. Sayre*, edited by L. van Zelst, pp. 201–224. Smithsonian Center for Materials Research and Education, Suitland, Maryland.

Neff, Hector, and Donna M. Glowacki. 2002. Ceramic Source Determination by Instrumental Neutron Activation Analysis in the American Southwest. In *Ceramic Production and Circulation in the Greater Southwest: Source Determination by INAA and Complementary Mineralogical Investigations*, edited by D. M. Glowacki and H. Neff, pp. 1–14. Cotsen Institute of Archaeology Monograph 44. Cotsen Institute of Archaeology at UCLA, Los Angeles.

Neitzel, Jill E. 2000. What Is a Regional System? In *The Archaeology of Regional Interaction: Religion, Warfare, and Exchange across the American Southwest and Beyond*, edited by M. Hegmon, pp. 25–40. University Press of Colorado, Boulder.

Nelson, Margaret C., Stephanie Kulow, Matthew A. Peeples, Michelle Hegmon, and Ann P. Kinzig. 2011. Resisting Diversity in Small Scale Societies: A Long-Term Archaeological Study. *Ecology and Society* 16(1): article 25.

Nesbitt, Paul H. 1938. *Starkweather Ruin*. Publications in Anthropology No. 6. Logan Museum, Beloit, Wisconsin.

Neuzil, Anna A. 2001. Ceramics and Social Dynamics: Technological Style and Corrugated Ceramics during the Pueblo III to Pueblo IV Transition, Silver Creek, Arizona. Unpublished M.A. thesis, University of Arizona.

———. 2005. Corrugated Ceramics and Migration in the Pueblo III to Pueblo IV Transition, Silver Creek, Arizona. *Kiva* 71(1): 101–124.

———. 2008. *In the Aftermath of Migration: Renegotiating Ancient Identity in Southeastern Arizona.* Anthropological Papers 73. University of Arizona Press, Tucson.

Neuzil, Anna A., and Patrick D. Lyons. 2005. *An Analysis of Whole Vessels from the Mills Collection Curated at Eastern Arizona College, Thatcher, Arizona.* Technical Report No. 2005-001. Center for Desert Archaeology, Tucson.

Nexon, Daniel H. 2009. *The Struggle for Power in Early Modern Europe: Religious Conflict, Dynastic Empires, and International Change.* Princeton University Press, Princeton, New Jersey.

Norton, Jay B., Jonathan A. Sandor, and Carleton S. White. 2003. Hillslope Soils and Organic Matter Dynamics within a Native American Agroecosystem on the Colorado Plateau. *Soil Science Society of America Journal* 67(1): 225–234.

Oakes, Yvonne R. 1999. Synthesis and Conclusions. In *Archaeology of the Mogollon Highlands: Settlement Systems and Adaptations,* edited by Y. R. Oakes and D. A. Zamora, pp. 295–318. Archaeology Notes 232, Vol. 6. Museum of New Mexico, Office of Archaeological Studies, Santa Fe.

Oliver, Pamela E., and Gerald Marwell. 1988. The Paradox of Group Size in Collective Action: A Theory of Critical Mass. *American Sociological Review* 53(1): 1–8.

Olson, Alan P. 1960. The Dry Prong Site, East Central Arizona. *American Antiquity* 26:185–204.

Ortman, Scott G. 1998. Corn Grinding and Community Organization in the Pueblo Southwest, A.D. 1150–1550. In *Migration and Reorganization: The Pueblo IV Period in the American Southwest,* edited by K. A. Spielmann, pp. 165–192. Anthropological Research Papers No. 51. Arizona State University, Tempe.

———. 2012. *Winds from the North: Tewa Origins and Historical Anthropology.* University of Utah Press, Salt Lake City.

Ostrom, Elinor. 2000. Collective Action and the Evolution of Social Norms. *Journal of Economic Perspectives* 14(3): 137–158.

———. 2010. Analyzing Collective Action. *Agricultural Economics* 41(1): 155–166.

Ownby, Mary F., Deborah L. Huntley, and Matthew A. Peeples. 2014. A Combined Approach: Using NAA and Petrography to Examine Ceramic Production and Exchange in the American Southwest. *Journal of Archaeological Science* 52:152–162.

Pachucki, Mark A., and Ronald L. Breiger. 2010. Cultural Holes: Beyond Relationality in Social Networks and Culture. *Annual Review of Sociology* 36:205–224.

Pailes, Matthew C. 2014. Social Network Analysis of Early Classic Hohokam Corporate Group Inequality. *American Antiquity* 79(3): 465–486.

Parkinson, William A. 2006. Tribal Boundaries: Stylistic Variability and Social Boundary Maintenance during the Transition to the Copper Age on the Great Hungarian Plain. *Journal of Anthropological Archaeology* 25:33–58.

Parsons, Elsie Clews. 1939. *Pueblo Indian Religion*. 2 vols. University of Chicago Press, Chicago.

Parsons, Talcott. 1937. *The Structure of Social Action*. McGraw Hill, New York.

Paynter, Robert. 1989. The Archaeology of Equality and Inequality. *Annual Review of Anthropology* 18:369–399.

Peckham, Stewart. 1969. *An Archaeological Site Inventory of New Mexico, Part 1*. Report on file, Laboratory of Anthropology, Museum of New Mexico.

Peckham, Stewart, Fred Wendorf, and Edwin N. Ferdon Jr. 1956. Excavations near Apache Creek, New Mexico. In *Highway Salvage Archaeology Volume 3*. New Mexico Highway Department and the Museum of New Mexico, Santa Fe.

Peeples, Matthew A. 2011. Identity and Social Transformation in the Prehispanic Cibola World: A.D. 1150–1325. Unpublished Ph.D. dissertation, Arizona State University.

———. 2014. Population History of the Zuni Region across the Protohistoric Transition: Migration, Gene Flow, and Social Transformation. In *Building Transnational Archaeologies*, edited by E. Villalpando and R. H. McGuire, pp. 93–109. Arizona State Museum Archaeological Series 209. Arizona State Museum and the University of Arizona, Tucson.

Peeples, Matthew A., and W. Randall Haas Jr. 2013. Brokerage and Social Capital in the Prehispanic U.S. Southwest. *American Anthropologist* 115(3): 232–247.

Peeples, Matthew A., Barbara J. Mills, W. Randall Haas Jr., Jeffery J. Clark, and John M. Roberts Jr. 2016. Analytical Challenges for the Application of Social Network Analysis in Archaeology. In *The Connected Past: Challenging Networks in Archaeology and History*, edited by T. Brughmans, A. Collar, and F. Coward, pp. 59–84. Oxford University Press, Oxford.

Peeples, Matthew A., and John M. Roberts Jr. 2013. To Binarize or Not to Binarize: Relational Data and the Construction of Archaeological Networks. *Journal of Archaeological Science* 40(7): 3001–3010.

———. 2012. Refining Correspondence Analysis-Based Ceramic Seriation of Regional Data Sets. *Journal of Archaeological Science* 39(8): 2818–2827.

Peeples, Matthew A., Gregson Schachner, and Edgar K. Huber. 2012. Rethinking Pithouse Communities across the Greater Zuni Region. In *Southwestern Pithouse Communities, AD 200–900*, edited by L. C. Young and S. A. Herr, pp. 166–180. University of Arizona Press, Tucson.

Pierce, Christopher. 2005. The Development of Corrugated Pottery in Southwestern Colorado. *Kiva* 71(1): 79–100.

Plog, Fred. 1983. Political and Economic Alliances on the Colorado Plateaus, A.D. 400–1450. In *Advances in World Archaeology, Volume II*, edited by F. Wendorf and A. E. Close, pp. 289–330. Academic Press, New York.

Plog, Fred, and Steadman Upham. 1983. The Analysis of Prehistoric Political Organization. In *Development of Political Organization in Native North America*, edited by E. Tooker and M. Fried, pp. 199–213. American Ethnological Society, Washington, D.C.

Plog, Stephen. 1980. *Stylistic Variation in Prehistoric Ceramics: Design Analysis in the American Southwest*. Cambridge University Press, Cambridge.

Pohl, J. 2004. Regional Identity. In *International Encyclopedia of the Social and Behavioral Sciences*, edited by N. J. Smelser and P. B. Baltes, pp. 12917–12922. Elsevier, Amsterdam.

Polletta, Francesca, and James M. Jasper. 2001. Collective Identity and Social Movements. *Annual Review of Sociology* 27:283–305.

Potter, James M. 1997. Communal Ritual, Feasting, and Social Differentiation in Late Prehistoric Zuni Communities. Unpublished Ph.D. dissertation, Arizona State University.

———. 1998. The Structure of Open Space in Late Prehistoric Settlements in the Southwest. In *Migration and Reorganization: The Pueblo IV Period in the American Southwest*, edited by K. A. Spielmann, pp. 137–164. Anthropological Papers No. 51. Arizona State University, Tempe.

———. 2000. Pots, Parties, and Politics: Communal Feasting in the American Southwest. *American Antiquity* 65(4): 471–492.

Powers, Robert P., William B. Gillespie, and Stephen H. Lekson. 1983. *The Outlier Survey: A Regional View of Settlement in the San Juan Basin*. Reports of the Chaco Center No. 3. Division of Cultural Resources, National Park Service, Albuquerque.

Preucel, Robert W. 2005. Ethnicity and Southwestern Archaeology. In *Southwestern Archaeology in the Twentieth Century*, edited by L. Cordell and D. Fowler, pp. 174–193. University of Utah Press, Salt Lake City.

Rapoport, Amos. 1982. *The Meaning of the Built Environment: A Nonverbal Communication Approach*. SAGE, Beverly Hills, California.

———. 1990. *History and Precedent in Environmental Design*. Plenum Press, New York.

Rautman, Alison. 1993. Resource Variability, Risk, and the Structure of Social Networks: An Example from the Prehistoric Southwest. *American Antiquity* 58(3): 403–424.

Reid, J. Jefferson. 1989. A Grasshopper Perspective on the Mogollon of the Arizona Mountains. In *Dynamics of Southwest Prehistory*, edited by L. S. Cordell and G. J. Gumerman, pp. 65–97. Smithsonian Institution Press, Washington, D.C.

Reid, J. Jefferson, and Barbara K. Montgomery. 1998. The Brown and the Gray: Pots and Population Movement in East-Central Arizona. *Journal of Anthropological Research* 54(4): 447–459.

Reid, J. Jefferson, J. R. Welsh, B. K. Montgomery, and Maria Nieves Zedeño. 1996. A Demographic Overview of the Late Pueblo III Period in the Mountains of East Central Arizona. In *The Prehistoric Pueblo World, A.D. 1150–1300*, edited by M. Adler, pp. 73–85. University of Arizona Press, Tucson.

Reid, J. Jefferson, and Stephanie Whittlesey. 2010. *Prehistory, Personality, and Place: Emil W. Haury and the Mogollon Controversy*. University of Arizona Press, Tucson.

Riggs, Charles R., Jr. 2001. *The Architecture of Grasshopper Pueblo*. University of Utah Press, Salt Lake City.

———. 2005. Late Ancestral Pueblo or Mogollon Pueblo? An Architectural Perspective on Identity. *Kiva* 70:323–348.

Rinaldo, John B. 1941. Conjectures on the Independent Development of the Mogollon Culture. *American Antiquity* 7:5–19.

———. 1959. *Foote Canyon Pueblo, Eastern Arizona*. Fieldiana: Anthropology 49(2). Field Museum of Natural History, Chicago.

———. 1964. Notes on the Origins of Historic Zuni Culture. *Kiva* 29:86–98.

Rinaldo, John B., and Elaine A. Bluhm. 1956. *Late Mogollon Pottery Types of the Reserve Area*. Fieldiana: Anthropology 7. Field Museum of Natural History, Chicago.

Roberts, Frank H. H., Jr. 1929. *Shabik'eschee Village: A Late Basket Maker Site in the Chaco Canyon*. Bulletin 92. Bureau of American Ethnology, Smithsonian Institution, Washington, D.C.

———. 1932. *The Village of the Great Kivas on the Zuni Reservation, New Mexico*. Bulletin 111. Bureau of American Ethnology, Smithsonian Institution, Washington, D.C.

———. 1939. *Archaeological Remains in the Whitewater District, Eastern Arizona*. Bulletin 121. Bureau of American Ethnology, Smithsonian Institution, Washington, D.C.

Roberts, John M., Jr., Barbara J. Mills, Jeffery J. Clark, W. Randall Haas Jr., Deborah L. Huntley, and Meaghan A. Trowbridge. 2012. A Method for Chronological Apportioning of Ceramic Assemblages. *Journal of Archaeological Science* 39(5): 1513–1520.

Robinson, David G. 1992. Pueblo Period Societal Differentiation in the Middle San Francisco River Valley Region, West-Central New Mexico. Unpublished Ph.D. dissertation, University of Texas.

Robinson, Hugh L. 2005. Feasting, Exterior Bowl Decoration, and Public Space in the Northern San Juan, A.D.1240–1300. Unpublished M.A. thesis, Washington State University.

Robinson, W. S. 1951. A Method for Chronologically Ordering Archaeological Deposits. *American Antiquity* 16(4): 293–301.

Roney, John R. 1996. The Pueblo III Period in the Eastern San Juan Basin and Acoma-Laguna Area. In *The Prehistoric Pueblo World, A.D. 1150–1350*, edited by M. A. Adler, pp. 145–169. University of Arizona Press, Tucson.

Roosens, Eugeen. 1989. *Creating Ethnicity: The Process of Ethnogenesis*. Sage, Newbury Park, California.

Roper, Donna C., Richard L. Josephs, and Margaret E. Beck. 2010. Determining Provenance of Shell-Tempered Pottery from the Central Plains Using Petrography and Oxidation Analysis. *Latin American Antiquity* 75:134–157.

Rudé, George. 1981. *The Crowd in History: A Study of Popular Disturbances in France and England, 1730–1848*. Lawrence and Wishart, London.

Ruppé, Reynold J. 1990. *The Acoma Culture Province*. Garland Publishing, Inc., New York.

Sackett, James R. 1977. The Meaning of Style in Archaeology: A General Model. *American Antiquity* 42(3): 369–381.

Sætersdal, Tore. 1999. Symbols of Cultural Identity: A Case Study from Tanzania. *African Archaeological Review* 16(2): 121–135.

Saitta, Dean J. 1994. The Political Economy and Ideology of Early Population Aggregation in Togeye Canyon, A.D. 1150–1250. In *Exploring Social, Political, and Economic Organization in the Zuni Region*, edited by T. L. Howell and T. Stone, pp. 47–60. Anthropological Research Papers No. 46. Arizona State University, Tempe.

Santoro, Marco. 2008. Framing Notes: An Introduction to "Catnets." *Sociologica* 1 (http://www.sociologica.mulino.it/doi/10.2383/26574).

Sassman, Kenneth E., and Wictoria Rudolphi. 2001. Communities of Practice in the Early Ceramic Traditions of the American Southeast. *Journal of Anthropological Research* 57(4): 407–425.

Schachner, Gregson. 2001. Ritual Control and Transformation in Middle-Range Societies: An Example from the American Southwest. *Journal of Anthropological Archaeology* 20:168–194.

———. 2006. The Decline of Zuni Glaze Ware Production in the Tumultuous Fifteenth Century. In *The Social Life of Pots: Glaze Wares and Cultural Dynamics in the Southwest, A.D. 1250–1680*, edited by J. A. Habicht-Mauche, S. A. Eckert, and D. L. Huntley, pp. 124–141. University of Arizona Press, Tucson.

———. 2007. Population Circulation and the Transformation of Ancient Cibola Communities. Unpublished Ph.D. dissertation, Arizona State University.

———. 2008. Imagining Communities in the Cibola Past. In *The Social Construction of Communities: Agency, Structure, and Identity in the Prehispanic Southwest*, edited by M. D. Varien and J. M. Potter, pp. 171–190. Archaeology and Society Series. Altamira Press, Lanham, Maryland.

———. 2012. *Population Circulation and the Transformation of Ancient Zuni Communities*. University of Arizona Press, Tucson.

Schachner, Gregson, Katelyn Bishop, and A. J. White. 2016. *Stone Axe Archaeological Survey, Apache County, Arizona*. Technical Report 1. UCLA Cotsen Institute, Los Angeles.

Schachner, Gregson, Dennis Gilpin, and Matthew A. Peeples. 2012. Alternative Trajectories during the Early Pueblo Period in the Little Colorado Drainage and Beyond. In *Crucible of Pueblos: The Early Pueblo Period in the Northern Southwest*, edited by R. H. Wilshusen, G. Schachner, and J. R. Allison, pp. 101–126. Cotsen Institute of Archaeology at UCLA, Los Angeles.

Schachner, Gregson, Deborah L. Huntley, and Andrew I. Duff. 2011. Changes in Regional Organization and Mobility in the Zuni Region of the American Southwest during the Pueblo III and IV Periods: Insights from INAA Studies. *Journal of Archaeological Science* 38:2261–2273.

Schachner, Gregson, and Keith W. Kintigh. 2004. Community Formation and Migration in the 13th Century El Morro Valley, New Mexico. Poster presented at the 69th Annual Meeting of the Society for American Archaeology, Montreal, Canada.

Schleher, Kari L., and Susan M. Ruth. 2005. Migration or Local Development? Technological Analysis of Corrugated Wares at the Pinnacle Ruin, Southwest New Mexico. *Pottery Southwest* 24(3–4): 2–14.

Schroeder, A. H., and Fred Wendorf. 1954. Excavations near Aragon, New Mexico. In *Highway Salvage Archaeology Volume 1*, pp. 53–65. Museum of New Mexico, Santa Fe.

Schwartz, Michael, and Paul Shuva. 1992. Resource Mobilization versus the Mobilization of People: Why Consensus Movements Cannot Be Instruments of Social Change. In *Frontiers in Social Movement Theory*, edited by A. D. Morris and C. McClurg Mueller, pp. 205–223. Yale University Press, New Haven, Connecticut.

Scott, John. 1991. *Social Network Analysis: A Handbook*. Sage, London.

Shapiro, Gary. 1984. Ceramic Vessels, Site Permanence, and Group Size: A Mississippian Example. *American Antiquity* 49(4): 696–712.

Shennan, Stephen J. (editor). 1989. *Archaeological Approaches to Cultural Identity*. Unwin and Hyman, London.

Shils, Edward. 1957. Primordial, Personal, and Sacred, Civil Ties. *British Journal of Sociology* 8(2): 130–145.

Siegel, David A. 2009. Social Networks and Collective Action. *American Journal of Political Science* 53(1): 122–138.

Sindbæk, Søren M. 2007. Networks and Nodal Points: The Emergence of Towns in Early Viking Age Scandinavia. *Antiquity* 81:119–132.

Skibo, James M. 1992. *Pottery Function: A Use-Alteration Perspective*. Plenum Press, New York.

Smail, D. L. 2000. *Imaginary Cartographies: Possession and Identity in Late Medieval Marseille*. Cornell University Press, Ithaca, New York.

Smiley, Terah L. 1952. *Four Late Prehistoric Kivas at Point of Pines, Arizona*. Social Science Bulletin 21. University of Arizona Press, Tucson.

Smith, Anthony D. 1981. *The Ethnic Revival in the Modern World*. Cambridge University Press, Cambridge.

———. 1984. Ethnic Myths and Ethnic Revivals. *European Journal of Sociology* 25: 283–305.

Smith, Jimmy E., II, Louis Robertson, Art Tawater, Bryan Jameson, and Glynn Osburn. 2009. *Techado Spring Pueblo: West-Central New Mexico*. Special Publications No. 3. LER & Sons Publications, Dallas, Texas.

Smith, Michael E. 2017. Social Science and Archaeological Enquiry. *Antiquity* 91(356): 520–528.

Smith, Michael E., Gary M. Feinman, Robert D. Drennan, Timothy Earle and Ian Morris. 2012. Archaeology as a Social Science. *Proceedings of the National Academy of Sciences* 109(20): 7617–7621.

Smith, Watson. 1972. *Prehistoric Kivas of Antelope Mesa: Northeastern Arizona*. Peabody Museum of Archaeology and Ethnology, Cambridge.

Smith, Watson, Richard B. Woodbury, and Nathalie F. Woodbury. 1966. *The Excavation of Hawikuh by Frederick Webb Hodge: Report of the Hendricks-Hodge Expedition, 1917–1923*. Contributions from the Museum of the American Indian, Heye Foundation No. 20, New York.

Snow, David H. 1983. Handedness, Technology and Symbolism in Anasazi Indented Corrugated Wares. In *Collected Papers in Honor of Charlie R. Steen*, edited by N. L.

Fox. Papers of the Archaeological Society of New Mexico No. 8. Archaeological Society of New Mexico, Albuquerque.

Solometo, Julia. 2004. The Conduct and Consequences of War: Dimensions of Conflict in East-Central Arizona. Unpublished Ph.D. dissertation, University of Michigan.

Somers, Margaret R. 1994. The Narrative Constitution of Identity: A Relational and Network Approach. *Theory and Society* 23(5): 605–649.

Somers, Margaret R., and Gloria D. Gibson. 1994. Reclaiming the Epistemological "Other": Narrative and the Social Construction of Identity. In *Social Theory and the Politics of Identity*, edited by C. Calhoun, pp. 37–99. Blackwell Publishers, Oxford.

Speakman, Robert J., and Hector Neff (editors). 2005. *Laser Ablation-ICP-MS in Archaeological Research*. University of New Mexico Press, Albuquerque.

Speth, John D. 1988. Do We Need Concepts like "Mogollon," "Anasazi," and "Hohokam" Today? A Cultural Anthropological Perspective. *Kiva* 53:205–209.

Spielmann, Katherine A. 1995. Glimpses of Gender in the American Southwest. *Journal of Anthropological Research* 51:91–102.

———. 1998. Ritual Influences on the Development of Rio Grande Glaze A Ceramics. In *Migration and Reorganization: the Pueblo IV Period in the American Southwest*, edited by K. A. Spielmann, pp. 253–262. Anthropological Research Papers 51. Arizona State University Press, Tempe.

———. 2002. Feasting, Craft Specialization, and the Ritual Mode of Production in Small Scale Societies. *American Anthropologist* 104(1): 195–207.

———. 2004. Clusters Revisited. In *The Protohistoric Pueblo World: A.D. 1275–1600*, edited by E. C. Adams and A. I. Duff, pp. 137–143. University of Arizona Press, Tucson.

Spielmann, Katherine A., Matthew A. Peeples, Donna M. Glowacki, and Andrew J. Dugmore. 2016. Early Warning Signals of Social Transformation: A Case Study from the U.S. Southwest. *PLoS One* 11(10): e0163685.

Spier, Leslie. 1917. *An Outline for a Chronology of Zuni Ruins*. Anthropological Papers of the American Museum of Natural History No. 18, Part 3. American Museum of Natural History, New York.

———. 1918. *Notes on Some Little Colorado Ruins*. Anthropological Papers of the American Museum of Natural History No. 18, Part 4. American Museum of Natural History, New York.

———. 1919. *Ruins in the White Mountains, Arizona*. Anthropological Papers of the American Museum of Natural History No. 18, Part 5. American Museum of Natural History, New York.

Stark, Barbara L., and John K. Chance. 2008. Diachronic and Multidisciplinary Perspectives on Mesoamerican Ethnicity. In *Ethnic Identity in Nahua Mesoamerica: The View from Archaeology, Art History, Ethnohistory, and Contemporary Ethnography*, edited by F. F. Berden, J. K. Chance, A. R. Sandstrom, B. L. Stark, J. M. Taggart, and E. Umberger, pp. 1–37. University of Utah Press, Salt Lake City.

Stark, Miriam T. (editor). 1998. *The Archaeology of Social Boundaries*. Smithsonian Institution Press, Washington, D.C.

———. 2006. Glaze Ware Technology, the Social Lives of Pots, and Communities of Practice in the Late Prehistoric Southwest. In *The Social Life of Pots: Glaze Wares and Cultural Transformation in the Late Precontact Southwest*, edited by J. A. Habicht-Mauche, S. L. Eckert, and D. L. Huntley, pp. 17–33. University of Arizona Press, Tucson.

Stark, Miriam T., Mark D. Elson, and Jeffrey J. Clark. 1998. Social Boundaries and Technical Choices in Tonto Basin Prehistory. In *The Archaeology of Social Boundaries*, edited by M. T. Stark, pp. 208–231. Smithsonian Institution Press, Washington, D.C.

Stebbins, Sara T., Dana Hartman, and Stephen G. Dosh (editors). 1986. *The Coronado Project Archaeological Investigations: Studies along the Coal Haul Railroad Corridor*. Museum of Northern Arizona, Flagstaff.

Stein, John R., and Stephen H. Lekson. 1992. Anasazi Ritual Landscapes. In *Anasazi Regional Organization and the Chaco System*, edited by D. E. Doyel, pp. 87–100. Anthropological Papers No. 5. Maxwell Museum of Anthropology, University of New Mexico, Albuquerque.

Sterba, Johannes H., Hans Mommsen, Georg Steinhauser, and Max Bichler. 2009. The Influence of Different Tempers on the Composition of Pottery. *Journal of Archaeological Science* 36:1582–1589.

Stokke, Hugo, and Marit Tjomsland. 1996. *Collective Identities and Social Movements*. Chr. Michelsen Institute, Bergen, Norway.

Stone, Tammy. 1986. An Examination of Mogollon Corrugated Pottery. In *Mogollon Variability*, edited by C. Benson and S. Upham, pp. 89–106. University Museum Occasional Papers No. 15. New Mexico State University, Las Cruces.

———. 2003. Social Identity and Ethnic Interaction in the Western Pueblos of the American Southwest. *Journal of Archaeological Method and Theory* 10(1): 31–67.

———. 2015. *Migration and Ethnicity in Middle-Range Societies*. University of Utah Press, Salt Lake City.

Stubbs, Stanley, and W. S. Stallings. 1953. *The Excavation of Pindi Pueblo, New Mexico*. Monographs of the School for American Research No. 18. School for American Research, Santa Fe.

Tainter, Joseph A., and Fred Plog. 1994. Strong and Weak Patterning in Southwestern Prehistory: The Formation of Puebloan Archaeology. In *Themes in Southwest Prehistory*, edited by G. J. Gumerman, pp. 165–181. School of American Research, Santa Fe.

Tarrow, Sidney. 1998. *Power in Movement: Social Movements and Contentious Politics*. Cambridge Studies in Comparative Politics. Cambridge University Press, Cambridge.

Tarrow, Sidney, and Doug McAdam. 2005. Scale Shift in Transnational Contention. In *Transnational Protest and Global Activism*, edited by D. della Porta and S. Tarrow, pp. 121–147. Rowman and Littlefield, Lanham, Maryland.

Tilly, Charles. 1978. *Mobilization to Revolution*. Addison-Wesley, Reading, Massachusetts.

———. 1998. Social Movements and (All Sorts of) Other Political Interactions—Local, National, and International—Including Identities. *Theory and Society* 27(4): 453–480.

———. 2001. Mechanisms in Political Processes. *Annual Review of Political Science* 4:21–41.

———. 2002. *Stories, Identities, and Political Change*. Rowman and Littlefield, Lanham, Maryland.

———. 2004a. Social Boundary Mechanisms. *Philosophy of the Social Sciences* 34(2): 211–236.

———. 2004b. *Social Movements: 1768–2004*. Paradigm Publishers, Boulder, Colorado.

———. 2005. *Identities, Boundaries, and Social Ties*. Paradigm Publishers, Boulder, Colorado.

Tomka, Marybeth. 1988. The Societal Implications of the Great Kivas at the WS Ranch Site, Alma, New Mexico. Unpublished M.A. thesis, University of Texas.

Torvinen, Andrea, Michelle Hegmon, Ann P. Kinzig, Margaret C. Nelson, Matthew A. Peeples, Karen G. Schollmeyer, Colleen Strawhacker, and Laura Swantek. 2016. Transformation without Collapse: Two Cases from the American Southwest. In *Archaeological Perspectives on Resilience, Revitalization, and Reorganization in Complex Societies*, edited by R. Faulseit, pp. 262–286. Southern Illinois University, Carbondale.

Trask, Garrett, and Matthew A. Peeples. 2011. Ceramic Design and Changing Scales of Social Interaction across the Cibola Region. Poster presented at the 76th Annual Meeting of the Society for American Archaeology, Sacramento, California.

Triadan, Daniela. 1997. *Ceramic Commodities and Common Containers: Production and Distribution of White Mountain Redware in the Grasshopper Region, Arizona*. Anthropological Papers 61. University of Arizona Press, Tucson.

———. 2006. Dancing Gods: Ritual, Performance, and Political Organization in the Prehistoric Southwest. In *Theaters of Power and Community: Archaeology of Performance and Politics*, edited by T. Inomata and L. Coben, pp. 159–186. Altamira Press, Walnut Creek, California.

Triadan, Daniela, Barbara J. Mills, and Andrew I. Duff. 2002. From Compositional to Anthropological: Fourteenth-Century Red-Ware Circulation and Its Implications for Pueblo Reorganization. In *Ceramic Production and Circulation in the Greater Southwest: Source Determination by INAA and Complementary Mineralogical Investigations*, edited by D. M. Glowacki and H. Neff, pp. 85–97. Cotsen Institute of Archaeology Monograph 44. Cotsen Institute of Archaeology at UCLA, Los Angeles.

Trigger, Bruce G. 1989. *A History of Archaeological Thought*. Cambridge University Press, Cambridge.

Turnbaugh, William A. 1979. Calumet Ceremonialism as a Nativistic Response. *American Antiquity* 44(4): 685–691.

Upham, Steadman. 1982. *Polities and Power: An Economic and Political History of the Western Pueblo*. Academic Press, New York.

Van Dyke, Ruth M. 1998. The Chaco Connection: Bonito Style Architecture in Outlier Communities. Unpublished Ph.D. dissertation, University of Arizona.

———. 2007. Great Kivas in Time, Space, and Society. In *The Architecture of Chaco Canyon*, edited by S. H. Lekson, pp. 93–126. University of Utah Press, Salt Lake City.

———. 2008. Temporal Scale and Qualitative Social Transformation at Chaco Canyon. *Cambridge Archaeological Journal* 18(1): 70–78.

Van Keuren, Scott. 2004. Crafting Feasts in the Prehispanic Southwest. In *Identity, Feasting, and the Archaeology of the Greater Southwest*, edited by B. J. Mills, pp. 192–209. University Press of Colorado, Boulder.

———. 2006. *Shumway Ruin and the Late Pre-Hispanic Period in East-Central Arizona*. Contributions in Science No. 8. Natural History Museum of Los Angeles, Los Angeles.

Van Keuren, Scott, Hector Neff, and Mark R. Agostini. 2013. Glaze-Paints, Technological Knowledge, and Ceramic Specialization in the Fourteenth-Century Pueblo Southwest. *Journal of Anthropological Archaeology* 32(4): 675–690.

Van West, Carla R., and David H. Greenwald. 2005. Introduction and Background. In *Fence Lake Project: Archaeological Data Recovery in the New Mexico Transportation Corridor and First Five-Year Permit Area, Fence Lake Coal Mine Project, Catron County, New Mexico, Volume 1: Introduction and Site Descriptions*, edited by

E. K. Huber and C. R. Van West, pp. 1.1–1.121. Technical Series No. 84. Statistical Research, Inc., Tucson.

Van West, Carla R., and Henri D. Grissino-Mayer. 2005. Dendroclimatic Reconstruction. In *Fence Lake Project: Archaeological Data Recovery in the New Mexico Transportation Corridor and First Five-Year Permit Area, Fence Lake Coal Mine Project, Catron County, New Mexico, Volume 3: Environmental Studies*, edited by E. K. Huber and C. R. Van West, pp. 33.1–33.130. Technical Series No. 84. Statistical Research, Inc., Tucson.

Varien, Mark D. 1990. *Excavations at Three Prehistoric Sites along Pia Mesa Road, Zuni Indian Reservation, McKinley County, New Mexico*. Zuni Archaeology Program Report No. 233. Zuni Archaeology Program, Pueblo of Zuni.

———. 1999. *Sedentism and Mobility in a Social Landscape: Mesa Verde and Beyond*. University of Arizona Press, Tucson.

———. 2000. Site NM:12:K3:101 Description. In *The Archaeology and Ethnohistory of Oak Wash, Zuni Indian Reservation, New Mexico*, edited by T. L. Howell, pp. 93–160. Zuni Cultural Resource Enterprise Report No. 664. Zuni Cultural Resource Enterprise, Pueblo of Zuni.

Veit, U. 1989. Ethnic Concepts in Prehistory: A Case Study on the Relationship between Cultural Identity and Archaeological Objectivity. In *Archaeological Approaches to Cultural Identity*, edited by S. J. Shennan, pp. 35–56. Unwin and Hyman, London.

Vivian, Gordon, and Paul Reiter. 1960. *The Great Kivas of Chaco Canyon*. School of American Research, Santa Fe.

Vivian, R. Gwinn. 1990. *The Chacoan Prehistory of the San Juan Basin*. Academic Press, San Diego.

Wallace, Anthony F. C. 1956. Revitalization Movements. *American Anthropologist* 58(2): 264–281.

Wallace, Henry D. 2014. Ritual Transformation and Cultural Revitalization: Explaining Hohokam in Pre–A.D. 1000 Southeastern Arizona. In *Between Mimbres and Hohokam: Exploring the Archaeology and History of Southeastern Arizona and Southwestern New Mexico*, edited by H. D. Wallace, pp. 433–499. Anthropological Papers No. 52. Archaeology Southwest, Tucson.

Warburton, Miranda, and Donna K. Graves. 1992. Navajo Springs, Arizona: Frontier Outlier or Autonomous Great House? *Journal of Field Archaeology* 19(1): 51–69.

Ware, John A. 2015. *A Pueblo Social History: Kinship, Sodality, and Community in the Northern Southwest*. School for Advanced Research Press, Santa Fe.

Wasley, William. 1959. Cultural Implications of Style Trends in Southwestern Prehistoric Pottery: Basketmaker III to Pueblo II in West-Central New Mexico. Unpublished Ph.D. dissertation, University of Arizona.

Wasserman, Stanley, and Katherine Faust. 1994. *Social Network Analysis: Methods and Applications*. Cambridge University Press, Cambridge.

Watson, Patty Jo, Steven A. LeBlanc, and Charles L. Redman. 1980. Aspects of Zuni Prehistory: Preliminary Report on Excavations and Survey in the El Morro Valley of New Mexico. *Journal of Field Archaeology* 7:201–218.

Weaver, Donald E. 1978. Prehistoric Population Dynamics and Environmental Exploration in the Manuelito Canyon District, Northwestern New Mexico. Unpublished Ph.D. dissertation, Arizona State University.

Wells, Peter S. 1998. Identity and Material Culture in the Later Prehistory of Central Europe. *Journal of Archaeological Research* 6(3): 239–298.

Wendorf, Fred. 1953. *Archaeological Studies in the Petrified Forest National Monument*. Museum of Northern Arizona, Flagstaff.

———. 1954. *Highway Salvage Archaeology Volume I*. New Mexico State Highway Department and Museum of New Mexico, Santa Fe.

———. 1956. *Highway Salvage Archaeology Volume II*. New Mexico State Highway Department and Museum of New Mexico, Santa Fe.

Wendorf, Fred, Nancy Fox, and Orian L. Lewis (editors). 1956. *Pipeline Archaeology: Reports of Salvage Operations in the Southwest on El Paso Natural Gas Company Projects, 1950–1953*. Laboratory of Anthropology and the Museum of Northern Arizona, Santa Fe and Flagstaff.

Westfall, Deborah A. 1981. *Prehistory of the St. Johns Area, East-Central Arizona: The TEP St. Johns Project*. Arizona State Museum Archaeological Series 153. University of Arizona Press, Tucson.

Wheat, Joe Ben. 1955. *Mogollon Culture Prior to A.D. 1000*. Memoirs of the American Anthropological Association No. 82 and Memoirs of the Society for American Archaeology No. 10. American Anthropological Association and Society for American Archaeology, Menosha, Wisconsin, and Salt Lake City.

White, Harrison. 1992. *Identity and Control: A Structural Theory of Social Action*. Princeton University Press, Princeton, New Jersey.

———. 2008a. Notes on the Constituents of Social Structure, Soc. Rel. 10—Spring '65. *Sociologica* 1 (http://www.sociologica.mulino.it/doi/10.2383/26576).

———. 2008b. *Identity and Control: How Social Formations Emerge*. Princeton University Press, Princeton, New Jersey.

Whittlesey, Stephanie. 2010. Fourteenth-Century Plazas and Great Kivas in East-Central Arizona: Ritual Spaces, Ideology, and Ethnicity. Paper presented at the 16th Biennial Mogollon Archaeology Conference, Las Cruces, New Mexico.

Wichlacz, Caitlin Anne. 2009. Complementary Compositional Analyses of Ceramics from Two Great House Communities in West-Central New Mexico. Unpublished M.A. thesis, Washington State University.

Wiessner, Polly. 1983. Style and Social Information in Kalahari San Projectile Points. *American Antiquity* 48(2): 253–276.

———. 1984. Reconsidering the Behavioral Basis for Style: A Case Study among the Kalahari San. *Journal of Anthropological Archaeology* 3(3): 190–234.

———. 1985. Style or Isochrestic Variation? A Reply to Sackett. *American Antiquity* 50:160–166.

———. 2002. The Vines of Complexity: Egalitarian Structures and the Institutionalization of Inequality among the Enga. *Current Anthropology* 43(2): 233–269.

Wiessner, Polly, and Akii Tumu. 1998. *Historical Vines: Enga Networks of Exchange, Ritual, and Warfare in Papua New Guinea*. Smithsonian Institution Press, Washington, D.C.

Wilcox, David R. 1988. Rethinking the Mogollon Concept. *Kiva* 53:205–209.

Wilcox, David R., David A. Gregory, and J. Brett Hill. 2007. Zuni in the Puebloan and Southwestern Worlds. In *Zuni Origins: Toward a New Synthesis of Southwestern Archaeology*, edited by D. A. Gregory and D. R. Wilcox, pp. 165–209. University of Arizona Press, Tucson.

Wilshusen, Richard H. 1989. Unstuffing the Estufa: Ritual Floor Features in Anasazi Pit Structures and Pueblo Kivas. In *The Architecture of Social Integration in Prehistoric Pueblos*, edited by W. D. Lipe and M. Hegmon, pp. 89–111. Occasional Paper No. 1. Crow Canyon Archaeological Center, Cortez, Colorado.

Wilson, C. Dean. 1994. Implications of Ceramic Resource Surveys in the Northern Mogollon Country. In *Mogollon VII: The Collected Papers of the 1992 Mogollon Conference Held in Las Cruces, New Mexico*, edited by P. Beckett, pp. 73–79. COAS Publishing and Research, Las Cruces, New Mexico.

———. 2007. Mogollon Pottery Production and Exchange. In *Zuni Origins: Toward a New Synthesis of Southwestern Archaeology*, edited by D. A. Gregory and D. R. Wilcox, pp. 239–246. University of Arizona Press, Tucson.

Wilson, C. Dean, and Patrick Severts. 1999. Clay Distribution, Use, and Pottery Production in the Northern Mogollon Highlands. In *Archaeology of the Mogollon Highlands: Settlement Systems and Adaptations*, edited by Y. R. Oakes and D. A. Zamora, pp. 131–138. Archaeology Notes 232, Vol. 4. Museum of New Mexico, Office of Archaeological Studies, Santa Fe.

Windes, Thomas C., and Dabney Ford. 1996. The Chaco Wood Project: The Chronometric Appraisal of Pueblo Bonito. *American Antiquity* 61(2): 295–310.

Wobst, H. Martin. 1977. Stylistic Behavior and Information Exchange. In *For the Director: Research Essays in Honor of James B. Griffen*, edited by C. E. Cleland, pp. 317–342. Anthropological Papers of the Museum of Anthropology 61. University of Michigan, Ann Arbor.

Wolf, Eric R. 1982. *Europe and the People without History*. University of California Press, Los Angeles.

Woodbury, Richard B. 1956. The Antecedents of Zuni Culture. In *Transactions of the New York Academy of Sciences, series 2*, vol. 18, pp. 557–563. New York Academy of Sciences, New York.

Woodbury, Richard B., and Nathalie F. Woodbury. 1956. Zuni Prehistory and El Morro National Monument. *Southwestern Lore* 21(4): 56–60.

Wozniak, Frank E., and Michael P. Marshall. 1991. *The Prehistoric Cebolla Canyon Community: An Archaeological Class III Inventory of 320 Acres of BLM Land at the Mouth of Cebolla Canyon*. Office of Contract Archaeology, University of New Mexico, Albuquerque.

Wright, David K. 2005. New Perspectives on Early Regional Interaction Networks of East African Trade: A View from Tsavo National Park, Kenya. *African Archaeological Review* 22(3): 111–140.

Yelvington, Kevin. 1991. Ethnicity as Practice? A Comment on Bentley. *Comparative Studies in Society and History* 33(1): 158–168.

Zamora, Dorothy A. 1999. LA 70185 (AR-03-06-03-00285), DZ Site. In *Archaeology of the Mogollon Highlands: Settlement Systems and Adaptations*, edited by Y. R. Oakes and D. A. Zamora, pp. 295–318. Archaeology Notes 232, Vol. 2. Museum of New Mexico, Office of Archaeological Studies, Santa Fe.

Zamora, Dorothy A., and Yvonne R. Oakes. 1999. LA 3279 (AR-03-06-03-00159), the Hough Site. In *Archaeology of the Mogollon Highlands: Settlement Systems and Adaptations*, edited by Y. R. Oakes and D. A. Zamora, pp. 5–78. Archaeology Notes 232, Vol. 2. Museum of New Mexico, Office of Archaeological Studies, Santa Fe.

Zedeño, Maria Nieves. 1994. *Sourcing Prehistoric Ceramics at Chodistaas Pueblo, Arizona: The Circulation of Pots and People in the Grasshopper Region*. Anthropological Papers 58. University of Arizona Press, Tucson.

———. 1995. The Role of Population Movement and Technology Transfer in the Manufacture of Southwestern Ceramics. In *Evolution of Ceramic Production in the*

*American Southwest*, edited by P. L. Crown and B. J. Mills, pp. 115–141. University of Arizona Press, Tucson.

———. 1998. Identifying Material Correlates for Ceramic Circulation in the Prehistoric Puebloan Southwest. *Journal of Anthropological Research* 54(4): 461–476.

———. 2002. Artifact Design, Composition, and Context: Updating the Analysis of Ceramic Circulation at Point of Pines, Arizona. In *Ceramic Production and Circulation in the Greater Southwest: Source Determination by INAA and Complementary Mineralogical Investigations*, edited by D. M. Glowacki and H. Neff, pp. 74–84. Cotsen Institute of Archaeology Monograph 44. Cotsen Institute of Archaeology at UCLA, Los Angeles.

Zhang, Qiaoping, and Isabelle Couloigner. 2005. A New Efficient K-Medoid Algorithm for Spatial Clustering. *Computational Science and Its Applications* 3,482:181–189.

Zier, Christian J. 1976. *Excavations near Zuni, New Mexico: 1973*. Museum of Northern Arizona Research Paper No. 2. Museum of Northern Arizona, Flagstaff.

# INDEX

# ABOUT THE AUTHOR

**Matthew A. Peeples** is an assistant professor of anthropology in the School of Human Evolution and Social Change at Arizona State University and research director of the ASU Center for Archaeology and Society. His research draws on models and methods from the comparative social sciences (in particular, social network analyses) to explore how and why societies emerge, transform, or dissolve over the long term. He conducts field and lab research primarily in the greater Cibola region.